Business
Plans
Handbook

Business Plans Handbook

A COMPILATION OF BUSINESS PLANS DEVELOPED BY INDIVIDUALS THROUGHOUT NORTH AMERICA

VOLUME

16

**Lynn M. Pearce,
Project Editor**

GALE
CENGAGE Learning

Detroit • New York • San Francisco • New Haven, Conn • Waterville, Maine • London

GALE
CENGAGE Learning™

Business Plans Handbook, Volume 16

Project Editor: Lynn M. Pearce

Product Manager: Jenai Drouillard

Product Design: Jennifer Wahi

Composition and Electronic Prepress: Evi Seoud

Manufacturing: Rita Wimberley

Editorial: Erin Braun

Gale
27500 Drake Rd.
Farmington Hills, MI, 48331-3535

ISBN-13: 978-14144-3908-2
ISBN-10: 1-4144-3908-3
1084-4473

Printed in the United States of America
1 2 3 4 5 6 7 13 12 11 10 09

Contents

Highlights

Business Plans Handbook, Volume 16 (BPH-16) is a collection of business plans compiled by entrepreneurs seeking funding for small businesses throughout North America. For those looking for examples of how to approach, structure, and compose their own business plans, *BPH-16* presents 20 sample plans, including plans for the following businesses:

- Automated Teller Machines (ATMs)
- Bed and Breakfast
- Beekeeping Business
- Car Wash and Car Detailing Business
- Counseling Practice
- Custom Carpentry Shop
- Day Camp Organizer
- Diner
- Domestic Services Provider
- Energy Efficiency Auditing Firm
- Gift Shop
- Home Organization Service
- House Cleaning
- Ice Cream Parlor
- Nature Photography Business
- Online Party–Planning Company
- Organic Cleaning Supplies
- Physical Therapy Practice
- Stable
- Wine Storage

FEATURES AND BENEFITS

BPH-16 offers many features not provided by other business planning references including:

- Twenty business plans, each of which represent an attempt at clarifying (for themselves and others) the reasons that the business should exist or expand and why a lender should fund the enterprise.
- Two fictional plans that are used by business counselors at a prominent small business development organization as examples for their clients. (You will find these in the Business Plan Template Appendix.)
- A directory section that includes: listings for venture capital and finance companies, which specialize in funding start-up and second-stage small business ventures, and a comprehensive

listing of Service Corps of Retired Executives (SCORE) offices. In addition, the Appendix also contains updated listings of all Small Business Development Centers (SBDCs); associations of interest to entrepreneurs; Small Business Administration (SBA) Regional Offices; and consultants specializing in small business planning and advice. It is strongly advised that you consult supporting organizations while planning your business, as they can provide a wealth of useful information.

- A Small Business Term Glossary to help you decipher the sometimes confusing terminology used by lenders and others in the financial and small business communities.

- A cumulative index, outlining each plan profiled in the complete Business Plans Handbook series.

- A Business Plan Template which serves as a model to help you construct your own business plan. This generic outline lists all the essential elements of a complete business plan and their components, including the Summary, Business History and Industry Outlook, Market Examination, Competition, Marketing, Administration and Management, Financial Information, and other key sections. Use this guide as a starting point for compiling your plan.

- Extensive financial documentation required to solicit funding from small business lenders. You will find examples of: Cash Flows, Balance Sheets, Income Projections, and other financial information included with the textual portions of the plan.

Introduction

Perhaps the most important aspect of business planning is simply doing it. More and more business owners are beginning to compile business plans even if they don't need a bank loan. Others discover the value of planning when they must provide a business plan for the bank. The sheer act of putting thoughts on paper seems to clarify priorities and provide focus. Sometimes business owners completely change strategies when compiling their plan, deciding on a different product mix or advertising scheme after finding that their assumptions were incorrect. This kind of healthy thinking and re-thinking via business planning is becoming the norm. The editors of *Business Plans Handbook, Volume 16 (BPH-16)* sincerely hope that this latest addition to the series is a helpful tool in the successful completion of your business plan, no matter what the reason for creating it.

This sixteenth volume, like each volume in the series, offers business plans used and created by real people. *BPH-16* provides 20 business plans. The business and personal names and addresses and general locations have been changed to protect the privacy of the plan authors.

NEW BUSINESS OPPORTUNITIES

As in other volumes in the series, *BPH-16* finds entrepreneurs engaged in a wide variety of creative endeavors. Examples include a proposal for automated teller machines, bed and breakfast, beekeeping business, and a car wash and car detailing business. In addition, several other plans are provided, including a counseling practice, custom carpentry shop, day camp organizer, diner, domestic services provider, and physical therapy practice, among others.

Comprehensive financial documentation has become increasingly important as today's entrepreneurs compete for the finite resources of business lenders. Our plans illustrate the financial data generally required of loan applicants, including Income Statements, Financial Projections, Cash Flows, and Balance Sheets.

ENHANCED APPENDIXES

In an effort to provide the most relevant and valuable information for our readers, we have updated the coverage of small business resources. For instance, you will find: a directory section, which includes listings of all of the Service Corps of Retired Executives (SCORE) offices; an informative glossary, which includes small business terms; and a cumulative index, outlining each plan profiled in the complete Business Plans Handbook series. In addition we have updated the list of Small Business Development Centers (SBDCs); Small Business Administration Regional Offices; venture capital and finance companies, which specialize in funding start-up and second-stage small business enterprises; associations of interest to entrepreneurs; and consultants, specializing in small business advice and planning. For your reference, we have also reprinted the business plan template, which provides a comprehensive overview of the essential components of a business plan and two fictional plans used by small business counselors.

SERIES INFORMATION

If you already have the first fifteen volumes of *BPH*, with this sixteenth volume, you will now have a collection of over 340 business plans (not including the one updated plan in the second volume, whose original appeared in the first, or the two fictional plans in the Business Plan Template Appendix section of the second, third, fourth, fifth, sixth, and seventh volumes); contact information for hundreds of organizations and agencies offering business expertise; a helpful business plan template; more than 1,500 citations to valuable small business development material; and a comprehensive glossary of terms to help the business planner navigate the sometimes confusing language of entrepreneurship.

ACKNOWLEDGEMENTS

The Editors wish to sincerely thank the contributors to *BPH-16*, including:

- Laura Becker
- Paul Greenland
- Kari Lucke

COMMENTS WELCOME

Your comments on *Business Plans Handbook* are appreciated. Please direct all correspondence, suggestions for future volumes of *BPH*, and other recommendations to the following:

Managing Editor, Business Product
Business Plans Handbook
Gale, a part of Cengage Learning
27500 Drake Rd.
Farmington Hills, MI 48331-3535
Phone: (248)699-4253
Fax: (248)699-8052
Toll-Free: 800-347-GALE
E-mail: BusinessProducts@cengage.com

Automated Teller Machines (ATMs)

Quick Cash Services

22 Bridge Rd.
Union City, New Jersey 07087

Laura Becker

Quick Cash Services will take advantage of the opportunity to supply ATM machines to areas that have few bank–owned ATM machines.

BUSINESS OVERVIEW

Mission

Quick Cash Services will take advantage of the opportunity to supply ATM machines to areas that have few bank–owned ATM machines. This includes placing ATM machines in convenience stores, supermarkets, and gas stations. The main objective will be to find locations that are under–banked (not served well by the banking community) and meet that demographics' needs for cash.

Objectives

Quick Cash Services' objective is to build a large portfolio of independently–owned ATM machines across the New York, New Jersey, and the Connecticut tri–state area. The company will continue to place ATM machines in under–banked urban areas, as well as other areas where there are few bank–owned ATM machines.

Business Strategy

ATM machines can be placed in high traffic locations such as convenience stores, supermarkets and gas stations. In addition, deals can be made with merchants to locate machines in other types of stores.

"Of the approximately 395,000 ATMs operating in the U.S. today, two–thirds are located in "off–premise" locations from financial institutions, mostly at merchants. About three–fourths of these off–premise ATMs (73 percent) are not bank–owned or branded [i.e., affiliated with a particular bank]. Such networks of ATM installations are due to independent sales organizations (ISOs) that market, install and manage machines to help merchants meet consumer needs for cash. Dispensing and incoming interchange fees are shared between the ISO's sponsoring bank, ATM processor (or "driver"), the ISO and the merchant. Approximately 27 million ATM transactions occur everyday."

EXECUTIVE SUMMARY

The independently–owned ATM machine business focuses on building a portfolio of machines that can be placed in strategic high foot-traffic locations. Revenue from the business is generated by charging a transaction fee when cash is dispensed from the machine. Usually the transaction fee, also known as the "surcharge" fee, is a fixed fee which ranges from $2 to $3 dollars per transaction. The smaller the cash withdrawal, the higher the percent return per transaction. This means that if two people withdraw cash from the same machine, one withdraws $20 dollars and the other withdraws $100 dollars, the person who withdraws $100 will pay a lower percentage transaction fee to withdraw cash ($2 / $20 = 10 percent versus $2/$100 = 1 percent). The larger the number of transactions, the more profitable the business becomes.

Since many bank–owned ATM machines offer their clients no fee transactions, it is important to pick locations that do not have a high number of bank ATM machines in the area. ATM machines can be purchased or leased and they require a merchant data processor to assist in processing bank card transactions. The industry is very much tied to cash. As new forms of payment continue to grow within the United States economy (for example debit card transactions), the need for cash will diminish. As long as people continue to need cash for their day to day lives, the ATM business will continue to flourish.

Here is a case study example of an ATM machine that is located in a busy sports bar in an urban area.

Case Study: ATM in a sports bar within a blue–collar metropolitan area

This ATM was installed in April 2006 and has been operating successfully since that time. The ATM owner does not pay for the phone line charge and pays the location owner a portion of the surcharge income.

	Start up costs
$3,465	Initial ATM cost
$ 500	Locator cost (amount paid to a professional salesperson for the location)
$ 100	Phone line installation (line is shared with location)
$4,065	**Total start up costs**

Year	# Transactions	Gross revenue	Startup	Expenses	Annual net profit
2006 (partial)	3,162	$ 6,324	$4,065	$3,162	($ 903)
2007	4,985	$12,462		$6,231	$5,431
2008	4,253	$10,632		$5,316	$5,016

Business Strategy

Quick Cash Services is an ATM provider for locations in urban and suburban areas with fairly dense populations. Each location will have relatively high day–to–day foot traffic. ATM machines are purchased or leased by Quick Cash Services and then installed in a supermarket, a convenience store, a gas station, or on the street. The business develops strong relationships with the owners of the locations where the ATM machines reside. The relationship is viewed as a partnership arrangement in which Quick Cash Services pays a small percent of the net profit from each machine to the location owner in exchange for a fixed rent price and a secure location.

START–UP DETAILS

New ATM machines can be purchased for between $3,000 to $6,000 depending on the model according to "How to Advice.com" and Franklin ATM.

Leasing options are also available and monthly payments can range from between $70 to $110 per month.

Servicing the ATM machines is the responsibility of the business as well. The business owner will need to select an independent sales organization (ISO) to process withdrawal transactions. The National Association of ATM ISOs and Operators will have lists of ISOs. The business owner will need to interview a number of companies and select an ISO to contract with (contracts are usually from one to several years). Setting up an account with a merchant service provider once selected usually takes approximately two weeks once the application is complete.

Quick Cash Services has a merchant account with First Data Corporation. The merchant provider has a relationship with the business' bank. Prior to setting up a merchant account, the business owner will need to set up a business account at a bank and discuss the type of the account with the bank and the accountant.

The business owner will also need to service the ATM machines on an ongoing basis including: regularly adding cash, fixing mechanical problems, and fixing software problems. A toll–free number is provided on all machines for customer service issues.

Owning and Operating an ATM Machine in a Merchant Store (either store–owned machine or placed in store by independent owner)

Basic Questions and Answers on Owning and Operating ATM Machines as a Store Merchant.

Benefits of having an ATM in your business or location

- Allows your customers access to their available cash from their debit, bank and credit cards.

- Keeps your customers in–house so they don't leave your location to get cash from a different ATM nearby.

- Increases retail sales by up to 50 percent of the amount withdrawn from your ATM.

- Reduces or eliminates the need to accept checks.

- Reduces credit card usage and credit card fees and expenses.

- Generates store traffic from walk–by traffic.

- Increases your customer satisfaction and loyalty.

- Free processing/no fees.

- Best of all you will receive surcharge revenue for every transaction.

How much revenue can you expect to generate from an ATM placement?

That generally depends on the amount of foot traffic your location has on a daily basis. The rule of thumb goes like this. 3 percent – 5 percent of the foot traffic that actually sees the ATM machine will use the ATM. So let's figure that you have a total of 300 people a day coming through your doors, and let's say that you are charging a $2.25 surcharge per valid withdrawal. If you take the middle road that 4 percent of the people that see the ATM machine will use it, you can count on your new automated teller machine to generate you a minimum of 360 transactions per month at $2.25 per valid withdrawal. That comes out to $810 per month or a total of $9,720 per year. All of that from one ATM machine at one location.

How secure are ATM machines from robbery?

ATM machines are broken down into two different types of ATM classifications:

Level 1 armored ATM: Level 1 ATMs are used primarily as outdoor ATMs, such as outdoor entertainment districts, outdoor flea markets, outdoor concert and events, etc.

Non–armored ATMs: Non–armored ATMs are used primarily for indoor locations that are closed to the public when employees are not present. (i.e. indoor malls, movie theaters, night clubs, restaurants, bars, etc.) Good examples of non–armored ATMs are the Triton 9100 ATM and the Tranax Mini Bank 1500 ATM.

Can I co–brand my ATM with my company/merchant name?

If the ATM machine is owned entirely by you (or if it's in the agreement with the owner), then yes you can.

MARKET ANALYSIS

The industry as a whole is a cash flow industry. Owners of ATM machines are looking for large numbers of transactions to return a robust return on capital. This means that for every dollar that is invested, the owner wants their original principal returned plus interest. The greater the turnover of capital, due to transactions, the greater the return on investment will be to the owner of the ATM machine. Most merchant service providers will credit the machines owner's account with the original principal plus the transaction fee within three business days. The fees for the merchant provider are generally debited from the ATM machines owners account on the fifth business day of the following month.

Currently, the ATM industry is in a relatively slow growth phase. There are several reasons for the slowdown in growth. First, there has been growth in the number of ATMs located outside of banks over the last decade. The average number of transactions generated per machine declined by 5 percent in 2005.

Second, there is growth in the popularity of surcharge–free networks in which banks/financial institutions agree not to charge members of various networks.

Third, there has been growth in the debit card sector. Debit cards can now be used in more and more retail operations which makes the need for cash on hand lower.

The early response in the industry was consolidation. Smaller players were being sold to medium and large–sized ATM fleet owners. Many ATM ISOs are looking for alternatives though. There has also been a lot of discussion about using the ATM machines for purposes other than simply dispensing cash, such as selling gift cards. That is still being looked at for potential opportunities as well as check imaging (depositing checks electronically without envelopes). In the near term the most promising opportunity for ATM ISOs is co–branding.

Co–branding is when ATM ISOs partner with financial institutions/banks. "The number one topic in ATMs these days is ATM co–branding," says Melissa Fox, a consultant with Boston–based Dove Consulting, a unit of Hitachi Consulting Corp. Fox recently completed a study on new business models for ATM deployment.

Co–branding occurs when a bank pays an ATM ISO to use the bank's brand on an ATM. The bank's customers can use the ISO–owned ATM without paying surcharges. To compensate the ISO for the loss of the surcharge and the interchange revenue from transactions made by bank's customers, the bank pays the ISO a monthly fee based on a number of factors, including the number of cards and machines in the region and the volume of transactions.

The bottom line is that, co–branding aside, there are still opportunities for ISOs in the under–banked areas of the country. These areas serve less affluent individuals who still deal primarily with cash. Their need for cash will continue to grow and therefore servicing this demographic is a strong niche.

There are other new revenue ideas as well, including using ATM machines to dispense gift cards. Better ATM Services offers technology to enable ATMs to dispense prepaid gift cards through the ATM cash tray. The gift card idea is in the early development stages and has not seen a lot of traction yet within the industry.

Global vs. Domestic Markets

The total size of the ATM machine business globally is 1.5 million machines as of 2006 according to ATMIA (Automated Teller Machine Information Association).

Growth in North America has been slowing while growth of machines in Asia has been increasing. The opportunity within the tri–state area would be to develop a portfolio of a few hundred ATM machines. The key to a successful ATM business is finding high traffic locations to place your machines. Locations for the machines are one of the highest barriers to entry. There are opportunities to purchase used machines and lease machines that will allow someone to begin the business with as little as $5,000. The initial investment will be used to either purchase or lease machines' as well as money to be used in the ATM machine. If you have a strong credit rating, your bank might lend you the capital you need to place cash in the ATM machine. If this is not an option, your initial investment will be the cash need to help your business function.

"In the tight business market that ATMs have become, managing your costs has become imperative," says John Clatworthy, Vice President, Sales and Marketing, Cash Connect. Installing the right type of ATM in the right location also should be a consideration, says Clatworthy. It doesn't make sense, for instance, to install a high–priced, sophisticated Diebold or NCR machine in a bowling alley. And for high–traffic locations, it makes sense to use an ATM with a large cash cassette so it won't have to be replenished.

Location, location, location

Finding the right location is probably the most important component of the business. The business owner will need to spend a lot of time investigating differing locations and meeting with merchants to find the right fit.

Franklin ATM has devised a statistical model that identifies predicted transactions by type of location.

Category	Variables analyzed	Predicted transaction range
Bars	12	50–800 per month
Gas stations	8	120–700 per month
Office buildings	6	50–400 per month
Convenience stores	6	80–600 per month
Bingo halls	in development	150–250 per month

COMPETITION

The competition within the ATM business is relatively strong. Most ATM machines will offer the same types of products and services. Quick Cash Services offers a machine that allows its clients to withdraw cash and check balances. Machines owned by banks will also allow clients to deposit money if the client has an account with that banking company. Prices for withdrawals of cash range from $1 dollar per transaction to as high as $3 dollars per transaction. Quick Cash Services has slightly different prices depending on the area where the ATM is situated and how many other ATM machines are in close vicinity. Machines that are generally the only ATM within a five block radius have transaction prices at $3, while machines that are within a close proximity to other ATMs are priced closer to $2 per transaction.

The largest ISO in the industry is Cardtronics, based in Houston, TX. Cardtronics operates the largest ATM network in the world with over 32,000 ATMs including significant networks in the United Kingdom and Mexico. Cardtronics has relationships with businesses such as 7–Eleven, Target, Walgreen's, CVS, Duane Reade, ExxonMobil and Chevron.

Cardtronics has jumped into the co–branding business described above by developing relationships with major financial institutions including J.P. Morgan Chase, PNC Financial Services Group Inc., HSBC Bank USA N.A., and Huntington Bancshares Inc.

According to a study done by Dove Consulting, 38 percent of ATM ISOs surveyed have at least one co–branding deal in place with a financial institution. Another 24 percent of ISOs are actively pursuing a co–branding agreement. Only 5 percent of ISOs surveyed said they were not interested in co–branding at all.

MARKETING & SALES

The business marketing strategy is to make sure the customers that frequent the supermarket or convenient store are aware that our services are available. The owner of the ATM machines should partner with the host locations to place advertisements inside and outside of their establishment to make customers aware of the ATM machine. This strategy has proven successful in convenient stores, gas stations and supermarkets. The costs of advertising within host locations are minor and in some cases the price is picked up by the host location.

OPERATIONS

Quick Cash Services is a family–owned and operated business. The business installs the machines, sets up the internet connections, and services the machines with cash on a regular basis. The ATM machines are connected to software which enables us to monitor their current cash balance, as well as alerting us if there is a mechanical problem.

Adding cash to the machines is something that the business owner can do on their own, by withdrawing money from the bank on that day. Machines are usually filled with approximately $5,000 in ten and twenty dollar bills. This will usually last for about a week to ten days depending on the traffic in the location. Keep in mind that there is sometimes a lag of up to three business days before the merchant service provider replaces the cash withdrawn from the ATM machine into the business bank account. The business owner should have $2,000 of reserve cash available for servicing at any time.

There is an 800 customer service phone number on every ATM machine. Usually calls are due to mechanical failures such as jammed cash or cash that will not dispense.

There is an alternative to withdrawing and loading the cash into the ATM machine as the business owner. There are a number of companies that offer secure cash loading services, as well as ATM machine maintenance. According to Brinks, they will handle all the operations of your ATM services for a percentage of the receipts. This percentage runs between 40–60 percent of the gross revenues—this is a good option for those that own many, many machines producing significant revenue.

There are also companies that provide financing for cash loads. For instance, ATM Business "rents" funds to ATM operators in maximum advances of one load per ATM (about $8,000 to $10,000) at an interest rate of prime plus 3 percent.

For the business owner who wants an ATM machine without managing its operation, there are companies that will provide comprehensive management services. NationalLink has a complete turn–key placement program; all you need to do is supply space and power, and NationalLink will do the rest. Under this program, the business owner receives a portion of the surcharge.

Fees

There are two types of fees that ATM owners receive. The surcharge (an ATM "usage" charge to customer withdrawing cash); and the interchange fee which is a fee the bank pays in part to the ATM owner and the processing network for each successful transaction.

A regular cash dispensing ATM machine collects "interchange" fees for each successful transaction it performs. Banks charge for using a non–bank ATM because the bank has to pay an "interchange fee"—typically about fifty cents—to the ATM owner, to cover its costs of providing and maintaining the ATM. (There's also a separate, smaller fee that goes to the ATM network.) The interchange fee is designed to cover the costs of operating the ATM, but it's only an estimate, so low–volume ATMs may end up losing money, while high–volume ATMs can turn a large profit, even without surcharges.

Therefore, the interchange is a fee that the cardholder's issuing bank pays to the network and ATM owners to cover processing costs. The networks and ATM owners keep a portion to cover their cost of providing network access into cardholder's banks. Without this service, there would be no way to get approval codes for transactions because banks don't just let anyone connect to their system. ATM business operators must be connected with a processing network who collects and distributes the transaction fees to the bank, the ATM owner and to the processing company.

Then, the processor keeps a portion of this money for administration costs, and shares a portion of it with their ISO, or distributor that setup the merchant location for service. This interchange does not come out of the surcharge, therefore the machine owner normally keeps 100 percent of the surcharge amount he collects on his machine because the processing is paid for by the interchange fee.

Interchange fees on card transactions amount to over $7.9 billion for ATM cash withdrawals.

There are two types of customer charges: the surcharge and the foreign fee. The surcharge fee may be imposed by the ATM owner (the "deployer" or Independent Sales Organization) and will be charged to the consumer using the machine. The foreign fee or transaction fee is a fee charged by the card issuer (financial institution, stored value provider) to the consumer for conducting a transaction outside of their network of machines in the case of a financial institution.

Equipment

The equipment needed to handle the operations of the business includes the following:

- ATM Machines
- Merchant Services Software
- Computer
- Ethernet Internet Connections

ATM Manufacturers

- *Tranax ATM Manufacturer:* Founded in 1986, Tranax is a leading innovator of retail ATM and self–service technology, serving the retail markets. Tranax has sold and supported more than 100,000 ATMs and self–service terminals throughout North America. Since 2006, Tranax started its own manufacturing, and has shipped over 20,000 ATM and self–service terminals. Tranax, headquartered in Hayward, California, became an independent operating company of Eltna Group in August 2008.

- *Triton ATM Manufacturer:* Triton is a major provider of off–premise ATMs and ATM management software globally. Triton ATMs are made in the USA.

- *WRG ATM Manufacturer:* WRG was founded in 1989 as a coin operated music and game operator.

- *Tidel ATM Manufacturer:* Tidel began in 1978 as part of the Southland Corporation (now known as 7–Eleven, Inc.) by inventing a robbery deterrent product that has become familiar to retail store operators everywhere—the Timed Access Cash Controller (TACC). Today there are over 250,000 TACCs working in retail locations throughout the world. In 1992, Tidel made history once again by introducing dial–up ATM technology to the commercial marketplace. Tidel set the standard for low–cost, high–reliability ATM performance and expanded the product line to include scalable ATMs and multimedia point–of–sale kiosks that could dispense everything from cash to stamps to event tickets. The success of Tidel's ATM platform didn't go without notice in the marketplace and among the larger players in the ATM world. As a result, Tidel and NCR Corporation entered into an asset purchase agreement in 2006 where Tidel sold all of its ATM products to NCR EasyPoint, LLC. Tidel originally released the Sentinel cash management system in 2002. This new product represented the next revolution in intelligent cash management, providing a host of features designed to provide users with real–time cash accountability. The Sentinel product line continues to move forward with its scalable platform that can incorporate the newest advances in cash management technology and unique user–specific features and peripherals. Tidel Engineering L.P. is a wholly owned subsidiary of Sentinel Technologies, Inc., a private holding company.

- *Diebold ATM Manufacturer:* For 150 years, Diebold has brought together a combination of innovation, expertise and quality service to become a global leader in providing integrated self–service, security systems and services. Headquartered in Canton, Ohio, Diebold employs more than

17,000 employees, with representation in more than 90 countries worldwide. In 2008, Diebold reported total revenue of $3.2 billion. Diebold is publicly traded on the New York Stock Exchange.

- *Hyosung–Nautilus ATM Manufacturer:* With over 27 years of experience in the industry, Nautilus Hyosung has developed proven technologies to help customers achieve greater effectiveness.

Hours of Operation

The business hours for the ATM business are flexible, but require a significant amount of time. Travel time between locations is a factor. Quick Cash Services uses the early morning hours to fill ATM machines with cash. Withdrawals from banks for cash to be loaded into ATM machines are generally done in the afternoon. If a maintenance call needs to be made, it is usually done in the morning, but could come at any time during the day.

This business can be run on a part–time basis with only a few machines. Staffing requirements will vary depending upon the number of machines deployed. One person can handle several machines, but if a larger network of machines is established, more personnel will be needed. Staffing also will vary depending on what part of the business is done by the owner versus outsourcing.

Professional Support

Initially there will be a need for legal advice when setting up the company that will conduct the business. This can be accomplished without a lawyer, but there are a number of nuances and some legal advice is recommended. There will likely always be a need for an accountant, since the number of transactions and the multiple types of taxes will be fairly complex.

Insurance

There are multiple types of insurance that are needed to run an efficient ATM business. The owner should purchase liability insurance. Kiosk specific insurance will run approximately $495 dollars per machine for $1 million dollars of liability, according to Arizona Central Insurance Company.

An owner can also purchase property insurance that runs approximately $500 per $10,000 of damage depending on the location of the machine. Cash can also be insured but rates can run as high as $1,000 per $10,000. Most ATM machine vendors self–insure their cash and keep amounts of less than $10,000 in a machine.

FINANCIAL ANALYSIS

	Year 1**	Year 2***	Year 3****
Revenue*	$29,200.00	$87,600.00	$160,600.00
Expenses			
Purchases	$12,000.00	$24,000.00	$ 30,000.00
Merchant service	$ 730.00	$ 2,190.00	$ 4,015.00
Insurance liability	$ 1,980.00	$ 5,940.00	$ 10,890.00
Property	$ 2,000.00	$ 6,000.00	$ 11,000.00
Internet	$ 2,400.00	$ 7,200.00	$ 13,200.00
Rent	$ 2,847.00	$ 8,541.00	$ 15,658.50
Accounting	$ 2,500.00	$ 2,500.00	$ 2,500.00
Legal	$ 1,500.00	$ 1,500.00	$ 1,500.00
Net income	**$ 3,243.00**	**$29,729.00**	**$ 71,836.50**

Assumptions:
**Year 1 assumes 4 ATM machines purchased
***Year 2 assumes 8 ATM machines purchased
****Year 3 assumes 10 ATM machines purchased

ATM machines are assumed to cost $3,000
Merchant Service takes approximately 5 cents per transaction.
Year 1 (10 transactions per day *5 cents *365 days *4 machines).
Rent is the amount an owner would pay a host location.

*Revenue is calculated by estimating the average transaction at $50, the average withdrawn amount per day ($500), and multiplying the transaction fee which is $2. ($500 / $50 * $2 = $20). This number is then multiplied by the number of days in a year and the number of ATM machines.

Bed and Breakfast

Rocheport Bed and Breakfast

123 Main St.
Rocheport, Missouri 65279

Kari Lucke

Olivia and Stan Jordan propose the opening of a luxurious yet competitively priced bed and breakfast inn in the historic town of Rocheport, Missouri.

EXECUTIVE SUMMARY

Olivia and Stan Jordan propose the opening of a new bed and breakfast inn in the historic town of Rocheport, Missouri. In order to stand out among other bed and breakfasts (B&Bs) in the area, the Jordans plan to make the Rocheport B&B the best and most luxurious while remaining competitive in terms of rates. They are able to do this based on the fact that they will do most of the remodeling work themselves, as well as all of the maintenance and service necessary for operation of the business. Olivia has a B.S. in culinary arts and thus is capable of producing outstanding meals, which is an extremely important aspect of a B&B. Stan has been a building contractor for 20 years and has the knowledge and skills to do most of the remodeling work as well as any ongoing maintenance. The Jordans aim is to provide a new place of rest and relaxation for residents from around the state and beyond.

Business Overview

A bed and breakfast inn is a small lodging establishment, usually a private home, that offers private bedrooms for rent; owners supply breakfast to their guests on the morning of their stay. B&Bs normally offer rooms with private bathrooms and/or a suite of rooms that share a bathroom. Breakfast is usually served in a dining room or the guests' rooms, and quality and presentation of the food is one of the key factors that distinguish the best B&Bs. Decor is also important; many B&Bs are historic buildings and incorporate Victorian or other historical decor and furnishings. Most owners live in the residence and manage the business themselves, although some may hire outside workers to clean the guest rooms. B&B owners must be friendly and willing to host a variety of people in their homes on an ongoing basis. Leisure travel dominates this sector of the inn-keeping business, attracting in particular guests who enjoy the cultural, historic, and unique aspects of B&Bs.

INDUSTRY AND MARKET

Industry Analysis

B&Bs represent a $3.4 billion industry, according to the Professional Association of Innkeepers International (PAII), and the industry is still growing. Whereas there were only 1,000 B&Bs in the United States serving about 1 million guests in 1990, by 2008 there were more than 20,000 serving over 50 million guests annually. According to a May 5, 2009, Time magazine article, "Americans have a wide array of lodgings to choose from when they take a vacation...Yet more and more people are flocking to bed-and-breakfast inns." As life becomes more complicated and Americans continue to search for ways to "get away from it all," B&Bs will continue to gain in popularity.

Market Analysis

The market for the Rocheport B&B consists of couples and individuals in the nearby town of Columbia, Missouri (population 94,000), as well as surrounding areas. Because Rocheport is located in the middle of the state, the metro areas of St. Louis (population 2.8 million) and Kansas City (population 2 million), both of which are a two-hour drive from Rocheport, are also considered important markets.

According to a Michigan State University study, most visitors to B&Bs are middle-aged, well-educated professionals in moderately high income brackets. About two-thirds of guests are couples. Eighty-two percent of the people surveyed indicated they were married, and about half had children at home. Newlyweds and empty-nesters accounted for a smaller portion of B&B guests.

Competition

Although there are three other B&Bs in Rocheport—Yates House B&B, School House B&B, and Amber House B&B—there are plenty of customers to go around, so to speak. The existing B&Bs are often hard to reserve, especially in the summer, due to high demand. Rocheport B&B may pick up those visitors who cannot get a reservation elsewhere, and then once the guests experience the service and accommodations the Jordans offer, it is highly likely that these people will come back as returning guests. Also, the fact that the Rocheport B&B is the village's newest inn should draw travelers who are interested in sampling a new place or who are attracted to new experiences and ventures.

PERSONNEL

Management

Olivia and Stan Jordan will manage the business on a day-to-day basis. Stan will perform all routine maintenance on the house and grounds, and Olivia will do all the cooking and cleaning. With Olivia's degree and experience with cooking, she will be able to plan and create extraordinary and creative breakfasts, which is a vital part of the B&B experience.

Professional and Advisory Support

The Jordans plan to join Bed & Breakfast Inns of Missouri (BBIM), which hosts an annual conference, provides a weekly state-specific newsletter on happenings in the industry, and manages an online forum of others in the business. Member inns can use the BBIM logo on marketing materials, showing that they have been inspected and approved by a reputable agency. The inspection and application fee is $100. BBIM also provides opportunities for free online marketing, including a listing on the BBIM site, which includes a link to the individual inn's web site and a variety of ways to search for inns, such as location, specialty, or route; gift certificates that are good only at BBIM inns; and a frequent guest program.

STRATEGIES

Business Strategy

To the Jordans, people who stay at the Rocheport B&B are houseguests, not customers. The Jordans' motivation to operate a B&B is based on their desire to meet new people and provide travelers and guests with a unique and enjoyable experience, as well as to use their skills and talents in a positive way. It is this philosophy that will make the Rocheport B&B a success. In this business, those who are in it for the money will not be successful, as they do not have the underlying enthusiasm or drive to provide what is essential to any good B&B: an interest in people and a willingness and desire to serve them well. However, those who do have this passion for interacting and serving other people—such as the Jordans—will accomplish and exceed their business goals as a result of their underlying motivations.

Growth Strategy

The most effective form of advertising for B&Bs, according to PAII, is word of mouth. The idea is that once guests experience the Rocheport B&B, they will tell others about it, and new business will be generated. In addition, online reviews have become a key factor in the industry. At such sites as BedandBreakfast.com, users rate inns they have visited based on guest rooms, service, value, cleanliness, and dining. A 2009 ComCore study showed that 25 percent of B&B guests surveyed viewed online reviews before deciding which B&B to visit, and 75 percent of those stated that the reviews significantly impacted their decision.

As the Jordans welcome more guests, their reputation as an excellent B&B in the Rocheport area will grow, due to both word–of–mouth promotion and positive online reviews. Such "free" marketing will bring new guests to their inn, and the Jordans can continue to build their client base. According to Harold Alexander of the University of Minnesota Extension as well as many others, "It's not unusual for guests to return again and again to favorite bed and breakfast...and develop long-lasting friendships with the owners."

PRODUCTS AND SERVICES

Description

The Rocheport Bed & Breakfast is located in Rocheport, Missouri, on the Missouri River. The home was built in 1915 and is listed on the National Register of Historic Places. With some moderate remodeling, the Rocheport B&B will become a four-bedroom inn. Each guest room will have its own private bathroom, and breakfast will be served in the main-level dining room or on the large, shaded, wood deck at the back of the house, depending on weather conditions.

The goal of the Rocheport B&B is to provide a quiet, relaxing, and enjoyable place to stay for guests looking for a romantic weekend away, a place to relax after a long day of shopping or on the trail, or just some "down time" away from the hustle and bustle of everyday life. The inn is within walking distance of several restaurants and the Katy Trail. The Katy Trail, originally part of the Missouri-Kansas-Texas rail line, is the longest state park in the country and a very popular destination for bicyclists as well as hikers. Rocheport is also home to Les Bourgeois Winery and several unique shops and antique stores.

Unique Features/Niche

The Rocheport B&B will stand out as the most accommodating and luxurious B&B in Rocheport. In addition to the standard B&B fare for upscale inns, such as exquisite decor, king-sized beds, luxurious bedding, private baths with showers, Wi-Fi, TV/DVD, radio/CD player, and refrigerator with complimentary beverages, the Jordans' inn will also provide the following amenities: a complimentary bottle of wine at arrival; homemade chocolate chip cookies in the afternoon; 24-hour coffee and tea; spa robes for all guests; free bike rental; a large library of both books and DVDs; and free shuttle services to village attractions. In addition, the inn will feature a multi-level wooden deck off the back of the house with tables, cushioned chairs, and a fire pit; an eight-person hot tub located on the bottom-level deck; and a two-person hammock under maple trees in the backyard. Every detail in the accommodations and surroundings, from the crystal chandeliers in the bedrooms to the c.1870 walnut table with seating for 10 in the dining room, will reflect the highest quality.

In the B&B industry, the quality of the hosts is also vital to an inn's success. Olivia and Stan both have an outgoing nature, never-ending energy, and a flare for conversation—characteristics that are critical to making guests feel instantly at ease and welcome.

Pricing

Room rates at the Rocheport B&B will be on par with the average rate charged by the other inns in the village. For Amber House, rates run from $149 to $239; for School House, $149 to $260; and for Yates House, $169 to $269.

The Rocheport B&B will offer four guest rooms, two with the amenities described under "Unique Features/Niche," at a rate of $169 per night, and two with these amenities plus a gas fireplace and a two-person Jacuzzi tub, at a rate of $259. Rates are reduced by $20 on all weekdays except Friday.

MARKETING AND SALES

Advertising and Promotion

When they are ready to open the inn, the Jordans will send a press release to local media regarding their new business and what it will offer. They will also run a quarter-page ad in the popular local monthly magazine *Inside Columbia*, which caters to the same market as the Rocheport B&B. Other forms of advertising will brochures, which will be distributed and placed in tourist information racks in key locations along Interstate 70 (which runs past Rocheport) and listings on web sites such as BBIM, mentioned under "Professional and Advisory Support," as well as similar web sites that provide free listing opportunities.

Cost

All of the marketing methods are low cost or free and have been proven effective for this type of business. Total upfront costs include the ad in *Inside Columbia* ($585) and 500 standard brochures ($125). Ongoing costs will occur when brochures need to be reprinted or updated but 500 copies are expected to last three years or longer.

OPERATIONS

Customers

As mentioned under "Market Analysis," most visitors to B&Bs are middle-aged, well educated, and work in a professional field earning moderately high incomes. Because Columbia is the nearest large town, it will be the focus of marketing efforts. The following statistics regarding the Columbia population are relevant:

- Individuals between the ages of 35 and 54—24%
- Couples with children under the age of 18—27%
- Households with incomes of $50,000 or more—40%

In addition, Columbia is home to two private four-year colleges and the state's flagship university, as well as three large hospitals. In 2008 *Forbes* magazine rated Columbia 11th on its list of Smartest Cities in America, based on the education levels of Columbia-area residents. Columbia also has the highest number of doctors per capita than any other city in the United States besides Rochester, Minnesota, where the Mayo Clinic is located. Such facts illustrate the kind of education and income levels that are typical of B&B visitors.

Columbia is not the only market, however, and the Rocheport B&B will welcome guests from around the United States as well as other countries.

Facility and Location

The Rocheport B&B is located at 213 First Street in Rocheport, Missouri. The location is zoned as commercial. The Jordans own the adjoining empty lot, which will be used for guest parking.

The location of the inn is ideal in that it is on the Katy Trail and the Missouri River and is within walking distance of shops and restaurants. Rocheport itself is an excellent location because it is only 2 miles off Interstate 70 and is in the middle of the state, allowing easy access from Kansas City and St. Louis, as well as providing a convenient place for people who are traveling I-70.

Currently the home consists of six bedrooms (two main level and four upper level) and two and a half bathrooms (one and a half main level and one upper level). The Jordans will occupy one of the main-floor bedrooms and the adjoining bathroom. The other main-floor bedroom will be furnished for guests. Remodeling on the main floor will consist of turning the half-bath into a full bath, with Jacuzzi tub, and adjoining it with the guest bedroom. Three of the bedrooms on the upper level will be furnished for guests, and one of the bedrooms will be converted into two bathrooms. The remaining bathroom upstairs will be remodeled to accommodate a two-person tub. Total cost of renovations is estimated to be $50,000.

Legal Environment

In Missouri, B&Bs are considered "lodging establishments" and thus must undergo an annual inspection by the Missouri Department of Health and Senior Services (DHSS). Owners must also submit to additional inspections if deemed necessary by the state. The DHSS then grants (or renews) an occupational license, good for one year. Relevant local ordinances include those regulating fire safety, electrical wiring, fireplaces, and plumbing, in addition to zoning regulations. B&B owners must also register the name of their business with the Missouri Secretary of State and obtain a business license from Boone County.

FINANCIAL ANALYSIS

The following two worksheets detail start-up costs and expected profits for the first three years. Loan payment is calculated based on a 7 percent fixed-rate commercial loan. First-year expected sales and food costs are based on the national average occupancy rates at B&Bs (40%); second- and third-year figures are based on an expected annual growth rate of about 10 percent. Expenses are calculated to increase by approximately 5 percent per year in addition to the increases incurred by accommodating more guests.

Start-Up Costs

Capital requirements	On hand	Needed
Legal fees, licenses	$ 0	$ 500
Furnishings, linens, and electronics for rooms	$ 2,000	$ 8,000
Business supplies	$ 500	$ 0
Other starting inventory (bicycles, toiletries, food and beverages)	$ 0	$ 5,000
Kitchen equipment, dishes	$ 500	$ 1,000
Outdoor furniture and amenities	$ 0	$ 3,000
Building renovations	$ 0	$ 50,000
Petty cash (working capital)	$ 500	$ 0
Directional and entrance signs	$ 0	$ 1,500
Parking lot preparation	$ 0	$ 2,000
Advertising	$ 0	$ 710
Totals	**$3,500**	**$71,710**

Worksheet 2: Sales and Earnings

	1st Year	2nd Year	3rd Year
Net sales	$125,000	$137,500	$151,250
Less expenses			
Loan payment	$ 1,400	$ 1,400	$ 1,400
Food	$ 5,840	$ 6,420	$ 7,350
Housekeeping/room supplies	$ 500	$ 750	$ 1,000
Utilities	$ 4,200	$ 4,620	$ 5,080
Repairs and maintenance	$ 600	$ 750	$ 1,000
Vehicle expenses (for shuttle)	$ 500	$ 625	$ 750
Insurance	$ 1,200	$ 1,320	$ 1,450
Total expenses	**$ 14,240**	**$ 15,885**	**$ 18,030**
Net profit before taxes	$110,760	$121,615	$133,220

Beekeeping Business

B. Strand's Bees

102 Georgetown Road
Montgomery Corners, Illinois 61022

Paul Greenland

B. Strand's Bees raises bees for the production of products such as honey and beeswax, and for crop pollination services.

EXECUTIVE SUMMARY

Business Overview

Owned by Bill Strand, B. Strand's Bees raises bees for the production of products such as honey and beeswax, and for crop pollination services. Our business relies on the performance of 500 honey bee colonies. Of these, some remain at our location in Montgomery Corners, Illinois, while other are relocated at different times throughout the season, depending on the needs of the orchards and farms to which we provide pollination services.

Savvy product marketing is critical for successful beekeepers. Over the years, the B. Strand's brand name has become well known in our region thanks to an identity and related product packaging designs developed by a local advertising agency. We market the majority of our products to well-heeled tourists who visit the neighboring town of Brendenwood, Illinois, where Bill Strand's wife operates a separate but affiliated gift shop operation called The Busy Bee.

B. Strand's is a relatively small operation. Our competitors include other beekeepers in northwestern Illinois who sell their products at farmers markets, organic food stores, and other locations, and rent their hives/provide pollination services to area orchards and farms.

MARKET ANALYSIS

Our operation is located in the town of Montgomery Corners, Illinois, in Davis County. We are only a short distance away from the historic town of Brendenwood, a popular tourist destination marked by nineteenth century architecture, unique shops, restaurants, B&Bs, wineries, and more.

The majority of the honey and beeswax that we produce is sold through a gift shop in Brendenwood named The Busy Bee, which sells candles, beeswax, honey, and bee-themed merchandise. Owned and operated by Bill Strand's wife, Leah Strand, this separate but affiliated retail business provides us with a unique channel to sell our offerings to tourists, many of whom have large disposable incomes.

Our competitors include other beekeepers in northwestern Illinois. Leading the competition is Webster's Bee Farm, a large commercial operation with 2,500 colonies. Super Bees (1,500 colonies) and Henry's Honey Haven (1,250 colonies) are two other sizable operations in our area. While most of our competitors market their offerings on a regional or national basis, we mainly focus on supplying our affiliated retail operation with branded products, and serving a few local orchards and farms.

INDUSTRY ANALYSIS

According to Midwestern State University's College of Agriculture, the United States is home to roughly 150,000 beekeepers. Collectively, they own about 3 million colonies of honey bees. Large commercial beekeeping operations maintain as many as 2,000 colonies.

The beekeeping industry provided limited employment opportunities during the mid-2000s. However, at that time a significant number of commercial beekeepers were nearing retirement, providing opportunities for new individuals to "learn the ropes" and take over their operations.

Many beekeepers belong to beekeeping clubs at the county level, or belong to one of three regional societies. These include the Heartland Apicultural Society, the Western Apicultural Society, and the Eastern Apicultural Society. At the national level, beekeepers may belong to either The American Honey Producers' Association or the American Beekeeping Federation.

MANAGEMENT

B. Strand's is headed by owner Bill Strand. Bill Strand acquired the operation in 2002 from his father-in-law, Stephen Goers, who established the business in 1984 under the name Bee Line Bees. Goers has since retired, but lends occasional assistance and expertise as needed. Strand's wife, Leah, who operates an affiliated gift shop in a neighboring town, also lends occasional assistance but is not an employee. Bill Strand is a member of both the American Honey Producers' Association and the American Beekeeping Federation.

PRODUCTS & SERVICES

Our operation produces approximately 30,000 pounds of extracted honey each year. The majority of this is packaged and sold as traditional liquid honey under our brand name. In addition to liquid honey, we also sell:

- Comb honey, which remains in the edible honeycomb.
- Whipped or creamed honey, which can be spread like butter.
- Chuck honey, which is liquid honey with pieces of honeycomb remaining in the jar.

We also sell beeswax to several area businesses that use it to produce candles, soaps, and other items.

Finally, we rent our bees out to a number of area farms and orchards throughout the spring and summer months.

OPERATIONS

B. Strand's Bees is located in a rural area, in close proximity to a number of orchards and farms to which we rent colonies for the purposes of pollination services. Our business is located on a plot of land that includes three outbuildings.

The success of B. Strand's Bees literally rests upon the wings of our bees. Specifically, we rely upon about 500 colonies of Italian honey bees. In addition to an excellent reputation for honey production, this type of bee resists disease more effectively than German bees and is less defensive, making it the bee stock of choice in the United States.

Our honey bees reside in beehives known as supers, or wooden boxes that contain a series of frames. Each colony consists of an egg-producing queen bee, hundreds of drones, and as many as 50,000 worker bees. On average, we are able to harvest about 75 to 80 pounds of honey from each colony per year.

Hives must be inspected on a regular basis to monitor production and detect potential problems. A number of pests pose potential threats to our business, including tracheal mites, varroa mites, wax moths, and small hive beetles. In addition, we must monitor hives for diseases such as European foulbrood and American foulbrood.

Although some may assume that beekeeping is a seasonal endeavor, we operate our business year-round. In the spring we focus on caring for old hives and establishing new ones. For hives with low food supplies, we provide them with a syrup consisting of sugar and water until they are able to begin producing honey. At this time we also acquire new bees from dealers and move them near sources of nectar, such as clover fields and orchards.

Honey is first harvested late in the spring or during the early summer months, at which time a mild, light-colored crop is produced. A second harvest follows in the fall, producing a darker, more flavorful honey. During the fall we prepare our hives for the winter months, at which time we perform maintenance on our equipment, analyze records, and engage in planning for the following season.

We utilize a wide range of equipment to carry out our operations. In addition to protective clothing, special tools, supers, and frames, we also rely upon a forklift, as well as a large truck used for making deliveries.

One important aspect of our operation is honey packaging, which is performed in a dedicated outbuilding. In addition to placing honey into jars, we also place our branded label onto containers. Labels include information such as the grade and weight of the honey, along with our contact information.

FINANCIAL ANALYSIS

Budget

Receipts	
Honey	$60,000
Pollination fees	
Spring hives	$12,500
Summer hives	$15,000
Wax	$ 500
Total receipts	**$88,000**
Variable costs	
Bees (replacement bees)	$ 4,500
Queens (replacement)	$ 1,200
Insurance	$ 500
Chemical for fume boards	$ 825
Jars	$ 9,500
Labels	$ 2,000
Marketing	$ 1,000
Parasite and disease control	$ 8,520
Registration fees	$ 100
Sugar	$ 1,250
Vehicle costs/maintenance	$ 5,750
Total variable costs	**$35,145**
Fixed costs	
Equipment	$ 9,500
Brood boxes and frames	
Extracting equipment	
Feeders	
Fume boards	
Hive tools/smokers	
Honey supers/frames	
Protective clothing	
Queen excluders	
Top, bottoms, and inner covers	
Facility Upkeep	$ 6,500
Total fixed costs	**$16,000**
Total costs	**$51,145**
Returns	
Returns over variable costs	$52,855
Net returns	$36,855

LEGAL

Per the Illinois Bees and Apiaries Act, our business is required to register our bee colonies with the Illinois Department of Agriculture, which provides free inspections in order to identify pests, diseases, and to recommend treatments. This service is provided as part of the Illinois Bees and Apiaries Program.

In addition to adhering to state regulations, we also have secured liability insurance from an agency recommended by the American Beekeeping Federation. Such coverage is necessary in the event of a lawsuit related to the consumption of our honey products, or in the event that a visitor to our facility has a negative reaction to a bee sting.

MARKETING & SALES

Over the years, the B. Strand's brand name has become well known in our region thanks to an identity and related product packaging designs developed by a local advertising agency many years ago.

Because the majority of our honey production is earmarked for resale through The Busy Bee, our affiliated retail operation in Brendenwood, Illinois, B. Strand's Bees does not engage in direct-to-consumer marketing. Beyond The Busy Bee, we have established relationships with several grocery stores and farmers markets in neighboring towns that carry our honey products.

On a similar note, little marketing is needed for our pollination services. Because the wild honey bee population has been severely impacted by pests and diseases, there is ample demand for our domestic honey bees. As an established operation, we have relationships in place with several area orchards and farms that rely upon our colonies for the pollination of pumpkins, apples, melons, blueberries, and cucumbers. Our marketing consists mainly of relationship building activities. Throughout the season, we pay occasional visits to the orchardists and farmers with whom we normally work in order to stay visible. On occasion, we bring complimentary honey products to them for their enjoyment, and take them out for lunch.

SWOT ANALYSIS

- Strengths: We are an established operation with a unique retail outlet through which we sell the majority of our honey and beeswax.

- Weaknesses: We are a relatively small beekeeping business, limiting our ability to provide pollination services to larger orchards and farms.

- Opportunities: Because pests and disease have virtually eliminated wild honey bees in our area, there is ample demand for pollination services provided by our domestic honey bees.

- Threats: Pests and disease are potential threats to our operation.

Car Wash and Car Detailing Business

Wash and Go

150 Merchant Rd.
Portland, Maine 04101

Laura Becker

Wash and Go provides a full service vehicle cleaning and detailing operation in Portland, Maine.

EXECUTIVE SUMMARY

Wash and Go will own and operate a car wash and car detailing business in Portland, Maine. The car wash will be an automatic process where customers will exit their vehicles and watch as the cars are professionally washed. Wash and Go also provides a car detailing service which accounts for additional revenue.

Independently owned car wash services, like Wash and Go, will provide a number of different vehicle cleaning services to clients. Revenue is produced from exterior washing, interior washing, detailing, and merchandise sales. Wash and Go offers a very high quality service and competes heavily on price with other car washes in the area. The customer base consists of individual car owners, fleet companies (which include taxi and limo companies) and car dealerships.

MARKET ANALYSIS

According to the International Carwash Association, the car wash industry can generally be organized along two lines: suppliers and retailers. Suppliers include providers of car washing equipment, solutions manufacturers and distributors. Retailers include car wash companies operating in one or more lines of business: self serve car wash; in–bay automatic (stationary automatic) car wash; or conveyor automatic car wash.

Professional car wash establishments are more ecologically–friendly relative to parking lot or driveway car washing. Water and cleaning fluid are routed to a treatment facility as opposed to the curve or drains, according to the International Carwash Association.

OPERATIONS

Car wash services can be stand alone entities, or operated as part of a group of automobile services or convenience stores. An example of car washing or detailing as one of many services is the oil lube shop.

Many oil lube shops offer car washes as one of the multitude of services they offer. Other examples of car washing services are automated service and self service car washes.

Wash and Go operates a conveyor automatic car wash service, which allows customers to hand off cars and watch as the cars are transported down a conveyor belt while having either individuals wash the cars or machines (brushes) wash the cars. Some customers prefer hand washed cars as they may eliminate the potential for slight scratches that may occur in brush washed facilities.

Hand washed car washes are usually more expensive, and cannot be as competitive on pricing. Self service washing provides for the car owner to wash a car at a facility that offers all of the necessary cleaning tools.

Types of Car Washes

When analyzing the decision to own a car wash business, one of the first decisions is to decide what type of car wash to establish. There are several options, as noted and described below.

Self service car wash

Customers wash their own vehicles in individual wash bays. These bays can either have self serve equipment or in–bay automatic equipment in them. The advantage of this type of car wash business is that there are low labor costs. Hours of car wash availability can be seven days a week, 24 hours a day.

Stand alone automatic car wash

When lot size is limited, a car wash business that uses only the in–bay automatic service may be preferable. The stand alone automatic car wash consists of one or two in–bay automatics and a vacuum and vending area.

Automatic car wash

There are three basic types of automatic car wash: touch, touch–free and conveyors.

A touch automatic car wash uses cloth or cloth–like materials to clean the car. A touch–free automatic car wash uses chemicals and high powered water sprays to clean the car. The conveyor system is a touch automatic car wash system that uses conveyor belts to pull cars through the system.

The touch automatic car wash system with conveyors can provide an exterior wash cycle and an interior wash.

There are three basic conveyor platforms including:

- Full Service Tunnel—The vehicle is cleaned inside and outside. The vehicle owner typically pays and then leaves the vehicle and goes to a waiting area while the vehicle is cleaned. This method is considered to be the premium offering; but it is also involves the most labor.

- Express Tunnel—Only the exterior of the vehicle is cleaned and vacuums may be offered to the customer after the car wash. The customer usually pays at a pay station prior to the tunnel and then remains in the vehicle during the car wash. This is a fast, low–priced tunnel car wash. This method has a goal of high volume and low costs for the operator.

- Flex Serve—The customer is offered an exterior car wash with the option for interior cleaning and detailing provided at an additional charge. The vehicle owner usually pays at a pay station prior to the tunnel and remains in their vehicle during the car wash. Those that wish to have their interior cleaned can either exit their vehicle and wait for the attendants to complete the interior cleaning or proceed to an area where self–vacuuming can be completed.

The benefits of tunnel car wash systems include high volume and high revenue potential and the ability to provide extra services such as detailing and quick lube for additional revenue opportunities.

Car wash and convenience store combination

In–bay automatics and self service car wash equipment can be a profitable addition to a convenience store operation, adding significant revenue to the entire operation.

Performing Site Analysis—Location, Location, Location

When setting up a car wash, it is extremely important to find the right location.

Lot Selection

- A good rule of thumb to follow concerning lot sizing is 100 to 120 feet deep X a minimum of 75 feet wide depending on the number of bays. (Typical 4 bay self–serve wash would require a lot 100 to 120 feet deep X 100 feet wide minimum).

- Good access from both directions of traffic flow is important.

- Ideal traffic speed should be under 40 mph.

- Lot size and shape will determine if you design a "Drive–in–back–out" or "Drive–through" building. (Income streams tend to favor the "drive–through" design).

- Ideal locations are near residential areas, apartment complexes or busy traffic flow routes.

- A good rule to follow regarding the cost of property is that the monthly lease payment should not exceed 15 percent of the gross monthly income of the wash.

Bay and Building Sizing

- Ideal bay size is 16 feet wide X 28 feet long (inside measurements).

- Typical pump room is 10 to15 feet wide X 28 feet length.

Building Placement

- Depending on specific codes, your building should be placed on the lot to allow for 1–2 cars minimum to be "stacked" behind each bay waiting to wash. Vacuums can be placed in this area but should not impede the normal flow into the bays.

- Make sure there are adequate drying and vacuuming areas that are out of the main traffic flow.

- Ideally, your bays should have a southern exposure to help reduce ice build–up in cold weather conditions.

- Local codes will also have "set–back" requirements on building placement.

Staff

The operations of a car wash facility are vital to the success of an automatic facility. A self service facility will require a few employees to assist occasionally in the washing process as well as employees to collect cash transactions. For an automatic facility, it is necessary to have employees assist in the cleaning process and to have an employee facilitate transactions. The employees needed in the Wash and Go facility are a facility manager, a wash reception person, a tire cleaner, a vacuum operator, one detailing cleaner, and at least six drying operators. All of these employees are paid on an hourly basis. Many of the staff generates a significant portion of their income from tips. The facility is open from 8a.m. to 6 p.m., seven days a week.

Cleaning Equipment

A car wash business needs to keep an inventory of cleaning fluid at all times. This includes chemicals that are mixed with waters to clean the exterior of automobiles as the vehicles move through the conveyor system.

Wash and Go purchases window cleaning fluid and detailing wax and keeps that in inventory as well. The business also needs to supply towels to the drying staff. There are many suppliers of cleaning supplies available. A leading supplier is Kleen–Rite Corporation.

Management and Control Software

It is a good idea to use management and control software to account for all transactions and to be able to analyze usage trends and patterns.

Professional Support

In setting up the Wash and Go operation, an outside attorney was hired to assist in establishing and incorporating the company.

A business will also need assistance from an insurance broker to attain the correct amount of liability insurance for the facility. Wash and Go works with a local banker to set up a revolving credit account and a payroll company to manage the payroll process. An outside accountant helps with books and records. Wash and Go set up a merchant account through First Data Corporation which allows the business to transact using credit cards.

FINANCIAL ANALYSIS

Revenue Projections—Bays

- Studies find that it takes a population base of 1,000–1,500 people to support one self serve bay.

- At this population level, the national average is approximately $1,350 per bay, per month of gross income for one self serve bay.

Revenue Projections—Vacuums

- The ideal number of vacuums to have is one and a half vacuums per one bay of self–serve.

- National average of revenue per vacuum is approximately $222 per vacuum per month in gross revenue.

Operating Cost Projections

Average operating costs is approximately 52 percent of gross income which includes 9.3 percent for attendant labor. (Lease payments, income tax, debt reduction or depreciation are not included).

Barriers to entry

The initial investment into a car wash will depend on whether you plan to purchase an existing facility or build a facility. An outright purchase can be financed through banks or credit unions, similar to financing of any small business. When building a facility, many factors will come into play.

For example, is there a facility that already exists? Will the owner have to build from scratch? Is the land available for lease? The land that Wash and Go decided on was available for lease and there was a vacant business on the property that had offered automobile lubrication.

The Wash and Go start up was based on these factors. Leases can range in prices depending on the location and area of the country. The Wash and Go lease, which is a three year lease, is $1,000 dollars per month. The business needed contracting work from a builder, and money to purchase water pumps, a conveyor belt, vacuums, cleaning fluids, drainage systems, computer terminal, and a cash register. The amount needed for start up, which includes money for employees was approximately $100,000.

OBJECTIVES

The Wash and Go business objective is to provide a superior car wash and detailing service to individuals and businesses in the Portland, Maine area. The strategy has been to focus on businesses and to provide an alternative to self cleaning automobiles.

Purchase Existing Establishment Versus Building New Establishment

One of the first decisions to make when establishing a car wash is to decide whether to purchase an already existing car wash establishment, or to build a new establishment on purchased or leased land.

Purchasing an existing facility may require a consultant to help evaluate the business and to determine a fair market value. Car wash facilities are normally valued by one of two methods. The first is to evaluate the adjusted monthly average income and create a multiple of 12–25 times this value. The second is to use a multiple of four to seven times the annual adjusted net income. Both of these methods of creating a market value excludes real estate, and subtracts lease or rental expenses to create the net value.

When purchasing an existing car wash, it is important to:

- Analyze existing facility, review demographics

- Observe and review entire operation in all departments

- Review management, equipment, improvements and property

- Analyze existing competition within a three mile radius

- Check with City Planning Department to determine if any new car washes are being planned or built

- Analyze existing marketing and advertising programs, bonus and commission schedules, any employee agreements, medical and pension plans, vendor agreements and sub–leases (if applicable)

- Analyze how extra services and sales may be added or upgraded

- Review property to determine what additional profit centers may be added, such as oil lube, smog testing, gasoline, express detailing, engine cleaning, convenience store, windshield repair, paint chip repair, etc.

- Review existing computer software for suitability

- Review operational income and expense statements

- Review Lease Agreement (if applicable) regarding lease terms, rent increases and other conditions that would affect buyer

- Assure that the property is free of toxic contamination. Provide recommendation if an Environmental Phase One is required

- Prepare a valuation of the business to use in determining a reasonable purchase price

- Provide a list of Conditions and Contingencies to be used in preparing an offer, escrow instructions and Purchase and Sale Agreement

- Analyze facility for possible State and Federal violations

- Provide handbooks, materials and forms to be used in the operation

- Provide new bonus and commission schedules, marketing and advertising programs, in the event business is purchased

- Review offers, purchase agreements, assist with negotiations, interact with buyer's attorney and accountant to protect the buyer's interest

- Assist buyer during due diligence period
- Provide a Business and Operational Plan for use by owner, management and, as required, by outside lenders if purchase is completed
- Provide lender's contacts for outside financing
- Provide insurance contacts for required coverage
- Provide unlimited telephone consultations with all parties involved

Prior to developing Wash and Go, management performed some simple market analysis to determine the ideal location to place the car wash establishment. It was concluded that a high traffic area would be the best location for the establishment. During the location analysis, there were no existing car wash facilities found within a three mile radius of Wash and Go's chosen location.

The Wash and Go facility is located approximately one mile from a major highway, and the main route in and out of Portland, Maine. It is also a wise idea to be in close proximity to local car dealerships. There are four dealerships within a one mile radius of Wash and Go, and one taxi service.

Close proximity to a highway allows customers to stop at the car wash on the way to and from work. During the five year period since Wash and Go opened, the business has undertaken several studies of consumer behavior and traffic patterns. The majority of Wash and Go's business during the weekdays is between 8 a.m. and 9 a.m. and 5 p.m. and 7 p.m. On the weekends, the business is busiest during the middle of the day from 11 a.m. to 3 p.m. This market analysis has helped to determine employment and operational requirements.

PRODUCTS & SERVICES

After finding the location, the next step was to decide on the type of car wash service to offer. Wash and Go is located near many local businesses, so it was decided to offer an automatic conveyor service (full service tunnel service) for customer convenience.

This will allow the business to approach both car dealerships and car services (taxi and limo) and offer car washing at a bulk discount rate. It was also decided that having a hand washed service compared to an automated wash service would be too costly.

Wash and Go then began the process of ordering the proper equipment for an automatic conveyor car wash, including automated brushes to wash cars.

Car Wash Equipment

D & S Car Wash Systems offers in–bay automatic systems such as Quicksilver Touchless and Odyssey Soft–Touch. In addition, D & S offers drive–through tunnel equipment such as the Quicksilver Express and the Odyssey Express. D & S offers a myriad of options for self–service equipment. In addition, D & S offers vacuums and other ancillary products.

For tunnel equipment used in conveyor car washes, Hanna Systems is another vendor. Hanna claims to have the broadest line of conveyor wash systems and components in the industry, including Soft Cloth, Light Foam, Hand Wash and Hi–Pressure Touchless conveyor systems.

Additional Equipment and Supply Providers

- Ryko Manufacturing Company
- American Car Wash Equipment and Supply

- PDQ

- Autobase

- Belanger Inc.

- Autec

- AOK

There is a web site for resale car wash equipment and supplies at Car Wash Consignments.com. The site connects buyers and sellers of used equipment and supplies.

COMPETITION

The nearest car wash service to Wash and Go is approximately four miles north of the facility. This facility is a self serve facility and does not compete directly for the same business. Wash and Go has a few different cleaning features and is priced competitively relative to other automated service facilities.

ADVERTISING

Prior to opening the business, it is helpful to advertise in a local newspaper or on local television. A direct mail campaign with introductory coupons is also helpful. The goal is to obtain as much customer information as possible in order to continually offer special promotions to draw in business.

FINANCIAL ANALYSIS

The bulk of Wash and Go's revenue is produced from full service car washes. Full service consists of an exterior car wash, interior cleaning and hand drying of an automobile. Exterior washes alone are less popular, and detailing produces the least amount of revenue.

Each service that Wash and Go offers has a different price which is listed below. The business' financials, which are broken out by year, contain information about the number of unit sales and the total revenue per service. The financials also list the cost of each service per unit sale. Expenses consist of rent, staff payroll, legal, insurance and accounting bills.

During the first year the operation had a loss of nearly $59,000. The second year of operation showed a gain of $16,400 before taxes. The third year showed a gain of over $101,000 before taxes.

Prices

Price list

Full wash	$ 15.00
Exterior wash	$ 9.00
Interior clean	$ 8.00
End user detail	$140.00
Business fleet washes	$ 10.00
Car dealership details	$ 70.00

Balance Sheet

	Year 1	Year 2	Year 3
Unit sales			
Full wash	1,500	3,500	5,500
Exterior wash	750	1,500	2,500
Interior clean	500	1,250	1,500
End user detail	150	225	350
Business fleet washes	1,500	3,000	5,000
Car dealership details	300	450	600
Revenue			
Full wash	$ 22,500.00	$ 52,500.00	$ 82,500.00
Exterior wash	$ 6,750.00	$ 13,500.00	$ 22,500.00
Interior clean	$ 4,000.00	$ 10,000.00	$ 12,000.00
End user detail	$ 21,000.00	$ 31,500.00	$ 49,000.00
Business fleet washes	$ 15,000.00	$ 30,000.00	$ 50,000.00
Car dealership details	$ 21,000.00	$ 31,500.00	$ 42,000.00
Total	**$ 90,250.00**	**$169,000.00**	**$258,000.00**
Cost of sales			
Full wash	$ 1,050.00	$ 2,450.00	$ 3,850.00
Exterior wash	$ 300.00	$ 600.00	$ 1,000.00
Interior clean	$ 150.00	$ 375.00	$ 450.00
End user detail	$ 450.00	$ 675.00	$ 1,050.00
Business fleet washes	$ 1,050.00	$ 2,100.00	$ 3,500.00
Car dealership details	$ 900.00	$ 1,350.00	$ 1,800.00
Total	**$ 3,900.00**	**$ 7,550.00**	**$ 11,650.00**
Expenses			
Administrative staff	$ 36,500.00	$ 36,500.00	$ 36,500.00
Hourly workers	$ 98,550.00	$ 98,550.00	$ 98,550.00
Rent	$ 12,000.00	$ 12,000.00	$ 12,000.00
Legal	$ 5,000.00	$ 5,000.00	$ 5,000.00
Insurance	$ 3,000.00	$ 3,000.00	$ 3,000.00
Accounting	$ 2,000.00	$ 2,000.00	$ 2,000.00
Total	**$ −70,650.00**	**$ 8,100.00**	**$ 97,100.00**

Cash Flow Projections

Magic Wand Self Service and In–Bay Automatics Cash Flow Projection

Monthly income per bay in case of self service or in–bay automatic car wash can vary over a broad range from $1,500 to $15,000, depending on several parameters. If the car wash activity is good, it is a wise decision to convert a self service bay to an in–bay automatic bay system. This conversion can increase the number of cars washed per hour from four–five cars to 10–12 cars, marking threefold increase in revenue.

Magic Wand Tunnel Car Wash Cash Flow Projection

While a tunnel car wash is a fast and continuous car wash system, it has higher costs involved. It is particularly important to pay more attention to labor costs while estimating cost and revenue in this case, because tunnel car wash systems typically require presence of multiple staff on site.

Counseling Practice

Roper Counseling Services Inc.

4302 Welty St.
Stonefield Building, Ste. 750
Chicopee Bend, Colorado 80500

Paul Greenland

Roper Counseling Services provides individuals, groups, and families with confidential and effective treatments for a wide range of emotional and behavioral difficulties.

EXECUTIVE SUMMARY

Roper Counseling Services offers confidential and effective treatments for a wide range of emotional and behavioral difficulties. Specifically, our practice provides individual counseling services for children, adolescents, and adults. Group therapy is offered for people dealing with similar issues, such as eating disorders. Finally, we also provide both marital and family therapy.

Business Overview

Over the course of one's life, challenges and difficulties are inevitable. Individuals are often able to overcome difficult times and deal with challenges in successful, optimal ways. However, sometimes even effective coping strategies and the support of family and friends is not enough. Situations resulting from abusive relationships, traumatic childhoods, addictions, loss, and chemical imbalances can spiral out of control, requiring assistance from trained professionals. With nearly 25 years of experience, Roper Counseling Services has a broad range of professional expertise, allowing us to help troubled individuals in almost any situation.

Organizational Structure

Our practice is incorporated in the state of Colorado and employs three licensed psychologists with doctorate degrees from programs approved by the American Psychological Association, as well as three licensed clinical social workers.

Company History

Roper Counseling Services was established in 1985, when President Dr. George Roper first established his independent practice. Since that time, the business has grown at a measured pace. Until 2001, Roper Counseling Services was a partnership comprised of Dr. Roper and Dr. Renée Coates. Our growth was such that, by 2001, we had identified the need to add another practitioner. At that time, Dr. Mary Anne Townsend joined the business, which continued to grow.

Our burgeoning patient base, which grew largely through word-of-mouth referrals, as well as exposure from local, regional, and national speaking commitments, required us to add additional capacity. In 2008 we agreed to merge with an existing counseling practice named Evergreen Associates. This resulted in the addition of three licensed clinical social workers: Peter Mullen MSW, LCSW; Steven Vetro MSW, LCSW; and Halley Peterson MSW, LCSW. All three practitioners had established reputations in the community. By joining Roper Counseling Services, they enabled our practice to become the largest of its kind in the Chicopee Bend area.

MARKET ANALYSIS

Mental illnesses, as well as behavioral and emotional difficulties, are quite common throughout the population. For example, according to data issued by the American Psychiatric Association in 2006, each year approximately 20 percent of U.S. adults suffer from a diagnosable mental illness.

According to a national study conducted by PXPL Associates Inc. in April 2009, stress levels throughout the United States were at an all-time high. The research, which involved interviews with 2,347 people, revealed that 37 percent of individuals categorize their stress level as overwhelming. Sixty-four percent of respondents indicated that their stress levels were significantly higher compared to the same period the previous year. According to the study, overall economic uncertainty was the leading cause of stress (31%), followed by relationship problems (29%), and financial concerns (24%). Although most people have adequate support networks in place to deal with their stress, a significant portion of the population either lacks such support, or does not rely upon appropriate coping mechanisms.

Despite the fact that there is a strong market for the services offered by Roper Consulting Services, the partners realize that several barriers to our growth exist within the marketplace. These namely are a lack of awareness about mental illness, as well as a variety of misconceptions.

For example, according to a 2006 consumer survey on mental health conducted by the American Psychiatric Association, 44 percent of U.S. adults indicated that they know little or virtually nothing about mental illness. Furthermore, 33 percent believed that mental illnesses are caused by either personal or emotional weakness. Finally, some 24 percent of the population believed that, most of the time, personal or emotional strength is enough to overcome common mental illnesses.

INDUSTRY ANALYSIS

According to data from the Bureau of Labor Statistics, 166,000 psychologists were employed in 2006. By 2016, this number is projected to grow 15 percent, reaching 191,000. In addition, 595,000 social workers were employed 2006. That profession is projected to grow 22 percent by 2016, at which time the number of social workers will rise to 727,000. According to Colorado's Department of Regulatory Agencies, Division of Registrations, in 2009 the state was home to approximately 2,150 active licensed psychologists.

PERSONNEL

George M. Roper, Ph.D., President—Dr. Roper graduated in 1984 from the Massachusetts School of Professional Psychology, where he earned his doctorate degree in psychology. He earned a master's degree in psychology from South University in West Palm, Florida. Dr. Roper has been a mental health practitioner since 1978, providing services to individuals, couples, families, and groups. His special interests include stress management, co-dependent relationships, substance abuse, and marital therapy. Dr. Roper is a licensed psychologist and has been practicing in Colorado since 1985.

Renee Coates, Ph.D., Vice President—Dr. Coates earned Master's and Doctor of Psychology degrees from the University of the Rockies in Colorado Springs, graduating in 1990. Dr. Coates has worked in the counseling field since 1985, working mainly with individuals and couples. Her special interests include women's issues, depression, domestic violence, and marital therapy. Dr. Coates is a licensed psychologist and has been practicing in Colorado since 1985.

Mary Anne Townsend, Ph.D.—Dr. Townsend received her doctorate degree in 1997 from The Chicago School of Professional Psychology, as well as a master's degree in psychology from the University of Illinois in 1991, at which time she began working in the counseling field. A highly skilled practitioner, Dr. Townsend specializes in working with children and adolescents in both residential and outpatient settings. Dr. Townsend is especially interested in attention deficit hyperactivity disorder, grief- and loss-related issues, and anxiety. She is a licensed psychologist and has been practicing in Colorado since 2001.

Peter Mullen MSW, LCSW—With more than 20 years of experience, Peter is a graduate of The School of Social Work at Colorado State University, where he received his undergraduate and graduate degrees. He provides both individual and group therapy in a wide range of settings. Peter is especially interested in men's issues, parent-child conflicts, anxiety, eating disorders, and depression. He has been a licensed clinical social worker since 1989.

Steven Vetro MSW, LCSW—Steven received his BSW degree from the Arizona State University School of Social Work, and his MSW degree from the School of Social Work at Colorado State University. He has been serving our community for 15 years, providing individual, family, and group therapies. His areas of interest include personal and occupational stress, life balance, creativity enhancement, anger management, divorce and divorce recovery, blended families, and life transition issues. He has been a licensed clinical social worker since 1994.

Halley Peterson MSW, LCSW—After receiving her BSW degree from Illinois State University, Halley earned an MSW degree from the School of Social Work at Colorado State University in 1999. She offers individual, family, and group therapies. Halley specializes in working with older adults and their families, and focuses on grief and loss, isolation and loneliness, life transition issues, end-of-life issues, anxiety, and depression. She has been a licensed clinical social worker since 1999.

Eric Simms, Practice Manager—Our practice is especially fortunate to have Eric on-board. With an undergraduate education that includes double majors in accounting and marketing, he has the necessary skills to handle accounting, bookkeeping, and payroll for the practice, and also develops and executes marketing strategies needed to help us grow. Additionally, Eric manages professional licensure for all the counselors, ensuring that we remain in compliance, and also negotiates fee schedules with insurance companies, as well as area hospitals and counseling centers where we provide services.

Mary Sidwell, Administrative Assistant—Mary is responsible for greeting clients and other professionals when they enter our practice. She often is the first impression that people have of our business, and we value her exceptional interpersonal skills. She is especially gifted at dealing with individuals who can be challenging in various ways. Mary books appointments for clients and maintains schedules for our therapists. In addition, she handles all travel arrangements, orders office supplies and other items, maintains patient records, takes care of inbound and outgoing U.S. mail and overnight packages, and performs a wide range of other duties as needed.

Professional & Advisory Support

Roper Counseling Services relies upon the firm of Willington, Bradfield & Terell for legal services. Tax services are provided by Rocky Mountain Professional Services. In addition, our firm has established checking accounts with the Bank of Colorado, which also provides us with merchant card services, allowing us to take credit card payments from clients.

GROWTH STRATEGY

Our practice will rely on word-of-mouth referrals, as well as the marketing tactics outlined in the Marketing & Sales section of this plan, to achieve meaningful growth over the next five years. Based upon the growth that both of our practices have experienced over the past five years (prior to merging), the Bureau of Labor Statistics projections for our professions referenced in the Industry Analysis section of this plan, and our professional observations of the local market, we anticipate our patient base will grow at a compound annual rate of 3.5 percent over the next five years.

SERVICES

Roper Counseling Services provides assessment and treatments for a wide range of mental health issues, drawing from nearly 25 years of experience. Our specialties include:

- ADD/ADHD
- Abuse
- Anxiety
- Bipolar Disorder
- Career Issues
- Conduct Disorder
- Couples/Marital
- Creativity Enhancement
- Cultural Issues
- Depression
- Divorce
- Eating Disorders
- Gender Identity
- Grief
- Impulse or Habit Control
- Interpersonal Conflict
- Intimacy
- Isolation or Loneliness
- Life Balance
- Life Transition
- Men's Issues
- Obsessive Compulsive Disorder
- Oppositional Defiant Behavior
- Parent-child Conflicts
- Women's Issues

MARKETING & SALES

Practice Manager Eric Simms has developed a detailed marketing plan for our practice that includes specific tactics for furthering our growth. These include:

- Printed collateral describing our practice for prospective clients and referral sources.

- An ongoing, highly targeted direct mail campaign that promotes our capabilities to professional referral sources in a 20-mile radius surrounding our practice.

- An expanded Yellow Page advertisement with pictures of our counselors and a short list of common services offered.

- A professional networking strategy that involves membership in the local chamber of commerce and county medical society.

- Local, regional, and national public speaking engagements on a wide range of mental health topics.

- A regular presence on a weekly local radio program called On Your Mind, where callers can phone in and ask our counselors general questions on the air.

- A Web site with complete details about our practice, as well as a resource section where people can obtain general information about mental health issues. In addition, our site allows people to request their first appointment with us online.

OPERATIONS

Facility & Location

Following its merger with Evergreen Associates, Roper Counseling Services relocated its offices to the Stonefield Building. Located on the thriving east side of Chicopee Bend, with ample parking space and access to major highways and bus routes, this office complex is home to other professionals who may serve as new referral sources for us. These include several attorneys and physicians, as well as two social service agencies.

In addition to the benefits listed above, we chose to relocate to the Stonefield Building because the office space was already suitable for our specific needs. It previously was home to a burgeoning psychiatry practice that closed its doors when two of the partners retired, and another decided to relocate elsewhere. In addition to the main entrance accessible off the waiting area, a separate entrance is available for therapists and staff. In addition, the facility offers soundproof counseling rooms, as well as a large, secure space for records storage.

Billing & Payment

Roper Counseling Services accepts payments from private insurance plans, as well as self-payments from individuals. Unless clients make other arrangements with us ahead of time, we require payment at the time of service. In addition to personal checks, we also accept Visa, MasterCard, Discover, and American Express. We have an existing computerized billing system for mental health practitioners that tracks patient accounts and generates all necessary forms and statements.

Fees

The fees that we charge vary depending upon contracts negotiated with different insurance companies, hospitals, and other agencies. Due to the complexity associated with various contracts, this information is not normally included with our business plan. However, it can be provided upon request. Generally speaking, our fee schedule is comparable with other counseling practices in our market.

Hours of Operation

Regular appointments are offered by appointment only; walk-ins are not welcomed. However, we do leave several slots in our schedules open every day for clients with urgent needs. In addition, all of our counselors rotate on-call duty, so that one is always available at any time for emergencies. An answering service forwards relevant after-hours calls received via our main number to the counselor on-call's cell phone.

LEGAL

Colorado's Department of Regulatory Agencies, Division of Registrations, has minimum licensure requirements that must be met by both psychologists and social workers.

Our psychologists meet all necessary requirements, including:

- Doctoral degrees from American Psychological Association-approved programs.

- One year of supervised post-degree experience.

- Successfully passing an examination in psychology prescribed by the state's Board of Psychologist Examiners.

- Completion of a jurisprudence examination developed by the Board of Psychologist Examiners.

Our social workers also have met me minimum licensure requirements for their profession established by Colorado's Board of Social Work Examiners.

In addition to compliance with licensure requirements, our practice also has secured appropriate liability insurance coverage from Smithfield Insurance Associates.

FINANCIAL PROJECTIONS

In 2008, Roper Counseling Services and Evergreen Associates generated combined net income of approximately $91,635. A detailed breakdown can be seen in the following balance sheet, which covers the time period January 1, 2008 to December 31, 2008.

Income	
Billings	$625,413
Consulting	$128,460
Public speaking	$ 16,840
Royalty income	$ 6,780
Total income	**$777,493**
Expenses	
Salaries	$500,460
Utilities	$ 4,700
Rent	$ 27,600
Insurance	$ 21,540
401 K contributions	$ 32,529
Office supplies	$ 9,800
Marketing & advertising	$ 12,850
Telecommunications & internet	$ 4,980
Professional development	$ 33,980
Travel & entertainment	$ 13,280
Subscriptions & dues	$ 5,200
Repairs & maintenance	$ 1,289
Taxes	$ 17,650
Total expenses	**$685,858**
Net income	**$ 91,635**

Based on our analysis of the market, and taking current economic conditions into consideration, we are forecasting that net income for our expanded practice will grow at a compound annual rate of 4 percent for the next five years.

Year	Net Income
2009	$ 95,300
2010	$ 99,112
2011	$103,077
2012	$107,200
2013	$111,488

Custom Carpentry Shop

Choice Cut Carpentry Inc.

18765 Grattidge Way
Boston, Massachusetts 02106

Paul Greenland

Choice Cut Carpentry provides custom carpentry services to both individuals and businesses in the Boston area.

EXECUTIVE SUMMARY

Business Overview

Choice Cut Carpentry Inc. provides custom carpentry services in the Boston area. Specifically, we specialize in custom cabinetry and shelving projects. One other unique niche that sets us apart from other carpenters is the production of unique, decorative wooden boxes. In addition, we also offer workshops and educational seminars for amateur woodworkers and professional carpenters looking to learn new skills.

Incorporated in the state of Massachusetts, our business is owned by Douglas Fortune and his sons, Nicholas and Bradley Fortune. For over 25 years, Douglas has been doing part-time carpentry project work for individuals and businesses throughout Boston. During this time, he has developed a reputation for craftsmanship and quality.

Our target market is mainly comprised of upper-income individuals, mid-sized businesses, builders, architects, and several large corporations in the Boston area.

MARKET ANALYSIS

Our competitors include other carpentry shops throughout Boston. Many other shops offer some of the carpentry services that we provide. In addition, several of our competitors are large-sized shops that are able to take on projects of a scope that is beyond our capabilities. However, few carpentry shops offer the level of skill and craftsmanship that we provide. Our focus is on quality and detail. Many of the projects we work on are simply too customized for larger, production-focused shops to perform cost-effectively.

In addition, our educational programs provide us with a strong differential in our market. The only noteworthy competitor that we have in this area is a local community college, which offers a strong vocational program. However, that program is focused on teaching elementary woodworking skills to as many people as possible, while our program is focused on the principles of quality craftsmanship.

Finally, another key differential for our business is the production of custom designer boxes.

PRODUCTS & SERVICES

Custom Cabinets

Cabinets from Choice Cut Carpentry are of the highest quality, offering finer construction and a longer lifespan than semi-custom or stock cabinets. Because they are crafted specifically for a certain environment, situation, or application, our cabinets ensure the most efficient use of space. In addition, our customers benefit from great flexibility in designing their cabinets. We offer many options, from different wood types and hardware to stains and finishes. In addition, we also offer a wide range of lighting solutions for customers who wish to have lights inside of their cabinets.

Prior to construction, considerable time is devoted to understanding customer requirements and desires. When meeting with clients, we gain a complete understanding of what their storage challenges are and discuss various options and solutions with them. Ultimately, we produce computer-generated plans that depict how the proposed custom cabinets will look in their environment. In addition, we present a wide range of options to the customer pertaining to stains, finishes, hardware, and lighting.

Choice Cut Carpentry builds cabinets for virtually every situation or application. However, most of our work falls into one of the following categories:

- Bathroom Cabinets
- Computer Cabinets
- Display Cabinets
- DVD Storage Cabinets
- File Cabinets
- Garage Cabinets
- Kitchen Cabinets
- Laundry Room Cabinets
- Medicine Cabinets
- TV Cabinets
- Wardrobe Cabinets
- Wooden Cabinets

Custom Boxes

Douglas Fortune began making custom wooden boxes at the age of 13, carrying on a family tradition that began with his great-great-grandfather. The Fortune name is well-known throughout Boston for those seeking a wide range of custom-made boxes, including jewelry boxes.

As with cabinetry, we are capable of building just about any type of custom wooden box. Our customers almost always have very specific requirements when placing orders with us. Most of the boxes that reproduce fall into one of the following categories:

- Cigar Boxes
- Gift Boxes
- Golf Boxes
- Humidors
- Jewelry Boxes
- Puzzle & Game Boxes

- Tea Boxes
- Tea Chests
- Tool Boxes
- Tool Chests
- Toy Boxes
- Watch Boxes
- Wine Boxes

OPERATIONS

Location and Facilities

Custom Cut Carpentry is located between downtown Boston and the city's prestigious Beacon Hill area. Our location provides convenient access to upper-income individuals, the many commercial businesses that we serve, as well as Interstate 90 and other major highways.

Our carpentry shop is situated in an existing 625-square-foot structure, located on property that has been in the Fortune family for several generations. This is a significant advantage for our business, allowing us to operate in an expensive geographical area without having to lease or purchase property. Another advantage is that our facility is already set up and partially equipped for commercial woodworking. Aside from purchasing several new pieces of equipment and making minor physical improvements to the facility, our location is ready for business.

FINANCIAL ANALYSIS

Start-up budget

Advertising	$ 9,000
Materials	$ 35,000
Property improvements	$ 12,000
Miscellaneous items	$ 2,000
Legal	$ 1,800
Accounting	$ 1,200
Office supplies	$ 500
Woodworking equipment	$ 13,000
Office equipment	$ 400
Power/utilities	$ 4,000
Auto	$ 18,000
Fuel	$ 3,500
Meals	$ 500
Phone book ads	$ 1,200
Salaries	$ 90,000
Total	**$192,100**

The owners' investment is $125,000; the remaining balance of $67,100 will be secured from the bank as an operating line of credit.

Major Suppliers

Tools:

Choice Cut Carpentry relies upon national and international manufacturers for the supply of hand and power tools. Some of the hand tools that we rely upon are acquired at flea markets, estate sales, and highly specialized manufacturers. However, we purchase common hand and power tools from the following companies:

- Black and Decker Corp.
- Husqvarna AB
- Stanley Works
- Makita Corp.
- Robert Bosch AG Otelfingen
- WMH Tool Group Inc. (JET)
- Amana Tool
- St. James Bay Tool Co.

Lumber:

Our business uses a wide range of wood to produce products. The types of wood that we purchase include:

- American Black Walnut
- American Elm
- American White Oak
- Aromatic Red Cedar
- Aspen
- Bald Cypress
- Balsa
- Basswood
- Black Cherry
- Butternut
- Chestnut
- Douglas Fir
- Eastern White Pine
- Ebony
- Hickory
- Lauan
- Mahogany
- Pecan
- Poplar
- Red Oak
- Redwood
- Rosewood
- Southern Yellow Pine
- Spruce SPF
- Sugar Maple
- Sugar Pine

- Teak

- Western Hemlock

- Western Red Cedar

- White Ash

- White Oak

- Yellow Birch

We rely upon a number of different suppliers in the New England area, including:

- 4 Lumber Co., Eighty Four, Pennsylvania

- Allen Lumber Company Inc., Barre, Vermont

- American Lumber Company L.P., Hamburg, New York

- Applewood Lumber Co., Phoenixville, Pennsylvania

- Arlington Coal and Lumber Co., Arlington, Massachusetts

- Britton Lumber Company Inc., Fairlee, Vermont

- Brookside Lumber and Supply Co., Bethel Park, Pennsylvania

- Cape Cod Lumber Company Inc., Abington, Massachusetts

- Catawissa Lumber and Specialty, Catawissa, Pennsylvania

- Cersosimo Lumber Company Inc., Brattleboro, Vermont

- Crane Co., Stamford, Connecticut

- Futter Lumber Corp., Rockville Centre, New York

- Graebers Lumber Co., Fairless Hills, Pennsylvania

- GV Moore Lumber Company Inc., Ayer, Massachusetts

- Hancock Lumber Company Inc., Casco, Maine

- J.T. Lumber Newport, Rhode Island

- Jackson Lumber and Millwork Co., Lawrence, Massachusetts

- Lakeville Lumber, Lakeville, Massachusetts

- LaValley Lumber Company L.L.C., Sanford, Maine

- Lezzer Lumber Inc., Curwensville, Pennsylvania

- Massachusetts Lumber Co., Cambridge, Massachusetts

- Moose River Lumber Company Inc., Jackman, Maine

- National Lumber Co., Mansfield, Massachusetts

- Nickerson Lumber Co., Orleans, Massachusetts

- OC Cluss Lumber Co., Aliquippa, Pennsylvania

- Old Town Lumber Co., Kenduskeag, Maine

- Rex Lumber Co., Acton, Massachusetts

Hardware:

The hardware that our shop uses to produce custom cabinetry, as well as boxes, is obtained from a number of national and international suppliers, including:

- 3M
- A H Peter Meier
- Accuride
- Amerock
- Amerock Allison
- Amerock Galleria
- Berenson
- Blum
- Buck Snort Lodge
- Century Hardware
- CompX National Lock
- Grass
- Hera Lighting
- Ironaway
- Ives
- Kampel
- Knape and Vogt
- Laurey Hardware
- Mepla
- Precision Casewerk
- Quickscrews
- Rev-A-Shelf
- Rockford Process Control
- Salice
- Schaub and Company
- Soss
- Sugatsune

MANAGEMENT SUMMARY

Choice Cut Carpentry is owned by Douglas Fortune and his sons, Nicholas and Bradley Fortune. For over 25 years, Douglas has been doing part-time carpentry project work for individuals and businesses throughout Boston. During this time, he has developed a reputation for craftsmanship and quality.

When budget cuts prompted the elimination of industrial arts education at the suburban school district where Douglas had taught woodworking for 17 years, the circumstances presented him with the opportunity to apply his knowledge and experience in a new way, resulting in the formation of Choice Cut Carpentry.

Nicholas and Bradley Fortune began learning about woodworking at a very young age. Benefiting from their father's instruction, they developed into fine craftsmen and have assisted their father with many cabinetry and other woodworking projects. Following high school graduation, both Nicholas and Bradley pursued college courses in design, engineering, and CAD/CAM. These invaluable skills allow Choice Cut Carpentry to offer customers project plans created with the latest technology.

MARKETING & SALES

Because of his extensive prior experience performing project work for individuals and commercial enterprises, Douglas Fortune is well known for his carpentry skills. Prior to establishing his own business, word-of-mouth referrals generated more opportunities than he could accommodate on his own. With the help of his two sons, Choice Cut Carpentry will have the capacity to accommodate existing demand.

To generate new business, a marketing plan has been developed that focuses heavily on regular direct mailings to area architects, home builders, and unions. In addition to promoting our services, these mailings will also feature details about upcoming educational opportunities that our business offers. The mailings will promote our Web site, which contains detailed information about our services, educational offerings, and general information about custom cabinetry. Finally, our business will do a limited amount of newspaper advertising.

Advertising Budget

Based upon our marketing plan, the following advertising budget has been established:

- Direct Marketing—$4,500 annually

- Newspaper—$2,000 annually

- Interactive Marketing—$2,500 annually

Customers

Our target market is mainly comprised of upper-income individuals, mid-sized businesses, builders, architects, and several large corporations in the Boston area. Over the years, Douglas Fortune has established a reputation for service and quality within each of these categories. Particular niches that generate considerable business include builders and individuals seeking custom shelving and cabinetry for home theaters and DVD libraries, as well as consulting firms, individual attorneys, and mid-sized law firms in need of built-in bookshelves.

SWOT ANALYSIS

Business Feasibility & SWOT Analysis

- *Strengths:* The level of craftsmanship and quality offered by Choice Cut Carpentry, as well as our educational offerings, set us apart from competitors.

- *Weaknesses:* When competing for bids, other carpentry shops may beat us on price when dealing with customers who value cost savings over quality. In addition, we do not concentrate on very large projects.

- *Opportunities:* There is ample demand and growth potential among high-income customers and businesses in the Boston area who value quality craftsmanship and excellent customer service.

- *Threats:* Because our business is staffed by three highly-skilled individuals, any one of whom would be very difficult to replace, illnesses and injuries can threaten our ability to complete projects.

Day Camp Organizer
Camp in the Park

67 Shore Park Dr.
Oyster Bay, New Jersey 11771

Laura Becker

Camp in the Park will establish and operate daily camps for local, neighborhood children with traditional summer camp activities including swimming, music, art, and sports.

EXECUTIVE SUMMARY

Objectives

The objective is to establish a summer day camp for children who live in a neighborhood area. Specifically, there is a local village with a large municipal park containing a playground, pool, tennis courts, basketball courts, and fields. The camp will be provided for children who reside within the village.

Business Overview

Camp in the Park will provide traditional summer day camp activities including sports, music, art, music and swimming. The camp will be set up in a local park or other area with permission from the local authorities and regulatory agencies.

The camp can be run by a skeletal year–round staff which comprises the main management of the camp company. This management will oversee a much larger, seasonal staff. The camp management is responsible for all administrative functions of the camp including: hiring, regulatory requirements, securing food vendors and activity vendors for the camp, etc.

Once the camp season begins, the seasonal staff runs the operation on a daily basis. This would be an ideal business for local parents of camp-aged children, or perhaps school teachers who have summers free and would like to earn some additional money over the summer.

MARKET ANALYSIS

According to the National Camp Association (http://www.summercamp.org/), there are approximately 10,000 camps in the United States (of which roughly 60 percent are sleep–away camps). The majority of camps are privately–owned.

Over 95 percent of camp owners only own one camp since it is truly a hands–on enterprise.

The average camp tuition is $2,500 with the average number of children at a camp being 450. Therefore, the gross revenue of the average camp is approximately $1,125,000 ($2,500 x 450 campers).

$1,125,000 multiplied by 10,000 camps means that the total industry revenue is in the 11 billion dollar range.

More specifically, the American Camp Association (http://www.acacamps.org/) states that there are 6,200 nonprofit camps including religious organizations and youth agencies; and 2,300 privately–owned, for–profit operators.

Running a camp requires a tremendous investment in the infrastructure and overhead with such items as salaries, insurance, food, maintenance, activities and travel posing significant expenses.

Interestingly, the outlook for the camp industry is strong. In the last years, camps have become even stronger since there are many households with two working parents who need to provide entertainment and daycare for their children during their working hours. In addition, the advent of specialty camps—whether it be music, weight loss, or learning disabled camps—has broadened the camp market as well.

In a 1999 study, the American Camp Association found that over 50 percent of the respondents reported an average increase in enrollment of 9 percent from the previous year. Demographic trends would suggest that the demand for child–care options will continue to increase.

According to CampGroup (http://www.campgroup.com/camping.htm), "The universe of 12,000 camps is comprised of literally hundreds of different types of camps." CampGroup believes that the majority of camps fit into about 16 basic types of camps which include:

- Sleep–away camps and day camps

- Traditional camps (those who operate in a location whose primary purpose is the camp) and non–traditional camps (a local Y)

- General camps and specialty camps

- For–profit camps and not–for–profit camps

- Accredited camps and non–accredited camps

- Special population camps and general population camps

- Religious camps and non–sectarian camps

The American Camp Association provides accreditation for camps who meet certain criteria. According to CampGroup, although any summer camp can seek ACA accreditation, only 2,340 of the estimated 12,000 summer camps are ACA accredited. Of the 2,340 ACA accredited camps, approximately 25 percent are for–profit and 75 percent are not–for–profit.

There are sleep–away camps located in all 50 states but the largest concentrations are in California, New York and Pennsylvania. Day camps are also located across the country. The largest percentage of day camps are located in areas with large metropolitan areas such as California, Illinois, New Jersey, New York and Massachusetts.

MSG Accountants, Consultants and Business Valuations provided an industry report on "Day Camps" (http://www.msgcpa.com/general.php?category=Industry+Library&headline=Day+Camp) which states that "Although, each type of camp varies greatly in the types of activities it offers, camps generally provide a program consisting of outdoor activities, such as hiking, swimming, games, sports, arts and crafts, and programs designed to promote awareness of nature. Many camps in the industry have set themselves apart by emphasizing and specializing in specific camping programs."

Examples of different types of programs include:

- Sports

- Music

- Horseback Riding

- Outdoor Adventures

- Religion

- Special Needs

- At Risk Youths

- Weight Loss

- Theater

- Dance

Many localities are interested in establishing summer camps in the area because they can give a nice boost to the local economy. A summer day camp for children is a solid economic growth contributor for a local economy. There are significant employment opportunities; and of course, staff will buy things at local stores such as food and necessities.

COMPETITION

The competitive environment will depend greatly on the location of the community day camp. Camp in the Park faces competition from privately–owned day camps in the area. Generally speaking, the goal at Camp in the Park is to create a very similar environment to those of the privately–owned camps. The Camp in the Park fee structure is usually significantly lower than the other camps because it is not run to make a profit; and there are no year–round staff to pay. Hiring is done completely on a seasonal basis.

The other camps in the local area that Camp in the Park competes with are Pierce Country Day Camp (http://www.piercecamps.com/), North Shore Day Camp (http://www.northshoredaycamp.com/) and Crestwood Country Day Camp (http://www.crestwoodcountryday.com/).

PRODUCTS & SERVICES

Establishing the Camp

There are several steps involved in establishing a community summer day camp. This can be done in a variety of ways.

The approach that Camp in the Park has taken is to establish a Camp Board composed of volunteer parents. There are officers on the Board (president, vice president, treasurer and secretary). Alternatively, if the camp management is running the camp they are the ones to make these decisions.

The first step will be to set up a meeting with a corporate attorney to discuss the best legal status for the company (for instance, should the camp be a not–for–profit; or a for– profit organization, etc.). The attorney will also file the necessary documents to get the camp set up and to obtain a corporate seal and to create by–laws based on the interests of the board and the mission of the camp.

Depending on how the camp is set up, there may be funding available from government programs (particularly if the camp is a non–profit organization or if it is a specialty camp of some sort). It is worth investigating potential funding sources.

Examples of things that need to be decided include the following: Do officers need to be elected or appointed; how long should board members serve; do their children need to be attending camp, etc.

The mission of the camp will also be discussed, including:

- Age of campers (for instance, 3 year olds–10 year olds)

- General camp versus specialty camp (all activities or focus on the arts, etc.)

- Hours of operation; dates of operation

- Fees to be charged

- Salary structure for staff (base salary, bonuses)

Finding a Location

The Camp Board/Management will need to find a location to host the camp. Camp in the Park operates within a village neighborhood that has a Park. The Camp approached the Trustees of the Village to obtain permission to operate a Camp in the Park for residents of the Village.

When looking for a location, the selectors should bear in mind that the camp will need restroom facilities and significant outdoor space for sports and other activities. An indoor space for inclement weather days will also be needed.

A private or public park with permission obtained from the appropriate authorities is an ideal, low–cost location.

Hiring Staff

The camp will likely need a staff including a Director, Assistant Director, Group Leaders, Counselors, Lifeguards, Art Director, Music Director, Sports Director and any other area of interest the camp wishes to pursue.

Determining Fees for the Camp

This can be done by gauging what other camps in the area charge for tuition and then coming up with an appropriate fee schedule (either for the whole camp session; weekly; etc.)

Creating a Schedule of Activities for the Groups

The Board/Management should determine what activities should be offered at the camp. Then it is important to interview various providers to see who will best meet the camp's needs. For instance, if the camp is interested in providing music instruction, the camp board/management will want to interview several music directors.

Seeking Regulatory Approval with All Applicable Licenses

The camp operators will need to be sure to follow local regulations including obtaining all necessary inspections (such as from the Board of Health) and registrations.

OPERATIONS

Personnel

It is important to recruit staff that has experience working with children. For a fairly small community day camp, staff will be hired on a seasonal basis (just for the camp season). The camp operators will take care of the administrative issues throughout the rest of the year. The camp may wish to hire a certain number of teachers in addition to college age and high school age counselors. It is also important to ensure that the appropriate background checks are employed for all incoming staff.

This is a standard staff application:

Name: _____ SS#: _____

Address: _____

Home Phone: _____ Cell Phone:_____ E-Mail: _____

Birth Date: _____ Summer Age:_____ Are you a US Citizen? _____

High School Attended: _____ Year of Graduation _____

Colleges Attended: _____ Major:_____ Grade: _____

_____ Major: _____ Grade: _____

Can you swim? _____ Red Cross Certifications: WSI _____ ALS _____ First Aid _____

CPR Certifications: Comm _____ Infant _____ Adult _____ RTE _____

Are you available to work on _____and all weekdays (excluding Friday,

July 3rd) from Monday, June 29th through Friday, August 21st without any days off? _____

Do you have any impairments, physical, mental or medical which would interfere with your ability to satisfactorily perform the essential functions of

this job? _____

If yes, please explain _____

How did you hear about Day Camp in the Park? _____

Do you smoke? _____

Please list any experience you have had with children. _____

_____

Did you ever attend camp? If so, which? _____

If yes, what was your favorite experience? _____

Please list what land sports, water sports, arts & crafts and performing arts activities you are skilled in: _____

_____

References: Please list three contacts: school reference (i.e.: teacher, counselor), job supervisor, babysitting and any other relevant reference.

Name	Phone #	Relationship

Harassment The camp's policy is to prohibit all forms of harassment by our employees. This includes sexual, racial, religious, and other forms of harassment. Have you ever been accused of harassment of any person including, but not limited to, workplace harassment? Yes? No? Explain.

_____

Criminal Record Have you ever been convicted of a crime, other than a minor traffic offense?

If yes, please describe. Yes? No?

Explain

_____

I authorize investigation of all statements herein, including any checks of criminal records, and release the camp and all others from liability in connection with same. I also understand that misrepresentations or falsifications herein or in any other documents completed or submitted by the applicant will result in dismissal, regardless of the date of discovery by the camp.

_____   _____
Applicant's signature   Date

Staff Pay Scale

The following pay scale is an example of the pay scale of a camp on Long Island, New York named North Shore Day Camp. It is provided as a framework as compensation can vary greatly in different areas of the country and for different types of camps.

Pay scale

Grade	Base	Bonus	Total potential salary
11th Grade	$ 400	$600	$1,000
12th Grade	$1,100	$600	$1,700
College freshman	$1,500	$600	$2,100
College sophomore	$1,900	$600	$2,500
College junior	$2,200	$600	$2,800
College senior	$2,400	$600	$3,000
Adult staff	$2,500	$600	$3,100

Regulatory Approval—Department of Health

One of the first things the Camp Board will need to determine is who is responsible for licensing the camp in the area. Camp in the Park is licensed by The Health Department who inspects the camps at least twice a season to assure that all physical facilities are properly operated and maintained, and that adequate supervision exists to provide a healthy and safe environment in accordance with the New York State Sanitary Code. It also investigates reports of serious incidents of injury, illness and all allegations of abuse or maltreatment and, when requested, provides parents or guardians of prospective campers an opportunity to review inspection reports and required plans.

Each year the Nassau County Department of Health oversees the issuance of permits for approximately 150 camps, which will host in excess of 32,000 children. A summer day camp needs a permit to operate if it is occupied by children less than 16 years of age between June 1st and September 15th and is primarily for the purpose of outdoor organized group activities.

The Department of Health will also require that each camper has an up to date medical form on file (physical examination within the last year); and that the camp employs a Medical Director.

Indoor Facility

If the camp operators choose a local facility that has an indoor weather space there will be no need to do anything further. However, if the host property for the camp is in a park as Camp in the Park's is, then the camp operators may wish to look into purchasing or renting a large tent to provide a covered area for hot summer days. In addition, an indoor building for inclement weather days may be considered.

Depending on the size and number of tents required, the cost may run anywhere from $2,500 to $10,000.

Information Required from Campers

- Camper Profile (includes emergency contact information)

- Medical Forms: The Board of Health will likely mandate that current health forms are on file for all staff and campers.

Information Required from Staff

- Counselor Profile (includes emergency contact information)

- Medical Forms: The Board of Health will likely mandate that current health forms are on file for all staff and campers.

Schedule of Activities

The camp operators will decide what activities to offer in the camp. Some of these activities can be performed by in–house staff (such as time in the playground); while other activities may require an outside vendors (such as Yoga).

The camp operators will negotiate arrangements with all outside vendors including fees and schedule.

The camp should create a daily schedule to incorporate all of the activities. A sample schedule from Camp in the Park follows:

Camp Schedule

Age groups	9:00 to 9:15	9:20 to 9:55	10:00 to 10:35	10:40 to 11:15	11:20 to 11:55	12:00 to 12:35	12:40 to 1:15	1:20 to 1:55	2:00 to 2:35	2:40 to 3:15	3:20 to 4:00
3 Year olds (8)(B/G)	Drop-off & welcome	Soccer	Swim	Music	Lunch & tent games	Yoga	Pick-up @ tent	X	X	X	X
4 Year olds (19)(B/G)	Drop-off & welcome	Music	Yoga	Swim F	Lunch & tent games	Arts & crafts	Group	Swim I	Soccer	3:00 Pickup	X
5/6 Year olds (15)(G)	Drop-off & welcome	Playground	M U S I C	Group	Lunch & tent games	Soccer	Arts & crafts	Tennis 1:30–2:00	Swim I	Yoga	S W I M F
5/6 Year olds (19)(B)	Drop-off & welcome	Sports		Swim I	Yoga	Lunch & tent games	Playground	Soccer	Arts & crafts	Tennis 2:30–3:00	
7 Year olds (12)(G)	Drop-off & welcome	Sports	Music	Soccer	Swim I	Lunch & tent games	Yoga	Cheer-leading	Playground	S W I M F	Arts & crafts
8/9/10 Year olds (18)(G)	Drop-off & welcome	Arts & crafts	Swim I	Music	Soccer	Lunch & tent games	Tennis 1:00–1:30	Playground	Yoga		Cheer-leading
7/8 Year olds (13)(B)	Drop-off & welcome	Sports	Soccer	Arts & crafts	Music	Lunch & tent games	Swim I	Yoga	Tennis 2:00–2:30		Playground

ORGANIZATION

Camp Orientation—Counselors

It is a good idea to hold an orientation session prior to camp opening. Workshops can be conducted to teach staff how to handle various situations. It is also helpful to provide a Staff Training Manual that the staff can take home with them for further study.

CAMP IN THE PARK—STAFF TRAINING MANUAL

Being a Good Counselor

Counseling at camp is a big job. It is a huge step that you're taking, probably one of the biggest steps of your life. The step is from selfishness to selflessness; from self–centeredness to being centered on others. Because you are going to be in a leadership role, people will be noticing you. Campers will look up to

WITHDRAWN

you and follow your example. You will have to show them how to make good choices...not with a frown on your face because you don't like the food, not with a lack of cooperation with the program, not with a sloppy appearance, not by being late, but in good, positive ways. Some ways to be a positive example: encourage a shy camper to make a new friend, pitch in at cleanup time with a smile, and sing along with enthusiasm at campfires.

Regressive Pull

Sometimes the staff can be the biggest kids at camp, and this is not necessarily good. "Regressive pull" is what we call the influence children have on our behavior that comes from working with them intensely, and especially in groups. In other words, if you spend enough time with children, you start to look and act just like they do! Counselors need to remind themselves who is "bigger"—that is, who is the adult and who is the child. Counselors need to understand what their success in working with children will depend in part on being able to, in a sense, enter a child's world without giving up their own maturity.

Why Am I At Camp?

To Make New Friends

Camp is a special place where children learn to make a friend and how to be a friend. You, the counselors, are trained to make sure that campers start making friends as soon as they arrive, because camp is a community where kids work and play together, contribute and cooperate with each other. While campers might arrive with friends, it's not necessary for them to know anyone when the camp season begins. It's especially fun to have winter friends and summer friends! You give campers the opportunity to leave any concerns they have from school behind and reinvent themselves.

To Help Your Campers Try New Things

Camp is a special place where children can be involved in tons of activities—just about anything they can imagine is here. It's impossible to get bored because there's always something new to try. You will encourage campers to participate in activities from archery to arts and crafts, dance to nature.

To Help Children Practice Growing Up

Camp is a special place where kids can make their own decisions—you provide the limits and boundaries that help them feel safe. You will help your campers believe in themselves, listen to them, respect them, and teach them to make good choices. Camp is a place for kids to practice growing up—under your watchful eye!

To Coach Self–Confidence

Camp is a special place where you will encourage your campers to feel good about themselves. You will coach them to leave their comfort zones, take healthy risks, and then enjoy the rewards of personal achievement. You will teach your campers to say "You bet I can!" when they are faced with new challenges—and make them feel like an important part of a caring community.

To Build Physical and Emotional Safety Nets

Camp is a special place where you will establish the boundaries that create an envelope of physical and emotional safety around each camper—the environment that helps children feel secure and willing to try new activities and experiences. You will coach campers to make good decisions and reap the rewards.

To Teach New Skills

Camp is a special place for children to learn skills in all sorts of activities. Whether you're a boating counselor who shows campers how to paddle a canoe or a cabin counselor who learns right alongside your group, you will help your camper learn skills they won't find anywhere else! You will share your enthusiasm with your campers—and help them discover activities they never even knew they loved.

To Create a Community Where Children Are Listened to and Respected

Camp is a special place where children are respected and listened to. The camp experience is based on the building blocks of self–respect: belonging, learning, and contributing. You help create a community, and every member of the community is as important as any other. You coach cooperation and responsibility, enabling children to make their own choices within limits that keep them safe.

To Help Campers Have Fun

Last but not least, camp is a special place…for kids and counselors to have fun! You aren't a teacher giving exams or homework—first and foremost, you are here so that campers can enjoy a fun, successful summer while acquiring life–long skills.

ABOUT CAMP IN THE PARK

- All counselors should be on their feet while they are with their group unless the children are seated.

- Parent confidentiality should be maintained: ages, grade, enrollment forms, and your rules.

- Keep all group lists, schedules and attendance sheets in your attendance folder at all times.

- Any notes you wish to send home should be cleared by your supervisor.

- "Lost and Found" should be brought to Headquarters. Lost items are displayed daily during lineup. Please check boxes often for your campers' missing articles. Please make sure your campers have all items labeled.

- We are not responsible for anything that may be lost or stolen other than which is brought and signed for at the main office. Encourage campers to leave valuables at home.

- Radios and cell phones should not be brought on campus or on camp vehicles. This includes tape recorders, boxes, headphones, walkmen, watchmen, etc.

- Counselors should take a count of the children in their group often to be certain none of them has strayed.

- A careful attendance check must be taken daily at morning lineup.

- Although campers should be accompanied to the lavatory or drinking fountain, all campers should be shown the various locations of these during orientation. Campers must remain with the group unless accompanied by a staff member.

- Personal Profile sheets should be reviewed during the first week of camp and any important notations should be brought to the attention of the director, supervisor, and/or a nurse.

- Please observe the eating habits of your campers. Sometimes a camper's behavior may be conditioned by hunger and/or food allergies.

- Please consider individual needs for each camper to rest. If a camper appears abnormally tired, it should be reported to one of our nurses, as should any change in camper's physical being.

- If the temperature takes a sudden drop, please make certain the camper is dressed warmly and that extra clothing later is removed if the weather becomes warmer. The same care should be taken on rainy days to keep youngsters as dry as possible.

- Counselors should supervise personal cleanliness and hygiene to the campers where appropriate.

- All safety procedures and precautions should be discussed with campers and practiced at all times. These are itemized on the pages that follow.

- Sneakers must be worn by counselors and campers at all times.

- Campers should not be carried. Walk side–by–side, talk with campers, but don't carry them.

ABOUT THE BUDDY SYSTEM

At the beginning of each session and prior to any swimming activity, the swimming ability of each camper will be assessed by a Certified American Red Cross Water Safety Instructor.

Campers will be designated as either a swimmer or non–swimmer.

- Swimmers will be identified by wearing wristbands. Non–swimmers will NOT be issued wristbands.

- Appropriate swimming areas will be assigned to each of these groups.

- Non–swimmers will be limited to areas no deeper than chest height.

Other information includes:

- The ratio of lifeguards of bathers shall be at least 1 to 25.

- The ratio of counselors to bathers shall be at least 1 to 7.

- The designated Buddy System coordinator will oversee attendance accounting.

The coordinator will be at least 16 years of age, remain on duty at the facility entrance during the entire swim period, and have in his or her possession:

- A full alphabetical listing, noting group and swim level.

- A full set of alphabetical group lists.

- Alphabetical group lists by period.

Other regulations include:

- Upon entering the pool, all bathers will sit at the edge of the pool in the area they have been assigned to for recreational or instructional swim. Only after assessing that bathers are seated in their appropriate areas, and that lifeguards and counselors are in their assigned locations, will campers be directed to enter the pool(s).

- For all campers 6 years of age or older, buddies of the same swim abilities will be assigned at the beginning of each camp session. The buddy system will be in effect during all recreational swim. (If swimmers of differing abilities are "buddied," they may only swim in the appropriate area for the buddy of lower ability.)

- Buddy checks will be conducted a minimum of every 15 minutes.

A buddy check will be conducted as follows.

- Lifeguards in charge will give two whistle blows.

- All campers will maintain silence and move immediately to the nearest pool side.

- Lifeguards will scan pool for distressed swimmers and assistance rendered if needed. An all–clear signal will be given.

- Staff will take a head count in each area, and reconcile the account with the attendance posted with the buddy coordinator.

- If a swimmer is unaccounted for, the "lost swimmer" and/or "lost camper" plan will be activated.

- Once all campers are accounted for, the lifeguard in charge will give the signal to resume swimming.

DEFINING A COUNSELOR'S ROLE

The Role of Play

The role of a counselor has been described in many different ways—as a camper's best friend, as a kind of surrogate parent, or even as a coach. None of these analogies is perfect, because being a camp counselor has its own special characteristics and relationships. Since most counselors have not been parents, trying to be one may not be too meaningful.

There are also drawbacks to the concept of being a camper's best friend. Besides the ability to set limits with campers (for their own physical and emotional safety), a counselor would not confide in or share with a camper an aspect of his or her personal life as one might do with a friend. A counselor would not expect to get advice from or lean on a camper as one might a best friend. Finally, a counselor would not engage in certain kinds of activities with a camper that one might with friends. So, while a counselor can have a lot of fun and be enormously helpful to a child, being a best friend is a very different kind of relationship.

Another way to view the role of a counselor with children is as a wise, benevolent, and caring older brother or sister. An older brother or sister wouldn't let a younger sibling do something to hurt themselves or others. An older brother or sister would intervene when a younger sibling was getting too wound up. Older brothers and sisters care for their siblings and have fun with them and take interest in them while still being able to put on the brakes when needed. Also, unlike a friend, there are certain confidences or aspects of your private life you would not share with a younger brother or sister because it would be confusing, upsetting, or put too much of a burden on them. We all know that younger siblings can be curious. An older brother or sister would know this is natural, but would be careful not to share information that was essentially private.

The Decisions You Make

Being an effective counselor also means making sound decisions for your campers. The first question to ask yourself when making a decision that affects campers is: "Whose well–being am I serving—mine (I get to be popular; I get to have fun doing what I want to do; I get to be with my friends) or my campers?". A second question is: "What is the risk involved, and am I certain that everyone will be able to negotiate that risk and end up safe both emotionally and physically?" with the greatest of relationships and the best of intentions, if our decision–making endangers or compromises the safety of children, we have lost the trust given to us when we assumed the responsibilities of being a counselor.

Time You Spend

When it comes to the quality of time a counselor spends with campers, some tips that may help you be a more successful counselor include:

- The time you spend at the beginning of a session getting to know the campers and establishing a way of meeting as a group will pay dividends during the rest of the season. This is the time to establish routines, create a rapport, and win the trust of your campers.

- Make a ritual of meeting at the same time every day for five to ten minutes to simply acknowledge how helpful or considerate specific campers have been to one another during the day. This public recognition should become part of your group culture. It is especially effective when done at the end of the day.

- Allow your campers to solve problems as a group right from the start. For example, instead of you and your co–counselor imposing your system of clean–up jobs on the campers, have them brainstorm how the system should work. Remember, lay down your ground rules for the group problem–solving right from the start.

Challenging Times

When campers begin to show challenging behavior, think of their actions as nonverbal statements. Campers are usually expressing one of three to four statements with their misbehavior: they are seeking attention, power, revenge, or trying to protect themselves.

Take a Deep Breath

The first thing to do when responding to such behavior is to take a deep breath and ask yourself, "What is my intention with this camper?" That is, how do you want to come across? Many younger or inexperienced counselors are not aware of what their intention is and may seem angry or vindictive even when they are trying to be thoughtful or engaging. How you come across to campers will have tremendous effects on what results you get. Ask yourself if you are trying to get even, show the kid whose boss, punish the kid, or get to the bottom of things.

Stay Calm

Secondly, stay calm. If you are taking the camper's action personally, you will react out of anger or frustration and be less effective. Find out what the child is trying to get from his or her behavior. When kids act in such a way that they either get into trouble or push other children away, it can be powerful simply to say, "I understand what I think you are trying to do; let's see if we can do it in a way that doesn't get you in trouble or cause you to lose friends."

Helping children solve problems and learn social skills is easier if they think you have their best interests at heart. Camp is full of opportunities for children to learn new and more effective behaviors for getting what they want, like making and keeping friends and getting attention and recognition for their true accomplishments. Have a great summer!

Lunch/Snacks

Depending on whether the camp facility has a kitchen, the camp will have two options: either hire a cook to prepare lunch and snacks; or order food from outside vendors.

At Camp in the Park, the camp does not have cooking facilities so the camp uses two vendors during the week. One provides pizza and pasta; the other provides bagels and hamburgers.

For snacks, the camp can buy in bulk at a store like Costco that stocks pretzels, party mix, cereals, fruit, etc. Water can be provided by having a water cooler on site (such as Poland Spring).

Safety/First Aid Training

It will be important to identify several senior staff members to participate in safety and CPR training. In addition, the camp must stock a First Aid Kit and keep a log of any incidents.

Transportation

Parents and guardians will be responsible for dropping off and picking up children. Bus service will be provided for all off–site trips.

Insurance

A camp insurance program usually includes all lines of cover including property, liability, vehicles, workers' compensation, excess liability, camper medical, directors/officer's liability and more.

It will be at the camp's discretion how much insurance to purchase; but a general rule is the more coverage the camp can afford, the better. The camp should have a primary policy which will cover up to $1,000,000 per incident; and at least two incidents per year. The camp can also add excess liability insurance for any additional amount (such as up to $5,000,000).

Camper Accident/Medical Insurance is for camper incidents whereby the camp will provide insurance coverage to campers (for instance, if a camper breaks an arm) which covers out–of–pocket expenses for medical care.

There are several insurance providers that focus on the camp market. Some suggestions include:

- Amskier: Amskier is an administrator/broker in the insurance business. The company says that they act as a "partner" to the camp and refer to themselves as a direct insurer. Amskier advised on what types of insurance the camp should have and then finds underwriters for specific policies. Amskier also provides experts and workshops on issues such as child abuse and swimming safety.

- Markel

- Philadelphia Insurance Companies

- Ace

The camp operators will want to check insurance company ratings when choosing a provider to ensure stability of the insurance company. A.M. Best and S&P provide ratings among others.

Camp Pricing

The community summer camp should be priced competitively to attract as many campers as possible.

For the full eight–week session, Camp in the Park charges $3,000.

There is also a four–week option priced at $2,070.

The competing privately–owned camps in the area charge approximately $6,500 for the eight–week session.

MARKETING & SALES

Promoting the Camp

Camp can be provided to local residents through a mailing announcing the camp and the details and word-of-mouth. In addition, local flyers and ads can be placed throughout the town.

CUSTOMERS

Parent Orientation

It is a nice idea to hold a parent meeting prior to the beginning of camp to discuss the parent manual and answer any questions that parents may have. Things to go over at the meeting would include camp rules, hours, supplies needed and general safety tips.

Customer Service

The camp will have a camp phone with the camp director at all times. Parents can always contact the Director with any concerns. The camp also has an email address to which parents can forward questions.

The camp will provide important announcements by email as well as by flyers distributed to campers. All notifications will be posted at camp as well.

FINANCIAL ANALYSIS

Assumptions

85 campers at $3,000 for an 8 week summer
Insurance: includes liability, worker's compensation and
disability insurance (liability $1,000,000 per incident; excess
liability at $10,000,000)

Revenue	**$ 255,000.00**
Expenses	
Payroll-staff salaries and bonuses	$ 103,000.00
Music director	$ 2,800.00
Drama instructor	$ 3,000.00
Sports director and staff	$ 15,000.00
Tennis instructor	$ 4,500.00
Art instructor	$ 3,000.00
Yoga instructor	$ 4,000.00
Dance instructor	$ 3,000.00
Insurance (liability, worker's comp and disability)	$ 15,000.00
Village-license fee	$ 1,750.00
Accountant	$ 2,050.00
Taxes	$ 3,800.00
Safety training (first aid/CPR)	$ 2,000.00
Paper goods / first aid supplies	$ 3,000.00
Supplies / pool supplies	$ 4,000.00
Art supplies	$ 1,500.00
Tent	$ 10,000.00
Lunch / snacks	$ 10,000.00
Field trips with bus (3 to 4 per summer)	$ 6,400.00
Science events	$ 800.00
Wacky Wednesday entertainment	$ 2,000.00
Magician event	$ 1,000.00
Boy vs girl day	$ 400.00
Pajama day	$ 600.00
Olympic family night	$ 700.00
Total expenses	**$ 203,300.00**
Net profit	**$ 51,700.00**

Diner

Shoestrings

41238 S. Main St.
Rock Bend, Ohio 44300

Paul Greenland

Shoestrings is a traditional diner focused on serving breakfast and lunch to cost–conscious consumers.

EXECUTIVE SUMMARY

Business Overview

Shoestrings is a traditional diner focused on serving breakfast and lunch to cost–conscious consumers. Located in downtown Rock Bend, Ohio, the diner serves affordable sandwiches, soups, and desserts, as well as a limited selection of hot entrees. Shoestrings primarily caters to employees of businesses in the downtown area, which is being revitalized. A key differential will be a free "bottomless" basket of seasoned shoestring potatoes with every order for patrons who dine in. The recipe for this signature item comes from a well–known downtown diner that closed its doors during the 1980s.

Business Philosophy

At Shoestrings, our objective is to be a "home away from home" for our customers. We feel that everyone is entitled to a reasonably–priced, home–cooked meal in a friendly setting. At our diner, customers can relax with friends and coworkers while enjoying simple fare like peanut–butter–and–jelly sandwiches, chicken noodle soup, and banana cream pie. Shoestrings is an inviting place that offers a brief reprieve from a busy workday. We will put considerable effort into developing relationships with our customers and remembering important details about them.

MARKET ANALYSIS

Like other "rust belt" cities, Rock Bend, Ohio has struggled for several decades. Local manufacturers have closed their doors or relocated operations to countries where low–cost labor is in ample supply. Over the years, commercial and residential development activity began occurring away from the city's downtown area. In the wake of these developments, downtown Rock Bend was peppered with abandoned factories and empty office buildings. As local manufacturers began to struggle or cease operations, so did the service businesses that catered to their employees. Particularly hard hit were local restaurants and eateries.

The revitalization of Rock Bend began during the early 2000s, when Webster Aerospace Corp. announced plans to establish a large research and development facility in the downtown area. The company was attracted by tax incentives, the availability of affordable real estate, and most importantly, a local workforce that included one of the largest concentrations of engineers nationwide. Webster Aerospace served as a catalyst for the rebirth of downtown Rock Bend. In time, other defense and aerospace companies began establishing research and development offices in the area. In addition to research and development, companies also began to establish test facilities and hire specialized manufacturing workers to build prototypes of new systems and products.

A major development unfolded in 2009, when Platinum Worldwide Aerospace announced plans to relocate its headquarters to Rock Bend. In addition to relocating 750 workers, the company proceeded to hire 400 new employees. Platinum Worldwide's new headquarters will open its doors in January of 2010, bringing the total downtown workforce population to approximately 6,500. In advance of this significant development, a variety of new service–related businesses, including restaurants and eateries, are being planned in the area.

Several national fast food franchises, including McDonald's and Burger King, have been planned for downtown Rock Bend. In addition, we are aware of at least two upscale restaurants that will open in the next 12 months. With its focus on low–cost meals, personalized service, and of course, its signature potatoes, Shoestrings will be the only restaurant of its kind in Rock Bend.

According to data from the Rock Bend Economic Development Council, there are approximately 6,500 workers in the downtown area. Among respondents to a recent survey by DownTown Beat, a weekly online newsletter for people who live or work in downtown Rock Bend, 30 percent indicated that they eat out at least once per week. Based on the Economic Development Council's figures, this puts the size of the weekly downtown lunch crowd at approximately 1,950 people.

The DownTown Beat survey also asked readers about their lunchtime preferences when eating out. According to the survey, 5 percent were unsure, 30 percent preferred fast food chains, 50 percent indicated they like to dine out at locally–owned cafes and sandwich shops, and 15 percent indicated a preference for gourmet restaurants. Based on this data, we estimate that there are approximately 975 prospective customers in our market. During its first year, Shoestrings is confident that it will corner 20 percent of its market niche (195 customers per week).

Competition

With its focus on affordable meals and personalized service, and its signature potatoes, Shoestrings will be the only restaurant of its kind in Rock Bend.

Shoestrings will face competition from a number of eating and drinking places. These include the fast–food chain restaurants, McDonald's and Burger King, each of which is planning to open a new location in downtown Rock Bend.

Also vying for a share of the downtown lunch crowd's wallet is a small, locally–owned chain called That's a Wrap, which focuses mainly on sandwich wraps, soups, and baked goods. While this chain has developed a following, it has a more expensive (and limited) menu than Shoestrings, and caters to a more upscale demographic.

Presently, our main competition will come from Spike's Pub, a popular downtown bar that serves lunch food such as burgers and fries. However, this institution also offers a relatively limited menu compared to Shoestrings.

INDUSTRY ANALYSIS

According to data from the National Restaurant Association (NRA), the restaurant industry had sales of $566 billion in 2009. A leading private–sector employer, the industry provided jobs for approximately 13 million people who worked at about 945,000 locations that year.

The following NRA chart provides a breakdown of the industry by category:

Type of establishment	2009 Estimated sales (Billions)
Commercial	$516.00
Eating places	$377.90
Drinking places	$ 17.10
Managed services	$ 40.10
Lodging-place restaurants	$ 27.90
Retail, vending, recreation, mobile	$ 52.90
Other	$ 49.90

In 2009, the NRA forecasted that industry sales will increase 2.5 percent. Smaller, locally–owned establishments like Shoestrings are the driving force within the industry. In fact, NRA figures reveal that 91 percent of all eating and drinking places have less than 50 employees.

OPERATIONS

Organization

Shoestrings is owned and managed by Terry Croteau, who has 15 years of restaurant management experience. Prior to establishing Shoestrings, Croteau managed restaurants for several leading national chains in Chicago and Phoenix. He has formal training in restaurant management from the Washington–based Stanley Richfield Culinary Academy of Spokane, from which he graduated in 1993.

Croteau will be supported by Assistant Manager Annie Thompson, who has five years of experience managing a local family restaurant in the area.

Shoestrings's staff will consist of the following positions. Corresponding monthly salaries are provided.

- Owner/Manager (Terry Croteau): $1,950

- Assistant Manager (Annie Thompson): $1,350

- Waiter: $1,100

- Waitress: $1,100

- Part–Time Cook: $1,000

- Part–time Dishwasher: $800

With their management experience, Croteau and Thompson are qualified to provide any necessary training to employees of Shoestrings. Employees will be paid weekly on Fridays. Initially, we are not able to provide our employees with health insurance or retirement benefits, but will consider these benefits as our business continues to grow.

Professional and Advisory Support

Shoestrings has retained the local accounting firm of Smith & Weller to assist us with bookkeeping and tax responsibilities.

Commercial checking accounts have been established with Rock Bend Financial, a local bank that also is providing us with partial financing. Rock Bend Financial also has assisted us with the establishment of merchant accounts, so that we are able to accept credit card payments.

Suppliers

Shoestrings has negotiated supplier agreements with several local food–service wholesalers in Rock Bend that have a reputation for quality and reliability:

- Veggie Mania

- Rock Bend Meats

- Fantastic Fruit

In the event that one of the aforementioned specialty suppliers cannot meet our needs, the following national suppliers can both provide all of the food–service products that we require. In addition, these wholesalers will supply us with general cooking and restaurant supplies, such as napkins, salt and pepper, etc.:

- Marsh Food Products Corp.

- Brock's Food Supply Inc.

Hours

Shoestrings will be open Monday through Friday from 11:00 a.m. to 4:00 p.m.

Facility and Location

Shoestrings will be located at 41238 S. Main St.

Formerly home to a well–known local eatery, our location is a short walking distance from the majority of companies located in downtown Rock Bend.

The building in which Shoestrings is located is owned by Jeff Stevens, whose family operated the restaurant formerly located there. Stevens has agreed to rent the facility to Shoestrings for $900 per month.

Equipment

Although much of the equipment needed to operate the restaurant is already present, approximately $15,000 in capital purchases will be needed before we are ready for business, including:

- 1 sandwich refrigerator

- 2 commercial grills

- 1 meat slicer

- 1 bread slicer

- 1 commercial microwave oven

In addition, the establishment requires reupholstered booths, new tables, and new flooring, which will cost approximately $15,000.

GROWTH STRATEGY

Shoestrings plans to grow the business via a strategy comprised of traditional and, most importantly, word–of–mouth advertising.

Based on the aforementioned data from the Rock Bend Economic Development Council and the DownTown Beat survey, Shoestrings is confident that in the first year it will corner 20 percent of the weekly downtown Rock Bend lunch crowd that prefers to dine at locally–owned cafes and sandwich shops (195 customers per week).

Moving forward, we project that our market share will increase to 30 percent (293 customers per week) during our second year, and 35 percent (341 customers per week) during our third year.

PRODUCTS & SERVICES

Shoestrings has established the following menu, which will be revised based on customer feedback during the first year of operation. As previously mentioned, a key differential will be a free "bottomless" basket of seasoned shoestring potatoes served with every order (for customers who dine in).

Appetizers

- French Fries
- Onion Rings
- Nachos
- Pizza Bread
- Sweet Potato Fries
- Potato Chip Basket
- Chicken Quesadillas
- Vegetable Quesadilla
- Chicken Bruschetta

Soup of the Day

- Cup
- Bowl

Sandwiches

- Poorboy
- Cajun Chicken Melt
- Chicken Breast
- Rock Bend Burger
- Rock Bend Cheeseburger
- Hickory Burger
- Pizza Burger
- Bacon Cheeseburger
- Turkey Burger
- Veggie Burger
- Turkey Club
- Veggie Club
- Super Chicken Burrito
- Super Vegetable Burrito
- Super Steak Burrito

- Rock Bend BBQ
- Double Decker BLT
- Grilled Cheese
- Grilled Ham & Cheese
- PBJ

Salads

- Garden Salad
- Caesar Salad
- Southwestern Chicken Salad

Hot Entrees

- Turkey Pot Pie
- Meatloaf
- Braised Beef
- Roasted Chicken
- Vegetable Quiche

Beverages

- Coke
- Diet Coke
- Sprite
- Diet Sprite
- A&W Root Beer
- Iced Tea
- Lemonade
- Hot Tea
- Coffee
- Hot Chocolate
- Milk: Whole, Low–fat, Skim, and Chocolate
- Juices: Apple, Cranberry, and Grapefruit
- Waters: Bottled, Mineral, Sparkling

Homemade Desserts

- Apple Pie
- Pumpkin Pie
- Banana Cream Pie
- French Silk Pie

MARKETING & SALES

We will promote our signature shoestring potatoes in all marketing and advertising communications. According to research from the National Restaurant Association (NRA), 68 percent of adults believe that food available from restaurants offers taste and flavor sensations that are difficult to replicate in a home kitchen. This is certainly the case with our shoestring potatoes. The recipe for this signature item comes from a well–known downtown diner that closed its doors during the 1980s. Although that restaurant closed, the former owner has continued to sell the shoestring potatoes at local events and festivals over the last 20 years. They are a highly popular favorite among locals, and we anticipate they will be a key differential for our restaurant.

An annual marketing budget of $5,000 has been established for Shoestrings. Marketing tactics include:

1. Coupons and Specials: Every Wednesday, Shoestrings will distribute a free coupon sheet to its customers that include specials for the following week. We feel this tactic will be especially effective, given the current economic conditions and related need for consumers to watch their budgets. According to research from the NRA, 27 percent of adults pay more attention to specials and coupons than they did two years ago.

2. Print and Online Advertising: A regular advertising presence will be established in the DownTown Beat, a weekly online newsletter for people who live or work in downtown Rock Bend, as well as The Bend, a free weekly paper serving the downtown market. The estimated annual cost for a presence in these two publications is $3,500.

3. Web Site: Shoestrings will develop a simple Web site, which will be included as a link on a variety of local Web portals. The cost to develop our site is estimated at $500.

4. E–mail Marketing: A database of customer e–mail addresses will be developed. This will be used to communicate weekly specials and new menu items.

FINANCIAL ANALYSIS

As the following three–year statement illustrates, Shoestrings will record a $9,820 net loss during its first year. The operation will become profitable during its second year, with an estimated net profit of $47,117, followed by an estimated net profit of $73,932 during the third year.

Three-Year Income Statement

	Year 1	Year 2	Year 3
Average customer volume	10,140	15,236	17,732
Total revenues	$121,680	$182,832	$212,784
Total cost of goods	$ 13,450	$ 14,123	$ 14,829
Total expenses	$118,050	$121,592	$124,023
Net profit	($ 9,820)	$ 47,117	$ 73,932

Financing for Shoestrings will consist of a $30,000 commercial loan from Rock Bend Financial, which also has agreed to supply us with a $25,500 line of credit. In addition, Owner/Manager Terry Croteau is providing $20,000 from his personal savings.

Domestic Services Provider

Helping Hands Personal Services LLC

123 Market St.
Galena Park, Illinois 60444

Paul Greenland

Helping Hands Personal Services offers reliable, dependable domestic services to those who need a helping hand.

EXECUTIVE SUMMARY

Business Overview

Helping Hands Personal Services offers reliable, dependable domestic services to those who need a helping hand. Specifically, our business assists the elderly, disabled, and busy adults with light house-keeping, laundry, transportation, grocery shopping, companionship, errands, and meal preparation.

In addition, we offer professional assistance for individuals who need help understanding and resolving issues with Medicare, Medicaid, or private health insurance companies, as well as a referral service that connects individuals with community programs and other resources that our business does not provide directly.

Finally, our Technology Helper service attempts to bridge the technology gap that exists between younger and older adults. Our staff helps those not experienced with computers and the Internet with tasks such as buying and selling items on eBay, e-mail, and online shopping.

Organizational Structure

Helping Hands Personal Services has been established as a limited liability company in order to secure full limited liability for its three owners.

MARKET ANALYSIS

Helping Hands Personal Services will focus on three target markets. Our primary target market will be older adults with annual household incomes of $40,000 or more. However, we also will promote our services to adults with minor disabilities or physical limitations, as well as working adults with house-hold incomes of $100,000 or more. The community of Galena Park is a relatively affluent area, with above average household incomes.

Our primary target market is poised for explosive growth in the coming years. According to Older Americans 2008: Key Indicators of Well-Being, a report issued by the Federal Interagency Forum on

Aging-Related Statistics, the United States was home to approximately 37 million people over the age of 65 in 2006, representing 12 percent of the population. The size of this population is forecast to increase to 71.5 million people by 2030, at which time adults over age 65 will account for 20 percent of the U.S. population.

In addition to growing in numbers, our target market also is growing in terms of economic resources. According to the aforementioned report, some 15 percent of older adults lived below the poverty line in 1974. However, by 2006 this percentage had fallen to 9 percent. During this same time period, the number of older adults considered to be within the high income category increased from 18 percent to 29 percent, while those considered to be low income decreased from 35 percent to 26 percent.

Generally speaking, the aging baby boomer segment will be a key driver of growth in our target market in the coming years.

Competition

Beyond individuals who offer some of the same services that our business offers, our main source of competition will be Lennox House, a local community agency that offers a mid-sized domestic services program. Another strong competitor is Comfort Care, a national provider of in-home care with approximately 270 independently owned and operated offices throughout the world. There is a Comfort Care franchise within range of our local market that provides many of the same services we offer, including grocery shopping, companionship, light housekeeping, meal preparation, and transportation.

PERSONNEL

Management

The owners of Helping Hands Personal Services have a unique blend of experience that qualifies them for success within their industry niche.

Kathy Stammers, MSN, MBA: A hospital staff nurse for more than 25 years, Kathy Stammers has extensive experience caring for geriatric and disabled patients, and she understands the challenges they face when trying to live independently. Kathy earned an undergraduate nursing degree from St. Anthony Nursing School in Petri, Wash., followed by a Masters of Science in Nursing degree from The Marcella Niehoff School of Nursing at Loyola University in Chicago, and a Masters of Business Administration from the University of Phoenix.

Ross Caravelle, MSW: Ross also hails from the healthcare industry, where he spent 15 years working as a hospital social worker. In that role, Ross gained extensive experience helping patients and their families deal with a wide range of issues. Benefiting his role as a partner in Helping Hands Personal Services is his working knowledge of community agencies and resources in the Galena Park area. In his role as a hospital social worker, Ross regularly served as a liaison with various community programs and agencies, and helped to arrange and coordinate resources for patients and their families. He earned a Masters of Social Work degree from Temple University's School of Social Administration in Philadelphia.

Sherry Kendall: After working for seven years as the human resources manager for a mid-sized landscaping company, Sherry Kendall applied her knowledge of health insurance to secure a job as a registration/insurance specialist at Abington Community Hospital in Chicago. In that role, she was responsible for overseeing a staff that verified insurance information, conducted patient interviews, and made various financial arrangements. She has extensive knowledge about reviewing itemized charges on hospital bills, communicating with physicians and their office staff, completing insurance claim forms, troubleshooting and correcting erroneous insurance claims, and dealing with third-party insurance companies and government agencies (e.g., Medicaid and Medicare). Sherry has an Associates Degree from Clark Community College in Rexford, Ill.

Staffing

In addition to its three founding partners, Helping Hands Personal Services will initially employ a staff of five full-time and 15 part-time employees. Although we do not provide patient care services, we require that all of our staff members receive training to become certified nursing assistants. This basic training will prepare all of our staff to assist customers who need help with more involved personal services, such as bathing or transferring from bed to chair. In addition, all of our staff must pass criminal background checks, have valid Illinois driver's licenses, and pass a basic skills competency exam that we have developed specifically for our business.

We have made arrangements to promote job offerings through the career planning offices at a local community college, as well as a four-year college, that offer programs in the field of human services.

Professional & Advisory Support

Our business has selected the firm of Smithfield, Luke, and Moran to provide us with legal services. Specifically, this law firm has experience in both employment and franchise law, which will help us to effectively deal with labor issues and support future growth and if and when we are in a position to expand beyond our local market by offering franchises in other locations. Specialized Accounting LLC has been retained to provide tax advisory services.

GROWTH STRATEGY

During its first three years of operations, Helping Hands Personal Services will focus on growing locally. A graduate research methods class at Parkville University recently conducted an independent analysis of our local market in order to determine both initial and projected demand. The results of this research, which was drawn from a statistically significant survey of Galena Park residents over age 65, indicate that the total market demand for our services is approximately 460 customers, representing 1,840 service hours weekly.

Based on the estimated market share held by our competitors, as well as our initial start-up capital, we are confident in our ability to support 100 customers during our first year, or 400 service hours weekly. Due to considerable untapped potential in the market, and because our overhead is low and we plan to reinvest as much profit as possible into the business, we estimate that our customer base will grow at a compound annual rate of approximately 37 percent during its first three years:

- Year 1: 100 customers

- Year 2: 137 customers

- Year 3: 188 customers

In years four and five, we anticipate the implementation of a regional growth strategy, marked by the formation of company-owned satellite locations in Wisconsin, Michigan, and Iowa. We will concentrate our efforts on communities with higher-than-average household incomes. Our plan will be to apply the same staffing model, whereby we rely upon local colleges and universities as sources of potential employees.

Long-range growth plans call for the potential expansion of our business via a franchise model. Early expansion will be concentrated within the midwestern United States, in order to minimize the geographic distance between franchisees, company-owned offices, and our headquarters.

SERVICES

Helping Hands Personal Services will offer a variety of services for customers, depending on their needs. Many of the services we provide will fall into one of the following major categories:

Light Housekeeping—Our staff performs basic housekeeping tasks for customers, including vacuuming, dusting, and mopping. Extensive cleaning jobs, such as window washing, are not provided.

Laundry—Our staff will clean laundry and linens in the customer's home or at a local Laundromat.

Transportation—Transportation services are provided to doctor appointments and other locations using the customer's insured vehicle.

Companionship—This service involves our staff spending time with customers and their families. The preparation of simple meals and other basic domestic tasks is included, as well as assistance with grooming, and personal care.

Personal Shopping—Based on lists and instructions provided by the customer, our staff will run errands to local stores, shopping malls, and grocery stores and make purchases on their behalf.

Technology Helper—Staff will provide basic computer skills training to customers, including Internet use. For customers who wish to take advantage of modern technology but have no desire to learn about computing, our staff will bridge the gap for them by providing research services. Examples include buying and selling items on eBay, maintaining a presence on social networking sites, assisting with e-mail correspondence with friends and family members, ordering merchandise from e-commerce Web sites, filling out government forms online, and online bill payment. To assist customers without computers, certain staff members will be equipped with laptop computers that connect to the free municipal wireless network that is accessible anywhere in the community of Galena Park.

Insurance Assistance—Professional assistance is available to those who are having difficulty navigating the insurance system, and sorting out issues related to Medicare and Medicaid. This premium service is offered by our partners at a rate of $45 per hour.

Referral/Resource Service—The partners of Helping Hands Professional Services also provide professional assistance to those who may benefit from programs provided by local, regional, state, or national organizations and agencies. At a rate of $45 per hour, we will perform custom research based on a customer's needs, helping them to identify appropriate services, make contact with the right individuals, and fill out any necessary paperwork.

MARKETING & SALES

We have identified a number of key marketing tactics to drive the growth of our business. These mainly focus on the target market of older adults, as well as the children of older adults who purchase services for their parents. Among the key tactics we have identified are:

- *Presentations to local companies.* Our partners will arrange to make presentations at large and mid-sized organizations throughout the Galena Park area. Our objective will be to reach working adults who seek services for their older parents.

- *Brochure.* An attractive, four-color capabilities brochure will be developed to promote our business. In addition to serving as a leave-behind item following live sales presentations, the brochure also can be given to people requesting information about our services.

- *Newspaper Advertising.* We will run regular newspaper ads in The Senior Times, a local free newspaper serving the senior market in Galena Park. This publication has a solid readership base, and the advertising rates are very affordable.

- *Internet Marketing.* Helping Hands Personal Services will maintain a regular presence on the World Wide Web. In addition to a Web site that provides basic information about our services, we also will maintain a presence on popular social networking sites, such as Facebook and Twitter, in order to initiate dialogue with adults who are decision makers for services used by their older parents.

OPERATIONS

Facility & Location

Helping Hands Personal Services has identified affordable, modest office space that will meet our needs during the first three years of operations. We have strategically located our office near the local colleges from which we hope to hire staff.

Billing & Payment

We require that all customers contract with us for a two-hour minimum per week. Customers are required to pre-pay for two weeks of service. Our office will generate monthly statements, with payment due within 30 days of the statement date. In addition to personal checks, we also accept Visa, MasterCard, Discover, and American Express. We have purchased a simple "out-of-the-box" billing system to maintain customer accounts. This software allows us to generate all necessary forms and statements.

Fees

A simplified billing structure allows us to provide most services at a flat rate of $25 per hour.

Hours of Operation

Helping Hands Personal Services will provide services around-the-clock, depending on a customer's needs and the availability of our staff members. Our office will maintain regular hours, from 8:00 AM to 4:30 PM, Monday through Friday. An answering service will be available to take calls after hours. In the event of an emergency, one of the managing partners will be available at all times.

FINANCIAL PROJECTIONS

Based on an average charge of $25 per hour for services rendered, we estimate that our first-year gross revenues will total $520,000. With a projected compound annual growth rate of 37 percent, we estimate revenues and net profits will increase significantly during the first three years of operations, providing us with the necessary capital for growth within our local market, and initial seed money to commence our regional growth plan in year four.

Three-Year Income Statement

	Year 1	Year 2	Year 3
Average customer volume	100	137	188
Total revenue	$520,000	$712,400	$975,988
Total expenses	$449,418	$516,831	$594,355
Net profit	$ 70,582	$195,569	$381,633

The following is an estimated balance sheet for our first year of operations:

First-year balance sheet

Income	
Total income	**$520,000**
Expenses	
Salaries	$380,000
Utilities	$ 2,900
Rent	$ 11,700
Insurance	$ 11,740
Equipment	$ 6,250
Office supplies	$ 3,950
Marketing & advertising	$ 14,380
Telecommunications	$ 2,300
Travel & entertainment	$ 2,450
Subscriptions & dues	$ 450
Repairs & maintenance	$ 500
Taxes	$ 15,784
Total expenses	**$449,418**
Net income	$ 70,582

Helping Hands Personal Services has applied for a $150,000 commercial loan from The Bank of Galena Park, from which the business also hopes to secure a reasonable line of credit. In addition, the owners are collectively providing $120,000 of their own money as start-up capital.

Energy Efficiency Auditing Firm

Energy Physicians

130 Hewitt Ave.
Long Beach, California 90805

Laura Becker

Energy Physicians performs residential and commercial energy efficiency audits and recommends ways to reduce energy consumption and save money.

EXECUTIVE SUMMARY

Mission Statement

Energy Physicians was created to help educate members of its community in an effort to become more energy independent. By analyzing energy usage in a residential or a commercial space, Energy Physicians will help its customers reduce energy costs and help reduce energy emissions.

Business Overview

Energy Physicians assists its customers in reducing the amount of electricity, natural gas or petroleum (heating oil or propane) that they use during the course of a year. The aim is to save money by reducing consumption and to take advantage of any tax incentives available. Energy Physicians has three business areas including: Energy Efficiency Audits; Customized Rebate Overview; and Alternative Systems Recommendations and Design. A representative assignment would include an initial consultation which is free, and then a full scale audit of the residence or commercial space at a flat rate price. The audit will examine all energy consumption and will design a program to mitigate energy usage and apply for tax rebates from federal, state and local governments. In addition, the company will recommend Alternative Energy Systems when applicable.

The energy consulting business has been a lucrative endeavor since the deregulation of natural gas and electricity in the early 1990s. After gasoline, heating oil, and natural gas had record high prices in the summer of 2008, there has been a renewed focus in the United States to mitigate energy expenses. There have been many improvements over the last decade in energy efficiency. Lighting, washing machines, dishwashers, driers, and television sets are all categorized by their energy efficiency rating. In many states around the country, utilities, states and local governments will offer rebates and tax incentives to end–users who use energy efficient products. The Obama Administration has increased the stakes in energy efficiency by adding language to the Stimulus Bill that creates tax incentives for individuals and companies that make improvements that are deemed energy efficient.

Energy Efficiency Auditors, such as Energy Physicians, have knowledge of the current incentives and an ability to create energy savings within customers' homes or businesses. This is the backbone of the consulting reports that are created after audits. Energy Physicians provides a full scale energy audit that will focus on multiple areas in order to save money and reduce consumption. A robust report will allow our customers to see specifically where they are spending their money by analyzing their bills and examining the interior and exterior of their residential or business property. In addition to creating a template for savings, Energy Physicians will determine if a customer's space will benefit from alternative sources of energy such as solar, wind or geothermal processes. Our knowledge and contacts in the alternative energy markets will allow us to educate our customers and give them a level of comfort with this beneficial, relatively new, technology.

BUSINESS STRATEGY

Energy Physicians is a family–owned business that focuses on residential and commercial customers within a 300 mile radius of Long Beach, California. We believe that the ability to enhance energy efficiency is in the earliest stages of development. Efficiency will come in products that use electricity, natural gas and petroleum, as well as, with processes that create heat and air conditioning. We believe that not only will our customers be interested in saving money, but they will also be interested in creating fewer emissions created by current energy processes. We are very enthusiastic about our current and future business prospects.

The energy efficiency business is important in multiple ways. First, the business' efforts to improve the way customers use energy is important environmentally. In addition, since most people are interested in saving money on gasoline, it is helpful to teach them how they can save money with slight changes to the products they use in their home or office.

Objectives

Energy Physicians' objectives are to be at the forefront of energy efficiency changes; and to steer customers in an energy–efficient direction so that they can save money, and help to have eco–friendly energy. The business aims to increase its customer base from high double digits to high triple digits over the next three years.

OPERATIONS

The Energy Efficiency Auditing business is broken down into two main areas: Field Consultants and Administration.

1. **Field Consultants:** Field consultants are the staff who speak to our clients and perform the auditing of residential and commercial space. Since these people are the face of our organization, it is imperative that they have a strong knowledge of energy efficiency, as well as a good bedside manner. Field consultants need to take a two prong training course prior to visiting clients alone. We have designed our own training tools, which are gathered and updated quarterly to keep field consultants up–to–date with the newest tools to create an energy efficient environment. Our training materials can be viewed online, and we ask consultants to pass an exam prior to making their first accompanied visit to a client. We also have new consultants make ten accompanied audits with an experienced consultant prior to taking on independent work. During an initial consultation, field consultants are instructed not to press new clients to purchase an energy audit, but there is definitely a need for consultants to sell their knowledge and the reputation of our company.

2. **Administration:** The business administration team consists of a financial bookkeeper who handles payroll, employee benefits, and invoicing and bill payment. This person works in conjunction with our office manager, who handles appointments, system issues, and customer support.

Energy Physicians opened its doors in November of 2005. The business started with three people and currently has twenty–five employees.

Certification

Auditors should receive certification from The Association of Energy Engineers. The Association conducts the testing for the Certified Energy Manager CEM (www.aeecenter.org/certification/CEMpage.htm).

Competition

The majority of the competition in the energy efficiency audit business will come from other energy efficiency auditors; alternative energy companies; and utilities.

When looking at the three segments of the business, none of the existing competitors currently overlap all three of these business lines.

Other energy auditors will provide audits but will not suggest alternative companies or implement rebates.

Alternative energy companies such as Solar Photovoltaic or Wind Power will perform a consultation to determine how much a customer can save and how long it will take to break even on any initial investment (in most states with a rebate system the current break even period is approximately seven years).

We feel that combining all of our expertise in all three business lines will allow us to balance the current needs of customers with the initial goal of saving customers money in the short term rather than over the long term. The business philosophy is that by generating customers' current cash flow within efficient products and rebates; then they are more likely to all alternative products in the future which will save them additional money.

MARKET ANALYSIS

The energy efficiency industry consists of energy conservation and alternative energy programs. Beyond the financial goals of running a business, industry goals are to move the United States away from petroleum–oriented energy sources and toward natural energy sources. Energy efficiency is a growth industry. The growth will be seen in several areas. For instance, the Obama Administration has made their intentions clear by promising to create a significant number of "green" jobs that will become available over the next few years. In addition, industry growth will come in the form of rebates and incentives in the proposed 2009 fiscal budget.

The energy efficiency industry over the short term will continue to grow at a steady pace. We believe that as prices of electricity, natural gas and petroleum continue to climb, there will be a greater incentive for businesses and residents to find ways to save on energy and power. Over the long term the industry will be able to grow geometrically. As the United States begins to enact programs that allow people to save money using alternative power and energy, the need for consultants to direct businesses and residents to companies that provide alternative energy will continue to increase. As Energy Efficiency Auditors, Energy Physicians has great expertise in the rebate and incentive market. The business's contacts within the alternative energy community will the business to help customers adapt and take advantage of the upcoming change to an alternative energy and power world.

According to the Department of Energy, the United States will invest $3.2 billion dollars into energy efficiency and conservation (http://www.eere.energy.gov). This funding will support energy audits and energy efficiency retrofits in residential and commercial buildings; the development and implementation of advanced building codes and inspections; and the creation of financial incentive programs for energy efficiency improvements (www.doe.gov).

The barriers to entry in the energy efficiency business are relatively low, and the costs to start a new auditing business are approximately $10,000 dollars. These costs would include the following:

- Purchase Inspection Equipment

- Blower Door Testing—an adjustable frame door vital to testing for air leaks (*US News and World Reports*, November 10, 2008)

- Infrared camera—allows auditor to identify less obvious energy leaks

PRODUCTS & SERVICES

Energy Physicians offers three different services within the energy efficiency business. The three services are:

- Energy Efficiency Audit

- Customized Rebate Overview

- Alternative Systems Design

Energy Efficiency Audit

After an initial consultation, an audit is performed which solves the issue of energy measurement. The energy audit report can be used as a starting point for Energy Management Plans, Retrofitting Existing Systems and Designing a new Energy Process (www.pqa.net).

Energy Physicians performs two types of audits. The basic audit consists of historical statistical analysis of past consumption and energy pricing on the residential or commercial facility. After the historical statistical analysis is performed, field consultants will perform a walk–through audit. The walk–through provides information on the facility's energy use profiles and an assessment of the energy systems and equipment. Field consultants will also gather information on the building conditions, process equipment and conditions of temperatures, pressures, flows and leaks (www.pqa.net).

The other audit is an Advanced Technical Audit which provides a historical analysis; a walk–through audit; and a report on complex energy consumption. This detailed analysis focuses on consumption and performance. The study answers the question of why the consumption is so high and a relative rating on performance. The studies can include details on heat loss and computer simulations on how to mitigate this problem. The study will also recommend product and systems that can be used to create a more energy efficient facility.

Customized Rebate Overview

Initially, Energy Physicians presents a report to a customer that analyzes the Energy Star Government Program (http://www.energystar.gov/). This program focuses on residential and commercial products that use less energy and are eligible for rebates. Products in more than sixty categories are eligible for the ENERGY STAR. They use less energy, save money, and help protect the environment (www.energystar.gov). A typical household spends more than $2,000 on energy per year according to the Department of Energy. Energy Star products will normally consume 33 percent less energy during the course of a year.

Next, Energy Physicians provides guidance on all of the state and federal incentives that are deemed beneficial for the customer. Most of the rebates are listed on the Department of Energy's website and are listed by state.

Alternative System Design

Our last business line is geared to the client that is interested in future saving and an investment into their home or office space. Alternative energy solutions include: Solar Panel Installation for electricity or hot water; Wind Energy Solutions for electricity and hot water, and Geothermal solutions for heat and hot water. Many states have subsidies that will provide most of the upfront costs for the different alternative energy solutions. The federal government also issues a tax credit that can be used to mitigate the upfront cost of alternative systems.

Prior to the initial consultation, Energy Physicians can enter a customer's zip code into the company's Solar or Wind calculator. This calculator with provide the field consultant with the information needed to discuss the saving a customer will incur and the length of time to recoup the initial costs of a new alternative systems. As consultants, we educate customers on electricity consumption and teach them how to use our calculator.

The solar or wind calculator will tell you:

- How much a solar system will cost for your house

- What tax credits, rebates and other incentives are available to you

- Potential financing costs and energy savings

Pricing

Pricing for each line of business should be competitive with current market rates. According to the New York State Energy Research and Development Authority, costs for businesses run from $100 to $400 depending on energy consumption. Residential facilities cost an average of $250.

Energy Physicians offers a rebate program which costs the customer an additional $100, plus 30 percent of rebates received. The company files the rebates for customers and mails them to the applicable agency.

Energy Physicians offers an alternative energy program which costs an additional $100. The business has a referral arrangement with partners who provide and install alternative systems.

MARKETING & SALES

The marketing and sales effort is multi–pronged:

- Website—The business must provide users with a user–friendly, customer–focused interface.

- Advertising on Field Consultants' cars—Since most business is conducted at client sites, Energy Physicians advertises on the consultants' cars which provide contact information, including website address, email and phone numbers. The company name, Energy Physicians, is relatively easy to remember and the phone number is easy to remember.

FINANCIAL ANALYSIS

Profit and Loss Estimates

Revenue		Year 1	Year 2
Energy audits			
Residential	$250 per audit	$ 13,000.00	$ 39,000.00
Business	$400 per audit	$ 8,000.00	$ 16,000.00
Energy rebates	$100 per audit	$ 2,600.00	$ 7,800.00
	Receive 10% of customer savings	$ 5,460.00	$ 16,380.00
Alternative systems	$100 per job	$ 500.00	$ 1,500.00
Referral to equipment provider	$300 per referral	$ 1,500.00	$ 4,500.00
Total revenue		**$31,060.00**	**$85,180.00**
Expenses			
Inspection equipment purchases			
Blower door		$ 10,000.00	$ —
Infrared camera		$ 2,000.00	$ —
Website design		$ 4,000.00	$ —
Website hosting		$ 360.00	$ 360.00
Vehicle leasing—field consultants		$ 1,800.00	$ 2,700.00
Office rent		$ —	$ 18,000.00
Total expenses		**$18,160.00**	**$21,060.00**
Net income		$12,900.00	$ 64,120.00

Gift Shop

The Busy Bee

102 Main Street
Brendenwood, Illinois 61025

Paul Greenland

The Busy Bee is a unique, eclectic, bee-themed gift shop.

EXECUTIVE SUMMARY

Business Overview

The Busy Bee is a unique, eclectic, bee-themed gift shop business that is owned and operated by Leah Strand. The business is located in the historic town of Brendenwood, Illinois, a popular tourist destination marked by nineteenth century architecture, unique shops, restaurants, B&Bs, wineries, and more.

Our business' flagship product is B. Strand's Honey, which is supplied by B. Strand's Bees, a commercial beekeeping business owned by Leah Strand's husband, Bill, in nearby Montgomery Corners, Illinois. In addition, we sell a wide range of bee-themed merchandise and edible items, along with a typical offering of gift items, greeting cards, candy, sandwiches, and beverages, which are obtained from various wholesalers.

Currently in its fifth year of operations, The Busy Bee has developed a strong following among the affluent tourists who visit Brendenwood each year.

MARKET ANALYSIS

Our primary service area is Brendenwood, Illinois, a popular tourist destination marked by nineteenth century architecture, unique shops, restaurants, B&Bs, wineries, and more. Specifically, we compete for consumers in the immediate vicinity of downtown Brendenwood.

The area on and around Main Street includes approximately 350 establishments, including 70 retailers. Of these, about 10 are gift shops similar in size to our operation, but with a different focus; our establishment is unique in its offering of bee-themed products. Specifically, the B. Strand's brand name has become well known in our region due to strong marketing efforts in recent years.

Beyond other area gift shops, we face competition from larger retail enterprises in the area, including a nearby Cracker Barrel Old Country Store, which offers a few of the same honey-related products and gift items that we sell.

According to a survey conducted by the City of Brendenwood, the Brendenwood Downtown Business Owners Association, the Jackson County Economic Development Council, and the consulting firm Rogers

Associates, retail sales within the City of Brendenwood totaled $12 million in 2008. This reflects a five-year annual growth rate of 4.5 percent. Due to weak economic conditions, growth is expected to remain flat in 2009, increase 1.5 percent in 2010, 2.5 percent in 2011, 3.5 percent in 2012, and 4.5 percent in 2013.

In addition to individual marketing efforts by area businesses, the Brendenwood Downtown Business Owners Association conducts an annual marketing campaign to attract affluent tourists from nearby cities, including the Chicago and Milwaukee markets.

INDUSTRY ANALYSIS

During the mid-2000s, players within the gift, novelty, and souvenir stores industry generated annual sales of approximately $21 billion, according to the Small Business Development Center National Information Clearinghouse. At that time, the industry included some 85,700 establishments and provided employment for about 300,000 people.

MANAGEMENT

The Busy Bee is owned and operated by Leah Strand. Prior to establishing her own business, Leah earned an Associates degree in business management from North Central Community College in 1993. Her retail career began in college. After working in the gift shop at North Central Community College for two years, she secured a position with nearby Good Shepherd Hospital, working first as a retail clerk. In 1995 Strand was promoted to supervisor of the hospital's main gift shop. In 2000, she was promoted to manager of guest services, which included management of two gift shops, as well as a coffee shop and sandwich shop.

Strand's love of bees came from her father, Stephen Goers, who established a bee keeping business in 1984 called Bee Line Bees. Goers has since retired, but sold the operation to Leah's husband, Bill Strand, in 2002. Three years later, in 2005, Leah decided to combine her business management experience with her love of bees and establish a retail enterprise to help her husband sell honey and related products.

PRODUCTS & SERVICES

Edible Honey Products
- Packaged Liquid Honey
- Comb Honey (in the edible honeycomb)
- Whipped or Creamed Honey (spreadable/butter-like)
- Chunk Honey (liquid honey with pieces of honeycomb remaining in the jar)
- Honey Wine
- Honey Beer
- Honeybee Pollen
- Sweet Natural Honey Candy
- Honey Sticks (apple, blueberry, cherry, grape, lemon, peppermint, pure clover, raspberry, strawberry, watermelon, root beer, banana, piña colada, licorice, and peach)
- Honey Straws (apple, blueberry, cherry, grape, lemon, peppermint, pure clover, raspberry, strawberry, watermelon, root beer, banana, piña colada, licorice, and peach)

Health & Beauty Products
- Alpine Swiss Honey Soap
- Royal Jelly
- Country Honey Soap
- Beeswax Hand Cream (unscented, lilac-, lavender-, and rose-scented)
- Beeswax Lip Balm

Deli
Sandwiches
- Roast Beef
- Pastrami
- Corned Beef
- Honey Smoked Ham
- Honey Smoked Turkey Breast

Available on a variety of breads, including:
- White
- Wheat
- Rye
- Croissant
- Bagel
- French

Cheese selections include:
- Cheddar
- Colby
- Colby Jack
- Feta
- Mozzarella
- Muenster
- Provolone
- Swiss
- White American
- Yellow American

Salads
- Chicken Salad
- Crab Salad
- Tuna Salad
- Egg Salad
- Potato Salad

- Macaroni Salad
- Baked Beans
- Cole Slaw
- ortellini Salad

Home Décor

- Beeswax Candles (beehive, bees, votive, cone, rope, star, cylindrical, rectangular, and spherical designs)
- Porcelain Figurines
- Decorative Pillows
- Throw Rugs
- Wall Hangings
- Yard Ornaments
- Clocks
- Statues & Statuettes
- Picture Frames
- Bookends
- Paperweights
- Glasses
- Plates
- Coffee Mugs

Greeting Cards

- Birthday
- Blank
- Engagement
- General Humor
- Get Well
- I Love You
- Missing You
- New Baby
- Wedding

Beverages

- Bottled Water
- Cafe Latte
- Chinese Tea
- Coffee
- Fruit Drinks
- Fruit Flavored Sodas

- Green Tea
- Lemon Tea
- Milk
- Milk Tea
- Soft Drinks

Candy

- Blow Pops
- Bottle Caps
- Chewing Gum
- Gummi Bears
- Jolly Rancher
- Nerds
- Now & Later
- Sugar Daddy
- Tangy Taffy

OPERATIONS

Facility and Location

The Busy Bee is located in a leased, 2,000-square-foot storefront on Main Street in downtown Brendenwood. This retail space was already equipped for operations at the time the business was established. Its previous occupant operated a combination gift shop/sandwich shop, and closed the business due to retirement.

Personnel

In addition to Leah Strand, The Busy Bee employs two seasonal part-time workers.

Suppliers

Beyond honey and related products supplied by B. Strand's Bees, The Busy Bee has negotiated supplier agreements with several regional food-service wholesalers, as well as a variety of national and international merchandise wholesalers.

Too extensive to list within this plan, our supplier list is very large. For example, within the greeting card category alone, we buy from the following suppliers:

- American Card Products
- American-Made Greeting Cards
- Blue Mountain Arts, Inc.
- CardSenders
- Cardstar
- Continental Cards, Inc.
- Emotions Greeting Cards

- Floral Poetry Greeting Cards
- Fusion Designs
- Heart & Mind Greetings
- InterGreet.com
- Karen Cole Paper
- Luvapet Specialty Company
- Marcel Schurman
- NancyB...Cards
- Notes & Queries
- Running Rhino & Co.
- Sianscript
- Simon Elvin Cards
- Sliding Pillar Press
- Snafu Designs
- Wishing Well Studios
- Your True Greetings

Hours

The Busy Bee is open Monday through Sunday from Memorial Day through October 31st, which is Brendenwood's peak tourist season. We are open on weekends during most of the off-season, but are closed on major holidays and during the months of January and February. Our hours of operation generally are 10:00 a.m. to 7:00 p.m.

Equipment

The following equipment was acquired from the previous occupant:

- 1 sandwich refrigerator
- 1 meat slicer
- 1 bread slicer
- 1 commercial microwave oven
- 1 refrigerated deli case
- 1 cash register
- 15 product display cases
- Shelving for product display
- 1 in-store music system
- 10 café-style tables
- 40 café-style chairs

FINANCIAL ANALYSIS

Sales

Sales Forecast

	2009	2010	2011
Cards	$ 15,896	$ 16,373	$ 16,864
Health & beauty	$ 18,961	$ 19,529	$ 20,116
Deli	$ 21,540	$ 22,186	$ 22,852
Candy	$ 12,540	$ 12,916	$ 13,303
Edible honey products	$ 35,869	$ 36,945	$ 38,053
Beverages	$ 19,654	$ 20,244	$ 20,951
Home décor	$ 25,863	$ 26,664	$ 27,464
Total sales	**$150,323**	**$154,857**	**$159,603**

Profit and Loss

Pro Forma Profit and Loss

	2009	2010	2011
Sales	$150,323	$154,857	$159,603
Direct cost of sales	$ 39,073	$ 40,636	$ 42,261
Total cost of sales	$ 39,073	$ 40,636	$ 42,261
Gross margin	$111,250	$114,221	$117,342
Expenses			
Payroll	$ 52,500	$ 54,600	$ 56,074
Sales and marketing and other expenses	$ 5,500	$ 6,000	$ 6,500
Depreciation	$ 3,250	$ 3,250	$ 3,250
Leased equipment	$ 463	$ 463	$ 463
Utilities	$ 3,700	$ 4,280	$ 4,650
Insurance	$ 3,800	$ 4,150	$ 4,500
Rent	$ 12,500	$ 12,500	$ 12,500
Payroll taxes	$ 7,875	$ 8,190	$ 8,411
Other	$ 850	$ 1,000	$ 1,000
Total operating expenses	$ 90,438	$ 94,433	$ 97,348
Net profit	**$ 21,587**	**$ 19,788**	**$ 19,994**

LEGAL

The Busy Bee is incorporated in the State of Illinois, and has obtained appropriate business and liability insurance policies. Our business is represented by the Brendenwood-based law firm Wade & Potter.

MARKETING & SALES

Our honey products are very popular with customers. Over the years, the B. Strand's brand name has become well known in our region thanks to an identity and related product packaging designs developed by a local advertising agency many years ago.

Event marketing is an important part of our operation. For the past 10 years, the city of Brendenwood has hosted an annual fall festival, which effectively marks the end of the tourist season. For the past four years, The Busy Bee and B. Strand's Bees have served as flagship sponsors of this event, which has adopted the name Brendenwood Honey Harvest Festival.

The Busy Bee has a strong retail presence at the festival, where we sell liquid honey and other edible honey products. In addition, the event provides us with an opportunity to provide free product samples to tourists, distribute coupons related to our end-of-year sale, add new customers to our mailing list, and help to further build the B. Strand's Bees brand name.

In addition to the Brendenwood Honey Harvest Festival, The Busy Bee participates in event marketing efforts at several parades throughout the season, including a Memorial Day parade, a Fourth of July parade, and a Labor Day parade.

Besides event marketing, we regularly distribute coupons and flyers to area hotels and B&Bs in order to entice their customers to pay us a visit.

We also are a regular advertiser in The Brendenwood Guide, a weekly tourist publication that is distributed to area merchants and lodging places.

Finally, one particularly innovative marketing tactic is our use of a yellow, bee-themed Volkswagen Bug, which has been designed to look like a giant bee. The vehicle is an effective attention-getter with area tourists.

SWOT ANALYSIS

- *Strengths:* We are unique in our market, and serve as the exclusive retail distributor for an established, popular brand of honey.

- *Weaknesses:* Leah Strand is the brains behind The Busy Bee, but also spends a great deal of her time on operational matters, making the development of growth strategies a challenge.

- *Opportunities:* Due to our popularity and a growing, loyal customer base that returns each season, we are positioned for future expansion as economic conditions improve.

- *Threats:* We are subject to the impact of economic conditions on consumers' discretionary spending. In addition, the beekeeping business that supplies our popular liquid honey is a relatively small enterprise, and is subject to risks such as poor crops due to pests and diseases.

Home Organization Service

Break Free Organizing

43 Bleak St.
Missouri City, Missouri 64072

Kari Lucke

Break Free Organizing is devoted to helping people organize their homes so that they can reduce stress, increase productivity, and improve their quality of life.

EXECUTIVE SUMMARY

Mission

Break Free Organizing is devoted to helping people organize their homes so that they can reduce stress, increase productivity, and improve their quality of life.

Business Overview

Julie McDonald, B.A., is owner and sole proprietor of Break Free Organizing. She serves the mid–Missouri community by aiding people who want to become more organized in their daily lives. The premise of the business is that many people feel trapped by their surroundings and lack of organizing skills and overwhelmed at the prospect of change. Julie acts as a guide to people who need help getting started, as well as those who need ongoing services. Although Julie will purchase organizing supplies for customers, the business is based on a service, not products.

The professional organizing industry has exploded in recent years. The National Association of Professional Organizers, founded in 1985, now has 4,200 members and a growing number of consumers who seek their services.

The philosophy at Break Free Organizing is "A cluttered house is a cluttered mind" and "A place for everything, and everything in its place." We believe that by helping people become more organized, we free them from stress, allow them more time for their families, and improve their quality of life.

Break Free Organizing adheres to the ethic principles of the National Organization of Professional Organizers (NAPO), which are as follows:

- I will serve my clients with integrity, competence, and objectivity and will treat them with respect and courtesy.

- I will offer services in those areas in which I am qualified and will accurately represent those qualifications in both verbal and written communications.

- When unable or unqualified to fulfill requests for services, I will make every effort to recommend the services of other qualified organizers and/or other qualified professionals.

- I will advertise my services in an honest manner and will represent the organizing profession accurately.

- I will keep confidential all client information, both business and personal, including that which may be revealed by other organizers.

- I will use proprietary client information only with the client's permission.

- I will keep client information confidential and not use it to benefit myself or my firm, or reveal this information to others.

- I will decide independently and communicate to my client in advance my fees and expenses and will charge fees and expenses that I deem reasonable, legitimate, and commensurate with my experience, the services I deliver, and the responsibility I accept.

- I will make recommendations for products and services with my client's best interests in mind.

- I will seek and maintain an equitable, honorable, and cooperative association with other NAPO members and will treat them with respect and courtesy.

- I will respect the intellectual property rights (materials, titles, and thematic creations) of my colleagues, and other firms and individuals, and will not use proprietary information or methodologies without permission.

- I will act and speak on a high professional level so as not to bring discredit to the organizing profession.

MARKET ANALYSIS

Americans have been taking on more demands and commitments in their work and personal lives but have gained no extra time to deal with them. The result is an everyday environment of chaos and clutter that robs people of precious time and induces even more stress than already present due to overbooked schedules and, sometimes, just too much stuff. The professional organizing industry was created to help these people bring peace and order to their lives.

Several studies have illustrated the need for professional organizing services in America. For example:

- A 2008 study by NAPO showed that 55 percent of respondents would save 16 minutes to 1 hour a day—or two to 15 days a year—if they were more organized.

- A recent *Real Simple* magazine survey showed that women waste an average of 55 minutes a day looking for things they know they have but can't find.

- The Small Business Administration reported that 80 percent of papers that are filed are never looked at again.

- The life of the average American is becoming more, not less, complicated, which sets the stage for major growth in the professional organizing industry.

Our market consists of upper–middle and upper–class families, specifically women, in Columbia and surrounding areas. Columbia's population grew from 69,000 in 1990 to approximately 94,000 in 2007. The population of Boone County, which includes the towns of Ashland, Centralia, and Hallsville, is around 146,000. The median household income of Columbia residents is $42,163, with a race distribution of 83 percent White, 9 percent Black, and 8 percent other. Fifteen percent of the Boone County population has an annual income of $100,000 or more.

Many professional organizers choose to specialize in one or more areas. Common areas of specialty include home offices, closets, garages, children's spaces, and business offices, as well as packing and moving. Break Free Organizing focuses on helping women, usually with children, and the major living areas in their homes—entryways, bedrooms, kitchens, and living areas, While the ideal goal for people may be to have their entire house organized, right down to the last closet, we try to help those people who are far from that, people who can't get out the door in the morning because they can't find their car keys or because the kids can't find their homework or their shoes. These are the people we seek to serve.

Competition

Only a handful of professional organizers operate out of Columbia, Missouri, and little information is available about their services. An online search brings up only three local businesses: Organization Plus and Packed, Stacked & Labeled; and Organize It...One Room at a Time. Closets by Design advertises as an organization service but focuses on closet storage and the sale and installation of their high–end storage units.

MANAGEMENT SUMMARY

According to the NAPO, a good professional organizer has the following characteristics:

- Ability to ask the right questions to understand what a client wants and needs
- Ability to listen and infer what a client means
- Ability to customize organizational systems to meet client needs
- Ability to teach and transfer basic organizing skills
- Ability to visualize spatially and see the big picture
- Ability to break goals down into manageable steps
- Ability to categorize and plan ahead
- Ability to use technology to support organizing efforts
- Physical and mental endurance
- Compassion
- Responsibility
- Professionalism

Julie McDonald has all of these characteristics, as well as a bachelor of arts degree in business from the University of Missouri. She was employed as an administrative assistant at two different University Physicians clinics for eight years. During that time, Julie dealt with people on a daily basis and learned to be diplomatic, trustworthy, and efficient. All of these characteristics are important attributes of a good professional organizer. Diplomacy and trustworthiness are especially vital. Many people who invite professional organizers into their homes are embarrassed about their living situation, and the organizer must be able to coach and help the person without being judgmental or critical. Julie has these skills as well as the business acumen to manage the financial and record–keeping aspects of the position.

Professional and Advisory Support

Julie is a member of the National Association for Professional Organizers (NAPO), which provides educational and business resources for the industry. She is working on becoming certified by the organization, and expects to complete the requirements for the certification by June 2009. In addition, Julie has taken several classes offered by NAPO, including PO–001T: Introduction to Professional Organizing, PO–101T: Starting an Organizing Business, and PO–102T: Fundamental Organizing Principles.

BUSINESS STRATEGY

Professional organizing is a service industry. Our aim is not to sell products but to provide services to clients who need them. Although some industries must advertise to convince customers that they need the service that they provide, professional organizers must advertise to convince customers that their business is the best one to provide the services the clients already knows he or she needs. In other words, it is not difficult to convince a overworked and harried working mother that she needs to get organized—and help doing it; the objective is to convince her that (a) Break Free Organizing is the best place to find that help, and (b) it will be well worth the money she invests. Once we have a client, our goal is to provide what he or she needs and wants in a timely, affordable, and professional manner.

PRODUCTS & SERVICES

Break Free Organizing adheres to standards set by the National Association of Professional Organizers (NAPO). According to the NAPO website, "A professional organizer enhances the lives of clients by designing custom organizing systems and processes and by transferring organizing skills. A professional organizer also educates the public on organizing solutions and the resulting benefits."

Pricing

The fees for services provided by Break Free Organizing are based on a per–hour cost. Nationwide, professional organizers charge anywhere from $40 an hour to $200 an hour, according to NAPO. Based on the demographics of Columbia, Missouri, rates for services provided by Break Free Organizing will be $75 an hour. This includes time spent working in the client's home as well as meeting with the client and completing necessary paperwork and/or prepatory work.

MARKETING & SALES

Advertising

The main means of promotion of the business will be a website, brochures, and advertising in the local media, including the monthly "door mail" packet, which is delivered to homes throughout Columbia, and the local newspaper, the *Columbia Daily Tribune*. We will also run an ad in the CenturyTel yellow pages. Word of mouth will become a major form of advertising once clients use the services and pass the information along to their friends and family.

Cost

The cost for the Yellow Page ad is $500 twice a year. Fees for advertising in door mail run approximately $100 a month. We will print 200 brochures twice a year at a cost of 50 cents per brochure. The cost of the website is minimal at approximately $100 a year.

OPERATIONS

Customers

Our target customers are women ages 25 to 50 who still have children living at home. Average household income of target customers is $100,000 and up. According to current demographics, this constitutes approximately 15 percent of the population of Columbia, or 14,100 individuals.

Hours

Break Free Organizing will operate on an appointment basis. The business phone will ring in the owner's home and be answered 24/7 by a person or an answering machine.

Services

The basic procedure is as follows: After a potential client contacts Julie, she meets with the client in his or her home and together they devise a plan of action. Julie then creates a contract that specifies exactly what services she will perform and the estimated cost. After the contract is finalized and signed, Julie and the client agree on a time when Julie will arrive for the first appointment and any following appointments if necessary. Jobs may last anywhere from a couple of hours for one room to several days for an entire house.

A sample job is illustrated below.

Charlene, a wife and mother of two children, ages 8 and 12, calls Julie asking for help getting organized. She is not sure what part of her house needs it the most, but she knows her main problem is getting the kids and herself out the door on time in the morning. She has limited funds for the project. Julie sets up a time to meet Charlene in her home, and at that time Charlene shows Julie the house and answers Julie's questions about the current situation and what Charlene would like to see happen. Based on her observations and the information Charlene provides her, Julie suggests that organizing the entryway, where the family enters and exists the home, and the adjoining coat closet will provide the family with the most benefits. The area is piled with coats, shoes, paperwork, old phone books, electronics, and many other items that do not "have a home." When Julie returns at the designated time, she and Charlene together handle each item in the entryway and closet and place it one of three piles: Keep, Give Away, or Throw Away. After they have gone through everything in the area, the Throw Away pile is taken out to the garage, where the trash is collected, and the Give Away is stowed in the back of Charlene's mini van for transporting to the Salvation Army or other charity. The items in the Keep pile are then sorted into categories, and anything that does not belong in the entryway is put away somewhere else in the house. With only the remaining Keep items left, Charlene and Julie devise a plan for where things will go. Julie suggests an inexpensive table with space for outgoing mail, gloves and hats, keys, cell phones, and other items that the family needs to take out the door with them every day. With Charlene's approval, Julie purchases and installs the table, and the two of them put away the items that belong there. The coat closet is left open for coats and the vacuum cleaner, which was previously sitting in the dining room because there was no room for it in the closet. Julie also installs hooks for the children's school backpacks. After three hours, the area is organized and the job done. Julie provides Charlene with a "reminder" sheet that lists what the family must do in order to make the area work efficiently for them. Sometimes this involves changes in behavior or habits, and the reminder sheet is a hard copy that Charlene can use when explaining the new system to her family. Julie then provides an invoice to Charlene for $225, and Charlene writes a check.

Facility and Location

Because Julie operates her business out of her home, additional space is not required. All of the paperwork and deskwork is done in Julie's home office.

Legal Environment

For protection of herself and her business, Julie carries business insurance through NAPOSure.com. The program is underwritten by the Philadelphia Companies and includes liability and bonding protection.

FINANCIAL ANALYSIS

Start–up costs for the business are minimal and cover only advertising, contracts, and a small amount of storage supplies. Other ongoing expenses would include gas and maintenance on Julie's vehicle and insurance. For the first year, while she is gaining clients, Julie predicts she will complete 40 hours of work a month. The following year, after she has gained more clients, she expects to work 60 hours a month, and the third year, 80. Because Julie expects word of mouth to provide advertising after the first year, she does not expect to increase her adverting costs in years 2 and 3. However, the price of advertising will likely increase by approximately 10 percent each year. Vehicle costs are figured at 25, 27, and 30 cents per mile in year 1, 2, and 3, respectively, with mileage increasing each year (year 1: 3,600 miles; year 2: 4,800 miles; year 3: 6,500 miles). Julie intends to keep her hourly rate at $75 for the first three years.

Professional Organizer 1

	2009–2010	2011–2012	2013–2014
Projected income	$36,000	$54,000	$72,000
Projected advertising costs	2,500	2,750	3,025
Projected vehicle costs	900	1,296	1,950
Projected insurance costs	1,200	1,200	1,200
Profit	$31,400	$48,754	$65,825

House Cleaning

Mid-Missouri Maid Service

4500 Stonecreek Drive
Columbia, Missouri 65201

Kari Lucke

Mid-Missouri Maid Service (MMS) will be a local house cleaning service operating out of Columbia, Missouri.

INTRODUCTION

Executive Summary

Mid-Missouri Maid Service (MMS) will be a local house cleaning service operating out of Columbia, Missouri. Owned and operated by Olivia and Scott Jones, MMS will serve upper-middle and upper-income families who own their own home in Columbia, as well as older people who cannot or prefer not to clean their own home. Couples, especially two-income couples with children, are the primary target market, as they tend to have the least amount of time to spend house cleaning. It is not hard to convince such couples that a house cleaning service will benefit them, and MMS's ability to schedule a cleaning appointment almost immediately after gaining a new client will help those clients feel confident about and happy with their decision to hire MMS.

Business Philosophy

The philosophy at MMS is that having a clean home improves a family's quality of life, and Olivia's goal is to help families realize, both mentally and physically, that condition. Olivia finds great satisfaction in bringing peace of mind and a sense of relief and contentment to people who want a clean house but do not have the time or the inclination to do it themselves.

Goals and Objectives

- Gain a small client base on which MMS can build in the first three months of business.

- Have enough clients within the first year to justify the hiring of two more employees.

- Earn net revenues of $70,000 the first year of business.

Organization Structure

MMS is a sole proprietorship owned and operated by Olivia and Scott Jones. Initially, all cleaning will be done by Olivia and two part-time employees. Scott will handle all accounting and bookkeeping, including payroll and taxes, scheduling, and customer service issues.

INDUSTRY AND MARKET

Industry Analysis

According to American Demographics, about 10 percent of Americans hire someone else to clean their home. In addition, a report released by the Home Cleaning Centers of America (HCCA) in 2007 showed that residential house cleaning has become one of the fastest-growing industries in the country. The industry had $20 billion in annual revenue, and HCCA predicted growth rates of 20 percent per year.

In 2008 the U.S. Census Bureau reported 1.5 million people employed as maid / house cleaners; 29 percent of these were employed by private households. The Census Bureau also predicted a growth rate (14 percent) through 2016. According to the 2009-10 edition of the Occupational Outlook Handbook, "Much of the growth in these occupations will come from cleaning residential properties. As families become more pressed for time, they increasingly hire cleaning and handyman services to perform a variety of tasks in their homes. Also, as the population ages, older people will need to hire cleaners to help maintain their houses."

Competition

There are several house cleaning businesses in Columbia, including Merry Maids and numerous individually owned agencies. However, the market is not saturated, and quality of service is an important issue for those looking for cleaning services. Whereas Merry Maids is one of the larger companies in town, it also has had some negative publicity, both locally and nationally. In addition, according to research by the House Cleaning Alliance (www.house-cleaning-alliance.com), people searching for house cleaners on the Internet select business that are classified as "not a franchise" over those who are deemed "thorough," "dependable," "careful," and "affordable." In other words, according to this report, people prefer a cleaning business that is not a franchise. Also, if they hire a franchise cleaning company, clients can often end up with different people cleaning their house every time, which can result in inconsistency, and franchised workers are trained to follow a set protocol, regardless of individual conditions, which can result in less effective results.

In order to compete with Merry Maids and individually owned business such as Casa Bonita House Cleaning, Tiger Maids, and Housecleaning Specialists, MMS will focus on providing quality services for an affordable price.

PERSONNEL

Management

Scott Jones will handle the day-to-day business of MMS, including scheduling appointments, providing estimates, and handling all bookkeeping and other support activities for the cleaning work done by Olivia and the staff. Scott has an associate's degree in business from Moberly Area Community College and has the knowledge and skills needed to keep the business on track. Olivia is a high school graduate and has worked as a house cleaner for three different companies over the past several years, including Merry Maids, House Cleaning Plus, and Maid for Hire.

Staffing

Other than Olivia and John, MSS will employ two part-time workers, each of whom will work 20 hours a week. To find these employees, Olivia and John will conduct a thorough search using the local newspaper and online job sites. Because Columbia is home to two four-year colleges and a major state university, the demand for part-time jobs is high, so there should be no lack of applications. The more important factor will be the quality of the people Olivia and John choose to hire. They will conduct background and reference checks on all potential employees so as to ensure, as much as possible, that the people they do hire are dependable, trustworthy, and willing and able to do what is required.

When a hiring decision is made, employees will receive a detailed job description and sign an agreement stating that their first month of employment is on a probation basis. If during the training period the person is not able to complete the duties as required, he or she will be released from employment, and a new employee will be sought. Olivia will conduct hands-on training. Several people have agreed to let her clean their house at no charge in exchange for using the home as a training ground for the new employees. Each new employee will clean a minimum of two houses with Olivia before he or she is considered ready to go out on a real job. Employees will carry a written checklist with them to each home in order to ensure each job is completed correctly.

Employees will be paid $12 an hour, which is a competitive salary for the sector. No insurance or vacation time will be included, as is most common with part-time jobs.

Professional and Advisory Support

Because Scott will take care of all accounting and tax issues for the company, the only professional support needed by MMS upfront will be an insurance agent (Patricia Willsmeyer, State Farm) and a lawyer (George Smith, Smith & Johnston Associates), for any legal issues that may arise.

BUSINESS STRATEGY

The strategy for conducting business is as follows: Scott will visit each interested client's home to gather information needed to provide an estimate and inform the client (via a brochure) of the services that MMS will provide, then he will follow up—within two days—by phone or e-mail with the actual estimate. If the client agrees to use the service, Scott will take the service contract to the client's home for signing; at the same time, they will set up a schedule of cleaning, based on the customer's needs. All information will be input into Scott's computer using the industry-specific software program, Maid Manager Pro 5.0. Olivia will accompany Scott on this home visit so that she can introduce herself to the client and answer any questions about the cleaning process. After a client has been contracted, Olivia and one employee will follow up with the cleaning based on the schedule that has been set up.

PRODUCTS AND SERVICES

Description

MMS will provide residential cleaning services to households in the Columbia area. Basic house cleaning services include dusting furniture and removing cobwebs; sweeping, vacuuming, and/or mopping floors; cleaning and disinfecting bathrooms, kitchens, and laundry rooms; picking up and straightening living areas; and performing other cleaning duties as requested or contracted. Whereas other cleaning services can do the same basic job, MMS will do it consistently (the same people will clean the same homes, even as the business expands) and well. Consistent quality service is vital to keeping customers, and MMS will make this one of the primary focuses of business.

Pricing

All estimates will be determined by a formula made available through a software program designed specifically for the industry. Scott inputs all factors, including number of bedrooms and bathrooms, square footage, number of pets and/or children, and so forth, and the program calculates how long it should take to clean the house. As a baseline, MMS charges $30 an hour. Using the figure gained from the program, Scott can determine an accurate estimate, which then becomes the amount charged to the customer for each cleaning. For example, a typical 2500-square-foot, 3 bedroom/2 bath home housing a family of four would cost $100 to clean. This figure can be adjusted based on customer preferences such as having only certain rooms cleaned, having additional cleaning tasks completed, or other variations. The frequency of cleaning (e.g., biweekly, weekly) also factors into the cost, as more frequent cleaning results in less work each time.

MMS pricing is comparable with individually owned competitors and lower than that for franchises such as Merry Maids, which charges approximately $150 for a one-time cleaning of a home with pets and children.

MARKETING AND SALES

Advertising and Promotion

MMS will use a web site and brochures as its main forms of advertising. The web site will list services included, reasons to use a cleaning service—as well as reasons to use MMS—and other pertinent information. A photo of Scott, Olivia, and, later, the other employees will be posted to give customers a personal link to the company. Photos will also be used to inspire and convince potential customers that they would benefit from the service. Brochures will contain the same basic information as the web site in a condensed and printed form. Another form of advertising will consist of signs for vehicles, which will be placed on cars driven by Scott, Olivia, and employees.

Word of mouth is considered another form of advertising. As people use MMS's services and are satisfied, they will recommend the company to friends and family. Word of mouth is considered one of the most effective means of advertising for this type of company.

Cost

Advertising costs are expected to be minimal and include approximately $100 for web site fees and $250 a year for brochure printing.

Image

"Professional" is an important characteristic of a house cleaning company. Sometimes this is a challenge if other local companies have given a different impression. For MMS, professionalism is the number–one focus of image. Quality that is consistent is also key and a characteristic that is hard to find in residential cleaning companies. Finally, price is a part of a company's image, and MMS will exhibit competitive prices for exceptional service. Focusing on these three factors—professionalism, consistent quality, and value—MMS will build an image that will set them apart from other cleaning companies.

OPERATIONS

Customers

According WorkEnders, Inc., people who hire outside cleaning help are typically dual-income households, professional single adults, high-income single-parent families, or affluent empty-nesters or retirees. (The latter category represents a smaller portion of the market in Columbia due to the city's relatively young population.) Typically, clients range in age from 35 to 65 years old and have household incomes of $75,000 or more annually. The following is a breakdown of the related demographics for Columbia:

Characteristic	Population	Percentage of population
Ages 35 to 65	28,200	30%
Homeowners	44,180	47%
Annual income $75,000 or more	25,380	27%

Equipment

MMS will provide all cleaning supplies and equipment. Equipment will include vacuum cleaners, buckets, mops, cleaning solutions, rags and sponges, and other necessary cleaning supplies.

Hours

Cleaning services will be provided Monday through Saturday from 7 a.m. to 4 p.m. and will be determined by the clients' needs and schedules.

Facility and Location

The business will be operated out of the Jones's home at 4500 Stonecreek Drive, Columbia, Missouri.

Legal Environment

All employees of MMS will be licensed and bonded.

FINANCIAL ANALYSIS

Initial start-up costs are as follows:

Start-up expenses	Cost
Equipment	$1000
Cleaning supplies	$ 250
Office supplies	$ 250
Uniforms	$ 100
Brochures	$ 250
Vehicle signs	$ 100
Computer hardware and software	$ 500
Insurance	$ 200
Business license	$ 100
Total start-up expenses	**$2750**

Funding for start-up costs will be provided by money from a personal savings account.

First year monthly expenses	Cost
Cleaning supplies	$ 100
Office supplies	$ 50
Salaries	$1920
Vehicle costs	$ 200
Insurance	$ 50
Other	$ 100
Total monthly expenses, first year	**$2420**

Estimated incomes are based on low figures using the average cost of $100 per cleaning.

Year	No. houses cleaned weekly	No. houses cleaned biweekly	No. houses one-time clean	Total no. houses/ cleanings per year	Total net income	Minus taxes	Total gross income
Year 1	5	15	5	25 / 710	$ 71,000	$21,300	$ 49,700
Year 2	10	20	10	40 / 1160	$116,000	$34,800	$ 81,200
Year 3	15	25	15	55 / 1550	$155,000	$46,500	$108,500

Ice Cream Parlor

SonnyScoops

725 Shore Dr.
Brooks Falls, Minnesota 55008

Paul Greenland

SonnyScoops is a popular ice cream shop in Brooks Falls, Minnesota.

EXECUTIVE SUMMARY

Business Overview

SonnyScoops is a popular ice cream shop in Brooks Falls, Minnesota.

In 2009, Paul Richardson agreed to acquire an existing ice cream retail business in Brooks Falls, Minnesota, named SonnyScoops, which has been in business for 22 years. Its well-known owner, Sonny Massari, is selling the business due to retirement.

SonnyScoops is a fixture in Brooks Falls. Located across from Sandy Beach on the shores of Silver Lake, this ice cream shop is very popular with tourists and locals alike during the summer months. Although sales are strongest during the summer, SonnyScoops enjoys an established customer base year-round. In addition to its location across from a popular beach, the ice cream shop is one block away from an elementary school, a middle school, and a high school. In addition, it also is within close geographic proximity to two popular parks, as well as a youth/community center.

Business Philosophy

SonnyScoops is the destination of choice for the coolest treats in town. Our commitment to our customers means providing quality ice cream and frozen desserts in a fun, family-friendly environment.

MARKET ANALYSIS

The town of Brooks Falls, Minnesota, is located northwest of Minneapolis, near the town of Brainerd. The area includes many lakes and resorts that attract tourists for fishing, camping, biking, swimming, boating, and more.

In 2002 a new competitor named Buster's Ice Cream Palace opened its doors several blocks away. However, because of its better location and established reputation, the impact on SonnyScoops' market share was minimal. Difficult economic conditions ultimately forced this primary competitor to close its doors midway through the summer 2008 season. In 2010, Paul Richardson plans to further strengthen

SonnyScoops' position of market leadership by expanding the business' product selection and sales reach (via the addition of mobile operations).

Other competition comes from established national franchises such as Dairy Queen and McDonald's. Once again, our geographic location serves us well in this regard, because Dairy Queen is located 1/2 mile from our establishment. McDonald's is only two blocks away, however, putting that restaurant within easy walking distance from the beach and other popular locations. For consumers in search of food and dessert, this puts us at a slight disadvantage.

INDUSTRY ANALYSIS

Manufacturers and distributors in our industry are represented by the International Ice Cream Association, which recognizes National Ice Cream Month in July. According to the association, the U.S. ice cream industry generates more than $21 billion in sales each year, and uses approximately 9 percent of the milk produced by the nation's dairy farmers.

According to data from the National Restaurant Association (NRA), the restaurant industry had sales of $566 billion in 2009. A leading private-sector employer, the industry provided jobs for approximately 13 million people who worked at about 945,000 locations that year. Our establishment is part of the Retail, Vending, Recreation, Mobile segment of the industry, which generated sales of $52.9 billion in 2009.

PERSONNEL

Management

SonnyScoops is owned and managed by Paul Richardson, a retired schoolteacher from St. Paul, Minnesota. Prior to establishing SonnyScoops, Richardson operated a mobile ice cream business for eight years in the Twin Cities. This was the perfect business opportunity during the summer months when he wasn't teaching school. Richardson has owned a vacation property in Brooks Falls for 15 years. The opportunity to purchase SonnyScoops dovetailed nicely with his experience in the ice cream business and plans to relocate permanently to Brooks Falls.

Richardson will be assisted by his wife, Jane, who has seven years of retail management experience. Most recently, she managed a local concession business at an indoor sports complex in the Twin Cities.

Staffing

In addition to the Richardsons, SonnyScoops will employ a staff of four part-time employees.

Professional and Advisory Support

SonnyScoops has retained the local accounting firm of Lane & Heller to assist us with bookkeeping and tax responsibilities.

Commercial checking accounts have been established with Brooks Falls Bank, a local bank that also is providing us with partial financing. Brooks Falls Bank also has assisted us with the establishment of merchant accounts, so that we are able to accept credit card and debit card payments.

GROWTH STRATEGY

SonnyScoops has historically offered 24 flavors of ice cream, as well as a limited selection of novelties. Moving forward, Paul Richardson has plans to double the business' selection of ice cream products and novelties, add a wide selection of water ice, and add a mobile sales operation consisting of a portable ice cream cart and an ice cream truck.

The new mobile operations will allow the business to capitalize on additional sales from Memorial Day to Labor Day. Specifically, the ice cream cart will offer novelties and a limited selection of ice cream at a nearby soccer field. The ice cream truck will frequent three nearby subdivisions, as well as a beach on the other side of the lake.

PRODUCTS & SERVICES

Beginning with the 2010 summer season, SonnyScoops will offer the following expanded lineup of ice cream and other frozen desserts:

Ice Cream & Sherbet
Banana

Banana Fudge

Banana Split

Banana Strawberry

Black Raspberry

Black Raspberry Sherbet

Blue Moon

Butter Almond

Butter Pecan

Butterfinger

Butterscotch

Cherry Vanilla

Chocolate

Chocolate Chip

Chocolate Chip Cookie Dough

Chocolate Macadamia Nut

Chocolate Peanut Butter

Coconut Fudge

Coffee

Cookies & Cream

Double Chocolate

Double Oreo

French Vanilla

Grasshopper

Heath Bar Crunch

Lemon Sherbet

Lime Sherbet

M&M

Mint Chocolate Chip

Mocha Chocolate Chip

Mud Pie

Orange Creamy

Orange Sherbet

Peach

Peanut Butter Cup Fudge

Peppermint Stick

Pistachio

Pralines & Cream

Rainbow Sherbet

Rice Krispy Treat

Rocky Road

Snicker Doodle

Strawberry

Vanilla

Vanilla Chocolate Chip

Vanilla Fudge

Vanilla Peanut Butter Cup

White Chocolate Raspberry

Ices

Banana

Black Cherry

Black Raspberry

Blue Raspberry

Bubble Gum

Cherry

Chocolate

Coconut

Cotton Candy

Grape

Lemon Lime

Mango

Orange

Orange Creamy

Passion Fruit

Peach

Pina Colada

Pineapple

Rootbeer

Red Raspberry

Sour Apple

Strawberry

Strawberry Kiwi

Strawberry Lemonade

Tangerine

Vanilla

Watermelon

Novelties

Creamsicles

Fudgesicles

Popsicles

Klondike Bars

Dove Bars

Snicker Bars

Rocket Push-Ups

Ice Cream Sandwiches

Vanilla Ice Cream Bar

Chocolate Ice Cream Bar

Strawberry Shortcake Stick

Vanilla Ice Cream Cup

Chocolate Ice Cream Cup

Strawberry Ice Cream Cup

Sugar-Free Ice Cream Cups

MARKETING & SALES

A comprehensive marketing plan has been developed for SonnyScoops. The plan includes both short-term and ongoing tactics.

Short-Term Tactics

In the short-term, a number of promotions and activities are planned around the re-launch of the business in the summer of 2010. Specifically, we will host three "Free Ice Cream Day" events during the Memorial Day, Fourth Of July, and Labor Day holiday weekends. This will allow us to get maximum exposure during peak tourist weekends. Each weekend (on Friday and Saturday), we will offer free junior-size, single-scoop servings of all our ice cream flavors from 7:00 to 9:00 p.m. Moving forward, we will offer the same promotion every year on the Fourth of July weekend, budget permitting.

In addition, during our first year of operations, we will pass out a limited number of coupons for free one-scoop ice cream cones. Distribution will occur on Sandy Beach, in an effort to generate additional foot traffic to our business. As with the "Free Ice Cream Day" promotion, we may continue this tactic if it proves to be a cost-effective means of increasing our customer base.

Ongoing Tactics

We plan to use certain marketing tactics on a regular basis to promote our business. These include the following.

Radio Advertising—During the summer, SonnyScoops will advertise with our market's Top 40 radio station, which has a strong listener base and is broadcast daily at Sandy Beach. We plan to offer regular on-promotions to drive foot traffic to our business during times of the day that are typically slow.

Event Marketing—Each year, SonnyScoops will host monthly beach volleyball tournaments at Sandy Beach.

Print Advertising—There are two main newspapers in our market: the Brooks Falls Gazette and the Sandy Beach Shopper. SonnyScoops will run regular advertisements in both publications, in order to promote weekly specials. In addition, we will offer occasional buy-one-get-one-free coupons during periods when business is slow.

OPERATIONS

Suppliers

SonnyScoops will purchase its products from several suppliers. The bulk of our ice cream and sherbet will be purchased from Nick & Cody Ice Cream Corp., allowing us to offer the popular Nick & Cody's brand.

In addition, we will acquire the supplies needed for our ice water frozen desserts, as well as novelties, from one of the three following regional suppliers:

- Martial Distribution
- Peterson Foods
- GDC Corp.

Hours

SonnyScoops will operate seven days a week, Memorial Day through Labor Day, from noon to 10:00 p.m. Throughout the rest of the year, we will close at 5:00 p.m. Monday through Thursday, and at 9:00 p.m. on Friday and Saturday. We will be closed on Sundays.

Facility and Location

SonnyScoops is located in a 1,000-square-foot storefront at 725 Shore Dr. For its first five years of operations, Paul Richardson has agreed to lease the storefront from the previous owner, Sonny Massari.

Equipment

Although much of the equipment needed to operate the restaurant is already present, approximately $21,300 in capital purchases will be needed before we are ready for business, including the following expenses, as noted below.

To expand our product lineup, we will need to purchase three additional 12-bucket ice cream display cases at a cost of $3,000 each.

There also will be costs for adding mobile operations to the business. Purchased at a cost of $1,800, the ice cream cart consists of a 7-cubic-foot electric freezer with a battery life of 10 hours.

The ice cream truck is a 2003 Ford E150, purchased at a cost of $10,500. It includes a high-top roof, 20-cubic-foot freezer, digital music system with speaker and microphone, Plexiglas slide windows and serving shelf, a five-foot canopy, as well as a menu display.

FINANCIAL ANALYSIS

Following are projected figures for our first year of operations.

Sales

Ice cream	$63,067
Ice water	$17,520
Novelties	$13,728
Total sales	**$94,315**

Pro Forma Profit & Loss

Sales	$ 94,315
Total cost of sales	$ 33,901
Gross margin	$ 60,413
Expenses	
Payroll	$ 35,000
Sales and marketing	$ 8,520
Utilities	$ 4,300
Vehicle	$ 4,500
Business loan	$ 5,000
Insurance	$ 750
Rent	$ 6,500
Total operating expenses	$ 64,570
Net profit	**($ 4,157)**

Based on our best estimate, we expect our net profit to increase at a compound annual rate of 7 percent through 2014. We expect to break even during our third year of operations.

Financing for SonnyScoops will consist of a $40,000 commercial loan from Brooks Falls Bank, which also has agreed to supply us with a $15,000 line of credit. In addition, Owner/Manager Paul Richardson is providing $30,000 from his personal savings.

Nature Photography Business

Shutterbugs Inc.

24 Williams St. North
Appleton, Wisconsin 54296

Paul Greenland

Shutterbugs is a nature photography business specializing in macro or close-up photography.

EXECUTIVE SUMMARY

Business Overview

Shutterbugs is a nature photography business specializing in macro or close-up photography. Our specialty includes photographing insects, arachnids, and unique textures found on objects like seeds, fruit, and leaves. We sell photographs to a variety of customers, including magazines, book publishers, stock photography agencies, and museums.

Incorporated in the state of Wisconsin, Shutterbugs is owned by photographer Jeff Thomas. Prior to starting his own photography business, Thomas spent 15 years working as an in-house photographer for a large corporation. Convinced that his prospects for success as a nature photographer are very good, Thomas has decided to pursue nature photography on a full-time basis by establishing Shutterbugs.

MARKET ANALYSIS

According to data from the U.S. Bureau of Labor Statistics, there were approximately 122,000 photographers employed in 2006. Of these, half were self-employed. The majority of these photographers worked for advertising agencies, commercial and portrait photography studios, newspapers, and magazines. Based on this information, it is reasonable to assume that the number of professional nature photographers is comparatively small.

Although the playing field may be somewhat smaller than in other areas of photography, Shutterbugs' competitors hail from all corners of the world. The advent of digital photography has made it much easier for individuals to enter the field and submit their work electronically. Focusing on macro photography and specializing in arachnids and insects provides Shutterbugs with key differentials that set us apart from other nature photographers.

In the photography business, individuality is highly prized, and unique photos are more important to editors and than a photographer's educational background or professional designations. Because magazine editors, book publishers, stock photography agencies, and museums have purchased photographs from Thomas on a regular basis over the past five years, he has developed a reputation for his work and is confident that he has a strong foothold in a competitive market.

PRODUCTS & SERVICES

Nature Photography

After completing photo shoots that may result in hundreds or thousands of images, Thomas selects the very best ones, performs photo editing, and uploads them to his digital portfolio, which current and prospective customers can access for viewing.

In addition, certain images may be submitted to photo stock agencies, which resell them and provide Thomas with royalty income that varies depending on how the images are used. For example, he receives larger royalties if an image is used on a book cover, as opposed to being used as a small thumbnail image in a magazine article.

Although Thomas sometimes works on assignment, he normally pursues photo shoots on his own and populates his portfolio with a steady stream of new images. Broad subject categories include:

- Amphibians

- Arachnids

- Crustaceans

- Earth

- Fruit

- Ice & Snow

- Insects

- Mammals

- Plants

- Reptiles

- Rocks & Sand

- Trees

- Water

Within each broad category, there are numerous sub-categories. Because arachnids and insects are Shutterbugs' specialty, the number of images that customers can choose from is quite large.

Examples of the types of arachnids we have photographed include:

- Garden Spiders

- Jumping Spiders

- Golden Silk Orb Weaver (Banana Spider)

- Ghost Spiders

- Lynx Spiders

- Sheet-web Weavers

- Hacklemesh Weavers

- Wolf Spiders

Examples of the types of insects we have photographed include:

- American Plum Borers
- Ants
- Aphids
- Armyworms
- Asiatic Garden Beetles
- Asiatic Oak Weevils
- Aster Leafhoppers
- Bagworms
- Bark Beetles
- Beet Webworms
- Billbugs
- Black Cherry Aphids
- Blister Beetles
- Boxelder Bugs
- Butterflies
- Caterpillars
- Cherry Fruitworms
- Colorado Potato Beetles
- Douglas Fir Bark Beetles
- Eastern Tent Caterpillars
- Elm Leaf Beetles
- Flies
- Harvestmen (daddy long legs)
- Japanese Beetles
- Leafhoppers
- Locusts
- Mexican Bean Beetles
- Millipedes
- Mosquitos
- Moths
- Red-banded Leaf Rollers
- Springtails
- Stink Bugs
- Weevils
- Willow Galls
- Wireworms

Commercial Photography

Shutterbugs performs commercial photography on a periodic basis to Jeff Thomas' former employer. At this time, the business does not pursue commercial assignments from other parties.

Classes & Workshops

In addition to teaching nature photography courses at a local community college, Shutterbugs will host classroom and field-based macro photography workshops for small groups of both aspiring and experienced nature photographers. Offered four times per year, these will be offered at one of three forest preserves in Wisconsin.

OPERATIONS

Location and Facilities

Jeff Thomas lives in a rural area, which provides ample opportunities for photographing various subjects in nature without having to travel. Even so, Thomas travels throughout the United States in search of specific photography subjects.

Thomas has devoted an existing outbuilding on his property to Shutterbugs. The building includes a loft where he will perform photo editing and perform general business tasks. The main level of the building includes a small space for classroom instruction, as well as an area for performing macro photography. The remainder of the main level space is devoted to equipment and gear storage.

Special Equipment

Over the course of his career, Jeff Thomas has amassed much of the equipment needed for his business. However, additional equipment and supplies will need to be purchased. Important items include outdoor gear such as:

- Snowshoes
- Windproof/Waterproof Clothing
- Head Gear
- Hand Warmer Packets
- Umbrellas
- Headlamps
- Bug Repellent
- Sunscreen
- Screen Bug Hat
- Hiking Boots
- Winter Boots
- Backpacks
- Ski Poles

New photography equipment that must be purchased includes:

- Camera Bodies
- Lenses
- Tripods

- Lens Reversing Attachment
- Reflectors
- Flash Memory Cards
- Batteries
- Filters

FINANCIAL ANALYSIS

Following is an estimated three-year balance sheet for shutterbugs:

Income	2010	2011	2012
Commercial photography	$25,000	$ 27,500	$ 28,500
Education & instruction	$10,000	$ 10,500	$ 11,000
Royalties	$14,500	$ 23,500	$ 26,200
Licensing	$25,500	$ 45,000	$ 55,000
Total income	**$75,000**	**$106,500**	**$120,700**
Expenses			
Marketing	$ 2,000	$ 1,500	$ 1,500
Photography supplies	$ 1,000	$ 1,500	$ 1,750
Miscellaneous	$ 500	$ 1,000	$ 1,000
Office supplies	$ 300	$ 300	$ 300
Legal	$ 750	$ 1,000	$ 1,500
Accounting	$ 400	$ 450	$ 500
Photography equipment	$ 8,500	$ 5,500	$ 5,500
Computer technology/software	$ 2,000	$ 1,000	$ 1,000
Utilities	$ 1,400	$ 1,600	$ 1,800
Automotive	$ 2,500	$ 3,500	$ 4,500
Fuel	$ 6,500	$ 8,500	$ 9,500
Meals	$ 3,500	$ 4,000	$ 4,500
Salary	$30,000	$ 55,000	$ 65,000
Outdoor apparel/gear	$ 3,500	$ 1,000	$ 1,500
Health & liability insurance	$12,000	$ 14,000	$ 16,000
Total expenses	**$74,850**	**$ 99,850**	**$115,850**
Net income	**$ 150**	**$ 6,650**	**$ 4,850**

The owners' investment is $25,000, which will provide a financial cushion during the first year of operations. The business will essentially break even during its first year, and turn a modest profit in years two and three.

MANAGEMENT SUMMARY

Shutterbugs is owned by photographer Jeff Thomas. Prior to starting his own photography business, Thomas spent 15 years working as an in-house photographer for a large corporation. In that role, he photographed everything from architecture and machinery to products and people. In particular, he developed special expertise photographing very small machine components.

Nature photography has always been Thomas' true passion. Recently, he celebrated the publication of *Small World*, a coffee table book featuring a collection of close-up pictures taken over a period of five years. Based on the success of that project, his publisher contracted him to compile a similar book called *Along Came the Spiders*.

Convinced that his prospects for success are very good, Thomas has decided to pursue nature photography on a full-time basis by establishing Shutterbugs. His former employer has retained him on a freelance basis, providing a steady stream of project work. In addition, he has been hired to teach nature photography classes at a local community college. Together, this situation will provide him with enough work to generate a steady stream of income while putting more effort toward nature photography.

MARKETING & SALES

Shutterbugs will generate new business by continually pitching samples of Jeff Thomas' work to prospective customers. A brief but high-impact proposal, consisting of a query letter and a four-color sample sheet, will be developed and used for reaching out to museums, nature magazines, and book publishers. The proposal will include instructions for accessing our online portfolio. In addition, Shutterbugs will continuously submit new images to leading stock image libraries, which will allow our business to generate a regular stream of income.

In keeping with our marketing strategy, the following advertising budget has been established:

- Query Letters & Proposals—$500 annually
- Web Site/Online Portfolio—$1,500 annually

SWOT ANALYSIS

Business Feasibility & SWOT Analysis

- *Strengths:* Shutterbugs will begin operations with a solid base of initial contacts, as well as a steady stream of work from Jeff Thomas' former employer.

- *Weaknesses:* Although macro photography and our focus on insects and spiders is a key differential, it also significantly limits the types of photography we offer and the assignments we work on.

- *Opportunities:* There always is a strong market for exceptionally unique photographs, which we have a strong reputation for. By devoting more time to nature photography, our foothold within this market niche will only become stronger.

- *Threats:* The success of Shutterbugs rests solely upon the shoulders of Jeff Thomas. In the event of an injury or illness, of which there is an increased risk (due to the dangerous environments in which he sometimes has to work), no other employees exist to generate income for the business.

Online Party–Planning Company

Theme Party in a Box

140 Eastminster Ln.
Riverhead, New York 11901

Laura Becker

Theme Party in a Box will provide website access to all–in–one theme parties for children. Everything that is needed for the party is sent by mail directly to a home. During difficult economic times, these parties will be cost–efficient and time–saving.

EXECUTIVE SUMMARY

Theme Party in a Box (TPB) offers everything someone would need to throw a birthday party for a child aged 1–12. The objective is to provide every element of the party in one box so that a parent can efficiently and inexpensively hold a child's party at home.

It is one–stop–shopping from a website. The customer picks a theme, and orders a box that comes with everything needed for a party. This includes costumes, decorations, paper goods, games/activities/crafts, a shopping list for themed foods, and party favors at a low cost.

Instructional photos and step–by–step directions are included to guide the customer through each step of the party. The Theme Party in a Box website also provides instructional videos of actual parties with each theme. As the business grows, the owner hopes to provide live chat capability to answer questions and make suggestions.

Market Analysis

Until the recent economic downturn, celebrating a child's birthday became almost a competitive sport for many parents. "Celebrating a child's birthday has evolved into something much larger than blowing out candles on a cake. Especially, it seems, in New York, there are particular pressures that have made the event a revealing challenge to the ingenuity and social skills of parent and child, and sometimes to their entire relationship. Many children here grow accustomed by the age of 3 to having 10 or 20 of their closest friends gather for cake and favors, at the very least, and often additional attractions, from a singing clown to a tuxedo–clad magician at part of a gymnasium or museum set aside for them, if not the Plaza or a double–decker bus. Fanned by the 80's wave of conspicuous consumption, the latest generation's parties tend to be ornate, intense and expensive: $200 for the magician or clown, $100 for a party room somewhere, as much as $200 for a cake. ("The Birthday Boom," *New York Times*, January 22, 1995).

"There is a keeping–up–with–the–Joneses mentality," said children's party planner Leesa Zelken of Santa Monica, California–based *Send in the Clowns*. "(Parents) tell me, 'I need to do more. I want to do it better'," than their neighbors. (Melinda Fulmer, MSN, Money, http://articles.moneycentral.msn.com/CollegeAndFamily/RaiseKids/KidsPartiesatSpareNoExpensePrices.aspx)

According to Hallmark, Americans spend more than $10 billion a year on birthday gifts. On birthday parties themselves, parents spend billions more. (Association of Baltimore Area Grantmakers, February 2008, http://www.abagmd.org)

In "Children's Birthday Parties in Contemporary America" (*Nanzan Review of American Studies*, Volume 23 (2001): 83–91, Yasue Kuwahara) the author makes clear that after reviewing results from two questionnaires sent to parents that children's birthday parties have become competitive for parents and are a new form of "conspicuous consumption." In other cultures, birthday parties are about the children, but recently in the United States the parties are about the parents showing off their wealth. Parents can spend up to $1,000 for a party at a local party franchise such as a gym, bowling alley, claymaking studio, dance studio, etc.

Traditionally there are a lot of options for children's birthday parties including holding the party outside of the home at a location such as a children's gym, movie theater, bowling alley, etc. These options can cost up to $1,000 for an average party.

If parents choose to hold a birthday party in the home they have many party places they can purchase items from, including various web sites (i.e. www.orientaltrading.com; www.partysupplydirect, www.partycity.com) and party retail locations such as Party City.

Recession

During the economic downturn, many parents are looking for alternatives. It is possible to provide parents with the same convenience of have a one–stop–shopping location and service, by sending them everything they need in one simple, easy–to–use box at a low cost—approximately $150. More and more people are going back to the idea of the "old–fashioned party."

"The days of over–the–top, birthday party ideas for kids are over. With increasing prices and income staying steady, parents need to find ways to throw their kids affordable birthday parties." www.associatedcontent.com, July, 2008, "How to Throw a Free Birthday Party for Kids That's Still Fun").

There is currently no one–stop web site that offers everything a parent needs to host a child's birthday party at a reasonable all–in–one price. Thus, came the idea for Theme Party in a Box.

COMPETITION

There is currently one company in the United States offering a similar service, although not identical. The company offers a web site located at www.birthdayinabox.com. However, this website only provides pieces of the puzzle, such as decorations, party supplies, etc. It is not an all–inclusive service.

There are only a few web sites offering party planning from start to finish—but none are as inclusive as the Theme Party in a Box.

PRODUCTS & SERVICES

Customers will visit the web site located at www.themepartyinabox.com. All a customer needs to do is choose the theme for the party. Once chosen, the customer will receive a box with everything included for a party, such as:

1. Party Invitations
2. Thank–you cards
3. Goodie bags with party favors

4. Theme costumes

5. Face paint supplies

6. Tattoos

7. Paper goods including plates, utensils, cups, napkins

8. Decorations including table centerpiece, tablecloth

9. Balloons

10. Party Door/Street Sign

11. Games/Activities with step–by–step instructions

12. Instructional video/photos

13. Themed food shopping list

14. Birthday cake decorations

BUSINESS STRATEGY

- Start creating inventory for the business

- Need to source party materials at lowest cost possible

- Party Themes—Establish themes for boys and girls for different age ranges between 1 and 12.

- Design user–friendly, easy–to–use web site with search categories including theme, age, girl/boy, etc.

EXAMPLE: THEME PARTY IN A BOX–PIZZA PARTY

Age recommendation: 5 and up

Pizza Party Supplies
- 8 invitations: $1.99

- 20 red paper plates: $4.99

- 24 red plastic forks: $1.79

- 20 12–ounce red cups: $1.99

- 50 red napkins: $1.59

- 1 red tablecloth: $1.59

- Pizza Sticks: $1.45/4 sheets

- 18 balloons in pizza colors (red, yellow, lime green): $2.69

- Total $18.08

Food Supplies
The total cost for pizza is $3/pizza, including premade dough, tomato sauce and toppings. Per party, the totoal cost of food is $35, which includes both the pizzas and cake ingredients.

Party Favors
Assuming 8 children per party, the cost of party favors will be approxsimately $15 per party.

Pizza Party Games and Activities

Toss Dough Like Pro

Divide the kids into pairs. Give each pair a ball of dough and challenge them to toss the dough just like a real pizza chef. Have the kids form two lines with teammates facing each other. Toss the ball of dough between the teammates, and after each toss, have them take a step backward. When a team drops the dough, they are out.

I'm Making a Pizza Game

Players form a circle and take turns saying: "I'm making a pizza and it will have (fill in blank)." The first person fills in the blank with an item for their pizza like anchovies, cheese, etc. Then the next person says, "I'm making a pizza and it will have blank," repeat what the first person said, and add an item. When a player forgets an item previously named, he/she is out of the game. The game is over when all players have had a turn. Or, you can keep going around, and as players forget items, the circle will get smaller and the game ends when only one player is left.

Pizza Box Folding

Purchase several unfolded pizza boxes from a local pizzeria. Divide the kids into teams and give each team an equal amount of boxes. The object of the game is to be the first team to get all of their boxes folded, in the shortest amount of time, with only one teammate folding at a time.

Dough Boy

Inflate small round balloons. Divide children into teams of 3–5 children. Each team will designate a member to be its "Dough Boy." Divide the balloons equally between the teams. Each Dough Boy pulls on an adult–sized sweatshirt and sweatpants over his/her clothes. When you say "Go," each team has two minutes to try to stuff as many balloons into their Dough Boy's clothes as possible. When the time expires, remove the balloons from each Dough Boy one at a time, counting to determine which team had the most balloons stuffed in their Dough Boy.

Categories

The children sit on the floor in a circle. One person is chosen as the leader. The leader begins by selecting a category such as "types of dessert" or "things in a kitchen." He/she starts a slap, clap, snap rhythm by slapping his/her knees twice, clapping twice and snapping his/her fingers twice. Everyone joins in the rhythm. The leader then says one category item such as "ice cream." Play continues clockwise, moving to the leader's left. Play continues until someone is unable to think of an item, misses the beat, or repeats what someone else already said. When someone misses, that player can begin a new category. For a more competitive game, the person that misses can be eliminated. Continue until you have one winner.

Baking

Make and Bake

Now it's time for the kids to really make and enjoy their own pizza. You may want to purchase prepared pizza dough from a supermarket, or use "Boboli" pizza crusts. You'll need standard toppings: cheese, sauces, pepperoni, onions, olives etc.

Have the children knead dough, then put it in a bowl and let it sit for about one hour. This will allow the dough to rise. Have the children "punch" down the dough to get any air out. Roll the dough (coat the rolling pin and surface with flour). Have the children add tomato sauce to the dough and spread it around the surface. Have different pizza toppings laid out in bowls so the children can choose what they want to add (mozzarella cheese, pepperoni, peppers, mushrooms, meatballs, etc.). The best way to cook pizza at home is on a pizza stone, which can be purchased at any kitchen or home goods store. Heat the pizza stone for about 20 minutes at 425 degrees. Put the pizza in the oven and let it cook at 425 degrees for 15 or 20 minutes. You will know it is done when the cheese starts to bubble and turn brown.

The above pizza can also be made with already prepared pizza dough bought from a supermarket or local pizzeria. Parents can also use "Boboli" pizza crusts, or substitute pizza bagels.

Pizza Cake

Bake a 12–14 inch round yellow sheet cake (made in a cake or pizza pan). Top with red frosting not quite to the edge of the cake (sauce). Top with white chocolate chips (cheese), strawberries, blueberries, kiwi, etc. Place the cake into a real pizza box with the lid propped open.

Arts and Crafts

Decorator Chefs

Use fabric markers and smocks, white chef's hats, oven mitts, or aprons. Have each child use fabric markers to decorate his/her own chef items to take home. Suggestions for decorating include: having each child draw his/her name, favorite food items, kitchen utensils, names of spices and restaurant logos.

Party Favors

Provide goody bags with candy and pizza stickers. Children will also take home their decorated pizza boxes and chef hats/aprons, etc.

OPERATIONS

Web Site

Objectives

- Design a Website

- Create user–friendly, bright, fun pages that are easily searchable by categories such as: Age of Child; Party Themes; Girl/Boy

- Put instructional video on website—password protected. Once customer pays, gets access to step–by–step instructions.

Web site design can be done either by the business owner—after learning some html coding—or by hiring a design firm. Web design firms would be able to get a website like this started for approximately $5,000–$10,000.

Search Engine Optimization

A significant percentage (approximately 85 percent) of website traffic comes from search engines, so it is important to consider this in website development. There are ways to increase website traffic such as submitting your site to search engines; and advertising techniques that will trigger your ad by keyword and highlight your listing above the rest. The Google web site has many helpful programs for small business owners for ad placement and ranking results, etc.

Monthly Hosting

There will be a monthly fee of approximately $30 for hosting the website.

Customer Support

The owner can set up a toll free phone number that will be directed to the owner's home/office phone. Typical services cost a little as $9.95 per month, and include such things as:

- One Toll Free or Local Number

- 100 Call Minutes

- Unlimited Extensions (sales department, accounts department, etc.)

- Month–to–month service

FINANCIAL ANALYSIS

Product Pricing

The business owner would take into account the cost of the party supplies described above and estimate the sales volume for the first three years. The cost of the web site development and customer support must also be considered.

Average price to host party at third–party facility: $500–$700.

Price of themed party in a box: $150

Profit and Loss Projections for Year 1 and Year 2

The figures below assume 8 children per party.

	Year 1	Year 2
Income		
Sales revenue—$150/Box	$30,000.00	$52,500.00
Cost of sales	$18,616.00	$24,828.00
Party supplies—$18.08 each	$ 3,616.00	$ 6,328.00
Party favors—$15/party for 8 children	$ 3,000.00	$ 5,250.00
Party food (if included)—$35/party	$ 7,000.00	$ 12,250.00
Web site design	$ 5,000.00	$ 1,000.00
Shipping (each box $4.95)	$ 990.00	$ 1,732.50
Gross profit	**$ 11,384.00**	**$ 27,672.00**
Operating expenses		
Salaries	$ —	$ —
Home office rent	$ —	$ —
Web site monthly hosting—$30/month	$ 360.00	$ 360.00
Customer service phone support—$9.95/month	$ 119.40	$ 119.40
Marketing and sales	$ 2,500.00	$ 2,500.00
	$ 2,979.40	$ 2,979.40
Income from operations	**$ 8,404.60**	**$24,692.60**
Taxes		
Net profit		

Organic Cleaning Supplies

Green Home Care Solutions

3400 Fox Ridge Drive
Columbia, Missouri 65201

Kari Lucke

Green Home Care Solutions is committed to providing customers with high-quality organic and earth-friendly cleaning and personal care products that people can use with peace of mind.

INTRODUCTION

Mission Statement

Green Home Care Solutions is committed to providing customers with high-quality organic and earth-friendly cleaning and personal care products that people can use with peace of mind, knowing that its parent company, Warhols, strictly adheres to a green business and production strategy and that the products cause no harm to the environment.

Executive Summary

Green Home Care Solutions is a home-based, direct sales business that sells organic and environmentally safe home and personal care products person-to-person and via the Internet. As the sole proprietor, John Clinton purchases the products at wholesale prices from Warhols, a large and well-established company based in Irvine, California, and then sells them at retail prices to consumers in the mid-Missouri area.

Goals and Objectives

As the sole proprietor of Green Home Care Solutions, John Clinton has enunciated several specific goals for his first year of business:

- Provide sample products and brochures to 25 new customers a month.

- Sell $2000 worth of products monthly.

- Attend and promote the business at two trade shows: the Columbia Home Show in May and the Mid-Missouri Business Expo in October.

- Establish and maintain an up-to-date, informative, and user-friendly website for Green Home Care Solutions.

Company History

Warhols, Green Home Care Solutions' parent company, was established in 1902 as a home goods general store in San Francisco, California. After two decades of success as a retail store, Warhols moved from a location-based business to a direct selling business and started selling products door-to-door. By

1950 it was growing as a very successful company that provided products to 5,000 associates for retail sale. In 2007, Warhols had grown to represent 30,000 associates nationwide.

INDUSTRY AND MARKET

Industry Analysis

The direct selling industry, also called network marketing, consists of independent entrepreneurs who buy products at wholesale prices and then earn a profit by selling them at retail. According to the Direct Selling Association, in 2007 sales in the industry reached $30.8 billion in the United States and $114 billion worldwide.

Market Analysis

According to the Direct Selling Association, more than 74 percent of Americans purchased products or services through direct selling in 2007. In addition to the increasing popularity of this method of purchase, a 2008 study by the Natural Marketing Institute (NMI) found that more consumers are incorporating organic products into their lifestyles. NMI found that, across six organic product categories, total U.S. household penetration rose from 57 percent in 2006 to 59 percent in 2007, and the percentage of Americans who used organic products consistently increased from 16 percent to 18 percent in the same time period. This number is expected to continue to increase.

Competition

Products that are considered competition for those sold by Green Home Care Solutions include such brands as Green Works and Nature's Source cleaners, sold in discount chain stores such as Wal-Mart. Although the prices of these products are slightly less than Green Home Care Solutions', they do not last as long and contain more water and other filler ingredients.

A comparison of the price, contents, and number of uses for comparable off-the-shelf products is presented in the brochure for Green Home Care Solutions' cleaning products, showing customers that, even though the price of the former may be somewhat less upfront, they save more money using Green Home Care Solutions' products, as well as achieve better results.

Convenience is another benefit of buying from Green Home Care Solutions. The products can be ordered online or over the phone, and they are delivered to the customers' homes.

PERSONNEL

Management

John Clinton is the sole proprietor of Green Home Care Solutions. He has a bachelor of arts degree in business from the University of Missouri and thus has a good background for the daily operation of a direct selling operation. He also has excellent interpersonal skills—another requirement for working with customers—gained from his position as fiscal officer in the Finance Department for the University, a position that he held for five years. Most important, however, is John's tenacity. Direct selling requires self-motivation and persistence, traits that John has exhibited both in his personal and his work life.

Professional and Advisory Support

Warhols is a member of the Direct Selling Association, a national trade association. The association's mission statement is "To protect, serve and promote the effectiveness of member companies and the independent business people they represent. To ensure that the marketing by member companies of products and/or the direct sales opportunity is conducted with the highest level of business ethics and service to consumers." As an associate of Warhols, John has access to all of the company's resources, including weekly and monthly publications, an annual conference, and online tools and advice. Also, executive staff of Warhols act as mentors to sales associates such as John who are just starting out in business. Each new Warhols associate is assigned an adviser for the first year. Through this relationship, John obtains expert direction and advice as he establishes his business.

STRATEGIES

Business Strategy

Green Home Care Solutions follows a green strategy set by Warhols—not just in the products, but in everyday business as well. For example, all packaging materials are biodegradable and lightweight, all printed materials use soy-based ink, and as much communication as possible is done via e-mail or other non-paper method. In addition, Warhols packages its products using gravity-fed filling processes. In other words, gravity feeds, rather than less energy-efficient means such as conveyor belts, are used to put the product into the package.

Growth Strategy

Growth in Green Home Care Solutions is based on repeat business. The philosophy is that once customers try the products, they will like them and continue to purchase them. Getting people to try the product is the first step, and John accomplishes this in a number of ways. For example, anyone who visits John's website can request a free catalog and a free sample of a select number of products. John then mails these to the interested client and follows up via telephone or e-mail in about a week to ensure that the customer received the packet and to ask whether the person is interested in ordering. John also attends certain trade shows and exhibits, during which he provides samples, catalogs, brochures, and other information about the product to potential clients.

PRODUCTS AND SERVICES

Description

Green Home Care Solutions sells a variety of products for the home and consumer, including cleaning supplies, laundry detergent and supplies, personal care items such as soap, indoor plant treatments, aromatherapy items, and other related items. All of the products are certified organic and/or environmentally friendly. They are created from biodegradable plant and vegetable ingredients and do not contain any of the toxic and harmful added elements that many other products do, such as dyes and perfumes, chlorine, enzymes, and artificial coloring. Also, Warhols uses no animal testing on any of its products.

Unique Features/Niche

The fact that Green Home Care Solutions' products are organic and environmentally friendly sets them apart from many other products. Because of statistics such as the following, Americans are becoming more aware of the detrimental effects of non-organic products:

- The average American uses about 25 gallons of toxic, hazardous chemical products per year in his or her home, most of which are found in household cleaning products.

- More than 7 million accidental poisonings occur each year in the United States; 75 percent involve children under the age of 6.

- The toxic chemicals in household cleaners are three times more likely to cause cancer than air pollution.

- Of chemicals commonly found in homes, 150 have been linked to allergies, birth defects, cancer, and psychological abnormalities.

- More than 32 million pounds of household cleaning products are poured down the drain each day nationwide. Many of these cleaners' toxic substances, which are not adequately removed by sewage treatment plants, are returned to the rivers from which cities draw their drinking water.

Pricing

Prices of the products are based on wholesale prices set by Warhols plus 30 percent. In other words, if John purchases a box of laundry soap for $8.00 from Warhols, he sells it to the customer for $10.40. A complete list of products and prices is available on request.

MARKETING AND SALES

Advertising and Promotion

The main forms of advertising used by Green Home Care Solutions are brochures/catalogs and a website. John hands out brochures and catalogs to all interested customers at the two annual trade shows he attends; he also leaves them at places potential customers visit, such as grocery stores, health stores, beauty salons, malls, and other such locations.

One means of promotion that is cost-free is the experience John and his wife gain by using the products themselves. Because he uses the products, John can give first-hand information to customers regarding the uses, quality, and life cycle of the products.

Cost

Warhols provides catalogs at a nominal price of 50 cents each. The company also provides a free template for a brochure, which John customizes on his computer and then prints at a local copy shop. Average price for brochures is between 25 and 50 cents each, depending on format and use of color. John purchases approximately 100 catalogs twice per year and prints 50 copies of brochures for Green Home Care Solutions four times a year, with one new brochure for each season. This allows John to personalize the brochure and target customers based on needs that are common during certain times of the year.

All promotional materials list John's website address, which is available for anyone to access. Cost of the domain for the website is $25 a month. John maintains the website himself, so no additional labor costs are involved.

The cost of the samples and brochures that are mailed to people who visit John's website, as mentioned in Section 4.2, vary but average around $50 per month ($2 per mailing times 25 customers). Costs for advertising per year are thus approximately $100 for catalogs, $300 for the website, $100 for brochures, and $600 for sample mailings, for a total of $1,100 per year.

Image

The image portrayed by Green Care Home Solutions is exemplified by its slogan, "Clean Home, Clean Earth." The idea is to make people feel good about cleaning with organic products, so that they can have a clean home without harming the environment. Customers are also encouraged to be proud to be using products that are made by a company that is striving to converse energy and reduce waste.

OPERATIONS

Customers

The customers for Green Home Care Solutions are middle- to upper-income individuals ages 25 to 55 in the mid-Missouri area, especially in and around Columbia, who own their own homes. Although anyone can buy the products, research by Warhols has determined that these are the people who are most likely to be interested in buying organic home products. Columbia is a town of approximately 94,000. The median household income of Columbia residents is $42,163, with a race distribution of 83 percent White, 9 percent Black, and 8 percent other. Forty percent of residents are between the ages of 25 and 50, Green Home Care Solutions' target age range. Forty-seven percent of Columbians own their own home. As a relatively liberal and young population, Columbia is the ideal location to sell organic products.

Suppliers

Warhols is Green Home Care Solutions' sole supplier. Warhols is a well-established and reputable company that has been in business for more than 100 years. Approximately 30,000 associates in the United States sell the Warhols product line, which consists of 250 different products.

Equipment

Because Green Home Care Solutions is based on an ordering system—the customer orders the product from the catalog or website—no inventory is necessary. However, John keeps some of his newest and best-selling products on hand to show to customers. He also purchases sample sizes of some items to give to customers.

Facility and Location

All business is conducted out of John's home, located at 3400 Fox Ridge Drive, Columbia, Missouri.

FINANCIAL ANALYSIS

Based on the goals John has set for the first year of business, the following profits and expenses are predicted.

Income	
Sales	$24,000
Expenses	
Promotional materials	$ 1,100
Inventory and samples	$ 500
Trade show booth rental	$ 500
Total first-year expenses	$ 2,100
Net profit	**$21,900**

Thus the profit from the first year of business is expected to be $21,900. As John grows his client base, profits should increase. Expenses will increase only due to inflation.

Physical Therapy Practice

Healing Hands Physical Therapy Inc.

27008 Gill St.
Dallas, Texas 75255

Paul Greenland

Healing Hands Physical Therapy is a holistic, wellness-focused physical therapy practice that helps individuals restore function and prevent disability following an illness or injury.

EXECUTIVE SUMMARY

Business Overview

From back and knee pain to tennis elbow and stiff shoulders, most people contend with physical setbacks at some point in their lifetime. These may result from sports-related injuries, overuse, occupational stress, surgery, and more. Oftentimes, individuals are able to recover from physical strain and injuries on their own. However, professional intervention is sometimes needed.

Healing Hands Physical Therapy is a holistic, wellness-focused physical therapy practice that helps individuals restore function and prevent disability following an illness or injury. Specifically, our trained, licensed physical therapists work under the order of a physician to improve the function of a patient's ligaments, joints, muscles, and nerves. Treatments primarily focus on improving flexibility, range of motion, and strength.

Although we rely on different types of equipment to deliver treatment, our practice emphasizes a hands-on treatment method or modality known as manual therapy. Our practice also offers services such as acupuncture, massage, and golf performance training, which are provided without a physician's referral.

With many years of combined experience, Healing Hands Physical Therapy has a unique blend of professional experience, allowing us to provide relief and improvement to patients in a wide range of situations.

Organizational Structure

Our practice is incorporated in the state of Texas and employs three licensed physical therapists—including owner Paul Irwin—who all hold degrees from programs accredited by the Commission on Accreditation in Physical Therapy Education. In addition, we employ a physical therapist assistant, a licensed massage therapist, and an administrative assistant.

MARKET ANALYSIS

Healing Hands Physical Therapy focuses on serving individuals with private health insurance, as well as upper-income individuals who are able to pay privately for our services.

Our geographic location in downtown Dallas, Texas, is well-suited for our target market, and puts us in close proximity to a large concentration of white-collar workers. In addition to 12 *Fortune 500* companies in the city proper, the larger Dallas-Fort Worth Metroplex area is home to more corporate headquarters than anywhere else in the nation. Our city's central business district alone was home to more than 135,000 employees during the mid-2000s. This figure is expected to exceed 138,000 in 2010 and total almost 150,000 in 2020. Our practice also is in close proximity to many physician offices, providing easy access to a strong referral base.

INDUSTRY ANALYSIS

According to projections from the U.S. Bureau of Labor Statistics, above average growth is projected for the physical therapy profession as a whole. From 2006 to 2016, employment of physical therapists is projected to grow 27 percent, increasing from 173,000 to 220,000. Among the factors contributing to the profession's growth are an increased interest in health promotion, as well as the aging of the population. In particular, the baby boom generation is a key market for the services we provide.

According to the Executive Council of Physical Therapy and Occupational Therapy Examiners, the state agency charged with licensing practitioners, 10,126 actively licensed physical therapists and 4,673 actively licensed physical therapy assistants were practicing in Texas as of February 2008.

PERSONNEL

Paul Irwin, PT, DPT, CSCS (Owner & President)—Paul holds a doctorate degree in physical therapy from Northern Central University. Specializing in the assessment and treatment of spinal problems, he holds a related certification from the McKenzie Institute. In addition, Paul is a Certified Strength and Conditioning Specialist. His other areas of clinical focus include: post-surgical conditions, orthopedic and musculoskeletal injuries, sports-related injuries, as well as golf-related injuries and conditioning. Paul has more than 18 years of experience as a physical therapist. Prior to establishing his own practice he worked at Pineview Health System, where he oversaw a staff of more than 25 people, including physical therapists, occupational therapists, and athletic trainers. Paul is a member of the American Physical Therapy Association.

Angela Jones, PT—Angela earned her physical therapy degree at Washington University, and started her career in Phoenix, Arizona, developing special expertise as a hand therapist. In this role, she focuses on patients with conditions such as arthritis, carpal tunnel syndrome, overuse syndromes, tendon injuries, and more. In addition to being a gifted therapist, Angela also has skills making custom splints and braces. In addition to her role as a physical therapist, Angela has an undergraduate degree in marketing. She uses her expertise in this area to handle marketing and advertising responsibilities for our practice. Angela is a member of the American Physical Therapy Association.

Michelle Christiansen, PT—Michelle trained as a physical therapist in Alaska, where she treated patients with a variety of orthopedic and musculoskeletal conditions. She has a very strong interest in manual therapy, and specializes in peripheral joint injuries. Before joining our practice, Michelle worked at Greenview Medical Center in Waller County, Texas, and at Northern Star hospital in Anchorage, Alaska. She also is a member of the American Physical Therapy Association.

Jennifer Thompson, LMT—Jennifer is a true asset to our practice, allowing us to provide a blend of services on a cash basis without a physician's referral. We often cross-sell her services to patients, giving them a complimentary massage at the end of the regular treatment, with hopes that they will become regular clients. Jennifer offers several different types of massage, including Shiatsu, classic Western, basic, deep tissue, hot stone, medical, and sports. Trained at the Dallas Academy of massage therapy, Jennifer is nationally certified and is licensed by Texas' Department of State Health Services.

Christine Roth, PTA—In addition to working as a physical therapist assistant, Christine has been an alternative medicine practitioner for 10 years. This aspect of her professional background brings another holistic element to our physical therapy practice. Specifically, Christine is a NCCAOM certified acupuncturist, and also has expertise in areas such as massage therapy, reflexology, and therapeutic touch.

Josephine Smith, Administrative Assistant—Josephine is usually the first person patients see when they enter our facility. Her cheerful disposition and strong organizational skills make her the "glue" that holds our practice together. Josephine is responsible for booking appointments and managing all of the therapists' schedules. While this task is somewhat simplified by the use of a special software program, she has in-depth knowledge about the way our practitioners work and the amount of time that various treatments will take. Josephine also is responsible for managing medical records and handling all other general office duties.

Professional & Advisory Support

We have retained the law firm of Johnson, Pratt & Weller to provide our practice with necessary legal services. In addition, tax and accounting services will be provided by Lone Star Accounting LLC. Business checking and merchant accounts (allowing us to accept credit card payments) have been opened with Texas National Bank.

GROWTH STRATEGY

Our physical therapists are fortunate to have established referral relationships with many Dallas-area physicians. We are confident that these relationships will be of immediate benefit to us during our first year of operations, allowing us to see a steady stream of patients. However, the staff of Healing Hands Physical Therapy understands how critical marketing is to the success of our practice and its future growth. With this in mind, we are committed to marketing our practice on a consistent basis, per the tactics outlined in the Marketing & Sales section of this plan.

Based on our physical therapists' combined knowledge of the local market, our unique holistic/spa-like approach, our plans to aggressively market the practice, and the Bureau of Labor Statistics' projections for the physical therapy profession referenced in the Industry Analysis section of this plan, we anticipate our patient base will grow at a compound annual rate of 7.5 percent during its first three years of operation.

SERVICES

Healing Hands Physical Therapy provides assessment and treatments for a wide range of injuries and physical conditions, drawing from several decades of combined experience. The treatments we offer include a number of modalities and techniques, such as:

- acupuncture
- aquatic therapy
- cold compresses
- electrical stimulation
- gait training
- hot packs

- massage

- mobilization/manipulation

- neuromuscular reeducation

- therapeutic exercises

- ultrasound

- video analysis (for golf performance)

- work hardening/conditioning

Several of our services are offered without a physician's referral. These include massage, acupuncture, and a golf clinic that helps golfers improve their performance and avoid injuries.

MARKETING & SALES

Our practice will take a two-pronged approach to focused growth. Because referrals from physicians are critical to our success, we will put a strong emphasis on tactics that allow us to stay visible with area physicians and their office staff.

In addition, we will take an "ask your doctor" consumer marketing approach, similar to that employed by pharmaceutical companies. Specifically, our approach will focus on generating awareness about our practice and its capabilities among individuals suffering from conditions such as back pain or knee pain, with a call-to-action encouraging consumers to see their doctor and request a referral if appropriate.

We have developed a marketing plan for our practice that includes several key tactics, including:

- Printed collateral for prospective clients and referral sources.

- A sustained, targeted direct mail campaign that promotes our capabilities to referring physicians in Dallas' central business district.

- An incentive program that offers a free 30-minute massage to existing or former patients who refer family members and friends to us.

- Sponsorship of golf performance clinics at area golf courses and country clubs.

- Relationship building initiatives (business lunches, dinners, etc.) with area golf pros and instructors to encourage referrals.

- Relationship building initiatives (business lunches, dinners, etc.) with area referring physicians and clinic nurses to encourage referrals.

- An expanded Yellow Page advertisement with a short list of common services offered.

- Advertising in the Dallas County Medical Society's *Dallas Medical Journal*, in order to stay visible among referring physicians.

- Advertising in local lifestyle magazines to reach our upscale target market.

- Radio advertising and occasional free massage giveaways.

- Free educational presentations, focused on ergonomics and proper body mechanics, for employees at local *Fortune 500* corporations.

- A Web site with complete details about our practice and its holistic philosophy.

OPERATIONS

Facility & Location

Healing Hands Physical Therapy is located within the Greater Dallas Professional Center, in the heart of downtown Dallas. Our 3,620-square-foot facility is situated in close proximity to where many affluent, white collar professionals work. It offers easy access to all major highways, and is only several blocks from the DART Rail. Appealing features include an open floorplan, many windows providing natural light, and 13-foot ceilings.

This facility is well situated for our needs, needing little modification. In order to transform the space into a natural, healing environment, we will purchase a wide range of plants, several fountains, and a sound system that will allow us to play soothing music. Additionally, we will have the facility painted in natural earth tones. We estimate the cost of these improvements will be $10,000.

Our largest capital investment is a $20,000 commercial therapy pool, which we will use for aquatic exercise and therapy. We have selected an above-ground pool with a modular design, allowing us to relocate it to a different facility in the future, if needed. A central part of our practice, the pool includes features like an underwater treadmill, hydrotherapy jets, a temperature control system, an underwater bench, stainless steel support bars, and stairs for easy access.

In addition, other start-up purchases include two treadmills, three exercise bikes, a universal machine, parallel bars, and a variety of smaller items such as leg and ankle weights, medicine balls, and core stabilization balls. These purchases will collectively cost about $12,500.

Billing & Payment

Healing Hands Physical Therapy accepts payments from private insurance plans, as well as self-payments from individuals. Unless clients make other arrangements with us ahead of time, we require payment at the time of service. In addition to personal checks, we also accept Visa, MasterCard, Discover, and American Express.

We have an existing computerized billing system for physical therapy practices that tracks patient accounts and generates all necessary forms and statements. This application includes a database of the diagnosis and procedure codes needed when submitting claims to insurance companies. In addition, the application tracks patient visits and flags us when we reached the maximum number of visits approved by a patient's insurance company.

Fees

The fees that we charge vary depending upon contract rates with different insurance companies. Due to the complexity associated with various contracts, this information is not normally included with our business plan. However, it can be provided upon request. Generally speaking, our fee schedule is comparable with other physical therapy practices in our market. On average, we are reimbursed at a rate of roughly $75 per patient visit.

Hours of Operation

Our practice is open from 7:30 a.m. to 6:30 p.m. Monday through Friday.

LEGAL

Our physical therapists and physical therapist assistants are all licensed by the Executive Council of Physical Therapy and Occupational Therapy Examiners, the state agency charged with licensing practitioners in the state of Texas. Additionally, we all carry appropriate business and professional liability insurance.

FINANCIAL PROJECTIONS

During its first year of operation, Healing Hands Physical Therapy will generate estimated net income of $117,699. A detailed breakdown can be seen in the following balance sheet, which covers the time period January 1, 2010 to December 31, 2010:

Income	
Patient care revenue	$507,000
Massage therapy revenue	$ 95,000
Public speaking	$ 3,400
Total income	**$605,400**
Expenses	
Salaries	$307,000
Utilities	$ 6,478
Rent	$ 39,000
Insurance	$ 15,693
401 K contributions	$ 15,350
Office supplies	$ 6,200
Marketing & advertising	$ 35,000
Telecommunications & internet	$ 4,980
Professional development	$ 24,000
Travel & entertainment	$ 3,800
Subscriptions & dues	$ 4,300
Repairs & maintenance	$ 1,100
Taxes	$ 24,800
Total expenses	**$487,701**
Net income	**$117,699**

The owners' investment is $75,000, which covers the $42,500 in start-up costs outlined in the Operations section of this plan, and provides cash-on-hand for operations as we establish our patient base during the first year. In addition, our practice also plans to secure an operating line of credit from Texas National Bank.

Based on our analysis of the market, we are forecasting that net income for our expanded practice will grow at a compound annual rate of 5.5 percent for the next three years:

Year	Net income
2010	$117,699
2011	$124,172
2012	$131,002

Stable

Miller Stables

4040 South Turtle Creek Lane
Columbia, Missouri 65203

Kari Lucke

Miller Stables LLC will provide a safe and accessible boarding facility at an affordable cost for horse owners who need a place to keep their horse(s). It will also offer excellent onsite care and related services.

INTRODUCTION

Mission Statement

Miller Stables LLC will provide a safe and accessible boarding facility at an affordable cost for horse owners who need a place to keep their horse(s). It will also offer excellent onsite care and related services.

Executive Summary

Jo Miller will own and manage Miller Stables, a boarding facility in the south Columbia, Missouri, area. Not all horse owners—or people who would like to own a horse—live on farms; these people need a place to keep their horse(s) that is physically safe for the animals and that offers necessary daily care for horses. Miller Stables will provide stalls and pasture, feed, water, and any necessary related care for horses whose owners currently do not have a place to house their horse or who are not satisfied with the boarding facility they are currently using.

Goals and Objectives

- To have 10 horses by the end of the first year of business, 15 by the end of the second, and 20 (capacity) by the end of the third

- To develop a reputation as a friendly, high–quality boarding facility in the Columbia area

Company History

Miller Stables was founded by Jo Miller in 1995 in Jefferson City, Missouri. Jo started by boarding three horses; by 2005 she had built her business to its capacity with 12 horses and a waiting list of clients. Jo and her husband Steve relocated to Columbia in 2009 due to Steve's obtaining employment at the University of Missouri. Jo would like to use the knowledge and experience she gained during the 14 years she owned and operated the stables in Jefferson City to establish a similar facility in the Columbia area.

INDUSTRY AND MARKET

Industry Analysis

According to the American Horse Council, the horse industry has grown 55 percent since 2000 and represents $39 billion in related revenues. The horse population has also increased—33 percent over the same time period—and is now 9.2 million. Specific statistics for Missouri show that there 281,000 horses in the state; 70 percent are used for showing and recreation. About 125,100 Missourians are involved in the horse industry in some way. A specific breed—the Missouri Fox Trotter—originated in the Ozark Mountains of Missouri in the late 1940s and continues to be a popular breed around the country.

Market Analysis

The market for Miller Stables includes the following:

- Horse owners in the Columbia area, especially the south

- Individuals and families who would like to own horses but do not have the proper facilities

- Horse owners who currently board their horse at a facility with which they are dissatisfied

Contrary to popular belief, horse ownership is not an elite activity enjoyed only the wealthy. The American Horse Council reports that approximately 34 percent of horse owners nationwide have a household income of less than $50,000. Only 28 percent have an annual income of over $100,000. Most (46 percent) horse owners have an annual income of between $25,000 and $75,000. Thus the target market is not limited to those in high income brackets. Columbia's population is approximately 94,000, and median household income $42,163.

Competition

The following facilities offer similar services to Miller Stables:

- Columbia Equestrian Center

- Brenda Benner Stables

- Palmer Stables

All of these are located north of Columbia city limits. Miller Stables will be the only organized horse boarding facility in the southern area.

PERSONNEL

Management

Jo Miller has a bachelor of science degree in equestrian science from Stephens College in Columbia, Missouri. She owned and operated a boarding facility in the Jefferson City area for 14 years, so she has both the knowledge of horses required as well as the acumen to manage the day–to–day business operations.

Staffing

Miller Stables will employ two part–time people to help clean stalls; feed, water, and turn out horses; and perform other related duties as needed. Because Columbia is home to three four–year colleges, one of which is known nationwide for its equestrian program (Stephens College), Jo expects no problems finding college students to work these jobs, especially if they are recruited from the equestrian program at Stephens, where many in the program are looking for hands–on experience in a stable in preparation for their future employment. The first year, stable hands will be paid $10 an hour and work 15 hours a week. As the business grows, additional staff will be hired.

Professional and Advisory Support

The following people and institutions will support the business:

- *Banker:* Paula Jones, Callaway Bank, 1515 West Broadway, Columbia

- *Accountant:* Tina Morgan, Accounting Plus, 400 I–70 Drive, Columbia

- *Insurance Agent:* Stephanie Williams, State Farm, 1700 Providence Road, Columbia

- *Attorney:* George Johnston, Johnston &? Associates, 2710 Stadium Drive, Columbia

- *Veterinarian:* David Parker, University of Missouri Equine Center, 3000 Highway 63, Columbia

- *Farrier:* Chris Mitchell, 3200 Rt. K, Columbia

GROWTH STRATEGY

Although initially Miller will provide boarding services only, after the first three years of business it will add other related services based on consumer demand. These could include horseback riding lessons, horse rental, and/or horse training. Jo Miller has the skills and knowledge required to incorporate these add–ons into the business and will do so based on what seems to draw the highest demand. This level of demand will be easy to determine from being aware of and listening to clients' and others' comments about the facility and what other services they would like to see offered. The extra services offered will also be determined by what the competitors provide and whether there is enough demand to justify adding the service.

PRODUCTS AND SERVICES

Description

Miller Stables will provide the following facilities:

- 60 acres pasture

- 60 x 100 foot indoor arena

- 100 x 200 foot lighted outdoor arena

- Space for horse trailer parking

- Easy access to Rockbridge State Park

- New barn

The new barn will include:

- 24 12 x 12 foot stalls, each with an automatic waterer, bedding, fan, and salt block

- Large tack room with lockers

- Full bathroom and dressing room

- Air–conditioned and heated lounge with tables/chairs and vending machine

- Wash bay

Services include:

- Daily turn out

- Daily stall cleaning

- Twice–daily feeding (grain and hay)

- Other services (grooming, vet visit, lunging) as requested

Unique Features/Niche

Miller Stables has the following advantages:

- Miller Stables is in an ideal location for a horse facility because it is adjacent to Rockbridge State Park, which covers about 2,000 acres and contains 15 miles of trails. Trail riding is a popular activity for many horse owners in mid–Missouri, and often boarding facilities do not have access to trails but rather are located on highways or other roadways not suitable for riding.

- Miller is located only 2 miles south of Columbia city limits off Route K and is an easy and quick drive for horse owners living in the south part of town.

- Miller will be the only organized horse boarding facility in south Columbia.

- Because Jo Miller lives on site, the horses under her care have 24–hour supervision, a factor that many horse owners consider important for their horses' safety and health.

- The barn in which the horses will be stalled is relatively new, built in 2006, and thus does not have safety and convenience issues that older barns may have.

- Miller has 60 acres of pasture, which are divided into twelve 5–acre paddocks, and two horses will be turned out for grazing on each paddock. Having only two horses per tract reduces the chances of them getting kicked, bitten, or otherwise hurt, as often happens in a herd, yet provides them with the same–species companionship that horses desire.

- Horses will be turned out to pasture for most of the day. Other stables do not turn the horses out and keep them confined in a stall a majority of the time. This can lead to cribbing, chewing wood, weaving, and other behavioral problems that can harm a horse's health. Horses were made to live outside, and although keeping them in a stall can protect them from weather and injury, as well as provide easy access for owners, it can also deprive horses of exercise, companionship, and fresh air. Miller Stables offers the owner the convenience of having the horse accessible while keeping the best interests of the horse in mind.

- No one likes spending half of his or her planned riding time chasing a horse around the pasture trying to catch it. Clients may call ahead when planning a trip to the stables, and Jo will bring his/her horse up from pasture and have it stalled so that the horse is available when the owner arrives.

- All fencing is made of plastic pipe, which enhances aesthetics while reducing chances of injury to the horses. Clients will be happy to find not one strand of barbed wire—a fencing material used often for horses but notorious for causing injury—on the property.

Pricing

The cost for full board, which includes stall cleaning, once a day turn out, and feed (grain once a day year–round and twice a day in the winter, a quality mix of alfalfa and timothy hay in the winter) is $300 per month. This is comparable to competitors who provide similar services.

Board will be due on the first of every month. After the fifth of the month, a $10 late fee will be charged for every five days board is not paid. These conditions are listed in the contract the boarder signs with Miller.

MARKETING AND SALES

Advertising and Promotion

Word–of–mouth is the best way to advertise in this business, but to gain a client base Miller will use the following methods of promotion:

- Website with list of services and fees, photos, customer testimonials
- Brochures, to be placed in local tack shops, feed stores, and western clothing stores

In addition, signs will be placed at the entrance to the property.

Cost

Start–up advertising costs will consist of printing 100 brochures and is estimated to be $250.

Image

Miller Stables' will advertise itself as "The Perfect Place for You and Your Horse" and strive to emphasize the advantages of its location, Jo's experience and friendliness, and the quality of the facilities.

OPERATIONS

Customers

Targeted customers include horse owners and those who would like to own horses but have no place to keep them who live on the south end of Columbia, as well as horse owners in other parts of town who are dissatisfied with their current boarding facility and find it worth the drive to Miller. The average client is female, ages 15 to 30, with a household income of more than $50,000. Although males are also welcome, girls and women are more likely to board horses. Columbia's population is about 94,000, and the median age of residents is 26.8. Forty–two percent of households earn more than $50,000 a year.

Suppliers

Suppliers include the following:

- *Feed:* Bourne Feed &? Supply, 411 I–70 Drive SE, Columbia
- *Hay:* Robert Coats Farm, 1200 High Point Lane, Columbia
- *Hay (Back–Up):* John Jacobs, 5600 Route E, Columbia
- *Horse Care Supplies:* MFA Inc., 780 Route B, Columbia

Equipment

Equipment includes the following:

- Tractor
- Pick–up truck
- Horse trailer
- Automatic waterers for stalls
- Fans for stalls
- Miscellaneous tack (halters, lead ropes, blankets)
- Wheelbarrows, shovels, pitchforks, brooms, buckets
- Water tanks and heaters for paddocks
- Fencing equipment

Hours

Miller Stables will be accessible to horse owners 24 hours a day, 7 days a week.

Facility and Location

Miller Stables is located at 4040 South Turtle Creek Lane, Columbia, Missouri. All necessary physical requirements, including barn, indoor arena, outdoor arena, and owners' home are already existing on site. Additional fencing will need to be installed to create the 5–acre paddocks.

Legal Environment

Miller Stables will use State Farm Insurance Company to purchase all necessary liability insurance. County health and environmental codes will be followed strictly.

FINANCIAL ANALYSIS

Because the Millers have already purchased the property and use it as their primary residence, the cost of the home, acreage, and outbuildings is not included in the total investment amount needed. Jo also owns some of the necessary equipment due to her previous involvement in the industry; she plans to obtain a business loan to fund the remainder.

Start Up Expenses

Start-Up Costs

Capital requirements	Already purchased	Need to fund
Property, including home	$750,000	$ 0
Tractor	$ 15,000	$ 0
Pick-up truck	$ 25,000	$ 0
Horse trailer	$ 8,000	$ 0
Automatic watering system	$ 0	$ 7,000
Fans	$ 0	$ 500
Extra tack	$ 0	$ 2,000
Stall-cleaning equipment	$ 0	$ 500
Water tanks and heaters	$ 0	$ 1,000
Fencing	$ 0	$10,000
Furniture, fixtures for lounge	$ 0	$ 2,000
Starting inventory: Salt blocks	$ 0	$ 100
Starting inventory: Grain	$ 0	$ 500
Starting inventory: Hay	$ 0	$ 300
Starting inventory: Bedding	$ 0	$ 500
Insurance	$ 0	$ 500
Entrance signs	$ 0	$ 500
Parking lot preparation	$ 0	$ 1,000
Advertising	$ 0	$ 250
Totals:	**$798,000**	**$26,650**

Earnings

Earnings estimates below are based on boarding 10 horses the first year, 15 the second, and 20 the third.

Earnings

	1st Year	2nd Year	3rd Year
Net sales	$36,000	$54,000	$72,000
Less expenses:			
Business loan payment	$ 3,600	$ 3,600	$ 3,600
Feed/hay/bedding/salt	$15,000	$22,500	$30,000
Salaries	$15,600	$20,800	$26,000
Repairs and maintenance	$ 1,000	$ 1,500	$ 2,000
Vehicle expenses	$ 500	$ 1,000	$ 1,500
Insurance	$ 1,000	$ 1,500	$ 2,000
Total expenses	$36,700	$50,900	$65,100
Net profit before taxes	**$ 700**	**$ 3,100**	**$ 6,900**

Wine Storage
Wine Portfolio Inc.

217 East Broad Street
West Hampton, New York 11977

Laura Becker

Wine Portfolio Inc. stores wine for wine auction houses, wine distributors, and private wine collectors.

BUSINESS OBJECTIVE AND DESCRIPTION

Wine Portfolio's objective is to broaden the appeal of its state-of-the-art wine storage facility. The company will continue to build strong relationships with wine auction houses and wine distributors that conduct business in the New York Area. In addition, the company is building a portfolio of customers who purchase and store their wine in a professional manner. This requires storing wine in a temperature-controlled environment that is constantly being monitored. Wine Portfolio provides first-rate customer service to customers including state-of-the-art inventory management systems; pick up and delivery of wines; and the buying and selling of wines on a consignment basis.

MISSION STATEMENT

Wine Portfolio was created to take advantage of the need for a facility to store wine in a professional manner. The company stores wine for its commercial and private customers; and allows customers to monitor wine portfolios via inventory management systems. The business objective is to be the premier wine storage company within the United States.

EXECUTIVE SUMMARY

The wine storage business focuses on building an inventory of wine, and creating value added products for clients. Revenue for the business is generated by charging a monthly fee for each bottle that is stored at one of the storage facilities. Bottles that differ in size from the standard 750 ML variety incur additional fees. The business also generates revenue from retrieving wines from distributors or vineyards. Deliveries of wines to customers help to generate income as well. Business growth is based on developing relationships throughout the wine community, which includes: wine auction houses, wine distributors (foreign and domestic) and wine collectors. As growth of wine consumption moves throughout the globe, the wine trade and wine transactions will grow in tandem. Growth of outsourcing wine storage by restaurants should also continue to grow.

There are two types of storage facilities: comingled wine which is generally for larger commercial use; and private wine storage (personal wine lockers) that is generally for smaller, private wine collectors. Wine Portfolio manages a comingled wine storage facility which provides full service to customers including wine monitoring, pick up, delivery, inventory management systems and buying and selling of wines on consignment.

BUSINESS OVERVIEW

Wine Portfolio is a commercial wine storage facility which provides storage and maintenance for comingled wines from various owners in a climate-controlled storage facility. This means that the wine is stored in a large room and there are no separate wine lockers for clients to visit. The business is a full-service offering meaning that all activity regarding the wine is taken care of by the operator of the facility. This includes turning the wine, viewing the wine or retrieving the wine. Inventory-management software for customers is provided as well.

Storage facilities such as Wine Portfolio's operate within large urban areas that are wine distribution centers. Cities such as New York, San Francisco, Los Angeles, and Chicago are strong candidates for comingled wine storage facilities such as this. This setup is also preferred in other large cities where the commercial space leases are at a premium.

The alternative to this type of comingled storage facility for wine collectors is to store wine in a storage facility that allows for individual wine space and the owners manage and maintain their own collection (that is, a personal locker type of experience). This type of individually-managed facility allows customers to store wine in a climate-controlled space and act as the sole operator of the wine. Inventory management software can be supplied, but the responsibility of monitoring the wine is the clients. These facilities are preferred in some circumstances because it allows free access to the wine that is stored and still provides a professional environment to store wine. This type of facility will be preferred mainly by private wine collections, and less by the auction houses and distributors.

INDUSTRY ANALYSIS

The growth of the wine storage industry is directly tied to the supply and demand for premium wines. Premium wines, for consumption or trade, are generally stored in a professional wine cellar or a professionally built home or business cellar. During the beginning of the current decade, wine storage has grown side by side with the increase in growth of premium wines. Wines from major terrier areas of France, Italy, Australia and the United States have grown substantially in value over the past five years. Even during the current economic crisis, premium wines purchases made in 2003 have more than doubled in value. The wine market in the United States, in terms of consumption, is forecasted to grow at a compound annual growth rate of about 7.7%, and 4% in value and volume terms between 2008 and 2012.

As global economies begin to recover, many economists believe that prices for hard assets and commodities will increase substantially. Wine has become commoditized, and should benefit from the flood of capital that central banks are distributing. The trading of wine has also increased over the past 10 years. As trading and auctions of wine continue to branch out across the United States and the globe, the need for professional storage of wine will grow as well. Auction houses such as Christie, Sotheby's, Ackerman and Morrel, and Zachy's all store wines that will be auctioned in professional storage facilities.

The table below is a list of wine auction houses.

Wine Auction Houses

Auction house	Wine investor score	City	URL	Buyers premium	Seller's premium	Minimum consignment	Auctions per year	Cost of catalogue (single)	Cost of catalogue (year)
Acker Merrall & Condit	94	New York	View website	19.5%	0%	Negotiable	8	$20	$150
Bonhams and Butterfields		San Francisco	View website	17%	Negotiable	Negotiable	7		
Christies		New York/ Los Angeles	View website	18.5%	Negotiable	Negotiable	10	$20	$190
Edward Roberts International		Chicago/ San Francisco	View website	17%	Negotiable	Negotiable	5	$25	
Hart Davis Hart		Chicago	View website	19.5%	Negotiable	Negotiable	5	$25	$ 80
Morrell & Company	92	New York	View website	18%	0%	$2,000	4	$15	$ 50
Sothebys		New York	View website	19.5%	Negotiable	Negotiable	6	$16	$123
The Chicago Wine Company		Chicago	View website	0%	Negotiable	Negotiable	12	$ 0	$ 0
Zachys		New York/ Los Angeles	View website	19%	Negotiable	Negotiable	9	$30	$160

MARKET ANALYSIS

The climate-control wine storage business is estimated to have revenues of approximately $113 million dollars per year according to "Vino Veritas." Climate-controlled storage makes up approximately .05 percent of the 1.6 billion square feet of storage on the market. This market is estimated to expand by 26 percent over the next 3 to 5 years. There is opportunity in both large urban communities, as well as, wealthy smaller towns within the United States.

The current market environment has been positive for the storage business. Current clients have continued to keep their wine in one location. Since the business is an annuity performance business with repetitive income, this has been a positive. The storage facilities are also taking business away from home storage units. A three hundred bottle temperature-controlled unit sells for approximately $4,000. Storage costs for three hundred bottles would be $500 dollars per year. During difficult financial times, professional storage facilities create better short-term value.

The barriers to entry within the wine storage business are relatively low. Securing a facility that will accommodate a temperature-controlled environment will be the largest expense. Most facilities are located in low rent areas. There will be some customization necessary which will depend on the business model employed. The basics needed will be to provide a space that can be temperature-controlled at 55 degrees Fahrenheit, humidity controlled at approximately 70%, with minimal light exposure, and have little to no vibrations. The owners of the business will also need access to a refrigerated truck to receive and deliver wine from customers assuming this is a service that will be provided.

Competition

The competition within the industry will be from companies that provide one of the two forms of service. There are very few companies that offer a comingled wine storage experience, along with a personal locker experience. A combined storage facility would offer the best of both worlds. The comingled storage facility usually offers a state-of-the-art inventory management system, along with top notch customer service. Some of these firms will also purchase or consign to sell your inventory. Vinfolio, a San Francisco wine storage facility, is a large comingled storage facility that offers inventory management, as well as, purchasing and sales options. The Wine Cellarage, a Bronx NY storage facility, is an example of a facility that offers storage and inventory, but does not offer consignment arrangements.

Existing Wine Storage Options

Company	Wine investor score	URL	State	City	Cost/case/ month
55 Degrees		View website	CA	St Helena	—
Adventures in Wine		View website	CA	San Francisco	—
Brix Wine Vault		View website	NY	Brooklyn	—
Desert Wine Cellars		View website	AZ	Scottsdale	—
Eastside Wine Storage		View website	WA	Seattle	—
El Camino Wine Storage		View website	CA	San Luis Obispo	—
Guarantee Wine Storage		View website	NY	New York	—
Kent Certified Wine		View website	IL	Chicago	—
LA Fine Arts & Wine Storage Co.		View website	CA	Los Angeles	—
Legend Cellars		View website	CA	Irvine	—
Marin Wine Vaults		View website	CA	San Raphael	$3.14
Morgan Manhatten		View website	NY	New York	—
Napa Valley Wine Storage		View website	CA	Napa	—
Napa Wine Lockers		View website	CA	Napa	$2.43
Portland Wine Storage		View website	OR	Portland	—
Seattle Wine Storage		View website	WA	Seattle	$1.74
Strongbox Wine Cellar		View website	IL	Chicago	—
The Wine Cellarage		View website	NY	Bronx	—
The Wine Storage Cave		View website	NY	Kingston	—
Vintage Wine Warehouse		View website	NY	New York	—
West Palm Wine		View website	FL	Tampa	—

PERSONNEL

The wine storage business is similar in many ways to most other storage businesses. Making money will depend on the owner's ability to secure an inexpensive lease in a large enough space and create revenues from storing wine. Direct expenses from personnel are low. Companies that comingle wine in one large storage facility need two people to be available to handle the operation. Managing inventory, which includes moving the inventory, and accounting for the inventory are the skills needed to provide a basic service. Additionally, the owners will need to perform bookkeeping, minor contract or insurance work and logistic or transportation work.

STRATEGIES

The wine storage business has two basic strategies. The first is a comingled storage facility that requires a large storage facility and a very strong inventory management system. This strategy is customer-oriented and has multiple business lines. The second strategy is a personal storage facility. This strategy is more similar to a standard storage business and requires minimal day to day interaction. Both strategies are viable on their own, but definitely can be combined to create a formidable business.

Comingled Storage Facility

Finding a large space where your lease is relatively low cost, is the first step in building a storage business using this strategy. Preferably, the storage space should be below ground. Below ground facilities have a natural cooling environment, and there is less of a need for heavy air conditioning or heat.

A case of wine is approximately one square foot, or half a cubic foot. With storage bins there are approximately two cases that call be stored using each cubic foot. A storage facility with 14 foot ceilings would be able to house twenty cases within a square foot of space. The revenue for storage range from $2.5 to $4 dollars per case which implies revenue from storage is between $50 to $80 dollars per square foot.

There are a number of different inventory management systems that can be purchased or leased. One example is Uncorked, which is $249 per year and it includes 2.7 million wines in its database as well as wine reviews.

The comingled facility as a stand alone business works well in large urban areas where space is at a premium. Delivery of wine to customers, as well as, a pickup service is a must. There is also a need to create a simple web site that will allow your customers to view the inventory of wine within the facility. The interior of the facility is open with multiple large storage bins, with levels to store wine. The practicality of storage at a comingled facility is much more important than how the storage facility is viewed.

Personal Locker Storage Facility

The business strategy is similar to personalized storage space. The owner will need to create different types of wine lockers that are different in size. This strategy will require some customization to create individual spaces that clients will deposit and retrieve their wine inventory. Most of these spaces have wood interiors, and can store between 200 and 15,000 bottles. Personal wine storage spaces can fluctuate depending on the area of the country they are located in. Small wine storage can be as low as $500 dollars per year for 36 cubic feet, to as high as $6,000 per year for large rooms according to the The Wine Hotel in Los Angeles.

PRODUCTS AND SERVICES

Each business line (comingled and personal lockers) will have specific products and services.

Comingled Wine Storage

The comingled wine storage facility will allow customers to ship wine from different regions of the country and the world to the facility based on specific state and local laws. The wine will be stored and inventoried. Clients will be able to view their wine within 48 hours of arrival to the facility. Taking digital pictures of the wine is a service that will be available. Customers will be able to request a delivery or schedule a pick up of their wine. This facility will offer shipping services of wine to almost anywhere in the world. The inventory system will also place an estimated value on the wine. If a client would like to consign the wine for sale, the facility will take on short term guaranteed sales as well as long term consignments. The guaranteed price will be a percentage of the estimate retail value of the wine minus a 20% commission. The long-term consigned price is a price designated by the customer. The customer will in turn pay a fee of 20% as commission for the sale of the wine.

Personal Locker Wine Storage

The personalized wine locker service is a locked temperature and climate-controlled environment. The area is secure and there will always be a person watching the facility. There will also be video cameras recording everyone who enters and exits the facility. Wine will be delivered and retrieved by the owners of the wine. This facility will offer a wine inventory system that will be leased to the customers. Taking inventory of the wine will be performed only by the owner of the wine or persons with permission that have access to the wine.

A niche within the industry is having a combined facility that allows customers to have private lockers as well as a comingled account.

Facilities can create value by offering a client a pricing structure where they can pay for either product in advance at a discount. Payment up front for one year has the advantage of receiving a

10% discount. Two year upfront payments will receive a 15% discount. Month to month payment requires a credit card to be on file. The minimum contract is six months, and each service offers a two year guaranteed lease.

MARKETING AND SALES

The Marketing and Sales effort will focus on multiple groups. The comingled facility will focus its marketing effort on distributors, auction houses, large retail sellers and private collectors with large collections of wine. Advertising the product will take place in magazines that focus on wine such as, *The Wine Spectator*, *The Wine Enthusiast*, and *Food and Wine*. It will also be important to develop relationships with some of the wine producers in areas of California, Washington State, and Oregon.

The marketing effort for personalized wine spaces will be targeted to many medium and smaller wine retailers, restaurants, and wine private collectors. It is important as well to advertise in the same major wine magazines.

OPERATIONS

The operational hours for the comingled facility will be slightly longer than normal business hours. The hours of 9 a.m. to 7 p.m. will allow the facility to receive all packages that will be delivered, and send all necessary items for a given business day. It will also be important to be open on Saturdays to allow customers to retrieve wine if necessary.

The operating house for the personalized spaces will be from 9 a.m. to 10 p.m. These hours will allow individuals the time to retrieve any wines they need over a broad period of time. Restaurants will also be able to retrieve wine if needed over a long time horizon.

Location

The comingled facility should be located within 60 miles of a major urban area. Locations around New York, Los Angeles, San Francisco, Dallas, Miami, Las Vegas will support this type of service. The personalized facility will be able to flourish in many smaller cities and suburban areas.

Licensing

Neither ype of facility will need a liquor license unless the facility is planning on offering consignment of wine.

FINANCIAL ANALYSIS

Revenues and expenses are broken out into two distinct services. The comingled service will have revenues based on attaining 500 cases of wine for storage. Additional revenues of $5,000 will be produced from delivery and retrieval of wines. Costs are broken down into lease costs, construction, climate control, advertising, legal, accounting and truck leasing. The second and third year's revenues are based on 2,000 cases of wine and 5,000 cases of wine respectively. Expenses are fixed over years two and three.

Revenues for the personal storage space are based on 40 cubic foot spaces that will be provided. The first year is based on 30 spaces leased. The second and third years are based on 100 and 200 spaces leased.

Comingled Wine Storage Facility

	Year 1	Year 2	Year 3
Revenue			
Storage	$ 48,000.00	$144,000.00	$ 192,000.00
Delivery	$ 5,000.00	$ 15,000.00	$ 25,000.00
Total revenue	$ 53,000.00	$159,000.00	$ 217,000.00
Expenses			
Construction	$ 20,000.00	$ —	$ —
Building lease—$4,000/month	$ 48,000.00	$ 48,000.00	$ 48,000.00
Air control—$500/month	$ 6,000.00	$ 6,000.00	$ 6,000.00
Advertising—$300/month	$ 3,600.00	$ 3,600.00	$ 3,600.00
Legal	$ 3,000.00	$ 3,000.00	$ 3,000.00
Accounting	$ 2,000.00	$ 2,000.00	$ 2,000.00
Truck lease	$ 6,000.00	$ 6,000.00	$ 6,000.00
Total expenses	**$ 88,600.00**	**$ 68,600.00**	**$ 68,600.00**
Net profit	($ 35,600.00)	$ 90,400.00	$148,400.00

Assumptions:
Year 1: 500 cases of wine
Year 2: 2,000 cases of wine
Year 3: 5,000 cases of wine
Lease: 3,000 square feet/60,000 cubic feet—$4,000/month

Personal Locker Wine Storage Facility

	Year 1	Year 2	Year 3
Revenue	$ 15,000.00	$50,000.00	$100,000.00
Expenses			
Construction	$ 20,000.00	$ —	$ —
Building lease—$1,500/month	$ 18,000.00	$18,000.00	$ 18,000.00
Air control—$200/month	$ 2,400.00	$ 2,400.00	$ 2,400.00
Advertising—$200/month	$ 2,400.00	$ 2,400.00	$ 2,400.00
Legal	$ 3,000.00	$ 3,000.00	$ 3,000.00
Accounting	$ 2,000.00	$ 2,000.00	$ 2,000.00
Total expenses	$ 47,800.00	$27,800.00	$ 27,800.00
Net profit	($32,800.00)	$22,200.00	$ 72,200.00

Assumptions:
Year 1: 30
Year 2: 100 lockers
Year 3: 200 lockers
Space: 40 cubic feet provided per locker
Lease: 1,000 square feet, 20,000 cubic feet

Business Plan Template

USING THIS TEMPLATE

A business plan carefully spells out a company's projected course of action over a period of time, usually the first two to three years after the start-up. In addition, banks, lenders, and other investors examine the information and financial documentation before deciding whether or not to finance a new business venture. Therefore, a business plan is an essential tool in obtaining financing and should describe the business itself in detail as well as all important factors influencing the company, including the market, industry, competition, operations and management policies, problem solving strategies, financial resources and needs, and other vital information. The plan enables the business owner to anticipate costs, plan for difficulties, and take advantage of opportunities, as well as design and implement strategies that keep the company running as smoothly as possible.

This template has been provided as a model to help you construct your own business plan. Please keep in mind that there is no single acceptable format for a business plan, and that this template is in no way comprehensive, but serves as an example.

The business plans provided in this section are fictional and have been used by small business agencies as models for clients to use in compiling their own business plans.

GENERIC BUSINESS PLAN

Main headings included below are topics that should be covered in a comprehensive business plan. They include:

Business Summary

Purpose
Provides a brief overview of your business, succinctly highlighting the main ideas of your plan.

Includes

- Name and Type of Business
- Description of Product/Service
- Business History and Development
- Location
- Market
- Competition
- Management
- Financial Information
- Business Strengths and Weaknesses
- Business Growth

Table of Contents

Purpose
Organized in an Outline Format, the Table of Contents illustrates the selection and arrangement of information contained in your plan.

Includes

- Topic Headings and Subheadings
- Page Number References

Business History and Industry Outlook

Purpose

Examines the conception and subsequent development of your business within an industry specific context.

Includes

- Start-up Information
- Owner/Key Personnel Experience
- Location
- Development Problems and Solutions
- Investment/Funding Information
- Future Plans and Goals
- Market Trends and Statistics
- Major Competitors
- Product/Service Advantages
- National, Regional, and Local Economic Impact

Product/Service

Purpose

Introduces, defines, and details the product and/or service that inspired the information of your business.

Includes

- Unique Features
- Niche Served
- Market Comparison
- Stage of Product/Service Development
- Production
- Facilities, Equipment, and Labor
- Financial Requirements
- Product/Service Life Cycle
- Future Growth

Market Examination

Purpose

Assessment of product/service applications in relation to consumer buying cycles.

Includes

- Target Market
- Consumer Buying Habits
- Product/Service Applications
- Consumer Reactions
- Market Factors and Trends
- Penetration of the Market
- Market Share
- Research and Studies
- Cost
- Sales Volume and Goals

Competition

Purpose

Analysis of Competitors in the Marketplace.

Includes

- Competitor Information
- Product/Service Comparison
- Market Niche
- Product/Service Strengths and Weaknesses
- Future Product/Service Development

Marketing

Purpose

Identifies promotion and sales strategies for your product/service.

Includes

- Product/Service Sales Appeal
- Special and Unique Features
- Identification of Customers
- Sales and Marketing Staff
- Sales Cycles
- Type of Advertising/ Promotion
- Pricing
- Competition
- Customer Services

Operations

Purpose

Traces product/service development from production/inception to the market environment.

Includes

- Cost Effective Production Methods
- Facility
- Location
- Equipment
- Labor
- Future Expansion

Administration and Management

Purpose

Offers a statement of your management philosophy with an in-depth focus on processes and procedures.

Includes

- Management Philosophy
- Structure of Organization
- Reporting System
- Methods of Communication
- Employee Skills and Training
- Employee Needs and Compensation
- Work Environment
- Management Policies and Procedures
- Roles and Responsibilities

Key Personnel

Purpose

Describes the unique backgrounds of principle employees involved in business.

Includes

- Owner(s)/Employee Education and Experience
- Positions and Roles
- Benefits and Salary
- Duties and Responsibilities
- Objectives and Goals

Potential Problems and Solutions

Purpose

Discussion of problem solving strategies that change issues into opportunities.

Includes

- Risks
- Litigation
- Future Competition
- Economic Impact
- Problem Solving Skills

Financial Information

Purpose

Secures needed funding and assistance through worksheets and projections detailing financial plans, methods of repayment, and future growth opportunities.

Includes

- Financial Statements
- Bank Loans
- Methods of Repayment
- Tax Returns
- Start-up Costs
- Projected Income (3 years)
- Projected Cash Flow (3 Years)
- Projected Balance Statements (3 years)

Appendices

Purpose

Supporting documents used to enhance your business proposal.

Includes

- Photographs of product, equipment, facilities, etc.
- Copyright/Trademark Documents
- Legal Agreements
- Marketing Materials
- Research and or Studies
- Operation Schedules
- Organizational Charts
- Job Descriptions
- Resumes
- Additional Financial Documentation

Fictional Food Distributor

Commercial Foods, Inc.

This plan demonstrates how a partnership can have a positive impact on a new business. It demonstrates how two individuals can carve a niche in the specialty foods market by offering gourmet foods to upscale restaurants and fine hotels. This plan is fictional and has not been used to gain funding from a bank or other lending institution.

3003 Avondale Ave.
Knoxville, TN 37920

STATEMENT OF PURPOSE

Commercial Foods, Inc. seeks a loan of $75,000 to establish a new business. This sum, together with $5,000 equity investment by the principals, will be used as follows:

- Merchandise inventory $25,000

- Office fixture/equipment $12,000

- Warehouse equipment $14,000

- One delivery truck $10,000

- Working capital $39,000

- Total $100,000

DESCRIPTION OF THE BUSINESS

Commercial Foods, Inc. will be a distributor of specialty food service products to hotels and upscale restaurants in the geographical area of a 50 mile radius of Knoxville. Richard Roberts will direct the sales effort and John Williams will manage the warehouse operation and the office. One delivery truck will be used initially with a second truck added in the third year. We expect to begin operation of the business within 30 days after securing the requested financing.

MANAGEMENT

A. Richard Roberts is a native of Memphis, Tennessee. He is a graduate of Memphis State University with a Bachelor's degree from the School of Business. After graduation, he worked for a major manufacturer of specialty food service products as a detail sales person for five years, and, for the past three years, he has served as a product sales manager for this firm.

B. John Williams is a native of Nashville, Tennessee. He holds a B.S. Degree in Food Technology from the University of Tennessee. His career includes five years as a product development chemist in gourmet food products and five years as operations manager for a food service distributor.

Both men are healthy and energetic. Their backgrounds complement each other, which will ensure the success of Commercial Foods, Inc. They will set policies together and personnel decisions will be made jointly. Initial salaries for the owners will be $1,000 per month for the first few years. The spouses of both principals are successful in the business world and earn enough to support the families.

They have engaged the services of Foster Jones, CPA, and William Hale, Attorney, to assist them in an advisory capacity.

PERSONNEL

The firm will employ one delivery truck driver at a wage of $8.00 per hour. One office worker will be employed at $7.50 per hour. One part-time employee will be used in the office at $5.00 per hour. The driver will load and unload his own trucks. Mr. Williams will assist in the warehouse operation as needed to assist one stock person at $7.00 per hour. An additional delivery truck and driver will be added the third year.

LOCATION

The firm will lease a 20,000 square foot building at 3003 Avondale Ave., in Knoxville, which contains warehouse and office areas equipped with two-door truck docks. The annual rental is $9,000. The building was previously used as a food service warehouse and very little modification to the building will be required.

PRODUCTS AND SERVICES

The firm will offer specialty food service products such as soup bases, dessert mixes, sauce bases, pastry mixes, spices, and flavors, normally used by upscale restaurants and nice hotels. We are going after a niche in the market with high quality gourmet products. There is much less competition in this market than in standard run of the mill food service products. Through their work experiences, the principals have contacts with supply sources and with local chefs.

THE MARKET

We know from our market survey that there are over 200 hotels and upscale restaurants in the area we plan to serve. Customers will be attracted by a direct sales approach. We will offer samples of our products and product application data on use of our products in the finished prepared foods. We will cultivate the chefs in these establishments. The technical background of John Williams will be especially useful here.

COMPETITION

We find that we will be only distributor in the area offering a full line of gourmet food service products. Other foodservice distributors offer only a few such items in conjunction with their standard product line. Our survey shows that many of the chefs are ordering products from Atlanta and Memphis because of a lack of adequate local supply.

SUMMARY

Commercial Foods, Inc. will be established as a foodservice distributor of specialty food in Knoxville. The principals, with excellent experience in the industry, are seeking a $75,000 loan to establish the business. The principals are investing $25,000 as equity capital.

The business will be set up as an S Corporation with each principal owning 50% of the common stock in the corporation.

Fictional Hardware Store

Oshkosh Hardware, Inc.

The following plan outlines how a small hardware store can survive competition from large discount chains by offering products and providing expert advice in the use of any product it sells. This plan is fictional and has not been used to gain funding from a bank or other lending institution.

123 Main St.
Oshkosh, WI 54901

EXECUTIVE SUMMARY

Oshkosh Hardware, Inc. is a new corporation that is going to establish a retail hardware store in a strip mall in Oshkosh, Wisconsin. The store will sell hardware of all kinds, quality tools, paint, and housewares. The business will make revenue and a profit by servicing its customers not only with needed hardware but also with expert advice in the use of any product it sells.

Oshkosh Hardware, Inc. will be operated by its sole shareholder, James Smith. The company will have a total of four employees. It will sell its products in the local market. Customers will buy our products because we will provide free advice on the use of all of our products and will also furnish a full refund warranty.

Oshkosh Hardware, Inc. will sell its products in the Oshkosh store staffed by three sales representatives. No additional employees will be needed to achieve its short and long range goals. The primary short range goal is to open the store by October 1, 1994. In order to achieve this goal a lease must be signed by July 1, 1994 and the complete inventory ordered by August 1, 1994.

Mr. James Smith will invest $30,000 in the business. In addition, the company will have to borrow $150,000 during the first year to cover the investment in inventory, accounts receivable, and furniture and equipment. The company will be profitable after six months of operation and should be able to start repayment of the loan in the second year.

THE BUSINESS

The business will sell hardware of all kinds, quality tools, paint, and housewares. We will purchase our products from three large wholesale buying groups.

In general our customers are homeowners who do their own repair and maintenance, hobbyists, and housewives. Our business is unique in that we will have a complete line of all hardware items and will be able to get special orders by overnight delivery. The business makes revenue and profits by servicing our customers not only with needed hardware but also with expert advice in the use of any product we sell. Our major costs for bringing our products to market are cost of merchandise of 36%, salaries of $45,000, and occupancy costs of $60,000.

Oshkosh Hardware, Inc.'s retail outlet will be located at 1524 Frontage Road, which is in a newly developed retail center of Oshkosh. Our location helps facilitate accessibility from all parts of town and reduces our delivery costs. The store will occupy 7500 square feet of space. The major equipment involved in our business is counters and shelving, a computer, a paint mixing machine, and a truck.

THE MARKET

Oshkosh Hardware, Inc. will operate in the local market. There are 15,000 potential customers in this market area. We have three competitors who control approximately 98% of the market at present. We feel we can capture 25% of the market within the next four years. Our major reason for believing this is that our staff is technically competent to advise our customers in the correct use of all products we sell.

After a careful market analysis, we have determined that approximately 60% of our customers are men and 40% are women. The percentage of customers that fall into the following age categories are:

Under 16: 0%
17-21: 5%
22-30: 30%
31-40: 30%
41-50: 20%
51-60: 10%
61-70: 5%
Over 70: 0%

The reasons our customers prefer our products is our complete knowledge of their use and our full refund warranty.

We get our information about what products our customers want by talking to existing customers. There seems to be an increasing demand for our product. The demand for our product is increasing in size based on the change in population characteristics.

SALES

At Oshkosh Hardware, Inc. we will employ three sales people and will not need any additional personnel to achieve our sales goals. These salespeople will need several years experience in home repair and power tool usage. We expect to attract 30% of our customers from newspaper ads, 5% of our customers from local directories, 5% of our customers from the yellow pages, 10% of our customers from family and friends, and 50% of our customers from current customers. The most cost effect source will be current customers. In general our industry is growing.

MANAGEMENT

We would evaluate the quality of our management staff as being excellent. Our manager is experienced and very motivated to achieve the various sales and quality assurance objectives we have set. We will use a management information system that produces key inventory, quality assurance, and sales data on a weekly basis. All data is compared to previously established goals for that week, and deviations are the primary focus of the management staff.

GOALS IMPLEMENTATION

The short term goals of our business are:

1. Open the store by October 1, 1994
2. Reach our breakeven point in two months
3. Have sales of $100,000 in the first six months

In order to achieve our first short term goal we must:

1. Sign the lease by July 1, 1994
2. Order a complete inventory by August 1, 1994

In order to achieve our second short term goal we must:

1. Advertise extensively in Sept. and Oct.
2. Keep expenses to a minimum

In order to achieve our third short term goal we must:

1. Promote power tool sales for the Christmas season
2. Keep good customer traffic in Jan. and Feb.

The long term goals for our business are:

1. Obtain sales volume of $600,000 in three years
2. Become the largest hardware dealer in the city
3. Open a second store in Fond du Lac

The most important thing we must do in order to achieve the long term goals for our business is to develop a highly profitable business with excellent cash flow.

FINANCE

Oshkosh Hardware, Inc. Faces some potential threats or risks to our business. They are discount house competition. We believe we can avoid or compensate for this by providing quality products complimented by quality advice on the use of every product we sell. The financial projections we have prepared are located at the end of this document.

JOB DESCRIPTION-GENERAL MANAGER

The General Manager of the business of the corporation will be the president of the corporation. He will be responsible for the complete operation of the retail hardware store which is owned by the corporation. A detailed description of his duties and responsibilities is as follows.

Sales

Train and supervise the three sales people. Develop programs to motivate and compensate these employees. Coordinate advertising and sales promotion effects to achieve sales totals as outlined in budget. Oversee purchasing function and inventory control procedures to insure adequate merchandise at all times at a reasonable cost.

Finance

Prepare monthly and annual budgets. Secure adequate line of credit from local banks. Supervise office personnel to insure timely preparation of records, statements, all government reports, control of receivables and payables, and monthly financial statements.

Administration

Perform duties as required in the areas of personnel, building leasing and maintenance, licenses and permits, and public relations.

Organizations, Agencies, & Consultants

A listing of Associations and Consultants of interest to entrepreneurs, followed by the ten Small Business Administration Regional Offices, Small Business Development Centers, Service Corps of Retired Executives offices, and Venture Capital and Finance Companies.

Associations

This section contains a listing of associations and other agencies of interest to the small business owner. Entries are listed alphabetically by organization name.

American Business Women's Association
9100 Ward Pkwy.
PO Box 8728
Kansas City, MO 64114-0728
(800)228-0007
E-mail: abwa@abwa.org
Website: http://www.abwa.org
Jeanne Banks, National President

American Franchisee Association
53 W Jackson Blvd., Ste. 1157
Chicago, IL 60604
(312)431-0545
E-mail: info@franchisee.org
Website: http://www.franchisee.org
Susan P. Kezios, President

American Independent Business Alliance
222 S Black Ave.
Bozeman, MT 59715
(406)582-1255
E-mail: info@amiba.net
Website: http://www.amiba.net
Jennifer Rockne, Director

American Small Businesses Association
206 E College St., Ste. 201
Grapevine, TX 76051
800-942-2722
E-mail: info@asbaonline.org
Website: http://www.asbaonline.org/

American Women's Economic Development Corporation
216 East 45th St., 10th Floor
New York, NY 10017
(917)368-6100
Fax: (212)986-7114
E-mail: info@awed.org
Website: http://www.awed.org
Roseanne Antonucci, Exec. Dir.

Association for Enterprise Opportunity
1601 N Kent St., Ste. 1101
Arlington, VA 22209
(703)841-7760
Fax: (703)841-7748
E-mail: aeo@assoceo.org
Website: http://www.micro
enterpriseworks.org
Bill Edwards, Exec.Dir.

Association of Small Business Development Centers
c/o Don Wilson
8990 Burke Lake Rd.
Burke, VA 22015
(703)764-9850
Fax: (703)764-1234
E-mail: info@asbdc-us.org
Website: http://www.asbdc-us.org
Don Wilson, Pres./CEO

BEST Employers Association
2505 McCabe Way
Irvine, CA 92614
(949)253-4080
800-433-0088
Fax: (714)553-0883
E-mail: info@bestlife.com
Website: http://www.bestlife.com
Donald R. Lawrenz, CEO

Center for Family Business
PO Box 24219
Cleveland, OH 44124
(440)460-5409
E-mail: grummi@aol.com
Dr. Leon A. Danco, Chm.

Coalition for Government Procurement
1990 M St. NW, Ste. 400
Washington, DC 20036
(202)331-0975
E-mail: info@thecgp.org
Website: http://www.coalgovpro.org
Paul Caggiano, Pres.

Employers of America
PO Box 1874
Mason City, IA 50402-1874
(641)424-3187
800-728-3187
Fax: (641)424-1673
E-mail: employer@employerhelp.org
Website: http://www.employerhelp.org
Jim Collison, Pres.

Family Firm Institute
200 Lincoln St., Ste. 201
Boston, MA 02111
(617)482-3045
Fax: (617)482-3049
E-mail: ffi@ffi.org
Website: http://www.ffi.org
Judy L. Green, Ph.D., Exec.Dir.

Independent Visually Impaired Enterprisers
500 S 3rd St., Apt. H
Burbank, CA 91502
(818)238-9321
E-mail: abazyn@bazyn
communications.com
http://www.acb.org/affiliates
Adris Bazyn, Pres.

International Association for Business Organizations
3 Woodthorn Ct., Ste. 12
Owings Mills, MD 21117
(410)581-1373
E-mail: nahbb@msn.com
Rudolph Lewis, Exec. Officer

International Council for Small Business
The George Washington University
School of Business and Public
Management
2115 G St. NW, Ste. 403
Washington, DC 20052
(202)994-0704
Fax: (202)994-4930
E-mail: icsb@gwu.edu
Website: http://www.icsb.org
Susan G. Duffy. Admin.

International Small Business Consortium
3309 Windjammer St.
Norman, OK 73072
E-mail: sb@isbc.com
Website: http://www.isbc.com

Kauffman Center for Entrepreneurial Leadership
4801 Rockhill Rd.
Kansas City, MO 64110-2046
(816)932-1000
E-mail: info@kauffman.org
Website: http://www.entreworld.org

National Alliance for Fair Competition
3 Bethesda Metro Center, Ste. 1100
Bethesda, MD 20814
(410)235-7116
Fax: (410)235-7116
E-mail: ampesq@aol.com
Tony Ponticelli, Exec.Dir.

National Association for the Self-Employed
PO Box 612067
DFW Airport
Dallas, TX 75261-2067
(800)232-6273
E-mail: mpetron@nase.org
Website: http://www.nase.org
Robert Hughes, Pres.

National Association of Business Leaders
4132 Shoreline Dr., Ste. J & H
Earth City, MO 63045
Fax: (314)298-9110
E-mail: nabl@nabl.com
Website: http://www.nabl.com/
Gene Blumenthal, Contact

National Association of Private Enterprise
PO Box 15550
Long Beach, CA 90815
888-224-0953

Fax: (714)844-4942
Website: http://www.napeonline.net
Laura Squiers, Exec.Dir.

National Association of Small Business Investment Companies
666 11th St. NW, Ste. 750
Washington, DC 20001
(202)628-5055
Fax: (202)628-5080
E-mail: nasbic@nasbic.org
Website: http://www.nasbic.org
Lee W. Mercer, Pres.

National Business Association
PO Box 700728
5151 Beltline Rd., Ste. 1150
Dallas, TX 75370
(972)458-0900
800-456-0440
Fax: (972)960-9149
E-mail: info@nationalbusiness.org
Website: http://www.national
business.org
Raj Nisankarao, Pres.

National Business Owners Association
PO Box 111
Stuart, VA 24171
(276)251-7500
(866)251-7505
Fax: (276)251-2217
E-mail: membershipservices@nboa.org
Website: http://www.rvmdb.com.nboa
Paul LaBarr, Pres.

National Center for Fair Competition
PO Box 220
Annandale, VA 22003
(703)280-4622
Fax: (703)280-0942
E-mail: kentonp1@aol.com
Kenton Pattie, Pres.

National Family Business Council
1640 W. Kennedy Rd.
Lake Forest, IL 60045
(847)295-1040
Fax: (847)295-1898
E-mail: lmsnfbc@email.msn.com
Jogn E. Messervey, Pres.

National Federation of Independent Business
53 Century Blvd., Ste. 250
Nashville, TN 37214
(615)872-5800
800-NFIBNOW
Fax: (615)872-5353
Website: http://www.nfib.org
Jack Faris, Pres. and CEO

National Small Business Association
1156 15th St. NW, Ste. 1100
Washington, DC 20005
(202)293-8830
800-345-6728
Fax: (202)872-8543
E-mail: press@nsba.biz
Website: http://www.nsba.biz
Rob Yunich, Dir. of Communications

PUSH Commercial Division
930 E 50th St.
Chicago, IL 60615-2702
(773)373-3366
Fax: (773)373-3571
E-mail: info@rainbowpush.org
Website: http://www.rainbowpush.org
Rev. Willie T. Barrow, Co-Chm.

Research Institute for Small and Emerging Business
722 12th St. NW
Washington, DC 20005
(202)628-8382
Fax: (202)628-8392
E-mail: info@riseb.org
Website: http://www.riseb.org
Allan Neece, Jr., Chm.

Sales Professionals USA
PO Box 149
Arvada, CO 80001
(303)534-4937
888-736-7767
E-mail: salespro@salesprofessionals-
usa.com
Website: http://www.salesprofessionals-
usa.com
Sharon Herbert, Natl. Pres.

Score Association - Service Corps of Retired Executives
409 3rd St. SW, 6th Fl.
Washington, DC 20024
(202)205-6762
800-634-0245
Fax: (202)205-7636
E-mail: media@score.org
Website: http://www.score.org
W. Kenneth Yancey, Jr., CEO

Small Business and Entrepreneurship Council
1920 L St. NW, Ste. 200
Washington, DC 20036
(202)785-0238
Fax: (202)822-8118
E-mail: membership@sbec.org
Website: http://www.sbecouncil.org
Karen Kerrigan, Pres./CEO

Small Business in Telecommunications

1331 H St. NW, Ste. 500
Washington, DC 20005
(202)347-4511
Fax: (202)347-8607
E-mail: sbt@sbthome.org
Website: http://www.sbthome.org
Lonnie Danchik, Chm.

Small Business Legislative Council

1010 Massachusetts Ave. NW, Ste. 540
Washington, DC 20005
(202)639-8500
Fax: (202)296-5333
E-mail: email@sblc.org
Website: http://www.sblc.org
John Satagaj, Pres.

Small Business Service Bureau

554 Main St.
PO Box 15014
Worcester, MA 01615-0014
(508)756-3513
800-343-0939
Fax: (508)770-0528
E-mail: membership@sbsb.com
Website: http://www.sbsb.com
Francis R. Carroll, Pres.

Small Publishers Association of North America

1618 W COlorado Ave.
Colorado Springs, CO 80904
(719)475-1726
Fax: (719)471-2182
E-mail: span@spannet.org
Website: http://www.spannet.org
Scott Flora, Exec. Dir.

SOHO America

PO Box 941
Hurst, TX 76053-0941
800-495-SOHO
E-mail: soho@1sas.com
Website: http://www.soho.org

Structured Employment Economic Development Corporation

915 Broadway, 17th Fl.
New York, NY 10010
(212)473-0255
Fax: (212)473-0357
E-mail: info@seedco.org
Website: http://www.seedco.org
William Grinker, CEO

Support Services Alliance

107 Prospect St.
Schoharie, NY 12157
800-836-4772

E-mail: info@ssamembers.com
Website: http://www.ssainfo.com
Steve COle, Pres.

United States Association for Small Business and Entrepreneurship

975 University Ave., No. 3260
Madison, WI 53706
(608)262-9982
Fax: (608)263-0818
E-mail: jgillman@wisc.edu
Website: http://www.ususbe.org
Joan Gillman, Exec. Dir.

Consultants

This section contains a listing of consultants specializing in small business development. It is arranged alphabetically by country, then by state or province, then by city, then by firm name.

Canada

Alberta

Common Sense Solutions

3405 16A Ave.
Edmonton, AB, Canada
(403)465-7330
Fax: (403)465-7380
E-mail: gcoulson@comsense
solutions.com
Website: http://www.comsensesolutions.
com

Varsity Consulting Group

School of Business
University of Alberta
Edmonton, AB, Canada T6G 2R6
(780)492-2994
Fax: (780)492-5400
Website: http://www.bus.ualberta.ca/vcg

Viro Hospital Consulting

42 Commonwealth Bldg., 9912 - 106
St. NW
Edmonton, AB, Canada T5K 1C5
(403)425-3871
Fax: (403)425-3871
E-mail: rpb@freenet.edmonton.ab.ca

British Columbia

SRI Strategic Resources Inc.

4330 Kingsway, Ste. 1600
Burnaby, BC, Canada V5H 4G7
(604)435-0627
Fax: (604)435-2782

E-mail: inquiry@sri.bc.ca
Website: http://www.sri.com

Andrew R. De Boda Consulting

1523 Milford Ave.
Coquitlam, BC, Canada V3J 2V9
(604)936-4527
Fax: (604)936-4527
E-mail: deboda@intergate.bc.ca
Website: http://www.ourworld.
compuserve.com/homepages/deboda

The Sage Group Ltd.

980 - 355 Burrard St.
744 W Haistings, Ste. 410
Vancouver, BC, Canada V6C 1A5
(604)669-9269
Fax: (604)669-6622

Tikkanen-Bradley

1345 Nelson St., Ste. 202
Vancouver, BC, Canada V6E 1J8
(604)669-0583
E-mail: webmaster@tikkanen
bradley.com
Website: http://www.tikkanenbradley.com

Ontario

The Cynton Co.

17 Massey St.
Brampton, ON, Canada L6S 2V6
(905)792-7769
Fax: (905)792-8116
E-mail: cynton@home.com
Website: http://www.cynton.com

Begley & Associates

RR 6
Cambridge, ON, Canada N1R 5S7
(519)740-3629
Fax: (519)740-3629
E-mail: begley@in.on.ca
Website: http://www.in.on.ca/~begley/
index.htm

CRO Engineering Ltd.

1895 William Hodgins Ln.
Carp, ON, Canada K0A 1L0
(613)839-1108
Fax: (613)839-1406
E-mail: J.Grefford@ieee.ca
Website: http://www.geocities.com/
WallStreet/District/7401/

Task Enterprises

Box 69, RR 2 Hamilton
Flamborough, ON, Canada L8N 2Z7
(905)659-0153
Fax: (905)659-0861

HST Group Ltd.
430 Gilmour St.
Ottawa, ON, Canada K2P 0R8
(613)236-7303
Fax: (613)236-9893

Harrison Associates
BCE Pl.
181 Bay St., Ste. 3740
PO Box 798
Toronto, ON, Canada M5J 2T3
(416)364-5441
Fax: (416)364-2875

TCI Convergence Ltd. Management Consultants
99 Crown's Ln.
Toronto, ON, Canada M5R 3P4
(416)515-4146
Fax: (416)515-2097
E-mail: tci@inforamp.net
Website: http://tciconverge.com/
index.1.html

Ken Wyman & Associates Inc.
64B Shuter St., Ste. 200
Toronto, ON, Canada M5B 1B1
(416)362-2926
Fax: (416)362-3039
E-mail: kenwyman@compuserve.com

JPL Business Consultants
82705 Metter Rd.
Wellandport, ON, Canada L0R 2J0
(905)386-7450
Fax: (905)386-7450
E-mail: plamarch@freenet.npiec.on.ca

Quebec

The Zimmar Consulting Partnership Inc.
Westmount
PO Box 98
Montreal, QC, Canada H3Z 2T1
(514)484-1459
Fax: (514)484-3063

Saskatchewan

Trimension Group
No. 104-110 Research Dr.
Innovation Place, SK, Canada S7N 3R3
(306)668-2560
Fax: (306)975-1156
E-mail: trimension@trimension.ca
Website: http://www.trimension.ca

Corporate Management Consultants
40 Government Road - PO Box 185
Prud Homme, SK, Canada, S0K 3K0
(306)654-4569

E-mail: gerald.rekve@corporate
managementconsultant.com
Website: http://www.Corporate
managementconsultants.com
Gerald Rekve

United states

Alabama

Business Planning Inc.
300 Office Park Dr.
Birmingham, AL 35223-2474
(205)870-7090
Fax: (205)870-7103

Tradebank of Eastern Alabama
546 Broad St., Ste. 3
Gadsden, AL 35901
(205)547-8700
Fax: (205)547-8718
E-mail: mansion@webex.com
Website: http://www.webex.com/~tea

Alaska

AK Business Development Center
3335 Arctic Blvd., Ste. 203
Anchorage, AK 99503
(907)562-0335
Free: 800-478-3474
Fax: (907)562-6988
E-mail: abdc@gci.net
Website: http://www.abdc.org

Business Matters
PO Box 287
Fairbanks, AK 99707
(907)452-5650

Arizona

Carefree Direct Marketing Corp.
8001 E Serene St.
PO Box 3737
Carefree, AZ 85377-3737
(480)488-4227
Fax: (480)488-2841

Trans Energy Corp.
1739 W 7th Ave.
Mesa, AZ 85202
(480)827-7915
Fax: (480)967-6601
E-mail: aha@clean-air.org
Website: http://www.clean-air.org

CMAS
5125 N 16th St.
Phoenix, AZ 85016

(602)395-1001
Fax: (602)604-8180

Comgate Telemanagement Ltd.
706 E Bell Rd., Ste. 105
Phoenix, AZ 85022
(602)485-5708
Fax: (602)485-5709
E-mail: comgate@netzone.com
Website: http://www.comgate.com

Moneysoft Inc.
1 E Camelback Rd. #550
Phoenix, AZ 85012
Free: 800-966-7797
E-mail: mbray@moneysoft.com

Harvey C. Skoog
PO Box 26439
Prescott Valley, AZ 86312
(520)772-1714
Fax: (520)772-2814

LMC Services
8711 E Pinnacle Peak Rd., No. 340
Scottsdale, AZ 85255-3555
(602)585-7177
Fax: (602)585-5880
E-mail: louws@earthlink.com

Sauerbrun Technology Group Ltd.
7979 E Princess Dr., Ste. 5
Scottsdale, AZ 85255-5878
(602)502-4950
Fax: (602)502-4292
E-mail: info@sauerbrun.com
Website: http://www.sauerbrun.com

Gary L. McLeod
PO Box 230
Sonoita, AZ 85637
Fax: (602)455-5661

Van Cleve Associates
6932 E 2nd St.
Tucson, AZ 85710
(520)296-2587
Fax: (520)296-3358

California

Acumen Group Inc.
(650)949-9349
Fax: (650)949-4845
E-mail: acumen-g@ix.netcom.com
Website: http://pw2.netcom.com/~janed/
acumen.html

On-line Career and Management Consulting
420 Central Ave., No. 314
Alameda, CA 94501

(510)864-0336
Fax: (510)864-0336
E-mail: career@dnai.com
Website: http://www.dnai.com/~career

Career Paths-Thomas E. Church & Associates Inc.
PO Box 2439
Aptos, CA 95001
(408)662-7950
Fax: (408)662-7955
E-mail: church@ix.netcom.com
Website: http://www.careerpaths-tom.com

Keck & Co. Business Consultants
410 Walsh Rd.
Atherton, CA 94027
(650)854-9588
Fax: (650)854-7240
E-mail: info@keckco.com
Website: http://www.keckco.com

Ben W. Laverty III, PhD, REA, CEI
4909 Stockdale Hwy., Ste. 132
Bakersfield, CA 93309
(661)283-8300
Free: 800-833-0373
Fax: (661)283-8313
E-mail: cstc@cstcsafety.com
Website: http://www.cstcsafety.com/cstc

Lindquist Consultants-Venture Planning
225 Arlington Ave.
Berkeley, CA 94707
(510)524-6685
Fax: (510)527-6604

Larson Associates
PO Box 9005
Brea, CA 92822
(714)529-4121
Fax: (714)572-3606
E-mail: ray@consultlarson.com
Website: http://www.consultlarson.com

Kremer Management Consulting
PO Box 500
Carmel, CA 93921
(408)626-8311
Fax: (408)624-2663
E-mail: ddkremer@aol.com

W and J PARTNERSHIP
PO Box 2499
18876 Edwin Markham Dr.
Castro Valley, CA 94546
(510)583-7751
Fax: (510)583-7645
E-mail: wamorgan@wjpartnership.com
Website: http://www.wjpartnership.com

JB Associates
21118 Gardena Dr.
Cupertino, CA 95014
(408)257-0214
Fax: (408)257-0216
E-mail: semarang@sirius.com

House Agricultural Consultants
PO Box 1615
Davis, CA 95617-1615
(916)753-3361
Fax: (916)753-0464
E-mail: infoag@houseag.com
Website: http://www.houseag.com/

3C Systems Co.
16161 Ventura Blvd., Ste. 815
Encino, CA 91436
(818)907-1302
Fax: (818)907-1357
E-mail: mark@3CSysCo.com
Website: http://www.3CSysCo.com

Technical Management Consultants
3624 Westfall Dr.
Encino, CA 91436-4154
(818)784-0626
Fax: (818)501-5575
E-mail: tmcrs@aol.com

RAINWATER-GISH & Associates, Business Finance & Development
317 3rd St., Ste. 3
Eureka, CA 95501
(707)443-0030
Fax: (707)443-5683

Global Tradelinks
451 Pebble Beach Pl.
Fullerton, CA 92835
(714)441-2280
Fax: (714)441-2281
E-mail: info@globaltradelinks.com
Website: http://www.globaltradelinks.com

Strategic Business Group
800 Cienaga Dr.
Fullerton, CA 92835-1248
(714)449-1040
Fax: (714)525-1631

Burnes Consulting
20537 Wolf Creek Rd.
Grass Valley, CA 95949
(530)346-8188
Free: 800-949-9021
Fax: (530)346-7704
E-mail: kent@burnesconsulting.com
Website: http://www.burnesconsulting.com

Pioneer Business Consultants
9042 Garfield Ave., Ste. 312
Huntington Beach, CA 92646
(714)964-7600

Beblie, Brandt & Jacobs Inc.
16 Technology, Ste. 164
Irvine, CA 92618
(714)450-8790
Fax: (714)450-8799
E-mail: darcy@bbjinc.com
Website: http://198.147.90.26

Fluor Daniel Inc.
3353 Michelson Dr.
Irvine, CA 92612-0650
(949)975-2000
Fax: (949)975-5271
E-mail: sales.consulting@fluordaniel.com
Website: http://www.fluordanielconsulting.com

MCS Associates
18300 Von Karman, Ste. 710
Irvine, CA 92612
(949)263-8700
Fax: (949)263-0770
E-mail: info@mcsassociates.com
Website: http://www.mcsassociates.com

Inspired Arts Inc.
4225 Executive Sq., Ste. 1160
La Jolla, CA 92037
(619)623-3525
Free: 800-851-4394
Fax: (619)623-3534
E-mail: info@inspiredarts.com
Website: http://www.inspiredarts.com

The Laresis Companies
PO Box 3284
La Jolla, CA 92038
(619)452-2720
Fax: (619)452-8744

RCL & Co.
PO Box 1143
737 Pearl St., Ste. 201
La Jolla, CA 92038
(619)454-8883
Fax: (619)454-8880

Comprehensive Business Services
3201 Lucas Cir.
Lafayette, CA 94549
(925)283-8272
Fax: (925)283-8272

The Ribble Group
27601 Forbes Rd., Ste. 52
Laguna Niguel, CA 92677

(714)582-1085
Fax: (714)582-6420
E-mail: ribble@deltanet.com

Norris Bernstein, CMC
9309 Marina Pacifica Dr. N
Long Beach, CA 90803
(562)493-5458
Fax: (562)493-5459
E-mail: norris@ctecomputer.com
Website: http://foodconsultants.com/
bernstein/

Horizon Consulting Services
1315 Garthwick Dr.
Los Altos, CA 94024
(415)967-0906
Fax: (415)967-0906

Brincko Associates Inc.
1801 Avenue of the Stars, Ste. 1054
Los Angeles, CA 90067
(310)553-4523
Fax: (310)553-6782

**Rubenstein/Justman Management
Consultants**
2049 Century Park E, 24th Fl.
Los Angeles, CA 90067
(310)282-0800
Fax: (310)282-0400
E-mail: info@rjmc.net
Website: http://www.rjmc.net

F.J. Schroeder & Associates
1926 Westholme Ave.
Los Angeles, CA 90025
(310)470-2655
Fax: (310)470-6378
E-mail: fjsacons@aol.com
Website: http://www.mcninet.com/
GlobalLook/Fjschroe.html

Western Management Associates
5959 W Century Blvd., Ste. 565
Los Angeles, CA 90045-6506
(310)645-1091
Free: (888)788-6534
Fax: (310)645-1092
E-mail: gene@cfoforrent.com
Website: http://www.cfoforrent.com

Darrell Sell and Associates
Los Gatos, CA 95030
(408)354-7794
E-mail: darrell@netcom.com

Leslie J. Zambo
3355 Michael Dr.
Marina, CA 93933
(408)384-7086

Fax: (408)647-4199
E-mail: 104776.1552@compuserve.com

Marketing Services Management
PO Box 1377
Martinez, CA 94553
(510)370-8527
Fax: (510)370-8527
E-mail: markserve@biotechnet.com

William M. Shine Consulting Service
PO Box 127
Moraga, CA 94556-0127
(510)376-6516

Palo Alto Management Group Inc.
2672 Bayshore Pky., Ste. 701
Mountain View, CA 94043
(415)968-4374
Fax: (415)968-4245
E-mail: mburwen@pamg.com

BizplanSource
1048 Irvine Ave., Ste. 621
Newport Beach, CA 92660
Free: 888-253-0974
Fax: 800-859-8254
E-mail: info@bizplansource.com
Website: http://www.bizplansource.com
Adam Greengrass, President

The Market Connection
4020 Birch St., Ste. 203
Newport Beach, CA 92660
(714)731-6273
Fax: (714)833-0253

Muller Associates
PO Box 7264
Newport Beach, CA 92658
(714)646-1169
Fax: (714)646-1169

International Health Resources
PO Box 329
North San Juan, CA 95960-0329
(530)292-1266
Fax: (530)292-1243
Website: http://www.futureof
healthcare.com

NEXUS - Consultants to Management
PO Box 1531
Novato, CA 94948
(415)897-4400
Fax: (415)898-2252
E-mail: jimnexus@aol.com

Aerospcace.Org
PO Box 28831
Oakland, CA 94604-8831

(510)530-9169
Fax: (510)530-3411
Website: http://www.aerospace.org

Intelequest Corp.
722 Gailen Ave.
Palo Alto, CA 94303
(415)968-3443
Fax: (415)493-6954
E-mail: frits@iqix.com

McLaughlin & Associates
66 San Marino Cir.
Rancho Mirage, CA 92270
(760)321-2932
Fax: (760)328-2474
E-mail: jackmcla@msn.com

**Carrera Consulting Group, a division
of Maximus**
2110 21st St., Ste. 400
Sacramento, CA 95818
(916)456-3300
Fax: (916)456-3306
E-mail: central@carreraconsulting.com
Website: http://www.carreraconsulting.com

**Bay Area Tax Consultants and Bayhill
Financial Consultants**
1150 Bayhill Dr., Ste. 1150
San Bruno, CA 94066-3004
(415)952-8786
Fax: (415)588-4524
E-mail: baytax@compuserve.com
Website: http://www.baytax.com/

AdCon Services, LLC
8871 Hillery Dr.
Dan Diego, CA 92126
(858)433-1411
E-mail: adam@adconservices.com
Website: http://www.adconservices.com
Adam Greengrass

California Business Incubation Network
101 W Broadway, No. 480
San Diego, CA 92101
(619)237-0559
Fax: (619)237-0521

G.R. Gordetsky Consultants Inc.
11414 Windy Summit Pl.
San Diego, CA 92127
(619)487-4939
Fax: (619)487-5587
E-mail: gordet@pacbell.net

Freeman, Sullivan & Co.
131 Steuart St., Ste. 500
San Francisco, CA 94105
(415)777-0707

Free: 800-777-0737
Fax: (415)777-2420
Website: http://www.fsc-research.com

Ideas Unlimited
2151 California St., Ste. 7
San Francisco, CA 94115
(415)931-0641
Fax: (415)931-0880

Russell Miller Inc.
300 Montgomery St., Ste. 900
San Francisco, CA 94104
(415)956-7474
Fax: (415)398-0620
E-mail: rmi@pacbell.net
Website: http://www.rmisf.com

PKF Consulting
425 California St., Ste. 1650
San Francisco, CA 94104
(415)421-5378
Fax: (415)956-7708
E-mail: callahan@pkfc.com
Website: http://www.pkfonline.com

Welling & Woodard Inc.
1067 Broadway
San Francisco, CA 94133
(415)776-4500
Fax: (415)776-5067

Highland Associates
16174 Highland Dr.
San Jose, CA 95127
(408)272-7008
Fax: (408)272-4040

ORDIS Inc.
6815 Trinidad Dr.
San Jose, CA 95120-2056
(408)268-3321
Free: 800-446-7347
Fax: (408)268-3582
E-mail: ordis@ordis.com
Website: http://www.ordis.com

Stanford Resources Inc.
20 Great Oaks Blvd., Ste. 200
San Jose, CA 95119
(408)360-8400
Fax: (408)360-8410
E-mail: sales@stanfordsources.com
Website: http://www.stanfordresources.com

Technology Properties Ltd. Inc.
PO Box 20250
San Jose, CA 95160
(408)243-9898
Fax: (408)296-6637
E-mail: sanjose@tplnet.com

Helfert Associates
1777 Borel Pl., Ste. 508
San Mateo, CA 94402-3514
(650)377-0540
Fax: (650)377-0472

Mykytyn Consulting Group Inc.
185 N Redwood Dr., Ste. 200
San Rafael, CA 94903
(415)491-1770
Fax: (415)491-1251
E-mail: info@mcgi.com
Website: http://www.mcgi.com

Omega Management Systems Inc.
3 Mount Darwin Ct.
San Rafael, CA 94903-1109
(415)499-1300
Fax: (415)492-9490
E-mail: omegamgt@ix.netcom.com

The Information Group Inc.
4675 Stevens Creek Blvd., Ste. 100
Santa Clara, CA 95051
(408)985-7877
Fax: (408)985-2945
E-mail: dvincent@tig-usa.com
Website: http://www.tig-usa.com

Cast Management Consultants
1620 26th St., Ste. 2040N
Santa Monica, CA 90404
(310)828-7511
Fax: (310)453-6831

Cuma Consulting Management
Box 724
Santa Rosa, CA 95402
(707)785-2477
Fax: (707)785-2478

The E-Myth Academy
131B Stony Cir., Ste. 2000
Santa Rosa, CA 95401
(707)569-5600
Free: 800-221-0266
Fax: (707)569-5700
E-mail: info@e-myth.com
Website: http://www.e-myth.com

Reilly, Connors & Ray
1743 Canyon Rd.
Spring Valley, CA 91977
(619)698-4808
Fax: (619)460-3892
E-mail: davidray@adnc.com

Management Consultants
Sunnyvale, CA 94087-4700
(408)773-0321

RJR Associates
1639 Lewiston Dr.
Sunnyvale, CA 94087
(408)737-7720
E-mail: bobroy@rjrassoc.com
Website: http://www.rjrassoc.com

Schwafel Associates
333 Cobalt Way, Ste. 21
Sunnyvale, CA 94085
(408)720-0649
Fax: (408)720-1796
E-mail: schwafel@ricochet.net
Website: http://www.patca.org

Staubs Business Services
23320 S Vermont Ave.
Torrance, CA 90502-2940
(310)830-9128
Fax: (310)830-9128
E-mail: Harry_L_Staubs@Lamg.com

Out of Your Mind...and Into the Marketplace
13381 White Sands Dr.
Tustin, CA 92780-4565
(714)544-0248
Free: 800-419-1513
Fax: (714)730-1414
E-mail: lpinson@aol.com
Website: http://www.business-plan.com

Independent Research Services
PO Box 2426
Van Nuys, CA 91404-2426
(818)993-3622

Ingman Company Inc.
7949 Woodley Ave., Ste. 120
Van Nuys, CA 91406-1232
(818)375-5027
Fax: (818)894-5001

Innovative Technology Associates
3639 E Harbor Blvd., Ste. 203E
Ventura, CA 93001
(805)650-9353

Grid Technology Associates
20404 Tufts Cir.
Walnut, CA 91789
(909)444-0922
Fax: (909)444-0922
E-mail: grid_technology@msn.com

Ridge Consultants Inc.
100 Pringle Ave., Ste. 580
Walnut Creek, CA 94596
(925)274-1990
Fax: (510)274-1956
E-mail: info@ridgecon.com
Website: http://www.ridgecon.com

Bell Springs Publishing
PO Box 1240
Willits, CA 95490
(707)459-6372
E-mail: bellsprings@sabernet
Website: http://www.bellsprings.com

Hutchinson Consulting and Appraisal
23245 Sylvan St., Ste. 103
Woodland Hills, CA 91367
(818)888-8175
Free: 800-977-7548
Fax: (818)888-8220
E-mail: r.f.hutchinson-cpa@worldnet.att.net

Colorado

Sam Boyer & Associates
4255 S Buckley Rd., No. 136
Aurora, CO 80013
Free: 800-785-0485
Fax: (303)766-8740
E-mail: samboyer@samboyer.com
Website: http://www.samboyer.com/

Ameriwest Business Consultants Inc.
PO Box 26266
Colorado Springs, CO 80936
(719)380-7096
Fax: (719)380-7096
E-mail: email@abchelp.com
Website: http://www.abchelp.com

GVNW Consulting Inc.
2270 La Montana Way
Colorado Springs, CO 80936
(719)594-5800
Fax: (719)594-5803
Website: http://www.gvnw.com

M-Squared Inc.
755 San Gabriel Pl.
Colorado Springs, CO 80906
(719)576-2554
Fax: (719)576-2554

Thornton Financial FNIC
1024 Centre Ave., Bldg. E
Fort Collins, CO 80526-1849
(970)221-2089
Fax: (970)484-5206

TenEyck Associates
1760 Cherryville Rd.
Greenwood Village, CO 80121-1503
(303)758-6129
Fax: (303)761-8286

Associated Enterprises Ltd.
13050 W Ceder Dr., Unit 11
Lakewood, CO 80228

(303)988-6695
Fax: (303)988-6739
E-mail: ael1@classic.msn.com

The Vincent Company Inc.
200 Union Blvd., Ste. 210
Lakewood, CO 80228
(303)989-7271
Free: 800-274-0733
Fax: (303)989-7570
E-mail: vincent@vincentco.com
Website: http://www.vincentco.com

Johnson & West Management Consultants Inc.
7612 S Logan Dr.
Littleton, CO 80122
(303)730-2810
Fax: (303)730-3219

Western Capital Holdings Inc.
10050 E Applwood Dr.
Parker, CO 80138
(303)841-1022
Fax: (303)770-1945

Connecticut

Stratman Group Inc.
40 Tower Ln.
Avon, CT 06001-4222
(860)677-2898
Free: 800-551-0499
Fax: (860)677-8210

Cowherd Consulting Group Inc.
106 Stephen Mather Rd.
Darien, CT 06820
(203)655-2150
Fax: (203)655-6427

Greenwich Associates
8 Greenwich Office Park
Greenwich, CT 06831-5149
(203)629-1200
Fax: (203)629-1229
E-mail: lisa@greenwich.com
Website: http://www.greenwich.com

Follow-up News
185 Pine St., Ste. 818
Manchester, CT 06040
(860)647-7542
Free: 800-708-0696
Fax: (860)646-6544
E-mail: Followupnews@aol.com

Lovins & Associates Consulting
309 Edwards St.
New Haven, CT 06511
(203)787-3367

Fax: (203)624-7599
E-mail: Alovinsphd@aol.com
Website: http://www.lovinsgroup.com

JC Ventures Inc.
4 Arnold St.
Old Greenwich, CT 06870-1203
(203)698-1990
Free: 800-698-1997
Fax: (203)698-2638

Charles L. Hornung Associates
52 Ned's Mountain Rd.
Ridgefield, CT 06877
(203)431-0297

Manus
100 Prospect St., S Tower
Stamford, CT 06901
(203)326-3880
Free: 800-445-0942
Fax: (203)326-3890
E-mail: manus1@aol.com
Website: http://www.RightManus.com

RealBusinessPlans.com
156 Westport Rd.
Wilton, CT 06897
(914)837-2886
E-mail: ct@realbusinessplans.com
Website: http://www.RealBusinessPlans.com
Tony Tecce

Delaware

Focus Marketing
61-7 Habor Dr.
Claymont, DE 19703
(302)793-3064

Daedalus Ventures Ltd.
PO Box 1474
Hockessin, DE 19707
(302)239-6758
Fax: (302)239-9991
E-mail: daedalus@mail.del.net

The Formula Group
PO Box 866
Hockessin, DE 19707
(302)456-0952
Fax: (302)456-1354
E-mail: formula@netaxs.com

Selden Enterprises Inc.
2502 Silverside Rd., Ste. 1
Wilmington, DE 19810-3740
(302)529-7113
Fax: (302)529-7442
E-mail: selden2@bellatlantic.net
Website: http://www.seldenenterprises.com

District of Columbia

Bruce W. McGee and Associates
7826 Eastern Ave. NW, Ste. 30
Washington, DC 20012
(202)726-7272
Fax: (202)726-2946

McManis Associates Inc.
1900 K St. NW, Ste. 700
Washington, DC 20006
(202)466-7680
Fax: (202)872-1898
Website: http://www.mcmanis-mmi.com

Smith, Dawson & Andrews Inc.
1000 Connecticut Ave., Ste. 302
Washington, DC 20036
(202)835-0740
Fax: (202)775-8526
E-mail: webmaster@sda-inc.com
Website: http://www.sda-inc.com

Florida

BackBone, Inc.
20404 Hacienda Court
Boca Raton, FL 33498
(561)470-0965
Fax: 516-908-4038
E-mail: BPlans@backboneinc.com
Website: http://www.backboneinc.com
Charles Epstein, President

Whalen & Associates Inc.
4255 Northwest 26 Ct.
Boca Raton, FL 33434
(561)241-5950
Fax: (561)241-7414
E-mail: drwhalen@ix.netcom.com

E.N. Rysso & Associates
180 Bermuda Petrel Ct.
Daytona Beach, FL 32119
(386)760-3028
E-mail: erysso@aol.com

Virtual Technocrats LLC
560 Lavers Circle, #146
Delray Beach, FL 33444
(561)265-3509
E-mail: josh@virtualtechnocrats.com;
info@virtualtechnocrats.com
Website: http://www.virtualtechnocrats.
com
Josh Eikov, Managing Director

Eric Sands Consulting Services
6193 Rock Island Rd., Ste. 412
Fort Lauderdale, FL 33319
(954)721-4767

Fax: (954)720-2815
E-mail: easands@aol.com
Website: http://www.ericsandsconsultig.com

Professional Planning Associates, Inc.
1975 E. Sunrise Blvd. Suite 607
Fort Lauderdale, FL 33304
(954)764-5204
Fax: 954-463-4172
E-mail: Mgoldstein@proplana.com
Website: http://proplana.com
Michael Goldstein, President

Host Media Corp.
3948 S 3rd St., Ste. 191
Jacksonville Beach, FL 32250
(904)285-3239
Fax: (904)285-5618
E-mail: msconsulting@compuserve.com
Website: http://www.media
servicesgroup.com

William V. Hall
1925 Brickell, Ste. D-701
Miami, FL 33129
(305)856-9622
Fax: (305)856-4113
E-mail: williamvhall@compuserve.com

F.A. McGee Inc.
800 Claughton Island Dr., Ste. 401
Miami, FL 33131
(305)377-9123

Taxplan Inc.
Mirasol International Ctr.
2699 Collins Ave.
Miami Beach, FL 33140
(305)538-3303

T.C. Brown & Associates
8415 Excalibur Cir., Apt. B1
Naples, FL 34108
(941)594-1949
Fax: (941)594-0611
E-mail: tcater@naples.net.com

RLA International Consulting
713 Lagoon Dr.
North Palm Beach, FL 33408
(407)626-4258
Fax: (407)626-5772

Comprehensive Franchising Inc.
2465 Ridgecrest Ave.
Orange Park, FL 32065
(904)272-6567
Free: 800-321-6567
Fax: (904)272-6750
E-mail: theimp@cris.com
Website: http://www.franchise411.com

Hunter G. Jackson Jr. - Consulting Environmental Physicist
PO Box 618272
Orlando, FL 32861-8272
(407)295-4188
E-mail: hunterjackson@juno.com

F. Newton Parks
210 El Brillo Way
Palm Beach, FL 33480
(561)833-1727
Fax: (561)833-4541

Avery Business Development Services
2506 St. Michel Ct.
Ponte Vedra Beach, FL 32082
(904)285-6033
Fax: (904)285-6033

Strategic Business Planning Co.
PO Box 821006
South Florida, FL 33082-1006
(954)704-9100
Fax: (954)438-7333
E-mail: info@bizplan.com
Website: http://www.bizplan.com

Dufresne Consulting Group Inc.
10014 N Dale Mabry, Ste. 101
Tampa, FL 33618-4426
(813)264-4775
Fax: (813)264-9300
Website: http://www.dcgconsult.com

Agrippa Enterprises Inc.
PO Box 175
Venice, FL 34284-0175
(941)355-7876
E-mail: webservices@agrippa.com
Website: http://www.agrippa.com

Center for Simplified Strategic Planning Inc.
PO Box 3324
Vero Beach, FL 32964-3324
(561)231-3636
Fax: (561)231-1099
Website: http://www.cssp.com

Georgia

Marketing Spectrum Inc.
115 Perimeter Pl., Ste. 440
Atlanta, GA 30346
(770)395-7244
Fax: (770)393-4071

Business Ventures Corp.
1650 Oakbrook Dr., Ste. 405
Norcross, GA 30093
(770)729-8000
Fax: (770)729-8028

Informed Decisions Inc.
100 Falling Cheek
Sautee Nacoochee, GA 30571
(706)878-1905
Fax: (706)878-1802
E-mail: skylake@compuserve.com

Tom C. Davis & Associates, P.C.
3189 Perimeter Rd.
Valdosta, GA 31602
(912)247-9801
Fax: (912)244-7704
E-mail: mail@tcdcpa.com
Website: http://www.tcdcpa.com/

Illinois

TWD and Associates
431 S Patton
Arlington Heights, IL 60005
(847)398-6410
Fax: (847)255-5095
E-mail: tdoo@aol.com

Management Planning Associates Inc.
2275 Half Day Rd., Ste. 350
Bannockburn, IL 60015-1277
(847)945-2421
Fax: (847)945-2425

Phil Faris Associates
86 Old Mill Ct.
Barrington, IL 60010
(847)382-4888
Fax: (847)382-4890
E-mail: pfaris@meginsnet.net

Seven Continents Technology
787 Stonebridge
Buffalo Grove, IL 60089
(708)577-9653
Fax: (708)870-1220

Grubb & Blue Inc.
2404 Windsor Pl.
Champaign, IL 61820
(217)366-0052
Fax: (217)356-0117

ACE Accounting Service Inc.
3128 N Bernard St.
Chicago, IL 60618
(773)463-7854
Fax: (773)463-7854

AON Consulting Worldwide
200 E Randolph St., 10th Fl.
Chicago, IL 60601
(312)381-4800
Free: 800-438-6487
Fax: (312)381-0240
Website: http://www.aon.com

FMS Consultants
5801 N Sheridan Rd., Ste. 3D
Chicago, IL 60660
(773)561-7362
Fax: (773)561-6274

Grant Thornton
800 1 Prudential Plz.
130 E Randolph St.
Chicago, IL 60601
(312)856-0001
Fax: (312)861-1340
E-mail: gtinfo@gt.com
Website: http://www.grantthornton.com

Kingsbury International Ltd.
5341 N Glenwood Ave.
Chicago, IL 60640
(773)271-3030
Fax: (773)728-7080
E-mail: jetlag@mcs.com
Website: http://www.kingbiz.com

MacDougall & Blake Inc.
1414 N Wells St., Ste. 311
Chicago, IL 60610-1306
(312)587-3330
Fax: (312)587-3699
E-mail: jblake@compuserve.com

James C. Osburn Ltd.
6445 N. Western Ave., Ste. 304
Chicago, IL 60645
(773)262-4428
Fax: (773)262-6755
E-mail: osburnltd@aol.com

Tarifero & Tazewell Inc.
211 S Clark
Chicago, IL 60690
(312)665-9714
Fax: (312)665-9716

Human Energy Design Systems
620 Roosevelt Dr.
Edwardsville, IL 62025
(618)692-0258
Fax: (618)692-0819

China Business Consultants Group
931 Dakota Cir.
Naperville, IL 60563
(630)778-7992
Fax: (630)778-7915
E-mail: cbcq@aol.com

Center for Workforce Effectiveness
500 Skokie Blvd., Ste. 222
Northbrook, IL 60062
(847)559-8777
Fax: (847)559-8778

E-mail: office@cwelink.com
Website: http://www.cwelink.com

Smith Associates
1320 White Mountain Dr.
Northbrook, IL 60062
(847)480-7200
Fax: (847)480-9828

Francorp Inc.
20200 Governors Dr.
Olympia Fields, IL 60461
(708)481-2900
Free: 800-372-6244
Fax: (708)481-5885
E-mail: francorp@aol.com
Website: http://www.francorpinc.com

Camber Business Strategy Consultants
1010 S Plum Tree Ct
Palatine, IL 60078-0986
(847)202-0101
Fax: (847)705-7510
E-mail: camber@ameritech.net

Partec Enterprise Group
5202 Keith Dr.
Richton Park, IL 60471
(708)503-4047
Fax: (708)503-9468

Rockford Consulting Group Ltd.
Century Plz., Ste. 206
7210 E State St.
Rockford, IL 61108
(815)229-2900
Free: 800-667-7495
Fax: (815)229-2612
E-mail: rligus@RockfordConsulting.com
Website: http://www.Rockford
Consulting.com

RSM McGladrey Inc.
1699 E Woodfield Rd., Ste. 300
Schaumburg, IL 60173-4969
(847)413-6900
Fax: (847)517-7067
Website: http://www.rsmmcgladrey.com

A.D. Star Consulting
320 Euclid
Winnetka, IL 60093
(847)446-7827
Fax: (847)446-7827
E-mail: startwo@worldnet.att.net

Indiana

Modular Consultants Inc.
3109 Crabtree Ln.
Elkhart, IN 46514

(219)264-5761
Fax: (219)264-5761
E-mail: sasabo5313@aol.com

Midwest Marketing Research
PO Box 1077
Goshen, IN 46527
(219)533-0548
Fax: (219)533-0540
E-mail: 103365.654@compuserve

Ketchum Consulting Group
8021 Knue Rd., Ste. 112
Indianapolis, IN 46250
(317)845-5411
Fax: (317)842-9941

**MDI Management
Consulting**
1519 Park Dr.
Munster, IN 46321
(219)838-7909
Fax: (219)838-7909

Iowa

McCord Consulting Group Inc.
4533 Pine View Dr. NE
PO Box 11024
Cedar Rapids, IA 52410
(319)378-0077
Fax: (319)378-1577
E-mail: smmccord@hom.com
Website: http://www.mccordgroup.com

Management Solutions L.C.
3815 Lincoln Pl. Dr.
Des Moines, IA 50312
(515)277-6408
Fax: (515)277-3506
E-mail: wasunimers@uswest.net

Grandview Marketing
15 Red Bridge Dr.
Sioux City, IA 51104
(712)239-3122
Fax: (712)258-7578
E-mail: eandrews@pionet.net

Kansas

Assessments in Action
513A N Mur-Len
Olathe, KS 66062
(913)764-6270
Free: (888)548-1504
Fax: (913)764-6495
E-mail: lowdene@qni.com
Website: http://www.assessments-
in-action.com

Maine

Edgemont Enterprises
PO Box 8354
Portland, ME 04104
(207)871-8964
Fax: (207)871-8964

Pan Atlantic Consultants
5 Milk St.
Portland, ME 04101
(207)871-8622
Fax: (207)772-4842
E-mail: pmurphy@maine.rr.com
Website: http://www.panatlantic.net

Maryland

Clemons & Associates Inc.
5024-R Campbell Blvd.
Baltimore, MD 21236
(410)931-8100
Fax: (410)931-8111
E-mail: info@clemonsmgmt.com
Website: http://www.clemonsmgmt.com

Imperial Group Ltd.
305 Washington Ave., Ste. 204
Baltimore, MD 21204-6009
(410)337-8500
Fax: (410)337-7641

Leadership Institute
3831 Yolando Rd.
Baltimore, MD 21218
(410)366-9111
Fax: (410)243-8478
E-mail: behconsult@aol.com

Burdeshaw Associates Ltd.
4701 Sangamore Rd.
Bethesda, MD 20816-2508
(301)229-5800
Fax: (301)229-5045
E-mail: jstacy@burdeshaw.com
Website: http://www.burdeshaw.com

Michael E. Cohen
5225 Pooks Hill Rd., Ste. 1119 S
Bethesda, MD 20814
(301)530-5738
Fax: (301)530-2988
E-mail: mecohen@crosslink.net

World Development Group Inc.
5272 River Rd., Ste. 650
Bethesda, MD 20816-1405
(301)652-1818
Fax: (301)652-1250
E-mail: wdg@has.com
Website: http://www.worlddg.com

Swartz Consulting
PO Box 4301
Crofton, MD 21114-4301
(301)262-6728

Software Solutions International Inc.
9633 Duffer Way
Gaithersburg, MD 20886
(301)330-4136
Fax: (301)330-4136

Strategies Inc.
8 Park Center Ct., Ste. 200
Owings Mills, MD 21117
(410)363-6669
Fax: (410)363-1231
E-mail: strategies@strat1.com
Website: http://www.strat1.com

Hammer Marketing Resources
179 Inverness Rd.
Severna Park, MD 21146
(410)544-9191
Fax: (305)675-3277
E-mail: info@gohammer.com
Website: http://www.gohammer.com

Andrew Sussman & Associates
13731 Kretsinger
Smithsburg, MD 21783
(301)824-2943
Fax: (301)824-2943

Massachusetts

Geibel Marketing and Public Relations
PO Box 611
Belmont, MA 02478-0005
(617)484-8285
Fax: (617)489-3567
E-mail: jgeibel@geibelpr.com
Website: http://www.geibelpr.com

Bain & Co.
2 Copley Pl.
Boston, MA 02116
(617)572-2000
Fax: (617)572-2427
E-mail: corporate.inquiries@bain.com
Website: http://www.bain.com

Mehr & Co.
62 Kinnaird St.
Cambridge, MA 02139
(617)876-3311
Fax: (617)876-3023
E-mail: mehrco@aol.com

Monitor Company Inc.
2 Canal Park
Cambridge, MA 02141

(617)252-2000
Fax: (617)252-2100
Website: http://www.monitor.com

Information & Research Associates
PO Box 3121
Framingham, MA 01701
(508)788-0784

Walden Consultants Ltd.
252 Pond St.
Hopkinton, MA 01748
(508)435-4882
Fax: (508)435-3971
Website: http://www.waldencon
sultants.com

Jeffrey D. Marshall
102 Mitchell Rd.
Ipswich, MA 01938-1219
(508)356-1113
Fax: (508)356-2989

Consulting Resources Corp.
6 Northbrook Park
Lexington, MA 02420
(781)863-1222
Fax: (781)863-1441
E-mail: res@consultingresources.net
Website: http://www.consulting
resources.net

Planning Technologies Group L.L.C.
92 Hayden Ave.
Lexington, MA 02421
(781)778-4678
Fax: (781)861-1099
E-mail: ptg@plantech.com
Website: http://www.plantech.com

Kalba International Inc.
23 Sandy Pond Rd.
Lincoln, MA 01773
(781)259-9589
Fax: (781)259-1460
E-mail: info@kalbainternational.com
Website: http://www.kalbainter
national.com

VMB Associates Inc.
115 Ashland St.
Melrose, MA 02176
(781)665-0623
Fax: (425)732-7142
E-mail: vmbinc@aol.com

The Company Doctor
14 Pudding Stone Ln.
Mendon, MA 01756
(508)478-1747
Fax: (508)478-0520

Data and Strategies Group Inc.
190 N Main St.
Natick, MA 01760
(508)653-9990
Fax: (508)653-7799
E-mail: dsginc@dsggroup.com
Website: http://www.dsggroup.com

The Enterprise Group
73 Parker Rd.
Needham, MA 02494
(617)444-6631
Fax: (617)433-9991
E-mail: lsacco@world.std.com
Website: http://www.enterprise-group.com

PSMJ Resources Inc.
10 Midland Ave.
Newton, MA 02458
(617)965-0055
Free: 800-537-7765
Fax: (617)965-5152
E-mail: psmj@tiac.net
Website: http://www.psmj.com

Scheur Management Group Inc.
255 Washington St., Ste. 100
Newton, MA 02458-1611
(617)969-7500
Fax: (617)969-7508
E-mail: smgnow@scheur.com
Website: http://www.scheur.com

I.E.E.E., Boston Section
240 Bear Hill Rd., 202B
Waltham, MA 02451-1017
(781)890-5294
Fax: (781)890-5290

Business Planning and Consulting Services
20 Beechwood Ter.
Wellesley, MA 02482
(617)237-9151
Fax: (617)237-9151

Michigan

Walter Frederick Consulting
1719 South Blvd.
Ann Arbor, MI 48104
(313)662-4336
Fax: (313)769-7505

Fox Enterprises
6220 W Freeland Rd.
Freeland, MI 48623
(517)695-9170
Fax: (517)695-9174
E-mail: foxjw@concentric.net
Website: http://www.cris.com/~foxjw

G.G.W. and Associates
1213 Hampton
Jackson, MI 49203
(517)782-2255
Fax: (517)782-2255

Altamar Group Ltd.
6810 S Cedar, Ste. 2-B
Lansing, MI 48911
(517)694-0910
Free: 800-443-2627
Fax: (517)694-1377

Sheffieck Consultants Inc.
23610 Greening Dr.
Novi, MI 48375-3130
(248)347-3545
Fax: (248)347-3530
E-mail: cfsheff@concentric.net

Rehmann, Robson PC
5800 Gratiot
Saginaw, MI 48605
(517)799-9580
Fax: (517)799-0227
Website: http://www.rrpc.com

Francis & Co.
17200 W 10 Mile Rd., Ste. 207
Southfield, MI 48075
(248)559-7600
Fax: (248)559-5249

Private Ventures Inc.
16000 W 9 Mile Rd., Ste. 504
Southfield, MI 48075
(248)569-1977
Free: 800-448-7614
Fax: (248)569-1838
E-mail: pventuresi@aol.com

JGK Associates
14464 Kerner Dr.
Sterling Heights, MI 48313
(810)247-9055
Fax: (248)822-4977
E-mail: kozlowski@home.com

Minnesota

Health Fitness Corp.
3500 W 80th St., Ste. 130
Bloomington, MN 55431
(612)831-6830
Fax: (612)831-7264

Consatech Inc.
PO Box 1047
Burnsville, MN 55337
(612)953-1088
Fax: (612)435-2966

Robert F. Knotek
14960 Ironwood Ct.
Eden Prairie, MN 55346
(612)949-2875

DRI Consulting
7715 Stonewood Ct.
Edina, MN 55439
(612)941-9656
Fax: (612)941-2693
E-mail: dric@dric.com
Website: http://www.dric.com

Markin Consulting
12072 87th Pl. N
Maple Grove, MN 55369
(612)493-3568
Fax: (612)493-5744
E-mail: markin@markinconsulting.com
Website: http://www.markin
consulting.com

**Minnesota Cooperation Office for
Small Business & Job Creation Inc.**
5001 W 80th St., Ste. 825
Minneapolis, MN 55437
(612)830-1230
Fax: (612)830-1232
E-mail: mncoop@msn.com
Website: http://www.mnco.org

Enterprise Consulting Inc.
PO Box 1111
Minnetonka, MN 55345
(612)949-5909
Fax: (612)906-3965

Amdahl International
724 1st Ave. SW
Rochester, MN 55902
(507)252-0402
Fax: (507)252-0402
E-mail: amdahl@best-service.com
Website: http://www.wp.com/amdahl_int

Power Systems Research
1365 Corporate Center Curve, 2nd Fl.
St. Paul, MN 55121
(612)905-8400
Free: (888)625-8612
Fax: (612)454-0760
E-mail: Barb@Powersys.com
Website: http://www.powersys.com

Missouri

**Business Planning and Development
Corp.**
4030 Charlotte St.
Kansas City, MO 64110
(816)753-0495

E-mail: humph@bpdev.demon.co.uk
Website: http://www.bpdev.demon.co.uk

CFO Service
10336 Donoho
St. Louis, MO 63131
(314)750-2940
E-mail: jskae@cfoservice.com
Website: http://www.cfoservice.com

Nebraska

**International Management Consulting
Group Inc.**
1309 Harlan Dr., Ste. 205
Bellevue, NE 68005
(402)291-4545
Free: 800-665-IMCG
Fax: (402)291-4343
E-mail: imcg@neonramp.com
Website: http://www.mgtcon
sulting.com

**Heartland Management Consulting
Group**
1904 Barrington Pky.
Papillion, NE 68046
(402)339-2387
Fax: (402)339-1319

Nevada

The DuBois Group
865 Tahoe Blvd., Ste. 108
Incline Village, NV 89451
(775)832-0550
Free: 800-375-2935
Fax: (775)832-0556
E-mail: DuBoisGrp@aol.com

New Hampshire

Wolff Consultants
10 Buck Rd.
Hanover, NH 03755
(603)643-6015

BPT Consulting Associates Ltd.
12 Parmenter Rd., Ste. B-6
Londonderry, NH 03053
(603)437-8484
Free: (888)278-0030
Fax: (603)434-5388
E-mail: bptcons@tiac.net
Website: http://www.bptconsulting.com

New Jersey

Bedminster Group Inc.
1170 Rte. 22 E
Bridgewater, NJ 08807

(908)500-4155
Fax: (908)766-0780
E-mail: info@bedminstergroup.com
Website: http://www.bedminster
group.com
Fax: (202)806-1777
Terry Strong, Acting Regional Dir.

Delta Planning Inc.
PO Box 425
Denville, NJ 07834
(913)625-1742
Free: 800-672-0762
Fax: (973)625-3531
E-mail: DeltaP@worldnet.att.net
Website: http://deltaplanning.com

Kumar Associates Inc.
1004 Cumbermeade Rd.
Fort Lee, NJ 07024
(201)224-9480
Fax: (201)585-2343
E-mail: mail@kumarassociates.com
Website: http://kumarassociates.com

John Hall & Company Inc.
PO Box 187
Glen Ridge, NJ 07028
(973)680-4449
Fax: (973)680-4581
E-mail: jhcompany@aol.com

Market Focus
PO Box 402
Maplewood, NJ 07040
(973)378-2470
Fax: (973)378-2470
E-mail: mcss66@marketfocus.com

Vanguard Communications Corp.
100 American Rd.
Morris Plains, NJ 07950
(973)605-8000
Fax: (973)605-8329
Website: http://www.vanguard.net/

ConMar International Ltd.
1901 US Hwy. 130
North Brunswick, NJ 08902
(732)940-8347
Fax: (732)274-1199

KLW New Products
156 Cedar Dr.
Old Tappan, NJ 07675
(201)358-1300
Fax: (201)664-2594
E-mail: lrlarsen@usa.net
Website: http://www.klwnew
products.com

ORGANIZATIONS, AGENCIES, & CONSULTANTS

PA Consulting Group
315A Enterprise Dr.
Plainsboro, NJ 08536
(609)936-8300
Fax: (609)936-8811
E-mail: info@paconsulting.com
Website: http://www.pa-consulting.com

Aurora Marketing Management Inc.
66 Witherspoon St., Ste. 600
Princeton, NJ 08542
(908)904-1125
Fax: (908)359-1108
E-mail: aurora2@voicenet.com
Website: http://www.auroramarketing.net

Smart Business Supersite
88 Orchard Rd., CN-5219
Princeton, NJ 08543
(908)321-1924
Fax: (908)321-5156
E-mail: irv@smartbiz.com
Website: http://www.smartbiz.com

Tracelin Associates
1171 Main St., Ste. 6K
Rahway, NJ 07065
(732)381-3288

Schkeeper Inc.
130-6 Bodman Pl.
Red Bank, NJ 07701
(732)219-1965
Fax: (732)530-3703

Henry Branch Associates
2502 Harmon Cove Twr.
Secaucus, NJ 07094
(201)866-2008
Fax: (201)601-0101
E-mail: hbranch161@home.com

Robert Gibbons & Company Inc.
46 Knoll Rd.
Tenafly, NJ 07670-1050
(201)871-3933
Fax: (201)871-2173
E-mail: crisisbob@aol.com

PMC Management Consultants Inc.
6 Thistle Ln.
Three Bridges, NJ 08887-0332
(908)788-1014
Free: 800-PMC-0250
Fax: (908)806-7287
E-mail: int@pmc-management.com
Website: http://www.pmc-management.com

R.W. Bankart & Associates
20 Valley Ave., Ste. D-2

Westwood, NJ 07675-3607
(201)664-7672

New Mexico

Vondle & Associates Inc.
4926 Calle de Tierra, NE
Albuquerque, NM 87111
(505)292-8961
Fax: (505)296-2790
E-mail: vondle@aol.com

InfoNewMexico
2207 Black Hills Rd., NE
Rio Rancho, NM 87124
(505)891-2462
Fax: (505)896-8971

New York

Powers Research and Training Institute
PO Box 78
Bayville, NY 11709
(516)628-2250
Fax: (516)628-2252
E-mail: powercocch@compuserve.com
Website: http://www.nancypowers.com

Consortium House
296 Wittenberg Rd.
Bearsville, NY 12409
(845)679-8867
Fax: (845)679-9248
E-mail: eugenegs@aol.com
Website: http://www.chpub.com

Progressive Finance Corp.
3549 Tiemann Ave.
Bronx, NY 10469
(718)405-9029
Free: 800-225-8381
Fax: (718)405-1170

Wave Hill Associates Inc.
2621 Palisade Ave., Ste. 15-C
Bronx, NY 10463
(718)549-7368
Fax: (718)601-9670
E-mail: pepper@compuserve.com

Management Insight
96 Arlington Rd.
Buffalo, NY 14221
(716)631-3319
Fax: (716)631-0203
E-mail: michalski@foodservice insight.com
Website: http://www.foodservice insight.com

Samani International Enterprises, Marions Panyaught Consultancy
2028 Parsons
Flushing, NY 11357-3436
(917)287-8087
Fax: 800-873-8939
E-mail: vjp2@biostrategist.com
Website: http://www.biostrategist.com

Marketing Resources Group
71-58 Austin St.
Forest Hills, NY 11375
(718)261-8882

Mangabay Business Plans & Development Subsidiary of Innis Asset Allocation
125-10 Queens Blvd., Ste. 2202
Kew Gardens, NY 11415
(905)527-1947
Fax: 509-472-1935
E-mail: mangabay@mangabay.com
Website: http://www.mangabay.com
Lee Toh, Managing Partner

ComputerEase Co.
1301 Monmouth Ave.
Lakewood, NY 08701
(212)406-9464
Fax: (914)277-5317
E-mail: crawfordc@juno.com

Boice Dunham Group
30 W 13th St.
New York, NY 10011
(212)924-2200
Fax: (212)924-1108

Elizabeth Capen
27 E 95th St.
New York, NY 10128
(212)427-7654
Fax: (212)876-3190

Haver Analytics
60 E 42nd St., Ste. 2424
New York, NY 10017
(212)986-9300
Fax: (212)986-5857
E-mail: data@haver.com
Website: http://www.haver.com

The Jordan, Edmiston Group Inc.
150 E 52nd Ave., 18th Fl.
New York, NY 10022
(212)754-0710
Fax: (212)754-0337

KPMG International
345 Park Ave.
New York, NY 10154-0102
(212)758-9700

Fax: (212)758-9819
Website: http://www.kpmg.com

Mahoney Cohen Consulting Corp.
111 W 40th St., 12th Fl.
New York, NY 10018
(212)490-8000
Fax: (212)790-5913

Management Practice Inc.
342 Madison Ave.
New York, NY 10173-1230
(212)867-7948
Fax: (212)972-5188
Website: http://www.mpiweb.com

Moseley Associates Inc.
342 Madison Ave., Ste. 1414
New York, NY 10016
(212)213-6673
Fax: (212)687-1520

Practice Development Counsel
60 Sutton Pl. S
New York, NY 10022
(212)593-1549
Fax: (212)980-7940
E-mail: pwhaserot@pdcounsel.com
Website: http://www.pdcounsel.com

Unique Value International Inc.
575 Madison Ave., 10th Fl.
New York, NY 10022-1304
(212)605-0590
Fax: (212)605-0589

The Van Tulleken Co.
126 E 56th St.
New York, NY 10022
(212)355-1390
Fax: (212)755-3061
E-mail: newyork@vantulleken.com

Vencon Management Inc.
301 W 53rd St.
New York, NY 10019
(212)581-8787
Fax: (212)397-4126
Website: http://www.venconinc.com

Werner International Inc.
55 E 52nd, 29th Fl.
New York, NY 10055
(212)909-1260
Fax: (212)909-1273
E-mail: richard.downing@rgh.com
Website: http://www.wernertex.com

Zimmerman Business Consulting Inc.
44 E 92nd St., Ste. 5-B
New York, NY 10128

(212)860-3107
Fax: (212)860-7730
E-mail: ljzzbci@aol.com
Website: http://www.zbcinc.com

Overton Financial
7 Allen Rd.
Peekskill, NY 10566
(914)737-4649
Fax: (914)737-4696

Stromberg Consulting
2500 Westchester Ave.
Purchase, NY 10577
(914)251-1515
Fax: (914)251-1562
E-mail: strategy@stromberg_consul
ting.com
Website: http://www.stromberg_
consulting.com

Innovation Management Consulting Inc.
209 Dewitt Rd.
Syracuse, NY 13214-2006
(315)425-5144
Fax: (315)445-8989
E-mail: missonneb@axess.net

M. Clifford Agress
891 Fulton St.
Valley Stream, NY 11580
(516)825-8955
Fax: (516)825-8955

Destiny Kinal Marketing Consultancy
105 Chemung St.
Waverly, NY 14892
(607)565-8317
Fax: (607)565-4083

Valutis Consulting Inc.
5350 Main St., Ste. 7
Williamsville, NY 14221-5338
(716)634-2553
Fax: (716)634-2554
E-mail: valutis@localnet.com
Website: http://www.valutisconsulting.com

North Carolina

Best Practices L.L.C.
6320 Quadrangle Dr., Ste. 200
Chapel Hill, NC 27514
(919)403-0251
Fax: (919)403-0144
E-mail: best@best:in/class
Website: http://www.best-in-class.com

Norelli & Co.
Bank of America Corporate Ctr.
100 N Tyron St., Ste. 5160

Charlotte, NC 28202-4000
(704)376-5484
Fax: (704)376-5485
E-mail: consult@norelli.com
Website: http://www.norelli.com

North Dakota

Center for Innovation
4300 Dartmouth Dr.
PO Box 8372
Grand Forks, ND 58202
(701)777-3132
Fax: (701)777-2339
E-mail: bruce@innovators.net
Website: http://www.innovators.net

Ohio

Transportation Technology Services
208 Harmon Rd.
Aurora, OH 44202
(330)562-3596

Empro Systems Inc.
4777 Red Bank Expy., Ste. 1
Cincinnati, OH 45227-1542
(513)271-2042
Fax: (513)271-2042

Alliance Management International Ltd.
1440 Windrow Ln.
Cleveland, OH 44147-3200
(440)838-1922
Fax: (440)838-0979
E-mail: bgruss@amiltd.com
Website: http://www.amiltd.com

Bozell Kamstra Public Relations
1301 E 9th St., Ste. 3400
Cleveland, OH 44114
(216)623-1511
Fax: (216)623-1501
E-mail: jfeniger@cleveland.bozellk
amstra.com
Website: http://www.bozellk
amstra.com

Cory Dillon Associates
111 Schreyer Pl. E
Columbus, OH 43214
(614)262-8211
Fax: (614)262-3806

Holcomb Gallagher Adams
300 Marconi, Ste. 303
Columbus, OH 43215
(614)221-3343
Fax: (614)221-3367
E-mail: riadams@acme.freenet.oh.us

Young & Associates
PO Box 711
Kent, OH 44240
(330)678-0524
Free: 800-525-9775
Fax: (330)678-6219
E-mail: online@younginc.com
Website: http://www.younginc.com

Robert A. Westman & Associates
8981 Inversary Dr. SE
Warren, OH 44484-2551
(330)856-4149
Fax: (330)856-2564

Oklahoma

Innovative Partners L.L.C.
4900 Richmond Sq., Ste. 100
Oklahoma City, OK 73118
(405)840-0033
Fax: (405)843-8359
E-mail: ipartners@juno.com

Oregon

INTERCON - The International Converting Institute
5200 Badger Rd.
Crooked River Ranch, OR 97760
(541)548-1447
Fax: (541)548-1618
E-mail: johnbowler@crookedriverranch.com

Talbott ARM
HC 60, Box 5620
Lakeview, OR 97630
(541)635-8587
Fax: (503)947-3482

Management Technology Associates Ltd.
2768 SW Sherwood Dr, Ste. 105
Portland, OR 97201-2251
(503)224-5220
Fax: (503)224-5334
E-mail: lcuster@mta-ltd.com
Website: http://www.mgmt-tech.com

Pennsylvania

Healthscope Inc.
400 Lancaster Ave.
Devon, PA 19333
(610)687-6199
Fax: (610)687-6376
E-mail: health@voicenet.com
Website: http://www.healthscope.net/

Elayne Howard & Associates Inc.
3501 Masons Mill Rd., Ste. 501

Huntingdon Valley, PA 19006-3509
(215)657-9550

GRA Inc.
115 West Ave., Ste. 201
Jenkintown, PA 19046
(215)884-7500
Fax: (215)884-1385
E-mail: gramail@gra-inc.com
Website: http://www.gra-inc.com

Mifflin County Industrial Development Corp.
Mifflin County Industrial Plz.
6395 SR 103 N
Bldg. 50
Lewistown, PA 17044
(717)242-0393
Fax: (717)242-1842
E-mail: mcide@acsworld.net

Autech Products
1289 Revere Rd.
Morrisville, PA 19067
(215)493-3759
Fax: (215)493-9791
E-mail: autech4@yahoo.com

Advantage Associates
434 Avon Dr.
Pittsburgh, PA 15228
(412)343-1558
Fax: (412)362-1684
E-mail: ecocba1@aol.com

Regis J. Sheehan & Associates
Pittsburgh, PA 15220
(412)279-1207

James W. Davidson Company Inc.
23 Forest View Rd.
Wallingford, PA 19086
(610)566-1462

Puerto Rico

Diego Chevere & Co.
Metro Parque 7, Ste. 204
Metro Office
Caparra Heights, PR 00920
(787)774-9595
Fax: (787)774-9566
E-mail: dcco@coqui.net

Manuel L. Porrata and Associates
898 Munoz Rivera Ave., Ste. 201
San Juan, PR 00927
(787)765-2140
Fax: (787)754-3285
E-mail: m_porrata@manuelporrata.com
Website: http://manualporrata.com

South Carolina

Aquafood Business Associates
PO Box 13267
Charleston, SC 29422
(843)795-9506
Fax: (843)795-9477
E-mail: rraba@aol.com

Profit Associates Inc.
PO Box 38026
Charleston, SC 29414
(803)763-5718
Fax: (803)763-5719
E-mail: bobrog@awod.com
Website: http://www.awod.com/gallery/business/proasc

Strategic Innovations International
12 Executive Ct.
Lake Wylie, SC 29710
(803)831-1225
Fax: (803)831-1177
E-mail: stratinnov@aol.com
Website: http://www.strategicinnovations.com

Minus Stage
Box 4436
Rock Hill, SC 29731
(803)328-0705
Fax: (803)329-9948

Tennessee

Daniel Petchers & Associates
8820 Fernwood CV
Germantown, TN 38138
(901)755-9896

Business Choices
1114 Forest Harbor, Ste. 300
Hendersonville, TN 37075-9646
(615)822-8692
Free: 800-737-8382
Fax: (615)822-8692
E-mail: bz-ch@juno.com

RCFA Healthcare Management Services L.L.C.
9648 Kingston Pke., Ste. 8
Knoxville, TN 37922
(865)531-0176
Free: 800-635-4040
Fax: (865)531-0722
E-mail: info@rcfa.com
Website: http://www.rcfa.com

Growth Consultants of America
3917 Trimble Rd.
Nashville, TN 37215

(615)383-0550
Fax: (615)269-8940
E-mail: 70244.451@compuserve.com

Texas

**Integrated Cost Management
Systems Inc.**
2261 Brookhollow Plz. Dr., Ste. 104
Arlington, TX 76006
(817)633-2873
Fax: (817)633-3781
E-mail: abm@icms.net
Website: http://www.icms.net

Lori Williams
1000 Leslie Ct.
Arlington, TX 76012
(817)459-3934
Fax: (817)459-3934

Business Resource Software Inc.
2013 Wells Branch Pky., Ste. 305
Austin, TX 78728
Free: 800-423-1228
Fax: (512)251-4401
E-mail: info@brs-inc.com
Website: http://www.brs-inc.com

Erisa Adminstrative Services Inc.
12325 Hymeadow Dr., Bldg. 4
Austin, TX 78750-1847
(512)250-9020
Fax: (512)250-9487
Website: http://www.cserisa.com

R. Miller Hicks & Co.
1011 W 11th St.
Austin, TX 78703
(512)477-7000
Fax: (512)477-9697
E-mail: millerhicks@rmhicks.com
Website: http://www.rmhicks.com

Pragmatic Tactics Inc.
3303 Westchester Ave.
College Station, TX 77845
(409)696-5294
Free: 800-570-5294
Fax: (409)696-4994
E-mail: ptactics@aol.com
Website: http://www.ptatics.com

Perot Systems
12404 Park Central Dr.
Dallas, TX 75251
(972)340-5000
Free: 800-688-4333
Fax: (972)455-4100
E-mail: corp.comm@ps.net
Website: http://www.perotsystems.com

ReGENERATION Partners
3838 Oak Lawn Ave.
Dallas, TX 75219
(214)559-3999
Free: 800-406-1112
E-mail: info@regeneration-partner.com
Website: http://www.regeneration-partners.com

**High Technology Associates - Division
of Global Technologies Inc.**
1775 St. James Pl., Ste. 105
Houston, TX 77056
(713)963-9300
Fax: (713)963-8341
E-mail: hta@infohwy.com

MasterCOM
103 Thunder Rd.
Kerrville, TX 78028
(830)895-7990
Fax: (830)443-3428
E-mail: jmstubblefield@master
training.com
Website: http://www.mastertraining.com

PROTEC
4607 Linden Pl.
Pearland, TX 77584
(281)997-9872
Fax: (281)997-9895
E-mail: p.oman@ix.netcom.com

Alpha Quadrant Inc.
10618 Auldine
San Antonio, TX 78230
(210)344-3330
Fax: (210)344-8151
E-mail: mbussone@sbcglobal.net
Website:http://www.a-quadrant.com
Michele Bussone

Bastian Public Relations
614 San Dizier
San Antonio, TX 78232
(210)404-1839
E-mail: lisa@bastianpr.com
Website: http://www.bastianpr.com
Lisa Bastian CBC

**Business Strategy Development
Consultants**
PO Box 690365
San Antonio, TX 78269
(210)696-8000
Free: 800-927-BSDC
Fax: (210)696-8000

Tom Welch, CPC
6900 San Pedro Ave., Ste. 147
San Antonio, TX 78216-6207

(210)737-7022
Fax: (210)737-7022
E-mail: bplan@iamerica.net
Website: http://www.moneywords.com

Utah

Business Management Resource
PO Box 521125
Salt Lake City, UT 84152-1125
(801)272-4668
Fax: (801)277-3290
E-mail: pingfong@worldnet.att.net

Virginia

Tindell Associates
209 Oxford Ave.
Alexandria, VA 22301
(703)683-0109
Fax: 703-783-0219
E-mail: scott@tindell.net
Website: http://www.tindell.net
Scott Lockett, President

Elliott B. Jaffa
2530-B S Walter Reed Dr.
Arlington, VA 22206
(703)931-0040
E-mail: thetrainingdoctor@excite.com
Website: http://www.tregistry.com/jaffa.htm

Koach Enterprises - USA
5529 N 18th St.
Arlington, VA 22205
(703)241-8361
Fax: (703)241-8623

Federal Market Development
5650 Chapel Run Ct.
Centreville, VA 20120-3601
(703)502-8930
Free: 800-821-5003
Fax: (703)502-8929

Huff, Stuart & Carlton
2107 Graves Mills Rd., Ste. C
Forest, VA 24551
(804)316-9356
Free: (888)316-9356
Fax: (804)316-9357
Website: http://www.wealthmgt.net

AMX International Inc.
1420 Spring Hill Rd. , Ste. 600
McLean, VA 22102-3006
(703)690-4100
Fax: (703)643-1279
E-mail: amxmail@amxi.com
Website: http://www.amxi.com

Charles Scott Pugh (Investor)
4101 Pittaway Dr.
Richmond, VA 23235-1022
(804)560-0979
Fax: (804)560-4670

John C. Randall and Associates Inc.
PO Box 15127
Richmond, VA 23227
(804)746-4450
Fax: (804)730-8933
E-mail: randalljcx@aol.com
Website: http://www.johncrandall.com

McLeod & Co.
410 1st St.
Roanoke, VA 24011
(540)342-6911
Fax: (540)344-6367
Website: http://www.mcleodco.com/

Salzinger & Company Inc.
8000 Towers Crescent Dr., Ste. 1350
Vienna, VA 22182
(703)442-5200
Fax: (703)442-5205
E-mail: info@salzinger.com
Website: http://www.salzinger.com

The Small Business Counselor
12423 Hedges Run Dr., Ste. 153
Woodbridge, VA 22192
(703)490-6755
Fax: (703)490-1356

Washington

Burlington Consultants
10900 NE 8th St., Ste. 900
Bellevue, WA 98004
(425)688-3060
Fax: (425)454-4383
E-mail: partners@burlingt
onconsultants.com
Website: http://www.burlington
consultants.com

Perry L. Smith Consulting
800 Bellevue Way NE, Ste. 400
Bellevue, WA 98004-4208
(425)462-2072
Fax: (425)462-5638

St. Charles Consulting Group
1420 NW Gilman Blvd.
Issaquah, WA 98027
(425)557-8708
Fax: (425)557-8731
E-mail: info@stcharlesconsulting.com
Website: http://www.stcharlescon
sulting.com

**Independent Automotive Training
Services**
PO Box 334
Kirkland, WA 98083
(425)822-5715
E-mail: ltunney@autosvccon.com
Website: http://www.autosvccon.com

Kahle Associate Inc.
6203 204th Dr. NE
Redmond, WA 98053
(425)836-8763
Fax: (425)868-3770
E-mail: randykahle@kahleassociates.com
Website: http://www.kahleassociates.com

Dan Collin
3419 Wallingord Ave N, No. 2
Seattle, WA 98103
(206)634-9469
E-mail: dc@dancollin.com
Website: http://members.home.net/
dcollin/

ECG Management Consultants Inc.
1111 3rd Ave., Ste. 2700
Seattle, WA 98101-3201
(206)689-2200
Fax: (206)689-2209
E-mail: ecg@ecgmc.com
Website: http://www.ecgmc.com

**Northwest Trade Adjustment
Assistance Center**
900 4th Ave., Ste. 2430
Seattle, WA 98164-1001
(206)622-2730
Free: 800-667-8087
Fax: (206)622-1105
E-mail: matchingfunds@nwtaac.org
Website: http://www.taacenters.org

Business Planning Consultants
S 3510 Ridgeview Dr.
Spokane, WA 99206
(509)928-0332
Fax: (509)921-0842
E-mail: bpci@nextdim.com

West Virginia

**Stanley & Associates Inc./
BusinessandMarketingPlans.com**
1687 Robert C. Byrd Dr.
Beckley, WV 25801
(304)252-0324
Free: 888-752-6720
Fax: (304)252-0470
E-mail: cclay@charterinternet.com

Website: http://www.Businessand-
MarketingPlans.com
Christopher Clay

Wisconsin

White & Associates Inc.
5349 Somerset Ln. S
Greenfield, WI 53221
(414)281-7373
Fax: (414)281-7006
E-mail: wnaconsult@aol.com

Small business administration regional offices

This section contains a listing of Small Business Administration offices arranged numerically by region. Service areas are provided. Contact the appropriate office for a referral to the nearest field office, or visit the Small Business Administration online at www.sba.gov.

Region 1

U.S. Small Business Administration
Region I Office
10 Causeway St., Ste. 812
Boston, MA 02222-1093
Phone: (617)565-8415
Fax: (617)565-8420
Serves Connecticut, Maine, Massachusetts, New Hampshire, Rhode Island, and Vermont.

Region 2

U.S. Small Business Administration
Region II Office
26 Federal Plaza, Ste. 3108
New York, NY 10278
Phone: (212)264-1450
Fax: (212)264-0038
Serves New Jersey, New York, Puerto Rico, and the Virgin Islands.

Region 3

U.S. Small Business Administration
Region III Office
Robert N C Nix Sr. Federal Building
900 Market St., 5th Fl.
Philadelphia, PA 19107
(215)580-2807
Serves Delaware, the District of Columbia, Maryland, Pennsylvania, Virginia, and West Virginia.

Region 4

U.S. Small Business Administration
Region IV Office
233 Peachtree St. NE
Harris Tower 1800
Atlanta, GA 30303
Phone: (404)331-4999
Fax: (404)331-2354
Serves Alabama, Florida, Georgia, Kentucky, Mississippi, North Carolina, South Carolina, and Tennessee.

Region 5

U.S. Small Business Administration
Region V Office
500 W. Madison St.
Citicorp Center, Ste. 1240
Chicago, IL 60661-2511
Phone: (312)353-0357
Fax: (312)353-3426
Serves Illinois, Indiana, Michigan, Minnesota, Ohio, and Wisconsin.

Region 6

U.S. Small Business Administration
Region VI Office
4300 Amon Carter Blvd., Ste. 108
Fort Worth, TX 76155
Phone: (817)684-5581
Fax: (817)684-5588
Serves Arkansas, Louisiana, New Mexico, Oklahoma, and Texas.

Region 7

U.S. Small Business Administration
Region VII Office
323 W. 8th St., Ste. 307
Kansas City, MO 64105-1500
Phone: (816)374-6380
Fax: (816)374-6339
Serves Iowa, Kansas, Missouri, and Nebraska.

Region 8

U.S. Small Business Administration
Region VIII Office
721 19th St., Ste. 400
Denver, CO 80202
Phone: (303)844-0500
Fax: (303)844-0506
Serves Colorado, Montana, North Dakota, South Dakota, Utah, and Wyoming.

Region 9

U.S. Small Business Administration
Region IX Office
330 N Brand Blvd., Ste. 1270
Glendale, CA 91203-2304
Phone: (818)552-3434
Fax: (818)552-3440
Serves American Samoa, Arizona, California, Guam, Hawaii, Nevada, and the Trust Territory of the Pacific Islands.

Region 10

U.S. Small Business Administration
Region X Office
2401 Fourth Ave., Ste. 400
Seattle, WA 98121
Phone: (206)553-5676
Fax: (206)553-4155
Serves Alaska, Idaho, Oregon, and Washington.

Small business development centers

This section contains a listing of all Small Business Development Centers, organized alphabetically by state/U.S. territory, then by city, then by agency name.

Alabama

Alabama SBDC
UNIVERSITY OF ALABAMA
2800 Milan Court Suite 124
Birmingham, AL 35211-6908
Phone: 205-943-6750
Fax: 205-943-6752
E-Mail: wcampbell@provost.uab.edu
Website: http://www.asbdc.org
Mr. William Campbell Jr, State Director

Alaska

Alaska SBDC
UNIVERSITY OF ALASKA - ANCHORAGE
430 West Seventh Avenue, Suite 110
Anchorage, AK 99501
Phone: 907-274 -7232
Fax: 907-274-9524
E-Mail: anerw@uaa.alaska.edu
Website: http://www.aksbdc.org
Ms. Jean R. Wall, State Director

American Samoa

American Samoa SBDC
AMERICAN SAMOA COMMUNITY COLLEGE
P.O. Box 2609
Pago Pago, American Samoa 96799
Phone: 011-684-699-4830
Fax: 011-684-699-6132
E-Mail: htalex@att.net
Mr. Herbert Thweatt, Director

Arizona

Arizona SBDC
MARICOPA COUNTY COMMUNITY COLLEGE
2411 West 14th Street, Suite 132
Tempe, AZ 85281
Phone: 480-731-8720
Fax: 480-731-8729
E-Mail: mike.york@domail.maricopa.edu
Website: http://www.dist.maricopa.edu.sbdc
Mr. Michael York, State Director

Arkansas

Arkansas SBDC
UNIVERSITY OF ARKANSAS
2801 South University Avenue
Little Rock, AR 72204
Phone: 501-324-9043
Fax: 501-324-9049
E-Mail: jmroderick@ualr.edu
Website: http://asbdc.ualr.edu
Ms. Janet M. Roderick, State Director

California

California - San Francisco SBDC
Northern California SBDC Lead Center
HUMBOLDT STATE UNIVERSITY
Office of Economic Development
1 Harpst Street 2006A, Siemens Hall
Arcata, CA, 95521
Phone: 707-826-3922
Fax: 707-826-3206
E-Mail: gainer@humboldt.edu
Ms. Margaret A. Gainer, Regional Director

California - Sacramento SBDC
CALIFORNIA STATE UNIVERSITY - CHICO
Chico, CA 95929-0765
Phone: 530-898-4598
Fax: 530-898-4734

E-Mail: dripke@csuchico.edu
Website: http://gsbdc.csuchico.edu
Mr. Dan Ripke, Interim Regional Director

California - San Diego SBDC
SOUTHWESTERN COMMUNITY
COLLEGE DISTRICT
900 Otey Lakes Road
Chula Vista, CA 91910
Phone: 619-482-6388
Fax: 619-482-6402
E-Mail: dtrujillo@swc.cc.ca.us
Website: http://www.sbditc.org
Ms. Debbie P. Trujillo, Regional Director

California - Fresno SBDC
UC Merced Lead Center
UNIVERSITY OF CALIFORNIA -
MERCED
550 East Shaw, Suite 105A
Fresno, CA 93710
Phone: 559-241-6590
Fax: 559-241-7422
E-Mail: crosander@ucmerced.edu
Website: http://sbdc.ucmerced.edu
Mr. Chris Rosander, State Director

California - Santa Ana SBDC
Tri-County Lead SBDC
CALIFORNIA STATE UNIVERSITY -
FULLERTON
800 North State College Boulevard, LH640
Fullerton, CA 92834
Phone: 714-278-2719
Fax: 714-278-7858
E-Mail: vpham@fullerton.edu
Website: http://www.leadsbdc.org
Ms. Vi Pham, Lead Center Director

California - Los Angeles Region SBDC
LONG BEACH COMMUNITY
COLLEGE DISTRICT
3950 Paramount Boulevard, Ste 101
Lakewood, CA 90712
Phone: 562-938-5004
Fax: 562-938-5030
E-Mail: ssloan@lbcc.edu
Ms. Sheneui Sloan, Interim Lead Center
Director

Colorado

Colorado SBDC
OFFICE OF ECONOMIC
DEVELOPMENT
1625 Broadway, Suite 170
Denver, CO 80202
Phone: 303-892-3864
Fax: 303-892-3848
E-Mail: Kelly.Manning@state.co.us

Website: http://www.state.co.us/oed/sbdc
Ms. Kelly Manning, State Director

Connecticut

Connecticut SBDC
UNIVERSITY OF CONNECTICUT
1376 Storrs Road, Unit 4094
Storrs, CT 06269-1094
Phone: 860-870-6370
Fax: 860-870-6374
E-Mail: richard.cheney@uconn.edu
Website: http://www.sbdc.uconn.edu
Mr. Richard Cheney, Interim State Director

Delaware

Delaware SBDC
DELAWARE TECHNOLOGY PARK
1 Innovation Way, Suite 301
Newark, DE 19711
Phone: 302-831-2747
Fax: 302-831-1423
E-Mail: Clinton.tymes@mvs.udel.edu
Website: http://www.delawaresbdc.org
Mr. Clinton Tymes, State Director

District of Columbia

District of Columbia SBDC
HOWARD UNIVERSITY
2600 6th Street, NW Room 128
Washington, DC 20059
Phone: 202-806-1550
Fax: 202-806-1777
E-Mail: hturner@howard.edu
Website: http://www.dcsbdc.com/
Mr. Henry Turner, Executive Director

Florida

Florida SBDC
UNIVERSITY OF WEST FLORIDA
401 East Chase Street, Suite 100
Pensacola, FL 32502
Phone: 850-473-7800
Fax: 850-473-7813
E-Mail: jcartwri@uwf.edu
Website: http://www.floridasbdc.com
Mr. Jerry Cartwright, State Director

Georgia

Georgia SBDC
UNIVERSITY OF GEORGIA
1180 East Broad Street
Athens, GA 30602
Phone: 706-542-6762
Fax: 706-542-6776
E-Mail: aadams@sbdc.uga.edu

Website: http://www.sbdc.uga.edu
Mr. Allan Adams, Interim State Director

Guam

Guam Small Business Development
Center
UNIVERSITY OF GUAM
Pacific Islands SBDC
P.O. Box 5014 - U.O.G. Station
Mangilao, GU 96923
Phone: 671-735-2590
Fax: 671-734-2002
E-mail: casey@pacificsbdc.com
Website: http://www.uog.edu/sbdc
Mr. Casey Jeszenka, Director

Hawaii

Hawaii SBDC
UNIVERSITY OF HAWAII - HILO
308 Kamehameha Avenue, Suite 201
Hilo, HI 96720
Phone: 808-974-7515
Fax: 808-974-7683
E-Mail: darrylm@interpac.net
Website: http://www.hawaii-sbdc.org
Mr. Darryl Mleynek, State Director

Idaho

Idaho SBDC
BOISE STATE UNIVERSITY
1910 University Drive
Boise, ID 83725
Phone: 208-426-3799
Fax: 208-426-3877
E-mail: jhogge@boisestate.edu
Website: http://www.idahosbdc.org
Mr. Jim Hogge, State Director

Illinois

Illinois SBDC
DEPARTMENT OF COMMERCE
AND ECONOMIC OPPORTUNITY
620 E. Adams, S-4
Springfield, IL 62701
Phone: 217-524-5700
Fax: 217-524-0171
E-mail: mpatrilli@ildceo.net
Website: http://www.ilsbdc.biz
Mr. Mark Petrilli, State Director

Indiana

Indiana SBDC
INDIANA ECONOMIC
DEVELOPMENT CORPORATION
One North Capitol, Suite 900
Indianapolis, IN 46204

Phone: 317-234-8872
Fax: 317-232-8874
E-mail: dtrocha@isbdc.org
Website: http://www.isbdc.org
Ms. Debbie Bishop Trocha, State Director

Iowa

Iowa SBDC
IOWA STATE UNIVERSITY
340 Gerdin Business Bldg.
Ames, IA 50011-1350
Phone: 515-294-2037
Fax: 515-294-6522
E-mail: jonryan@iastate.edu
Website: http://www.iabusnet.org
Mr. Jon Ryan, State Director

Kansas

Kansas SBDC
FORT HAYS STATE UNIVERSITY
214 SW Sixth Street, Suite 301
Topeka, KS 66603
Phone: 785-296-6514
Fax: 785-291-3261
E-mail: ksbdc.wkearns@fhsu.edu
Website: http://www.fhsu.edu/ksbdc
Mr. Wally Kearns, State Director

Kentucky

Kentucky SBDC
UNIVERSITY OF KENTUCKY
225 Gatton College of Business Economics Building
Lexington, KY 40506-0034
Phone: 859-257-7668
Fax: 859-323-1907
E-mail: lrnaug0@pop.uky.edu
Website: http://www.ksbdc.org
Ms. Becky Naugle, State Director

Louisiana

Louisiana SBDC
UNIVERSITY OF LOUISIANA - MONROE
College of Business Administration
700 University Avenue
Monroe, LA 71209
Phone: 318-342-5506
Fax: 318-342-5510
E-mail: wilkerson@ulm.edu
Website: http://www.lsbdc.org
Ms. Mary Lynn Wilkerson, State Director

Maine

Maine SBDC
UNIVERSITY OF SOUTHERN MAINE
96 Falmouth Street P.O. Box 9300
Portland, ME 04103
Phone: 207-780-4420
Fax: 207-780-4810
E-mail: jrmassaua@maine.edu
Website: http://www.mainesbdc.org
Mr. John Massaua, State Director

Maryland

Maryland SBDC
UNIVERSITY OF MARYLAND
7100 Baltimore Avenue, Suite 401
College Park, MD 20742
Phone: 301-403-8300
Fax: 301-403-8303
E-mail: rsprow@mdsbdc.umd.edu
Website: http://www.mdsbdc.umd.edu
Ms. Renee Sprow, State Director

Massachusetts

Massachusetts SBDC
UNIVERSITY OF MASSACHUSETTS
School of Management, Room 205
Amherst, MA 01003-4935
Phone: 413-545-6301
Fax: 413-545-1273
E-mail: gep@msbdc.umass.edu
Website: http://msbdc.som.umass.edu
Ms. Georgianna Parkin, State Director

Michigan

Michigan SBTDC
GRAND VALLEY STATE UNIVERSITY
510 West Fulton Avenue
Grand Rapids, MI 49504
Phone: 616-331-7485
Fax: 616-331-7389
E-mail: lopuckic@gvsu.edu
Website: http://www.misbtdc.org
Ms. Carol Lopucki, State Director

Minnesota

Minnesota SBDC
MINNESOTA SMALL BUSINESS DEVELOPMENT CENTER
1st National Bank Building
332 Minnesota Street, Suite E200
St. Paul, MN 55101-1351
Phone: 651-297-5773
Fax: 651-296-5287

E-mail: michael.myhre@state.mn.us
Website: http://www.mnsbdc.com
Mr. Michael Myhre, State Director

Mississippi

Mississippi SBDC
UNIVERSITY OF MISSISSIPPI
B-19 Jeanette Phillips Drive
P.O. Box 1848
University, MS 38677
Phone: 662-915-5001
Fax: 662-915-5650
E-mail: wgurley@olemiss.edu
Website: http://www.olemiss.edu/depts/mssbdc
Mr. Doug Gurley, Jr., State Director

Missouri

Missouri SBDC
UNIVERSITY OF MISSOURI
1205 University Avenue, Suite 300
Columbia, MO 65211
Phone: 573-882-1348
Fax: 573-884-4297
E-mail: summersm@missouri.edu
Website: http://www.mo-sbdc.org/index.shtml
Mr. Max Summers, State Director

Montana

Montana SBDC
DEPARTMENT OF COMMERCE
301 South Park Avenue, Room 114 / P.O. Box 200505
Helena, MT 59620
Phone: 406-841-2746
Fax: 406-444-1872
E-mail: adesch@state.mt.us
Website: http://commerce.state.mt.us/brd/BRD_SBDC.html
Ms. Ann Desch, State Director

Nebraska

Nebraska SBDC
UNIVERSITY OF NEBRASKA - OMAHA
60th & Dodge Street, CBA Room 407
Omaha, NE 68182
Phone: 402-554-2521
Fax: 402-554-3473
E-mail: rbernier@unomaha.edu
Website: http://nbdc.unomaha.edu
Mr. Robert Bernier, State Director

Nevada

Nevada SBDC
UNIVERSITY OF NEVADA - RENO
Reno College of Business
Administration, Room 411
Reno, NV 89557-0100
Phone: 775-784-1717
Fax: 775-784-4337
E-mail: males@unr.edu
Website: http://www.nsbdc.org
Mr. Sam Males, State Director

New Hampshire

New Hampshire SBDC
UNIVERSITY OF NEW HAMPSHIRE
108 McConnell Hall
Durham, NH 03824-3593
Phone: 603-862-4879
Fax: 603-862-4876
E-mail: Mary.Collins@unh.edu
Website: http://www.nhsbdc.org
Ms. Mary Collins, State Director

New Jersey

New Jersey SBDC
RUTGERS UNIVERSITY
49 Bleeker Street
Newark, NJ 07102-1993
Phone: 973-353-5950
Fax: 973-353-1110
E-mail: bhopper@njsbdc.com
Website: http://www.njsbdc.com/home
Ms. Brenda Hopper, State Director

New Mexico

New Mexico SBDC
SANTA FE COMMUNITY COLLEGE
6401 Richards Avenue
Santa Fe, NM 87505
Phone: 505-428-1362
Fax: 505-471-9469
E-mail: rmiller@santa-fe.cc.nm.us
Website: http://www.nmsbdc.org
Mr. Roy Miller, State Director

New York

New York SBDC
STATE UNIVERSITY OF NEW YORK
SUNY Plaza, S-523
Albany, NY 12246
Phone: 518-443-5398
Fax: 518-443-5275
E-mail: j.king@nyssbdc.org
Website: http://www.nyssbdc.org
Mr. Jim King, State Director

North Carolina

North Carolina SBDTC
UNIVERSITY OF NORTH CAROLINA
5 West Hargett Street, Suite 600
Raleigh, NC 27601
Phone: 919-715-7272
Fax: 919-715-7777
E-mail: sdaugherty@sbtdc.org
Website: http://www.sbtdc.org
Mr. Scott Daugherty, State Director

North Dakota

North Dakota SBDC
UNIVERSITY OF NORTH DAKOTA
1600 E. Century Avenue, Suite 2
Bismarck, ND 58503
Phone: 701-328-5375
Fax: 701-328-5320
E-mail: christine.martin@und.nodak.edu
Website: http://www.ndsbdc.org
Ms. Christine Martin-Goldman, State
Director

Ohio

Ohio SBDC
**OHIO DEPARTMENT
OF DEVELOPMENT**
77 South High Street
Columbus, OH 43216
Phone: 614-466-5102
Fax: 614-466-0829
E-mail: mabraham@odod.state.oh.us
Website: http://www.ohiosbdc.org
Ms. Michele Abraham, State Director

Oklahoma

Oklahoma SBDC
**SOUTHEAST OKLAHOMA STATE
UNIVERSITY**
517 University, Box 2584, Station A
Durant, OK 74701
Phone: 580-745-7577
Fax: 580-745-7471
E-mail: gpennington@sosu.edu
Website: http://www.osbdc.org
Mr. Grady Pennington, State Director

Oregon

Oregon SBDC
LANE COMMUNITY COLLEGE
99 West Tenth Avenue, Suite 390
Eugene, OR 97401-3021
Phone: 541-463-5250
Fax: 541-345-6006
E-mail: carterb@lanecc.edu

Website: http://www.bizcenter.org
Mr. William Carter, State Director

Pennsylvania

Pennsylvania SBDC
UNIVERSITY OF PENNSYLVANIA
The Wharton School
3733 Spruce Street
Philadelphia, PA 19104-6374
Phone: 215-898-1219
Fax: 215-573-2135
E-mail: ghiggins@wharton.upenn.edu
Website: http://pasbdc.org
Mr. Gregory Higgins, State Director

Puerto Rico

Puerto Rico SBDC
**INTER-AMERICAN UNIVERSITY
OF PUERTO RICO**
416 Ponce de Leon Avenue, Union Plaza,
Seventh Floor
Hato Rey, PR 00918
Phone: 787-763-6811
Fax: 787-763-4629
E-mail: cmarti@prsbdc.org
Website: http://www.prsbdc.org
Ms. Carmen Marti, Executive Director

Rhode Island

Rhode Island SBDC
BRYANT UNIVERSITY
1150 Douglas Pike
Smithfield, RI 02917
Phone: 401-232-6923
Fax: 401-232-6933
E-mail: adawson@bryant.edu
Website: http://www.risbdc.org
Ms. Diane Fournaris, Interim State Director

South Carolina

South Carolina SBDC
UNIVERSITY OF SOUTH CAROLINA
College of Business Administration
1710 College Street
Columbia, SC 29208
Phone: 803-777-4907
Fax: 803-777-4403
E-mail: lenti@moore.sc.edu
Website: http://scsbdc.moore.sc.edu
Mr. John Lenti, State Director

South Dakota

South Dakota SBDC
UNIVERSITY OF SOUTH DAKOTA
414 East Clark Street, Patterson Hall
Vermillion, SD 57069

Phone: 605-677-6256
Fax: 605-677-5427
E-mail: jshemmin@usd.edu
Website: http://www.sdsbdc.org
Mr. John S. Hemmingstad, State Director

Tennessee

Tennessee SBDC
TENNESSEE BOARD OF REGENTS
1415 Murfressboro Road, Suite 540
Nashville, TN 37217-2833
Phone: 615-898-2745
Fax: 615-893-7089
E-mail: pgeho@mail.tsbdc.org
Website: http://www.tsbdc.org
Mr. Patrick Geho, State Director

Texas

Texas-North SBDC
DALLAS COUNTY COMMUNITY COLLEGE
1402 Corinth Street
Dallas, TX 75215
Phone: 214-860-5835
Fax: 214-860-5813
E-mail: emk9402@dcccd.edu
Website: http://www.ntsbdc.org
Ms. Liz Klimback, Region Director

Texas-Houston SBDC
UNIVERSITY OF HOUSTON
2302 Fannin, Suite 200
Houston, TX 77002
Phone: 713-752-8425
Fax: 713-756-1500
E-mail: fyoung@uh.edu
Website: http://sbdcnetwork.uh.edu
Mr. Mike Young, Executive Director

Texas-NW SBDC
TEXAS TECH UNIVERSITY
2579 South Loop 289, Suite 114
Lubbock, TX 79423
Phone: 806-745-3973
Fax: 806-745-6207
E-mail: c.bean@nwtsbdc.org
Website: http://www.nwtsbdc.org
Mr. Craig Bean, Executive Director

Texas-South-West Texas Border Region SBDC
UNIVERSITY OF TEXAS - SAN ANTONIO
501 West Durango Boulevard
San Antonio, TX 78207-4415
Phone: 210-458-2742
Fax: 210-458-2464

E-mail: albert.salgado@utsa.edu
Website: http://www.iedtexas.org
Mr. Alberto Salgado, Region Director

Utah

Utah SBDC
SALT LAKE COMMUNITY COLLEGE
9750 South 300 West
Sandy, UT 84070
Phone: 801-957-3493
Fax: 801-957-3488
E-mail: Greg.Panichello@slcc.edu
Website:http://www.slcc.edu/sbdc
Mr. Greg Panichello, State Director

Vermont

Vermont SBDC
VERMONT TECHNICAL COLLEGE
PO Box 188, 1 Main Street
Randolph Center, VT 05061-0188
Phone: 802-728-9101
Fax: 802-728-3026
E-mail: lquillen@vtc.edu
Website: http://www.vtsbdc.org
Ms. Lenae Quillen-Blume, State Director

Virgin Islands

Virgin Islands SBDC
UNIVERSITY OF THE VIRGIN ISLANDS
8000 Nisky Center, Suite 720
St. Thomas, VI 00802-5804
Phone: 340-776-3206
Fax: 340-775-3756
E-mail: wbush@webmail.uvi.edu
Website: http://rps.uvi.edu/SBDC
Mr. Warren Bush, State Director

Virginia

Virginia SBDC
GEORGE MASON UNIVERSITY
4031 University Drive, Suite 200
Fairfax, VA 22030-3409
Phone: 703-277-7727
Fax: 703-352-8515
E-mail: jkeenan@gmu.edu
Website: http://www.virginiasbdc.org
Ms. Jody Keenan, Director

Washington

Washington SBDC
WASHINGTON STATE UNIVERSITY
534 E. Trent Avenue
P.O. Box 1495
Spokane, WA 99210-1495

Phone: 509-358-7765
Fax: 509-358-7764
E-mail: barogers@wsu.edu
Website: http://www.wsbdc.org
Mr. Brett Rogers, State Director

West Virginia

West Virginia SBDC
WEST VIRGINIA DEVELOPMENT OFFICE
Capital Complex, Building 6, Room 652
Charleston, WV 25301
Phone: 304-558-2960
Fax: 304-558-0127
E-mail: csalyer@wvsbdc.org
Website: http://www.wvsbdc.org
Mr. Conley Salyor, State Director

Wisconsin

Wisconsin SBDC
UNIVERSITY OF WISCONSIN
432 North Lake Street, Room 423
Madison, WI 53706
Phone: 608-263-7794
Fax: 608-263-7830
E-mail: erica.kauten@uwex.edu
Website: http://www.wisconsinsbdc.org
Ms. Erica Kauten, State Director

Wyoming

Wyoming SBDC
UNIVERSITY OF WYOMING
P.O. Box 3922
Laramie, WY 82071-3922
Phone: 307-766-3505
Fax: 307-766-3406
E-mail: DDW@uwyo.edu
Website: http://www.uwyo.edu/sbdc
Ms. Debbie Popp, Acting State Director

Service corps of retired executives (score) offices

This section contains a listing of all SCORE offices organized alphabetically by state/U.S. territory, then by city, then by agency name.

Alabama

SCORE Office (Northeast Alabama)
1330 Quintard Ave.
Anniston, AL 36202
(256)237-3536

SCORE Office (North Alabama)
901 South 15th St, Rm. 201
Birmingham, AL 35294-2060
(205)934-6868
Fax: (205)934-0538

SCORE Office (Baldwin County)
29750 Larry Dee Cawyer Dr.
Daphne, AL 36526
(334)928-5838

SCORE Office (Shoals)
612 S. COurt
Florence, AL 35630
(256)764-4661
Fax: (256)766-9017
E-mail: shoals@shoalschamber.com

SCORE Office (Mobile)
600 S Court St.
Mobile, AL 36104
(334)240-6868
Fax: (334)240-6869

SCORE Office (Alabama Capitol City)
600 S. Court St.
Montgomery, AL 36104
(334)240-6868
Fax: (334)240-6869

SCORE Office (East Alabama)
601 Ave. A
Opelika, AL 36801
(334)745-4861
E-mail: score636@hotmail.com
Website: http://www.angelfire.com/sc/score636/

SCORE Office (Tuscaloosa)
2200 University Blvd.
Tuscaloosa, AL 35402
(205)758-7588

Alaska

SCORE Office (Anchorage)
510 L St., Ste. 310
Anchorage, AK 99501
(907)271-4022
Fax: (907)271-4545

Arizona

SCORE Office (Lake Havasu)
10 S. Acoma Blvd.
Lake Havasu City, AZ 86403
(520)453-5951
E-mail: SCORE@ctaz.com
Website: http://www.scorearizona.org/lake_havasu/

SCORE Office (East Valley)
Federal Bldg., Rm. 104
26 N. MacDonald St.
Mesa, AZ 85201
(602)379-3100
Fax: (602)379-3143
E-mail: 402@aol.com
Website: http://www.scorearizona.org/mesa/

SCORE Office (Phoenix)
2828 N. Central Ave., Ste. 800
Central & One Thomas
Phoenix, AZ 85004
(602)640-2329
Fax: (602)640-2360
E-mail: e-mail@SCORE-phoenix.org
Website: http://www.score-phoenix.org/

SCORE Office (Prescott Arizona)
1228 Willow Creek Rd., Ste. 2
Prescott, AZ 86301
(520)778-7438
Fax: (520)778-0812
E-mail: score@northlink.com
Website: http://www.scorearizona.org/prescott/

SCORE Office (Tucson)
110 E. Pennington St.
Tucson, AZ 85702
(520)670-5008
Fax: (520)670-5011
E-mail: score@azstarnet.com
Website: http://www.scorearizona.org/tucson/

SCORE Office (Yuma)
281 W. 24th St., Ste. 116
Yuma, AZ 85364
(520)314-0480
E-mail: score@C2i2.com
Website: http://www.scorearizona.org/yuma

Arkansas

SCORE Office (South Central)
201 N. Jackson Ave.
El Dorado, AR 71730-5803
(870)863-6113
Fax: (870)863-6115

SCORE Office (Ozark)
Fayetteville, AR 72701
(501)442-7619

SCORE Office (Northwest Arkansas)
Glenn Haven Dr., No. 4
Ft. Smith, AR 72901
(501)783-3556

SCORE Office (Garland County)
Grand & Ouachita
PO Box 6012
Hot Springs Village, AR 71902
(501)321-1700

SCORE Office (Little Rock)
2120 Riverfront Dr., Rm. 100
Little Rock, AR 72202-1747
(501)324-5893
Fax: (501)324-5199

SCORE Office (Southeast Arkansas)
121 W. 6th
Pine Bluff, AR 71601
(870)535-7189
Fax: (870)535-1643

California

SCORE Office (Golden Empire)
1706 Chester Ave., No. 200
Bakersfield, CA 93301
(805)322-5881
Fax: (805)322-5663

SCORE Office (Greater Chico Area)
1324 Mangrove St., Ste. 114
Chico, CA 95926
(916)342-8932
Fax: (916)342-8932

SCORE Office (Concord)
2151-A Salvio St., Ste. B
Concord, CA 94520
(510)685-1181
Fax: (510)685-5623

SCORE Office (Covina)
935 W. Badillo St.
Covina, CA 91723
(818)967-4191
Fax: (818)966-9660

SCORE Office (Rancho Cucamonga)
8280 Utica, Ste. 160
Cucamonga, CA 91730
(909)987-1012
Fax: (909)987-5917

SCORE Office (Culver City)
PO Box 707
Culver City, CA 90232-0707
(310)287-3850
Fax: (310)287-1350

SCORE Office (Danville)
380 Diablo Rd., Ste. 103
Danville, CA 94526
(510)837-4400

SCORE Office (Downey)
11131 Brookshire Ave.
Downey, CA 90241
(310)923-2191
Fax: (310)864-0461

SCORE Office (El Cajon)
109 Rea Ave.
El Cajon, CA 92020
(619)444-1327
Fax: (619)440-6164

SCORE Office (El Centro)
1100 Main St.
El Centro, CA 92243
(619)352-3681
Fax: (619)352-3246

SCORE Office (Escondido)
720 N. Broadway
Escondido, CA 92025
(619)745-2125
Fax: (619)745-1183

SCORE Office (Fairfield)
1111 Webster St.
Fairfield, CA 94533
(707)425-4625
Fax: (707)425-0826

SCORE Office (Fontana)
17009 Valley Blvd., Ste. B
Fontana, CA 92335
(909)822-4433
Fax: (909)822-6238

SCORE Office (Foster City)
1125 E. Hillsdale Blvd.
Foster City, CA 94404
(415)573-7600
Fax: (415)573-5201

SCORE Office (Fremont)
2201 Walnut Ave., Ste. 110
Fremont, CA 94538
(510)795-2244
Fax: (510)795-2240

SCORE Office (Central California)
2719 N. Air Fresno Dr., Ste. 200
Fresno, CA 93727-1547
(559)487-5605
Fax: (559)487-5636

SCORE Office (Gardena)
1204 W. Gardena Blvd.
Gardena, CA 90247
(310)532-9905
Fax: (310)515-4893

SCORE Office (Lompoc)
330 N. Brand Blvd., Ste. 190
Glendale, CA 91203-2304

(818)552-3206
Fax: (818)552-3323

SCORE Office (Los Angeles)
330 N. Brand Blvd., Ste. 190
Glendale, CA 91203-2304
(818)552-3206
Fax: (818)552-3323

SCORE Office (Glendora)
131 E. Foothill Blvd.
Glendora, CA 91740
(818)963-4128
Fax: (818)914-4822

SCORE Office (Grover Beach)
177 S. 8th St.
Grover Beach, CA 93433
(805)489-9091
Fax: (805)489-9091

SCORE Office (Hawthorne)
12477 Hawthorne Blvd.
Hawthorne, CA 90250
(310)676-1163
Fax: (310)676-7661

SCORE Office (Hayward)
22300 Foothill Blvd., Ste. 303
Hayward, CA 94541
(510)537-2424

SCORE Office (Hemet)
1700 E. Florida Ave.
Hemet, CA 92544-4679
(909)652-4390
Fax: (909)929-8543

SCORE Office (Hesperia)
16367 Main St.
PO Box 403656
Hesperia, CA 92340
(619)244-2135

SCORE Office (Holloster)
321 San Felipe Rd., No. 11
Hollister, CA 95023

SCORE Office (Hollywood)
7018 Hollywood Blvd.
Hollywood, CA 90028
(213)469-8311
Fax: (213)469-2805

SCORE Office (Indio)
82503 Hwy. 111
PO Drawer TTT
Indio, CA 92202
(619)347-0676

SCORE Office (Inglewood)
330 Queen St.

Inglewood, CA 90301
(818)552-3206

SCORE Office (La Puente)
218 N. Grendanda St. D.
La Puente, CA 91744
(818)330-3216
Fax: (818)330-9524

SCORE Office (La Verne)
2078 Bonita Ave.
La Verne, CA 91750
(909)593-5265
Fax: (714)929-8475

SCORE Office (Lake Elsinore)
132 W. Graham Ave.
Lake Elsinore, CA 92530
(909)674-2577

SCORE Office (Lakeport)
PO Box 295
Lakeport, CA 95453
(707)263-5092

SCORE Office (Lakewood)
5445 E. Del Amo Blvd., Ste. 2
Lakewood, CA 90714
(213)920-7737

SCORE Office (Long Beach)
1 World Trade Center
Long Beach, CA 90831

SCORE Office (Los Alamitos)
901 W. Civic Center Dr., Ste. 160
Los Alamitos, CA 90720

SCORE Office (Los Altos)
321 University Ave.
Los Altos, CA 94022
(415)948-1455

SCORE Office (Manhattan Beach)
PO Box 3007
Manhattan Beach, CA 90266
(310)545-5313
Fax: (310)545-7203

SCORE Office (Merced)
1632 N. St.
Merced, CA 95340
(209)725-3800
Fax: (209)383-4959

SCORE Office (Milpitas)
75 S. Milpitas Blvd., Ste. 205
Milpitas, CA 95035
(408)262-2613
Fax: (408)262-2823

SCORE Office (Yosemite)
1012 11th St., Ste. 300
Modesto, CA 95354
(209)521-9333

SCORE Office (Montclair)
5220 Benito Ave.
Montclair, CA 91763

SCORE Office (Monterey Bay)
380 Alvarado St.
PO Box 1770
Monterey, CA 93940-1770
(408)649-1770

SCORE Office (Moreno Valley)
25480 Alessandro
Moreno Valley, CA 92553

SCORE Office (Morgan Hill)
25 W. 1st St.
PO Box 786
Morgan Hill, CA 95038
(408)779-9444
Fax: (408)778-1786

SCORE Office (Morro Bay)
880 Main St.
Morro Bay, CA 93442
(805)772-4467

SCORE Office (Mountain View)
580 Castro St.
Mountain View, CA 94041
(415)968-8378
Fax: (415)968-5668

SCORE Office (Napa)
1556 1st St.
Napa, CA 94559
(707)226-7455
Fax: (707)226-1171

SCORE Office (North Hollywood)
5019 Lankershim Blvd.
North Hollywood, CA 91601
(818)552-3206

SCORE Office (Northridge)
8801 Reseda Blvd.
Northridge, CA 91324
(818)349-5676

SCORE Office (Novato)
807 De Long Ave.
Novato, CA 94945
(415)897-1164
Fax: (415)898-9097

SCORE Office (East Bay)
519 17th St.
Oakland, CA 94612

(510)273-6611
Fax: (510)273-6015
E-mail: webmaster@eastbayscore.org
Website: http://www.eastbayscore.org

SCORE Office (Oceanside)
928 N. Coast Hwy.
Oceanside, CA 92054
(619)722-1534

SCORE Office (Ontario)
121 West B. St.
Ontario, CA 91762
Fax: (714)984-6439

SCORE Office (Oxnard)
PO Box 867
Oxnard, CA 93032
(805)385-8860
Fax: (805)487-1763

SCORE Office (Pacifica)
450 Dundee Way, Ste. 2
Pacifica, CA 94044
(415)355-4122

SCORE Office (Palm Desert)
72990 Hwy. 111
Palm Desert, CA 92260
(619)346-6111
Fax: (619)346-3463

SCORE Office (Palm Springs)
650 E. Tahquitz Canyon Way Ste. D
Palm Springs, CA 92262-6706
(760)320-6682
Fax: (760)323-9426

SCORE Office (Lakeside)
2150 Low Tree
Palmdale, CA 93551
(805)948-4518
Fax: (805)949-1212

SCORE Office (Palo Alto)
325 Forest Ave.
Palo Alto, CA 94301
(415)324-3121
Fax: (415)324-1215

SCORE Office (Pasadena)
117 E. Colorado Blvd., Ste. 100
Pasadena, CA 91105
(818)795-3355
Fax: (818)795-5663

SCORE Office (Paso Robles)
1225 Park St.
Paso Robles, CA 93446-2234
(805)238-0506
Fax: (805)238-0527

SCORE Office (Petaluma)
799 Baywood Dr., Ste. 3
Petaluma, CA 94954
(707)762-2785
Fax: (707)762-4721

SCORE Office (Pico Rivera)
9122 E. Washington Blvd.
Pico Rivera, CA 90660

SCORE Office (Pittsburg)
2700 E. Leland Rd.
Pittsburg, CA 94565
(510)439-2181
Fax: (510)427-1599

SCORE Office (Pleasanton)
777 Peters Ave.
Pleasanton, CA 94566
(510)846-9697

SCORE Office (Monterey Park)
485 N. Garey
Pomona, CA 91769

SCORE Office (Pomona)
485 N. Garey Ave.
Pomona, CA 91766
(909)622-1256

SCORE Office (Antelope Valley)
4511 West Ave. M-4
Quartz Hill, CA 93536
(805)272-0087
E-mail: avscore@ptw.com
Website: http://www.score.av.org/

SCORE Office (Shasta)
737 Auditorium Dr.
Redding, CA 96099
(916)225-2770

SCORE Office (Redwood City)
1675 Broadway
Redwood City, CA 94063
(415)364-1722
Fax: (415)364-1729

SCORE Office (Richmond)
3925 MacDonald Ave.
Richmond, CA 94805

SCORE Office (Ridgecrest)
PO Box 771
Ridgecrest, CA 93555
(619)375-8331
Fax: (619)375-0365

SCORE Office (Riverside)
3685 Main St., Ste. 350
Riverside, CA 92501
(909)683-7100

SCORE Office (Sacramento)
9845 Horn Rd., 260-B
Sacramento, CA 95827
(916)361-2322
Fax: (916)361-2164
E-mail: sacchapter@directcon.net

SCORE Office (Salinas)
PO Box 1170
Salinas, CA 93902
(408)424-7611
Fax: (408)424-8639

SCORE Office (Inland Empire)
777 E. Rialto Ave.
Purchasing
San Bernardino, CA 92415-0760
(909)386-8278

SCORE Office (San Carlos)
San Carlos Chamber of Commerce
PO Box 1086
San Carlos, CA 94070
(415)593-1068
Fax: (415)593-9108

SCORE Office (Encinitas)
550 W. C St., Ste. 550
San Diego, CA 92101-3540
(619)557-7272
Fax: (619)557-5894

SCORE Office (San Diego)
550 West C. St., Ste. 550
San Diego, CA 92101-3540
(619)557-7272
Fax: (619)557-5894
Website: http://www.score-sandiego.org

SCORE Office (Menlo Park)
1100 Merrill St.
San Francisco, CA 94105
(415)325-2818
Fax: (415)325-0920

SCORE Office (San Francisco)
455 Market St., 6th Fl.
San Francisco, CA 94105
(415)744-6827
Fax: (415)744-6750
E-mail: sfscore@sfscore.
Website: http://www.sfscore.com

SCORE Office (San Gabriel)
401 W. Las Tunas Dr.
San Gabriel, CA 91776
(818)576-2525
Fax: (818)289-2901

SCORE Office (San Jose)
Deanza College
208 S. 1st. St., Ste. 137
San Jose, CA 95113
(408)288-8479
Fax: (408)535-5541

SCORE Office (Silicon Valley)
84 W. Santa Clara St., Ste. 100
San Jose, CA 95113
(408)288-8479
Fax: (408)535-5541
E-mail: info@svscore.org
Website: http://www.svscore.org

SCORE Office (San Luis Obispo)
3566 S. Hiquera, No. 104
San Luis Obispo, CA 93401
(805)547-0779

SCORE Office (San Mateo)
1021 S. El Camino, 2nd Fl.
San Mateo, CA 94402
(415)341-5679

SCORE Office (San Pedro)
390 W. 7th St.
San Pedro, CA 90731
(310)832-7272

SCORE Office (Orange County)
200 W. Santa Anna Blvd., Ste. 700
Santa Ana, CA 92701
(714)550-7369
Fax: (714)550-0191
Website: http://www.score114.org

SCORE Office (Santa Barbara)
3227 State St.
Santa Barbara, CA 93130
(805)563-0084

SCORE Office (Central Coast)
509 W. Morrison Ave.
Santa Maria, CA 93454
(805)347-7755

SCORE Office (Santa Maria)
614 S. Broadway
Santa Maria, CA 93454-5111
(805)925-2403
Fax: (805)928-7559

SCORE Office (Santa Monica)
501 Colorado, Ste. 150
Santa Monica, CA 90401
(310)393-9825
Fax: (310)394-1868

SCORE Office (Santa Rosa)
777 Sonoma Ave., Rm. 115E
Santa Rosa, CA 95404

(707)571-8342
Fax: (707)541-0331
Website: http://www.pressdemo.com/community/score/score.html

SCORE Office (Scotts Valley)
4 Camp Evers Ln.
Scotts Valley, CA 95066
(408)438-1010
Fax: (408)438-6544

SCORE Office (Simi Valley)
40 W. Cochran St., Ste. 100
Simi Valley, CA 93065
(805)526-3900
Fax: (805)526-6234

SCORE Office (Sonoma)
453 1st St. E
Sonoma, CA 95476
(707)996-1033

SCORE Office (Los Banos)
222 S. Shepard St.
Sonora, CA 95370
(209)532-4212

SCORE Office (Tuolumne County)
39 North Washington St.
Sonora, CA 95370
(209)588-0128
E-mail: score@mlode.com

SCORE Office (South San Francisco)
445 Market St., Ste. 6th Fl.
South San Francisco, CA 94105
(415)744-6827
Fax: (415)744-6812

SCORE Office (Stockton)
401 N. San Joaquin St., Rm. 215
Stockton, CA 95202
(209)946-6293

SCORE Office (Taft)
314 4th St.
Taft, CA 93268
(805)765-2165
Fax: (805)765-6639

SCORE Office (Conejo Valley)
625 W. Hillcrest Dr.
Thousand Oaks, CA 91360
(805)499-1993
Fax: (805)498-7264

SCORE Office (Torrance)
3400 Torrance Blvd., Ste. 100
Torrance, CA 90503
(310)540-5858
Fax: (310)540-7662

SCORE Office (Truckee)
PO Box 2757
Truckee, CA 96160
(916)587-2757
Fax: (916)587-2439

SCORE Office (Visalia)
113 S. M St,
Tulare, CA 93274
(209)627-0766
Fax: (209)627-8149

SCORE Office (Upland)
433 N. 2nd Ave.
Upland, CA 91786
(909)931-4108

SCORE Office (Vallejo)
2 Florida St.
Vallejo, CA 94590
(707)644-5551
Fax: (707)644-5590

SCORE Office (Van Nuys)
14540 Victory Blvd.
Van Nuys, CA 91411
(818)989-0300
Fax: (818)989-3836

SCORE Office (Ventura)
5700 Ralston St., Ste. 310
Ventura, CA 93001
(805)658-2688
Fax: (805)658-2252
E-mail: scoreven@jps.net
Website: http://www.jps.net/scoreven

SCORE Office (Vista)
201 E. Washington St.
Vista, CA 92084
(619)726-1122
Fax: (619)226-8654

SCORE Office (Watsonville)
PO Box 1748
Watsonville, CA 95077
(408)724-3849
Fax: (408)728-5300

SCORE Office (West Covina)
811 S. Sunset Ave.
West Covina, CA 91790
(818)338-8496
Fax: (818)960-0511

SCORE Office (Westlake)
30893 Thousand Oaks Blvd.
Westlake Village, CA 91362
(805)496-5630
Fax: (818)991-1754

Colorado

SCORE Office (Colorado Springs)
2 N. Cascade Ave., Ste. 110
Colorado Springs, CO 80903
(719)636-3074
Website: http://www.cscc.org/score02/index.html

SCORE Office (Denver)
US Custom's House, 4th Fl.
721 19th St.
Denver, CO 80201-0660
(303)844-3985
Fax: (303)844-6490
E-mail: score62@csn.net
Website: http://www.sni.net/score62

SCORE Office (Tri-River)
1102 Grand Ave.
Glenwood Springs, CO 81601
(970)945-6589

SCORE Office (Grand Junction)
2591 B & 3/4 Rd.
Grand Junction, CO 81503
(970)243-5242

SCORE Office (Gunnison)
608 N. 11th
Gunnison, CO 81230
(303)641-4422

SCORE Office (Montrose)
1214 Peppertree Dr.
Montrose, CO 81401
(970)249-6080

SCORE Office (Pagosa Springs)
PO Box 4381
Pagosa Springs, CO 81157
(970)731-4890

SCORE Office (Rifle)
0854 W. Battlement Pky., Apt. C106
Parachute, CO 81635
(970)285-9390

SCORE Office (Pueblo)
302 N. Santa Fe
Pueblo, CO 81003
(719)542-1704
Fax: (719)542-1624
E-mail: mackey@iex.net
Website: http://www.pueblo.org/score

SCORE Office (Ridgway)
143 Poplar Pl.
Ridgway, CO 81432

SCORE Office (Silverton)
PO Box 480

Silverton, CO 81433
(303)387-5430

SCORE Office (Minturn)
PO Box 2066
Vail, CO 81658
(970)476-1224

Connecticut

SCORE Office (Greater Bridgeport)
230 Park Ave.
Bridgeport, CT 06601-0999
(203)576-4369
Fax: (203)576-4388

SCORE Office (Bristol)
10 Main St. 1st. Fl.
Bristol, CT 06010
(203)584-4718
Fax: (203)584-4722

SCORE office (Greater Danbury)
246 Federal Rd.
Unit LL2, Ste. 7
Brookfield, CT 06804
(203)775-1151

SCORE Office (Greater Danbury)
246 Federal Rd., Unit LL2, Ste. 7
Brookfield, CT 06804
(203)775-1151

SCORE Office (Eastern Connecticut)
Administration Bldg., Rm. 313
PO 625
61 Main St. (Chapter 579)
Groton, CT 06475
(203)388-9508

SCORE Office (Greater Hartford County)
330 Main St.
Hartford, CT 06106
(860)548-1749
Fax: (860)240-4659
Website: http://www.score56.org

SCORE Office (Manchester)
20 Hartford Rd.
Manchester, CT 06040
(203)646-2223
Fax: (203)646-5871

SCORE Office (New Britain)
185 Main St., Ste. 431
New Britain, CT 06051
(203)827-4492
Fax: (203)827-4480

SCORE Office (New Haven)
25 Science Pk., Bldg. 25, Rm. 366

New Haven, CT 06511
(203)865-7645

SCORE Office (Fairfield County)
24 Beldon Ave., 5th Fl.
Norwalk, CT 06850
(203)847-7348
Fax: (203)849-9308

SCORE Office (Old Saybrook)
146 Main St.
Old Saybrook, CT 06475
(860)388-9508

SCORE Office (Simsbury)
Box 244
Simsbury, CT 06070
(203)651-7307
Fax: (203)651-1933

SCORE Office (Torrington)
23 North Rd.
Torrington, CT 06791
(203)482-6586

Delaware

SCORE Office (Dover)
Treadway Towers
PO Box 576
Dover, DE 19903
(302)678-0892
Fax: (302)678-0189

SCORE Office (Lewes)
PO Box 1
Lewes, DE 19958
(302)645-8073
Fax: (302)645-8412

SCORE Office (Milford)
204 NE Front St.
Milford, DE 19963
(302)422-3301

SCORE Office (Wilmington)
824 Market St., Ste. 610
Wilmington, DE 19801
(302)573-6652
Fax: (302)573-6092
Website: http://www.scoredelaware.com

District of Columbia

SCORE Office (George Mason University)
409 3rd St. SW, 4th Fl.
Washington, DC 20024
800-634-0245

SCORE Office (Washington DC)
1110 Vermont Ave. NW, 9th Fl.

Washington, DC 20043
(202)606-4000
Fax: (202)606-4225
E-mail: dcscore@hotmail.com
Website: http://www.scoredc.org/

Florida

SCORE Office (Desota County Chamber of Commerce)
16 South Velucia Ave.
Arcadia, FL 34266
(941)494-4033

SCORE Office (Suncoast/Pinellas)
Airport Business Ctr.
4707 - 140th Ave. N, No. 311
Clearwater, FL 33755
(813)532-6800
Fax: (813)532-6800

SCORE Office (DeLand)
336 N. Woodland Blvd.
DeLand, FL 32720
(904)734-4331
Fax: (904)734-4333

SCORE Office (South Palm Beach)
1050 S. Federal Hwy., Ste. 132
Delray Beach, FL 33483
(561)278-7752
Fax: (561)278-0288

SCORE Office (Ft. Lauderdale)
Federal Bldg., Ste. 123
299 E. Broward Blvd.
Ft. Lauderdale, FL 33301
(954)356-7263
Fax: (954)356-7145

SCORE Office (Southwest Florida)
The Renaissance
8695 College Pky., Ste. 345 & 346
Ft. Myers, FL 33919
(941)489-2935
Fax: (941)489-1170

SCORE Office (Treasure Coast)
Professional Center, Ste. 2
3220 S. US, No. 1
Ft. Pierce, FL 34982
(561)489-0548

SCORE Office (Gainesville)
101 SE 2nd Pl., Ste. 104
Gainesville, FL 32601
(904)375-8278

SCORE Office (Hialeah Dade Chamber)
59 W. 5th St.
Hialeah, FL 33010

(305)887-1515
Fax: (305)887-2453

SCORE Office (Daytona Beach)
921 Nova Rd., Ste. A
Holly Hills, FL 32117
(904)255-6889
Fax: (904)255-0229
E-mail: score87@dbeach.com

SCORE Office (South Broward)
3475 Sheridian St., Ste. 203
Hollywood, FL 33021
(305)966-8415

SCORE Office (Citrus County)
5 Poplar Ct.
Homosassa, FL 34446
(352)382-1037

SCORE Office (Jacksonville)
7825 Baymeadows Way, Ste. 100-B
Jacksonville, FL 32256
(904)443-1911
Fax: (904)443-1980
E-mail: scorejax@juno.com
Website: http://www.scorejax.org/

SCORE Office (Jacksonville Satellite)
3 Independent Dr.
Jacksonville, FL 32256
(904)366-6600
Fax: (904)632-0617

SCORE Office (Central Florida)
5410 S. Florida Ave., No. 3
Lakeland, FL 33801
(941)687-5783
Fax: (941)687-6225

SCORE Office (Lakeland)
100 Lake Morton Dr.
Lakeland, FL 33801
(941)686-2168

SCORE Office (St. Petersburg)
800 W. Bay Dr., Ste. 505
Largo, FL 33712
(813)585-4571

SCORE Office (Leesburg)
9501 US Hwy. 441
Leesburg, FL 34788-8751
(352)365-3556
Fax: (352)365-3501

SCORE Office (Cocoa)
1600 Farno Rd., Unit 205
Melbourne, FL 32935
(407)254-2288

SCORE Office (Melbourne)
Melbourne Professional Complex
1600 Sarno, Ste. 205
Melbourne, FL 32935
(407)254-2288
Fax: (407)245-2288

SCORE Office (Merritt Island)
1600 Sarno Rd., Ste. 205
Melbourne, FL 32935
(407)254-2288
Fax: (407)254-2288

SCORE Office (Space Coast)
Melbourn Professional Complex
1600 Sarno, Ste. 205
Melbourne, FL 32935
(407)254-2288
Fax: (407)254-2288

SCORE Office (Dade)
49 NW 5th St.
Miami, FL 33128
(305)371-6889
Fax: (305)374-1882
E-mail: score@netrox.net
Website: http://www.netrox.net/~score/

SCORE Office (Naples of Collier)
International College
2654 Tamiami Trl. E
Naples, FL 34112
(941)417-1280
Fax: (941)417-1281
E-mail: score@naples.net
Website: http://www.naples.net/clubs/
score/index.htm

SCORE Office (Pasco County)
6014 US Hwy. 19, Ste. 302
New Port Richey, FL 34652
(813)842-4638

SCORE Office (Southeast Volusia)
115 Canal St.
New Smyrna Beach, FL 32168
(904)428-2449
Fax: (904)423-3512

SCORE Office (Ocala)
110 E. Silver Springs Blvd.
Ocala, FL 34470
(352)629-5959

Clay County SCORE Office
Clay County Chamber of Commerce
1734 Kingsdey Ave.
PO Box 1441
Orange Park, FL 32073
(904)264-2651
Fax: (904)269-0363

SCORE Office (Orlando)
80 N. Hughey Ave.
Rm. 445 Federal Bldg.
Orlando, FL 32801
(407)648-6476
Fax: (407)648-6425

SCORE Office (Emerald Coast)
19 W. Garden St., No. 325
Pensacola, FL 32501
(904)444-2060
Fax: (904)444-2070

SCORE Office (Charlotte County)
201 W. Marion Ave., Ste. 211
Punta Gorda, FL 33950
(941)575-1818
E-mail: score@gls3c.com
Website: http://www.charlotte-
florida.com/business/scorepg01.htm

SCORE Office (St. Augustine)
1 Riberia St.
St. Augustine, FL 32084
(904)829-5681
Fax: (904)829-6477

SCORE Office (Bradenton)
2801 Fruitville, Ste. 280
Sarasota, FL 34237
(813)955-1029

SCORE Office (Manasota)
2801 Fruitville Rd., Ste. 280
Sarasota, FL 34237
(941)955-1029
Fax: (941)955-5581
E-mail: score116@gte.net
Website: http://www.score-suncoast.org/

SCORE Office (Tallahassee)
200 W. Park Ave.
Tallahassee, FL 32302
(850)487-2665

SCORE Office (Hillsborough)
4732 Dale Mabry Hwy. N, Ste. 400
Tampa, FL 33614-6509
(813)870-0125

SCORE Office (Lake Sumter)
122 E. Main St.
Tavares, FL 32778-3810
(352)365-3556

SCORE Office (Titusville)
2000 S. Washington Ave.
Titusville, FL 32780
(407)267-3036
Fax: (407)264-0127

SCORE Office (Venice)
257 N. Tamiami Trl.
Venice, FL 34285
(941)488-2236
Fax: (941)484-5903

SCORE Office (Palm Beach)
500 Australian Ave. S, Ste. 100
West Palm Beach, FL 33401
(561)833-1672
Fax: (561)833-1712

SCORE Office (Wildwood)
103 N. Webster St.
Wildwood, FL 34785

Georgia

SCORE Office (Atlanta)
Harris Tower, Suite 1900
233 Peachtree Rd., NE
Atlanta, GA 30309
(404)347-2442
Fax: (404)347-1227

SCORE Office (Augusta)
3126 Oxford Rd.
Augusta, GA 30909
(706)869-9100

SCORE Office (Columbus)
School Bldg.
PO Box 40
Columbus, GA 31901
(706)327-3654

SCORE Office (Dalton-Whitfield)
305 S. Thorton Ave.
Dalton, GA 30720
(706)279-3383

SCORE Office (Gainesville)
PO Box 374
Gainesville, GA 30503
(770)532-6206
Fax: (770)535-8419

SCORE Office (Macon)
711 Grand Bldg.
Macon, GA 31201
(912)751-6160

SCORE Office (Brunswick)
4 Glen Ave.
St. Simons Island, GA 31520
(912)265-0620
Fax: (912)265-0629

SCORE Office (Savannah)
111 E. Liberty St., Ste. 103
Savannah, GA 31401
(912)652-4335

Fax: (912)652-4184
E-mail: info@scoresav.org
Website: http://www.coastalempire.com/
score/index.htm

Guam

SCORE Office (Guam)
Pacific News Bldg., Rm. 103
238 Archbishop Flores St.
Agana, GU 96910-5100
(671)472-7308

Hawaii

SCORE Office (Hawaii, Inc.)
1111 Bishop St., Ste. 204
PO Box 50207
Honolulu, HI 96813
(808)522-8132
Fax: (808)522-8135
E-mail: hnlscore@juno.com

SCORE Office (Kahului)
250 Alamaha, Unit N16A
Kahului, HI 96732
(808)871-7711

SCORE Office (Maui, Inc.)
590 E. Lipoa Pkwy., Ste. 227
Kihei, HI 96753
(808)875-2380

Idaho

SCORE Office (Treasure Valley)
1020 Main St., No. 290
Boise, ID 83702
(208)334-1696
Fax: (208)334-9353

SCORE Office (Eastern Idaho)
2300 N. Yellowstone, Ste. 119
Idaho Falls, ID 83401
(208)523-1022
Fax: (208)528-7127

Illinois

SCORE Office (Fox Valley)
40 W. Downer Pl.
PO Box 277
Aurora, IL 60506
(630)897-9214
Fax: (630)897-7002

SCORE Office (Greater Belvidere)
419 S. State St.
Belvidere, IL 61008
(815)544-4357
Fax: (815)547-7654

SCORE Office (Bensenville)
1050 Busse Hwy. Suite 100
Bensenville, IL 60106
(708)350-2944
Fax: (708)350-2979

SCORE Office (Central Illinois)
402 N. Hershey Rd.
Bloomington, IL 61704
(309)644-0549
Fax: (309)663-8270
E-mail: webmaster@central-illinois-
score.org
Website: http://www.central-illinois-
score.org/

SCORE Office (Southern Illinois)
150 E. Pleasant Hill Rd.
Box 1
Carbondale, IL 62901
(618)453-6654
Fax: (618)453-5040

SCORE Office (Chicago)
Northwest Atrium Ctr.
500 W. Madison St., No. 1250
Chicago, IL 60661
(312)353-7724
Fax: (312)886-5688
Website: http://www.mcs.net/~bic/

**SCORE Office (Chicago–Oliver Harvey
College)**
Pullman Bldg.
1000 E. 11th St., 7th Fl.
Chicago, IL 60628
Fax: (312)468-8086

SCORE Office (Danville)
28 W. N. Street
Danville, IL 61832
(217)442-7232
Fax: (217)442-6228

SCORE Office (Decatur)
Milliken University
1184 W. Main St.
Decatur, IL 62522
(217)424-6297
Fax: (217)424-3993
E-mail: charding@mail.millikin.edu
Website: http://www.millikin.edu/
academics/Tabor/score.html

SCORE Office (Downers Grove)
925 Curtis
Downers Grove, IL 60515
(708)968-4050
Fax: (708)968-8368

SCORE Office (Elgin)
24 E. Chicago, 3rd Fl.
PO Box 648
Elgin, IL 60120
(847)741-5660
Fax: (847)741-5677

SCORE Office (Freeport Area)
26 S. Galena Ave.
Freeport, IL 61032
(815)233-1350
Fax: (815)235-4038

SCORE Office (Galesburg)
292 E. Simmons St.
PO Box 749
Galesburg, IL 61401
(309)343-1194
Fax: (309)343-1195

SCORE Office (Glen Ellyn)
500 Pennsylvania
Glen Ellyn, IL 60137
(708)469-0907
Fax: (708)469-0426

SCORE Office (Greater Alton)
Alden Hall
5800 Godfrey Rd.
Godfrey, IL 62035-2466
(618)467-2280
Fax: (618)466-8289
Website: http://www.altonweb.com/
score/

SCORE Office (Grayslake)
19351 W. Washington St.
Grayslake, IL 60030
(708)223-3633
Fax: (708)223-9371

SCORE Office (Harrisburg)
303 S. Commercial
Harrisburg, IL 62946-1528
(618)252-8528
Fax: (618)252-0210

SCORE Office (Joliet)
100 N. Chicago
Joliet, IL 60432
(815)727-5371
Fax: (815)727-5374

SCORE Office (Kankakee)
101 S. Schuyler Ave.
Kankakee, IL 60901
(815)933-0376
Fax: (815)933-0380

SCORE Office (Macomb)
216 Seal Hall, Rm. 214

Macomb, IL 61455
(309)298-1128
Fax: (309)298-2520

SCORE Office (Matteson)
210 Lincoln Mall
Matteson, IL 60443
(708)709-3750
Fax: (708)503-9322

SCORE Office (Mattoon)
1701 Wabash Ave.
Mattoon, IL 61938
(217)235-5661
Fax: (217)234-6544

SCORE Office (Quad Cities)
622 19th St.
Moline, IL 61265
(309)797-0082
Fax: (309)757-5435
E-mail: score@qconline.com
Website: http://www.qconline.com/
business/score/

SCORE Office (Naperville)
131 W. Jefferson Ave.
Naperville, IL 60540
(708)355-4141
Fax: (708)355-8355

SCORE Office (Northbrook)
2002 Walters Ave.
Northbrook, IL 60062
(847)498-5555
Fax: (847)498-5510

SCORE Office (Palos Hills)
10900 S. 88th Ave.
Palos Hills, IL 60465
(847)974-5468
Fax: (847)974-0078

SCORE Office (Peoria)
124 SW Adams, Ste. 300
Peoria, IL 61602
(309)676-0755
Fax: (309)676-7534

SCORE Office (Prospect Heights)
1375 Wolf Rd.
Prospect Heights, IL 60070
(847)537-8660
Fax: (847)537-7138

SCORE Office (Quincy Tri-State)
300 Civic Center Plz., Ste. 245
Quincy, IL 62301
(217)222-8093
Fax: (217)222-3033

SCORE Office (River Grove)
2000 5th Ave.
River Grove, IL 60171
(708)456-0300
Fax: (708)583-3121

SCORE Office (Northern Illinois)
515 N. Court St.
Rockford, IL 61103
(815)962-0122
Fax: (815)962-0122

SCORE Office (St. Charles)
103 N. 1st Ave.
St. Charles, IL 60174-1982
(847)584-8384
Fax: (847)584-6065

SCORE Office (Springfield)
511 W. Capitol Ave., Ste. 302
Springfield, IL 62704
(217)492-4416
Fax: (217)492-4867

SCORE Office (Sycamore)
112 Somunak St.
Sycamore, IL 60178
(815)895-3456
Fax: (815)895-0125

SCORE Office (University)
Hwy. 50 & Stuenkel Rd. Ste. C3305
University Park, IL 60466
(708)534-5000
Fax: (708)534-8457

Indiana

SCORE Office (Anderson)
205 W. 11th St.
Anderson, IN 46015
(317)642-0264

SCORE Office (Bloomington)
Star Center
216 W. Allen
Bloomington, IN 47403
(812)335-7334
E-mail: wtfische@indiana.edu
Website: http://www.brainfreezemedia.
com/score527/

SCORE Office (South East Indiana)
500 Franklin St.
Box 29
Columbus, IN 47201
(812)379-4457

SCORE Office (Corydon)
310 N. Elm St.
Corydon, IN 47112

(812)738-2137
Fax: (812)738-6438

SCORE Office (Crown Point)
Old Courthouse Sq. Ste. 206
PO Box 43
Crown Point, IN 46307
(219)663-1800

SCORE Office (Elkhart)
418 S. Main St.
Elkhart, IN 46515
(219)293-1531
Fax: (219)294-1859

SCORE Office (Evansville)
1100 W. Lloyd Expy., Ste. 105
Evansville, IN 47708
(812)426-6144

SCORE Office (Fort Wayne)
1300 S. Harrison St.
Ft. Wayne, IN 46802
(219)422-2601
Fax: (219)422-2601

SCORE Office (Gary)
973 W. 6th Ave., Rm. 326
Gary, IN 46402
(219)882-3918

SCORE Office (Hammond)
7034 Indianapolis Blvd.
Hammond, IN 46324
(219)931-1000
Fax: (219)845-9548

SCORE Office (Indianapolis)
429 N. Pennsylvania St., Ste. 100
Indianapolis, IN 46204-1873
(317)226-7264
Fax: (317)226-7259
E-mail: inscore@indy.net
Website: http://www.score-
indianapolis.org/

SCORE Office (Jasper)
PO Box 307
Jasper, IN 47547-0307
(812)482-6866

**SCORE Office (Kokomo/Howard
Counties)**
106 N. Washington St.
Kokomo, IN 46901
(765)457-5301
Fax: (765)452-4564

SCORE Office (Logansport)
300 E. Broadway, Ste. 103
Logansport, IN 46947
(219)753-6388

SCORE Office (Madison)
301 E. Main St.
Madison, IN 47250
(812)265-3135
Fax: (812)265-2923

SCORE Office (Marengo)
Rt. 1 Box 224D
Marengo, IN 47140
Fax: (812)365-2793

SCORE Office (Marion/Grant Counties)
215 S. Adams
Marion, IN 46952
(765)664-5107

SCORE Office (Merrillville)
255 W. 80th Pl.
Merrillville, IN 46410
(219)769-8180
Fax: (219)736-6223

SCORE Office (Michigan City)
200 E. Michigan Blvd.
Michigan City, IN 46360
(219)874-6221
Fax: (219)873-1204

SCORE Office (South Central Indiana)
4100 Charleston Rd.
New Albany, IN 47150-9538
(812)945-0066

SCORE Office (Rensselaer)
104 W. Washington
Rensselaer, IN 47978

SCORE Office (Salem)
210 N. Main St.
Salem, IN 47167
(812)883-4303
Fax: (812)883-1467

SCORE Office (South Bend)
300 N. Michigan St.
South Bend, IN 46601
(219)282-4350
E-mail: chair@southbend-score.org
Website: http://www.southbend-score.org/

SCORE Office (Valparaiso)
150 Lincolnway
Valparaiso, IN 46383
(219)462-1105
Fax: (219)469-5710

SCORE Office (Vincennes)
27 N. 3rd
PO Box 553
Vincennes, IN 47591
(812)882-6440
Fax: (812)882-6441

SCORE Office (Wabash)
PO Box 371
Wabash, IN 46992
(219)563-1168
Fax: (219)563-6920

Iowa

SCORE Office (Burlington)
Federal Bldg.
300 N. Main St.
Burlington, IA 52601
(319)752-2967

SCORE Office (Cedar Rapids)
2750 1st Ave. NE, Ste 350
Cedar Rapids, IA 52401-1806
(319)362-6405
Fax: (319)362-7861
E:mail: score@scorecr.org
Website: http://www.scorecr.org

SCORE Office (Illowa)
333 4th Ave. S
Clinton, IA 52732
(319)242-5702

SCORE Office (Council Bluffs)
7 N. 6th St.
Council Bluffs, IA 51502
(712)325-1000

SCORE Office (Northeast Iowa)
3404 285th St.
Cresco, IA 52136
(319)547-3377

SCORE Office (Des Moines)
Federal Bldg., Rm. 749
210 Walnut St.
Des Moines, IA 50309-2186
(515)284-4760

SCORE Office (Ft. Dodge)
Federal Bldg., Rm. 436
205 S. 8th St.
Ft. Dodge, IA 50501
(515)955-2622

SCORE Office (Independence)
110 1st. St. east
Independence, IA 50644
(319)334-7178
Fax: (319)334-7179

SCORE Office (Iowa City)
210 Federal Bldg.
PO Box 1853
Iowa City, IA 52240-1853
(319)338-1662

SCORE Office (Keokuk)
401 Main St.
Pierce Bldg., No. 1
Keokuk, IA 52632
(319)524-5055

SCORE Office (Central Iowa)
Fisher Community College
709 S. Center
Marshalitown, IA 50158
(515)753-6645

SCORE Office (River City)
15 West State St.
Mason City, IA 50401
(515)423-5724

SCORE Office (South Central)
SBDC, Indian Hills Community College
525 Grandview Ave.
Ottumwa, IA 52501
(515)683-5127
Fax: (515)683-5263

SCORE Office (Dubuque)
10250 Sundown Rd.
Peosta, IA 52068
(319)556-5110

SCORE Office (Southwest Iowa)
614 W. Sheridan
Shenandoah, IA 51601
(712)246-3260

SCORE Office (Sioux City)
Federal Bldg.
320 6th St.
Sioux City, IA 51101
(712)277-2324
Fax: (712)277-2325

SCORE Office (Iowa Lakes)
122 W. 5th St.
Spencer, IA 51301
(712)262-3059

SCORE Office (Vista)
119 W. 6th St.
Storm Lake, IA 50588
(712)732-3780

SCORE Office (Waterloo)
215 E. 4th
Waterloo, IA 50703
(319)233-8431

Kansas

SCORE Office (Southwest Kansas)
501 W. Spruce
Dodge City, KS 67801
(316)227-3119

SCORE Office (Emporia)
811 Homewood
Emporia, KS 66801
(316)342-1600

SCORE Office (Golden Belt)
1307 Williams
Great Bend, KS 67530
(316)792-2401

SCORE Office (Hays)
PO Box 400
Hays, KS 67601
(913)625-6595

SCORE Office (Hutchinson)
1 E. 9th St.
Hutchinson, KS 67501
(316)665-8468
Fax: (316)665-7619

SCORE Office (Southeast Kansas)
404 Westminster Pl.
PO Box 886
Independence, KS 67301
(316)331-4741

SCORE Office (McPherson)
306 N. Main
PO Box 616
McPherson, KS 67460
(316)241-3303

SCORE Office (Salina)
120 Ash St.
Salina, KS 67401
(785)243-4290
Fax: (785)243-1833

SCORE Office (Topeka)
1700 College
Topeka, KS 66621
(785)231-1010

SCORE Office (Wichita)
100 E. English, Ste. 510
Wichita, KS 67202
(316)269-6273
Fax: (316)269-6499

SCORE Office (Ark Valley)
205 E. 9th St.
Winfield, KS 67156
(316)221-1617

Kentucky

SCORE Office (Ashland)
PO Box 830
Ashland, KY 41105
(606)329-8011
Fax: (606)325-4607

SCORE Office (Bowling Green)
812 State St.
PO Box 51
Bowling Green, KY 42101
(502)781-3200
Fax: (502)843-0458

SCORE Office (Tri-Lakes)
508 Barbee Way
Danville, KY 40422-1548
(606)231-9902

SCORE Office (Glasgow)
301 W. Main St.
Glasgow, KY 42141
(502)651-3161
Fax: (502)651-3122

SCORE Office (Hazard)
B & I Technical Center
100 Airport Gardens Rd.
Hazard, KY 41701
(606)439-5856
Fax: (606)439-1808

SCORE Office (Lexington)
410 W. Vine St., Ste. 290, Civic C
Lexington, KY 40507
(606)231-9902
Fax: (606)253-3190
E-mail: scorelex@uky.campus.mci.net

SCORE Office (Louisville)
188 Federal Office Bldg.
600 Dr. Martin L. King Jr. Pl.
Louisville, KY 40202
(502)582-5976

SCORE Office (Madisonville)
257 N. Main
Madisonville, KY 42431
(502)825-1399
Fax: (502)825-1396

SCORE Office (Paducah)
Federal Office Bldg.
501 Broadway, Rm. B-36
Paducah, KY 42001
(502)442-5685

Louisiana

SCORE Office (Central Louisiana)
802 3rd St.
Alexandria, LA 71309
(318)442-6671

SCORE Office (Baton Rouge)
564 Laurel St.
PO Box 3217
Baton Rouge, LA 70801

(504)381-7130
Fax: (504)336-4306

SCORE Office (North Shore)
2 W. Thomas
Hammond, LA 70401
(504)345-4457
Fax: (504)345-4749

SCORE Office (Lafayette)
804 St. Mary Blvd.
Lafayette, LA 70505-1307
(318)233-2705
Fax: (318)234-8671
E-mail: score302@aol.com

SCORE Office (Lake Charles)
120 W. Pujo St.
Lake Charles, LA 70601
(318)433-3632

SCORE Office (New Orleans)
365 Canal St., Ste. 3100
New Orleans, LA 70130
(504)589-2356
Fax: (504)589-2339

SCORE Office (Shreveport)
400 Edwards St.
Shreveport, LA 71101
(318)677-2536
Fax: (318)677-2541

Maine

SCORE Office (Augusta)
40 Western Ave.
Augusta, ME 04330
(207)622-8509

SCORE Office (Bangor)
Peabody Hall, Rm. 229
One College Cir.
Bangor, ME 04401
(207)941-9707

SCORE Office (Central & Northern Arroostock)
111 High St.
Caribou, ME 04736
(207)492-8010
Fax: (207)492-8010

SCORE Office (Penquis)
South St.
Dover Foxcroft, ME 04426
(207)564-7021

SCORE Office (Maine Coastal)
Mill Mall
Box 1105
Ellsworth, ME 04605-1105

(207)667-5800
E-mail: score@arcadia.net

SCORE Office (Lewiston-Auburn)
BIC of Maine-Bates Mill Complex
35 Canal St.
Lewiston, ME 04240-7764
(207)782-3708
Fax: (207)783-7745

SCORE Office (Portland)
66 Pearl St., Rm. 210
Portland, ME 04101
(207)772-1147
Fax: (207)772-5581
E-mail: Score53@score.maine.org
Website: http://www.score.maine.org/
chapter53/

SCORE Office (Western Mountains)
255 River St.
PO Box 252
Rumford, ME 04257-0252
(207)369-9976

SCORE Office (Oxford Hills)
166 Main St.
South Paris, ME 04281
(207)743-0499

Maryland

SCORE Office (Southern Maryland)
2525 Riva Rd., Ste. 110
Annapolis, MD 21401
(410)266-9553
Fax: (410)573-0981
E-mail: score390@aol.com
Website: http://members.aol.com/
score390/index.htm

SCORE Office (Baltimore)
The City Crescent Bldg., 6th Fl.
10 S. Howard St.
Baltimore, MD 21201
(410)962-2233
Fax: (410)962-1805

SCORE Office (Bel Air)
108 S. Bond St.
Bel Air, MD 21014
(410)838-2020
Fax: (410)893-4715

SCORE Office (Bethesda)
7910 Woodmont Ave., Ste. 1204
Bethesda, MD 20814
(301)652-4900
Fax: (301)657-1973

SCORE Office (Bowie)
6670 Race Track Rd.
Bowie, MD 20715
(301)262-0920
Fax: (301)262-0921

SCORE Office (Dorchester County)
203 Sunburst Hwy.
Cambridge, MD 21613
(410)228-3575

SCORE Office (Upper Shore)
210 Marlboro Ave.
Easton, MD 21601
(410)822-4606
Fax: (410)822-7922

SCORE Office (Frederick County)
43A S. Market St.
Frederick, MD 21701
(301)662-8723
Fax: (301)846-4427

SCORE Office (Gaithersburg)
9 Park Ave.
Gaithersburg, MD 20877
(301)840-1400
Fax: (301)963-3918

SCORE Office (Glen Burnie)
103 Crain Hwy. SE
Glen Burnie, MD 21061
(410)766-8282
Fax: (410)766-9722

SCORE Office (Hagerstown)
111 W. Washington St.
Hagerstown, MD 21740
(301)739-2015
Fax: (301)739-1278

SCORE Office (Laurel)
7901 Sandy Spring Rd. Ste. 501
Laurel, MD 20707
(301)725-4000
Fax: (301)725-0776

SCORE Office (Salisbury)
300 E. Main St.
Salisbury, MD 21801
(410)749-0185
Fax: (410)860-9925

Massachusetts

SCORE Office (NE Massachusetts)
100 Cummings Ctr., Ste. 101 K
Beverly, MA 01923
(978)922-9441
Website: http://www1.shore.net/~score/

SCORE Office (Boston)
10 Causeway St., Rm. 265
Boston, MA 02222-1093
(617)565-5591
Fax: (617)565-5598
E-mail: boston-score-20@worldnet.att.net
Website: http://www.scoreboston.org/

SCORE office (Bristol/Plymouth County)
53 N. 6th St., Federal Bldg.
Bristol, MA 02740
(508)994-5093

SCORE Office (SE Massachusetts)
60 School St.
Brockton, MA 02401
(508)587-2673
Fax: (508)587-1340
Website: http://www.metrosouth
chamber.com/score.html

SCORE Office (North Adams)
820 N. State Rd.
Cheshire, MA 01225
(413)743-5100

SCORE Office (Clinton Satellite)
1 Green St.
Clinton, MA 01510
Fax: (508)368-7689

SCORE Office (Greenfield)
PO Box 898
Greenfield, MA 01302
(413)773-5463
Fax: (413)773-7008

SCORE Office (Haverhill)
87 Winter St.
Haverhill, MA 01830
(508)373-5663
Fax: (508)373-8060

SCORE Office (Hudson Satellite)
PO Box 578
Hudson, MA 01749
(508)568-0360
Fax: (508)568-0360

SCORE Office (Cape Cod)
Independence Pk., Ste. 5B
270 Communications Way
Hyannis, MA 02601
(508)775-4884
Fax: (508)790-2540

SCORE Office (Lawrence)
264 Essex St.
Lawrence, MA 01840
(508)686-0900
Fax: (508)794-9953

SCORE Office (Leominster Satellite)
110 Erdman Way
Leominster, MA 01453
(508)840-4300
Fax: (508)840-4896

SCORE Office (Bristol/Plymouth Counties)
53 N. 6th St., Federal Bldg.
New Bedford, MA 02740
(508)994-5093

SCORE Office (Newburyport)
29 State St.
Newburyport, MA 01950
(617)462-6680

SCORE Office (Pittsfield)
66 West St.
Pittsfield, MA 01201
(413)499-2485

SCORE Office (Haverhill-Salem)
32 Derby Sq.
Salem, MA 01970
(508)745-0330
Fax: (508)745-3855

SCORE Office (Springfield)
1350 Main St.
Federal Bldg.
Springfield, MA 01103
(413)785-0314

SCORE Office (Carver)
12 Taunton Green, Ste. 201
Taunton, MA 02780
(508)824-4068
Fax: (508)824-4069

SCORE Office (Worcester)
33 Waldo St.
Worcester, MA 01608
(508)753-2929
Fax: (508)754-8560

Michigan

SCORE Office (Allegan)
PO Box 338
Allegan, MI 49010
(616)673-2479

SCORE Office (Ann Arbor)
425 S. Main St., Ste. 103
Ann Arbor, MI 48104
(313)665-4433

SCORE Office (Battle Creek)
34 W. Jackson Ste. 4A
Battle Creek, MI 49017-3505

(616)962-4076
Fax: (616)962-6309

SCORE Office (Cadillac)
222 Lake St.
Cadillac, MI 49601
(616)775-9776
Fax: (616)768-4255

SCORE Office (Detroit)
477 Michigan Ave., Rm. 515
Detroit, MI 48226
(313)226-7947
Fax: (313)226-3448

SCORE Office (Flint)
708 Root Rd., Rm. 308
Flint, MI 48503
(810)233-6846

SCORE Office (Grand Rapids)
111 Pearl St. NW
Grand Rapids, MI 49503-2831
(616)771-0305
Fax: (616)771-0328
E-mail: scoreone@iserv.net
Website: http://www.iserv.net/~
scoreone/

SCORE Office (Holland)
480 State St.
Holland, MI 49423
(616)396-9472

SCORE Office (Jackson)
209 East Washington
PO Box 80
Jackson, MI 49204
(517)782-8221
Fax: (517)782-0061

SCORE Office (Kalamazoo)
345 W. Michigan Ave.
Kalamazoo, MI 49007
(616)381-5382
Fax: (616)384-0096
E-mail: score@nucleus.net

SCORE Office (Lansing)
117 E. Allegan
PO Box 14030
Lansing, MI 48901
(517)487-6340
Fax: (517)484-6910

SCORE Office (Livonia)
15401 Farmington Rd.
Livonia, MI 48154
(313)427-2122
Fax: (313)427-6055

SCORE Office (Madison Heights)
26345 John R
Madison Heights, MI 48071
(810)542-5010
Fax: (810)542-6821

SCORE Office (Monroe)
111 E. 1st
Monroe, MI 48161
(313)242-3366
Fax: (313)242-7253

SCORE Office (Mt. Clemens)
58 S/B Gratiot
Mt. Clemens, MI 48043
(810)463-1528
Fax: (810)463-6541

SCORE Office (Muskegon)
PO Box 1087
230 Terrace Plz.
Muskegon, MI 49443
(616)722-3751
Fax: (616)728-7251

SCORE Office (Petoskey)
401 E. Mitchell St.
Petoskey, MI 49770
(616)347-4150

SCORE Office (Pontiac)
Executive Office Bldg.
1200 N. Telegraph Rd.
Pontiac, MI 48341
(810)975-9555

SCORE Office (Pontiac)
PO Box 430025
Pontiac, MI 48343
(810)335-9600

SCORE Office (Port Huron)
920 Pinegrove Ave.
Port Huron, MI 48060
(810)985-7101

SCORE Office (Rochester)
71 Walnut Ste. 110
Rochester, MI 48307
(810)651-6700
Fax: (810)651-5270

SCORE Office (Saginaw)
901 S. Washington Ave.
Saginaw, MI 48601
(517)752-7161
Fax: (517)752-9055

SCORE Office (Upper Peninsula)
2581 I-75 Business Spur
Sault Ste. Marie, MI 49783
(906)632-3301

SCORE Office (Southfield)
21000 W. 10 Mile Rd.
Southfield, MI 48075
(810)204-3050
Fax: (810)204-3099

SCORE Office (Traverse City)
202 E. Grandview Pkwy.
PO Box 387
Traverse City, MI 49685
(616)947-5075
Fax: (616)946-2565

SCORE Office (Warren)
30500 Van Dyke, Ste. 118
Warren, MI 48093
(810)751-3939

Minnesota

SCORE Office (Aitkin)
Aitkin, MN 56431
(218)741-3906

SCORE Office (Albert Lea)
202 N. Broadway Ave.
Albert Lea, MN 56007
(507)373-7487

SCORE Office (Austin)
PO Box 864
Austin, MN 55912
(507)437-4561
Fax: (507)437-4869

SCORE Office (South Metro)
Ames Business Ctr.
2500 W. County Rd., No. 42
Burnsville, MN 55337
(612)898-5645
Fax: (612)435-6972
E-mail: southmetro@scoreminn.org
Website: http://www.scoreminn.org/
southmetro/

SCORE Office (Duluth)
1717 Minnesota Ave.
Duluth, MN 55802
(218)727-8286
Fax: (218)727-3113
E-mail: duluth@scoreminn.org
Website: http://www.scoreminn.org

SCORE Office (Fairmont)
PO Box 826
Fairmont, MN 56031
(507)235-5547
Fax: (507)235-8411

SCORE Office (Southwest Minnesota)
112 Riverfront St.

Box 999
Mankato, MN 56001
(507)345-4519
Fax: (507)345-4451
Website: http://www.scoreminn.org/

SCORE Office (Minneapolis)
North Plaza Bldg., Ste. 51
5217 Wayzata Blvd.
Minneapolis, MN 55416
(612)591-0539
Fax: (612)544-0436
Website: http://www.scoreminn.org/

SCORE Office (Owatonna)
PO Box 331
Owatonna, MN 55060
(507)451-7970
Fax: (507)451-7972

SCORE Office (Red Wing)
2000 W. Main St., Ste. 324
Red Wing, MN 55066
(612)388-4079

SCORE Office (Southeastern Minnesota)
220 S. Broadway, Ste. 100
Rochester, MN 55901
(507)288-1122
Fax: (507)282-8960
Website: http://www.scoreminn.org/

SCORE Office (Brainerd)
St. Cloud, MN 56301

SCORE Office (Central Area)
1527 Northway Dr.
St. Cloud, MN 56301
(320)240-1332
Fax: (320)255-9050
Website: http://www.scoreminn.org/

SCORE Office (St. Paul)
350 St. Peter St., No. 295
Lowry Professional Bldg.
St. Paul, MN 55102
(651)223-5010
Fax: (651)223-5048
Website: http://www.scoreminn.org/

SCORE Office (Winona)
Box 870
Winona, MN 55987
(507)452-2272
Fax: (507)454-8814

SCORE Office (Worthington)
1121 3rd Ave.
Worthington, MN 56187
(507)372-2919
Fax: (507)372-2827

Mississippi

SCORE Office (Delta)
915 Washington Ave.
PO Box 933
Greenville, MS 38701
(601)378-3141

SCORE Office (Gulfcoast)
1 Government Plaza
2909 13th St., Ste. 203
Gulfport, MS 39501
(228)863-0054

SCORE Office (Jackson)
1st Jackson Center, Ste. 400
101 W. Capitol St.
Jackson, MS 39201
(601)965-5533

SCORE Office (Meridian)
5220 16th Ave.
Meridian, MS 39305
(601)482-4412

Missouri

SCORE Office (Lake of the Ozark)
University Extension
113 Kansas St.
PO Box 1405
Camdenton, MO 65020
(573)346-2644
Fax: (573)346-2694
E-mail: score@cdoc.net
Website: http://sites.cdoc.net/score/

Chamber of Commerce (Cape Girardeau)
PO Box 98
Cape Girardeau, MO 63702-0098
(314)335-3312

SCORE Office (Mid-Missouri)
1705 Halstead Ct.
Columbia, MO 65203
(573)874-1132

SCORE Office (Ozark-Gateway)
1486 Glassy Rd.
Cuba, MO 65453-1640
(573)885-4954

SCORE Office (Kansas City)
323 W. 8th St., Ste. 104
Kansas City, MO 64105
(816)374-6675
Fax: (816)374-6692
E-mail: SCOREBIC@AOL.COM
Website: http://www.crn.org/score/

SCORE Office (Sedalia)
Lucas Place
323 W. 8th St., Ste.104
Kansas City, MO 64105
(816)374-6675

SCORE office (Tri-Lakes)
PO Box 1148
Kimberling, MO 65686
(417)739-3041

SCORE Office (Tri-Lakes)
HCRI Box 85
Lampe, MO 65681
(417)858-6798

SCORE Office (Mexico)
111 N. Washington St.
Mexico, MO 65265
(314)581-2765

SCORE Office (Southeast Missouri)
Rte. 1, Box 280
Neelyville, MO 63954
(573)989-3577

SCORE office (Poplar Bluff Area)
806 Emma St.
Poplar Bluff, MO 63901
(573)686-8892

SCORE Office (St. Joseph)
3003 Frederick Ave.
St. Joseph, MO 64506
(816)232-4461

SCORE Office (St. Louis)
815 Olive St., Rm. 242
St. Louis, MO 63101-1569
(314)539-6970
Fax: (314)539-3785
E-mail: info@stlscore.org
Website: http://www.stlscore.org/

SCORE Office (Lewis & Clark)
425 Spencer Rd.
St. Peters, MO 63376
(314)928-2900
Fax: (314)928-2900
E-mail: score01@mail.win.org

SCORE Office (Springfield)
620 S. Glenstone, Ste. 110
Springfield, MO 65802-3200
(417)864-7670
Fax: (417)864-4108

SCORE office (Southeast Kansas)
1206 W. First St.
Webb City, MO 64870
(417)673-3984

Montana

SCORE Office (Billings)
815 S. 27th St.
Billings, MT 59101
(406)245-4111

SCORE Office (Bozeman)
1205 E. Main St.
Bozeman, MT 59715
(406)586-5421

SCORE Office (Butte)
1000 George St.
Butte, MT 59701
(406)723-3177

SCORE Office (Great Falls)
710 First Ave. N
Great Falls, MT 59401
(406)761-4434
E-mail: scoregtf@in.tch.com

SCORE Office (Havre, Montana)
518 First St.
Havre, MT 59501
(406)265-4383

SCORE Office (Helena)
Federal Bldg.
301 S. Park
Helena, MT 59626-0054
(406)441-1081

SCORE Office (Kalispell)
2 Main St.
Kalispell, MT 59901
(406)756-5271
Fax: (406)752-6665

SCORE Office (Missoula)
723 Ronan
Missoula, MT 59806
(406)327-8806
E-mail: score@safeshop.com
Website: http://missoula.bigsky.net/score/

Nebraska

SCORE Office (Columbus)
Columbus, NE 68601
(402)564-2769

SCORE Office (Fremont)
92 W. 5th St.
Fremont, NE 68025
(402)721-2641

SCORE Office (Hastings)
Hastings, NE 68901
(402)463-3447

SCORE Office (Lincoln)
8800 O St.
Lincoln, NE 68520
(402)437-2409

SCORE Office (Panhandle)
150549 CR 30
Minatare, NE 69356
(308)632-2133
Website: http://www.tandt.com/SCORE

SCORE Office (Norfolk)
3209 S. 48th Ave.
Norfolk, NE 68106
(402)564-2769

SCORE Office (North Platte)
3301 W. 2nd St.
North Platte, NE 69101
(308)532-4466

SCORE Office (Omaha)
11145 Mill Valley Rd.
Omaha, NE 68154
(402)221-3606
Fax: (402)221-3680
E-mail: infoctr@ne.uswest.net
Website: http://www.tandt.com/score/

Nevada

SCORE Office (Incline Village)
969 Tahoe Blvd.
Incline Village, NV 89451
(702)831-7327
Fax: (702)832-1605

SCORE Office (Carson City)
301 E. Stewart
PO Box 7527
Las Vegas, NV 89125
(702)388-6104

SCORE Office (Las Vegas)
300 Las Vegas Blvd. S, Ste. 1100
Las Vegas, NV 89101
(702)388-6104

SCORE Office (Northern Nevada)
SBDC, College of Business
Administration
Univ. of Nevada
Reno, NV 89557-0100
(702)784-4436
Fax: (702)784-4337

New Hampshire

SCORE Office (North Country)
PO Box 34

Berlin, NH 03570
(603)752-1090

SCORE Office (Concord)
143 N. Main St., Rm. 202A
PO Box 1258
Concord, NH 03301
(603)225-1400
Fax: (603)225-1409

SCORE Office (Dover)
299 Central Ave.
Dover, NH 03820
(603)742-2218
Fax: (603)749-6317

SCORE Office (Monadnock)
34 Mechanic St.
Keene, NH 03431-3421
(603)352-0320

SCORE Office (Lakes Region)
67 Water St., Ste. 105
Laconia, NH 03246
(603)524-9168

SCORE Office (Upper Valley)
Citizens Bank Bldg., Rm. 310
20 W. Park St.
Lebanon, NH 03766
(603)448-3491
Fax: (603)448-1908
E-mail: billt@valley.net
Website: http://www.valley.net/~score/

SCORE Office (Merrimack Valley)
275 Chestnut St., Rm. 618
Manchester, NH 03103
(603)666-7561
Fax: (603)666-7925

SCORE Office (Mt. Washington Valley)
PO Box 1066
North Conway, NH 03818
(603)383-0800

SCORE Office (Seacoast)
195 Commerce Way, Unit-A
Portsmouth, NH 03801-3251
(603)433-0575

New Jersey

SCORE Office (Somerset)
Paritan Valley Community College,
Rte. 28
Branchburg, NJ 08807
(908)218-8874
E-mail: nj-score@grizbiz.com.
Website: http://www.nj-score.org/

SCORE Office (Chester)
5 Old Mill Rd.
Chester, NJ 07930
(908)879-7080

**SCORE Office
(Greater Princeton)**
4 A George Washington Dr.
Cranbury, NJ 08512
(609)520-1776

SCORE Office (Freehold)
36 W. Main St.
Freehold, NJ 07728
(908)462-3030
Fax: (908)462-2123

SCORE Office (North West)
Picantinny Innovation Ctr.
3159 Schrader Rd.
Hamburg, NJ 07419
(973)209-8525
Fax: (973)209-7252
E-mail: nj-score@grizbiz.com
Website: http://www.nj-score.org/

SCORE Office (Monmouth)
765 Newman Springs Rd.
Lincroft, NJ 07738
(908)224-2573
E-mail: nj-score@grizbiz.com
Website: http://www.nj-score.org/

SCORE Office (Manalapan)
125 Symmes Dr.
Manalapan, NJ 07726
(908)431-7220

SCORE Office (Jersey City)
2 Gateway Ctr., 4th Fl.
Newark, NJ 07102
(973)645-3982
Fax: (973)645-2375

SCORE Office (Newark)
2 Gateway Center, 15th Fl.
Newark, NJ 07102-5553
(973)645-3982
Fax: (973)645-2375
E-mail: nj-score@grizbiz.com
Website: http://www.nj-score.org

SCORE Office (Bergen County)
327 E. Ridgewood Ave.
Paramus, NJ 07652
(201)599-6090
E-mail: nj-score@grizbiz.com
Website: http://www.nj-score.org/

SCORE Office (Pennsauken)
4900 Rte. 70

Pennsauken, NJ 08109
(609)486-3421

SCORE Office (Southern New Jersey)
4900 Rte. 70
Pennsauken, NJ 08109
(609)486-3421
E-mail: nj-score@grizbiz.com
Website: http://www.nj-score.org/

SCORE Office (Greater Princeton)
216 Rockingham Row
Princeton Forrestal Village
Princeton, NJ 08540
(609)520-1776
Fax: (609)520-9107
E-mail: nj-score@grizbiz.com
Website: http://www.nj-score.org/

SCORE Office (Shrewsbury)
Hwy. 35
Shrewsbury, NJ 07702
(908)842-5995
Fax: (908)219-6140

SCORE Office (Ocean County)
33 Washington St.
Toms River, NJ 08754
(732)505-6033
E-mail: nj-score@grizbiz.com
Website: http://www.nj-score.org/

SCORE Office (Wall)
2700 Allaire Rd.
Wall, NJ 07719
(908)449-8877

SCORE Office (Wayne)
2055 Hamburg Tpke.
Wayne, NJ 07470
(201)831-7788
Fax: (201)831-9112

New Mexico

SCORE Office (Albuquerque)
525 Buena Vista, SE
Albuquerque, NM 87106
(505)272-7999
Fax: (505)272-7963

SCORE Office (Las Cruces)
Loretto Towne Center
505 S. Main St., Ste. 125
Las Cruces, NM 88001
(505)523-5627
Fax: (505)524-2101
E-mail: score.397@zianet.com

SCORE Office (Roswell)
Federal Bldg., Rm. 237

Roswell, NM 88201
(505)625-2112
Fax: (505)623-2545

SCORE Office (Santa Fe)
Montoya Federal Bldg.
120 Federal Place, Rm. 307
Santa Fe, NM 87501
(505)988-6302
Fax: (505)988-6300

New York

SCORE Office (Northeast)
1 Computer Dr. S
Albany, NY 12205
(518)446-1118
Fax: (518)446-1228

SCORE Office (Auburn)
30 South St.
PO Box 675
Auburn, NY 13021
(315)252-7291

SCORE Office (South Tier Binghamton)
Metro Center, 2nd Fl.
49 Court St.
PO Box 995
Binghamton, NY 13902
(607)772-8860

SCORE Office (Queens County City)
12055 Queens Blvd., Rm. 333
Borough Hall, NY 11424
(718)263-8961

SCORE Office (Buffalo)
Federal Bldg., Rm. 1311
111 W. Huron St.
Buffalo, NY 14202
(716)551-4301
Website: http://www2.pcom.net/score/buf45.html

SCORE Office (Canandaigua)
Chamber of Commerce Bldg.
113 S. Main St.
Canandaigua, NY 14424
(716)394-4400
Fax: (716)394-4546

SCORE Office (Chemung)
333 E. Water St., 4th Fl.
Elmira, NY 14901
(607)734-3358

SCORE Office (Geneva)
Chamber of Commerce Bldg.
PO Box 587

Geneva, NY 14456
(315)789-1776
Fax: (315)789-3993

SCORE Office (Glens Falls)
84 Broad St.
Glens Falls, NY 12801
(518)798-8463
Fax: (518)745-1433

SCORE Office (Orange County)
40 Matthews St.
Goshen, NY 10924
(914)294-8080
Fax: (914)294-6121

SCORE Office (Huntington Area)
151 W. Carver St.
Huntington, NY 11743
(516)423-6100

SCORE Office (Tompkins County)
904 E. Shore Dr.
Ithaca, NY 14850
(607)273-7080

SCORE Office (Long Island City)
120-55 Queens Blvd.
Jamaica, NY 11424
(718)263-8961
Fax: (718)263-9032

SCORE Office (Chatauqua)
101 W. 5th St.
Jamestown, NY 14701
(716)484-1103

SCORE Office (Westchester)
2 Caradon Ln.
Katonah, NY 10536
(914)948-3907
Fax: (914)948-4645
E-mail: score@w-w-w.com
Website: http://w-w-w.com/score/

SCORE Office (Queens County)
Queens Borough Hall
120-55 Queens Blvd. Rm. 333
Kew Gardens, NY 11424
(718)263-8961
Fax: (718)263-9032

SCORE Office (Brookhaven)
3233 Rte. 112
Medford, NY 11763
(516)451-6563
Fax: (516)451-6925

SCORE Office (Melville)
35 Pinelawn Rd., Rm. 207-W
Melville, NY 11747
(516)454-0771

SCORE Office (Nassau County)
400 County Seat Dr., No. 140
Mineola, NY 11501
(516)571-3303
E-mail: Counse1998@aol.com
Website: http://members.aol.com/Counse1998/Default.htm

SCORE Office (Mt. Vernon)
4 N. 7th Ave.
Mt. Vernon, NY 10550
(914)667-7500

SCORE Office (New York)
26 Federal Plz., Rm. 3100
New York, NY 10278
(212)264-4507
Fax: (212)264-4963
E-mail: score1000@erols.com
Website: http://users.erols.com/score-nyc/

SCORE Office (Newburgh)
47 Grand St.
Newburgh, NY 12550
(914)562-5100

SCORE Office (Owego)
188 Front St.
Owego, NY 13827
(607)687-2020

SCORE Office (Peekskill)
1 S. Division St.
Peekskill, NY 10566
(914)737-3600
Fax: (914)737-0541

SCORE Office (Penn Yan)
2375 Rte. 14A
Penn Yan, NY 14527
(315)536-3111

SCORE Office (Dutchess)
110 Main St.
Poughkeepsie, NY 12601
(914)454-1700

SCORE Office (Rochester)
601 Keating Federal Bldg., Rm. 410
100 State St.
Rochester, NY 14614
(716)263-6473
Fax: (716)263-3146
Website: http://www.ggw.org/score/

SCORE Office (Saranac Lake)
30 Main St.
Saranac Lake, NY 12983
(315)448-0415

SCORE Office (Suffolk)
286 Main St.
Setauket, NY 11733
(516)751-3886

SCORE Office (Staten Island)
130 Bay St.
Staten Island, NY 10301
(718)727-1221

SCORE Office (Ulster)
Clinton Bldg., Rm. 107
Stone Ridge, NY 12484
(914)687-5035
Fax: (914)687-5015
Website: http://www.scoreulster.org/

SCORE Office (Syracuse)
401 S. Salina, 5th Fl.
Syracuse, NY 13202
(315)471-9393

SCORE Office (Utica)
SUNY Institute of Technology, Route 12
Utica, NY 13504-3050
(315)792-7553

SCORE Office (Watertown)
518 Davidson St.
Watertown, NY 13601
(315)788-1200
Fax: (315)788-8251

North Carolina

SCORE office (Asheboro)
317 E. Dixie Dr.
Asheboro, NC 27203
(336)626-2626
Fax: (336)626-7077

SCORE Office (Asheville)
Federal Bldg., Rm. 259
151 Patton
Asheville, NC 28801-5770
(828)271-4786
Fax: (828)271-4009

SCORE Office (Chapel Hill)
104 S. Estes Dr.
PO Box 2897
Chapel Hill, NC 27514
(919)967-7075

SCORE Office (Coastal Plains)
PO Box 2897
Chapel Hill, NC 27515
(919)967-7075
Fax: (919)968-6874

SCORE Office (Charlotte)
200 N. College St., Ste. A-2015

Charlotte, NC 28202
(704)344-6576
Fax: (704)344-6769
E-mail: CharlotteSCORE47@AOL.com
Website: http://www.charweb.org/business/score/

SCORE Office (Durham)
411 W. Chapel Hill St.
Durham, NC 27707
(919)541-2171

SCORE Office (Gastonia)
PO Box 2168
Gastonia, NC 28053
(704)864-2621
Fax: (704)854-8723

SCORE Office (Greensboro)
400 W. Market St., Ste. 103
Greensboro, NC 27401-2241
(910)333-5399

SCORE Office (Henderson)
PO Box 917
Henderson, NC 27536
(919)492-2061
Fax: (919)430-0460

SCORE Office (Hendersonville)
Federal Bldg., Rm. 108
W. 4th Ave. & Church St.
Hendersonville, NC 28792
(828)693-8702
E-mail: score@circle.net
Website: http://www.wncguide.com/score/Welcome.html

SCORE Office (Unifour)
PO Box 1828
Hickory, NC 28603
(704)328-6111

SCORE Office (High Point)
1101 N. Main St.
High Point, NC 27262
(336)882-8625
Fax: (336)889-9499

SCORE Office (Outer Banks)
Collington Rd. and Mustain
Kill Devil Hills, NC 27948
(252)441-8144

SCORE Office (Down East)
312 S. Front St., Ste. 6
New Bern, NC 28560
(252)633-6688
Fax: (252)633-9608

SCORE Office (Kinston)
PO Box 95

New Bern, NC 28561
(919)633-6688

SCORE Office (Raleigh)
Century Post Office Bldg., Ste. 306
300 Federal St. Mall
Raleigh, NC 27601
(919)856-4739
E-mail: jendres@ibm.net
Website: http://www.intrex.net/score96/score96.htm

SCORE Office (Sanford)
1801 Nash St.
Sanford, NC 27330
(919)774-6442
Fax: (919)776-8739

SCORE Office (Sandhills Area)
1480 Hwy. 15-501
PO Box 458
Southern Pines, NC 28387
(910)692-3926

SCORE Office (Wilmington)
Corps of Engineers Bldg.
96 Darlington Ave., Ste. 207
Wilmington, NC 28403
(910)815-4576
Fax: (910)815-4658

North Dakota

SCORE Office (Bismarck-Mandan)
700 E. Main Ave., 2nd Fl.
PO Box 5509
Bismarck, ND 58506-5509
(701)250-4303

SCORE Office (Fargo)
657 2nd Ave., Rm. 225
Fargo, ND 58108-3083
(701)239-5677

SCORE Office (Upper Red River)
4275 Technology Dr., Rm. 156
Grand Forks, ND 58202-8372
(701)777-3051

SCORE Office (Minot)
100 1st St. SW
Minot, ND 58701-3846
(701)852-6883
Fax: (701)852-6905

Ohio

SCORE Office (Akron)
1 Cascade Plz., 7th Fl.
Akron, OH 44308

(330)379-3163
Fax: (330)379-3164

SCORE Office (Ashland)
Gill Center
47 W. Main St.
Ashland, OH 44805
(419)281-4584

SCORE Office (Canton)
116 Cleveland Ave. NW, Ste. 601
Canton, OH 44702-1720
(330)453-6047

SCORE Office (Chillicothe)
165 S. Paint St.
Chillicothe, OH 45601
(614)772-4530

SCORE Office (Cincinnati)
Ameritrust Bldg., Rm. 850
525 Vine St.
Cincinnati, OH 45202
(513)684-2812
Fax: (513)684-3251
Website: http://www.score.
chapter34.org/

SCORE Office (Cleveland)
Eaton Center, Ste. 620
1100 Superior Ave.
Cleveland, OH 44114-2507
(216)522-4194
Fax: (216)522-4844

SCORE Office (Columbus)
2 Nationwide Plz., Ste. 1400
Columbus, OH 43215-2542
(614)469-2357
Fax: (614)469-2391
E-mail: info@scorecolumbus.org
Website: http://www.scorecolumbus.org/

SCORE Office (Dayton)
Dayton Federal Bldg., Rm. 505
200 W. Second St.
Dayton, OH 45402-1430
(513)225-2887
Fax: (513)225-7667

SCORE Office (Defiance)
615 W. 3rd St.
PO Box 130
Defiance, OH 43512
(419)782-7946

SCORE Office (Findlay)
123 E. Main Cross St.
PO Box 923
Findlay, OH 45840
(419)422-3314

SCORE Office (Lima)
147 N. Main St.
Lima, OH 45801
(419)222-6045
Fax: (419)229-0266

SCORE Office (Mansfield)
55 N. Mulberry St.
Mansfield, OH 44902
(419)522-3211

SCORE Office (Marietta)
Thomas Hall
Marietta, OH 45750
(614)373-0268

SCORE Office (Medina)
County Administrative Bldg.
144 N. Broadway
Medina, OH 44256
(216)764-8650

SCORE Office (Licking County)
50 W. Locust St.
Newark, OH 43055
(614)345-7458

SCORE Office (Salem)
2491 State Rte. 45 S
Salem, OH 44460
(216)332-0361

SCORE Office (Tiffin)
62 S. Washington St.
Tiffin, OH 44883
(419)447-4141
Fax: (419)447-5141

SCORE Office (Toledo)
608 Madison Ave, Ste. 910
Toledo, OH 43624
(419)259-7598
Fax: (419)259-6460

SCORE Office (Heart of Ohio)
377 W. Liberty St.
Wooster, OH 44691
(330)262-5735
Fax: (330)262-5745

SCORE Office (Youngstown)
306 Williamson Hall
Youngstown, OH 44555
(330)746-2687

Oklahoma

SCORE Office (Anadarko)
PO Box 366
Anadarko, OK 73005
(405)247-6651

SCORE Office (Ardmore)
410 W. Main
Ardmore, OK 73401
(580)226-2620

SCORE Office (Northeast Oklahoma)
210 S. Main
Grove, OK 74344
(918)787-2796
Fax: (918)787-2796
E-mail: Score595@greencis.net

SCORE Office (Lawton)
4500 W. Lee Blvd., Bldg. 100, Ste. 107
Lawton, OK 73505
(580)353-8727
Fax: (580)250-5677

SCORE Office (Oklahoma City)
210 Park Ave., No. 1300
Oklahoma City, OK 73102
(405)231-5163
Fax: (405)231-4876
E-mail: score212@usa.net

SCORE Office (Stillwater)
439 S. Main
Stillwater, OK 74074
(405)372-5573
Fax: (405)372-4316

SCORE Office (Tulsa)
616 S. Boston, Ste. 406
Tulsa, OK 74119
(918)581-7462
Fax: (918)581-6908
Website: http://www.ionet.net/~tulscore/

Oregon

SCORE Office (Bend)
63085 N. Hwy. 97
Bend, OR 97701
(541)923-2849
Fax: (541)330-6900

SCORE Office (Willamette)
1401 Willamette St.
PO Box 1107
Eugene, OR 97401-4003
(541)465-6600
Fax: (541)484-4942

SCORE Office (Florence)
3149 Oak St.
Florence, OR 97439
(503)997-8444
Fax: (503)997-8448

SCORE Office (Southern Oregon)
33 N. Central Ave., Ste. 216

Medford, OR 97501
(541)776-4220
E-mail: pgr134f@prodigy.com

SCORE Office (Portland)
1515 SW 5th Ave., Ste. 1050
Portland, OR 97201
(503)326-3441
Fax: (503)326-2808
E-mail: gr134@prodigy.com

SCORE Office (Salem)
416 State St. (corner of Liberty)
Salem, OR 97301
(503)370-2896

Pennsylvania

SCORE Office (Altoona-Blair)
1212 12th Ave.
Altoona, PA 16601-3493
(814)943-8151

SCORE Office (Lehigh Valley)
Rauch Bldg. 37
Lehigh University
621 Taylor St.
Bethlehem, PA 18015
(610)758-4496
Fax: (610)758-5205

SCORE Office (Butler County)
100 N. Main St.
PO Box 1082
Butler, PA 16003
(412)283-2222
Fax: (412)283-0224

SCORE Office (Harrisburg)
4211 Trindle Rd.
Camp Hill, PA 17011
(717)761-4304
Fax: (717)761-4315

SCORE Office (Cumberland Valley)
75 S. 2nd St.
Chambersburg, PA 17201
(717)264-2935

SCORE Office (Monroe County-Stroudsburg)
556 Main St.
East Stroudsburg, PA 18301
(717)421-4433

SCORE Office (Erie)
120 W. 9th St.
Erie, PA 16501
(814)871-5650
Fax: (814)871-7530

SCORE Office (Bucks County)
409 Hood Blvd.
Fairless Hills, PA 19030
(215)943-8850
Fax: (215)943-7404

SCORE Office (Hanover)
146 Broadway
Hanover, PA 17331
(717)637-6130
Fax: (717)637-9127

SCORE Office (Harrisburg)
100 Chestnut, Ste. 309
Harrisburg, PA 17101
(717)782-3874

SCORE Office (East Montgomery County)
Baederwood Shopping Center
1653 The Fairways, Ste. 204
Jenkintown, PA 19046
(215)885-3027

SCORE Office (Kittanning)
2 Butler Rd.
Kittanning, PA 16201
(412)543-1305
Fax: (412)543-6206

SCORE Office (Lancaster)
118 W. Chestnut St.
Lancaster, PA 17603
(717)397-3092

SCORE Office (Westmoreland County)
300 Fraser Purchase Rd.
Latrobe, PA 15650-2690
(412)539-7505
Fax: (412)539-1850

SCORE Office (Lebanon)
252 N. 8th St.
PO Box 899
Lebanon, PA 17042-0899
(717)273-3727
Fax: (717)273-7940

SCORE Office (Lewistown)
3 W. Monument Sq., Ste. 204
Lewistown, PA 17044
(717)248-6713
Fax: (717)248-6714

SCORE Office (Delaware County)
602 E. Baltimore Pike
Media, PA 19063
(610)565-3677
Fax: (610)565-1606

SCORE Office (Milton Area)
112 S. Front St.
Milton, PA 17847

(717)742-7341
Fax: (717)792-2008

SCORE Office (Mon-Valley)
435 Donner Ave.
Monessen, PA 15062
(412)684-4277
Fax: (412)684-7688

SCORE Office (Monroeville)
William Penn Plaza
2790 Mosside Blvd., Ste. 295
Monroeville, PA 15146
(412)856-0622
Fax: (412)856-1030

SCORE Office (Airport Area)
986 Brodhead Rd.
Moon Township, PA 15108-2398
(412)264-6270
Fax: (412)264-1575

SCORE Office (Northeast)
8601 E. Roosevelt Blvd.
Philadelphia, PA 19152
(215)332-3400
Fax: (215)332-6050

SCORE Office (Philadelphia)
1315 Walnut St., Ste. 500
Philadelphia, PA 19107
(215)790-5050
Fax: (215)790-5057
E-mail: score46@bellatlantic.net
Website: http://www.pgweb.net/score46/

SCORE Office (Pittsburgh)
1000 Liberty Ave., Rm. 1122
Pittsburgh, PA 15222
(412)395-6560
Fax: (412)395-6562

SCORE Office (Tri-County)
801 N. Charlotte St.
Pottstown, PA 19464
(610)327-2673

SCORE Office (Reading)
601 Penn St.
Reading, PA 19601
(610)376-3497

SCORE Office (Scranton)
Oppenheim Bldg.
116 N. Washington Ave., Ste. 650
Scranton, PA 18503
(717)347-4611
Fax: (717)347-4611

SCORE Office (Central Pennsylvania)
200 Innovation Blvd., Ste. 242-B
State College, PA 16803

(814)234-9415
Fax: (814)238-9686
Website: http://countrystore.org/
business/score.htm

SCORE Office (Monroe-Stroudsburg)
556 Main St.
Stroudsburg, PA 18360
(717)421-4433

SCORE Office (Uniontown)
Federal Bldg.
Pittsburg St.
PO Box 2065 DTS
Uniontown, PA 15401
(412)437-4222
E-mail: uniontownscore@lcsys.net

SCORE Office (Warren County)
315 2nd Ave.
Warren, PA 16365
(814)723-9017

SCORE Office (Waynesboro)
323 E. Main St.
Waynesboro, PA 17268
(717)762-7123
Fax: (717)962-7124

SCORE Office (Chester County)
Government Service Center, Ste. 281
601 Westtown Rd.
West Chester, PA 19382-4538
(610)344-6910
Fax: (610)344-6919
E-mail: score@locke.ccil.org

SCORE Office (Wilkes-Barre)
7 N. Wilkes-Barre Blvd.
Wilkes Barre, PA 18702-5241
(717)826-6502
Fax: (717)826-6287

SCORE Office (North Central Pennsylvania)
240 W. 3rd St., Rm. 227
PO Box 725
Williamsport, PA 17703
(717)322-3720
Fax: (717)322-1607
E-mail: score234@mail.csrlink.net
Website: http://www.lycoming.org/
score/

SCORE Office (York)
Cyber Center
2101 Pennsylvania Ave.
York, PA 17404
(717)845-8830
Fax: (717)854-9333

Puerto Rico

SCORE Office (Puerto Rico & Virgin Islands)
PO Box 12383-96
San Juan, PR 00914-0383
(787)726-8040
Fax: (787)726-8135

Rhode Island

SCORE Office (Barrington)
281 County Rd.
Barrington, RI 02806
(401)247-1920
Fax: (401)247-3763

SCORE Office (Woonsocket)
640 Washington Hwy.
Lincoln, RI 02865
(401)334-1000
Fax: (401)334-1009

SCORE Office (Wickford)
8045 Post Rd.
North Kingstown, RI 02852
(401)295-5566
Fax: (401)295-8987

SCORE Office (J.G.E. Knight)
380 Westminster St.
Providence, RI 02903
(401)528-4571
Fax: (401)528-4539
Website: http://www.riscore.org

SCORE Office (Warwick)
3288 Post Rd.
Warwick, RI 02886
(401)732-1100
Fax: (401)732-1101

SCORE Office (Westerly)
74 Post Rd.
Westerly, RI 02891
(401)596-7761
800-732-7636
Fax: (401)596-2190

South Carolina

SCORE Office (Aiken)
PO Box 892
Aiken, SC 29802
(803)641-1111
800-542-4536
Fax: (803)641-4174

SCORE Office (Anderson)
Anderson Mall
3130 N. Main St.

Anderson, SC 29621
(864)224-0453

SCORE Office (Coastal)
284 King St.
Charleston, SC 29401
(803)727-4778
Fax: (803)853-2529

SCORE Office (Midlands)
Strom Thurmond Bldg., Rm. 358
1835 Assembly St., Rm 358
Columbia, SC 29201
(803)765-5131
Fax: (803)765-5962
Website: http://www.scoremid
lands.org/

SCORE Office (Piedmont)
Federal Bldg., Rm. B-02
300 E. Washington St.
Greenville, SC 29601
(864)271-3638

SCORE Office (Greenwood)
PO Drawer 1467
Greenwood, SC 29648
(864)223-8357

SCORE Office (Hilton Head Island)
52 Savannah Trail
Hilton Head, SC 29926
(803)785-7107
Fax: (803)785-7110

SCORE Office (Grand Strand)
937 Broadway
Myrtle Beach, SC 29577
(803)918-1079
Fax: (803)918-1083
E-mail: score381@aol.com

SCORE Office (Spartanburg)
PO Box 1636
Spartanburg, SC 29304
(864)594-5000
Fax: (864)594-5055

South Dakota

SCORE Office (West River)
Rushmore Plz. Civic Ctr.
444 Mount Rushmore Rd., No. 209
Rapid City, SD 57701
(605)394-5311
E-mail: score@gwtc.net

SCORE Office (Sioux Falls)
First Financial Center
110 S. Phillips Ave., Ste. 200
Sioux Falls, SD 57104-6727

(605)330-4231
Fax: (605)330-4231

Tennessee

SCORE Office (Chattanooga)
Federal Bldg., Rm. 26
900 Georgia Ave.
Chattanooga, TN 37402
(423)752-5190
Fax: (423)752-5335

SCORE Office (Cleveland)
PO Box 2275
Cleveland, TN 37320
(423)472-6587
Fax: (423)472-2019

SCORE Office (Upper Cumberland Center)
1225 S. Willow Ave.
Cookeville, TN 38501
(615)432-4111
Fax: (615)432-6010

SCORE Office (Unicoi County)
PO Box 713
Erwin, TN 37650
(423)743-3000
Fax: (423)743-0942

SCORE Office (Greeneville)
115 Academy St.
Greeneville, TN 37743
(423)638-4111
Fax: (423)638-5345

SCORE Office (Jackson)
194 Auditorium St.
Jackson, TN 38301
(901)423-2200

SCORE Office (Northeast Tennessee)
1st Tennessee Bank Bldg.
2710 S. Roan St., Ste. 584
Johnson City, TN 37601
(423)929-7686
Fax: (423)461-8052

SCORE Office (Kingsport)
151 E. Main St.
Kingsport, TN 37662
(423)392-8805

SCORE Office (Greater Knoxville)
Farragot Bldg., Ste. 224
530 S. Gay St.
Knoxville, TN 37902
(423)545-4203
E-mail: scoreknox@ntown.com
Website: http://www.scoreknox.org/

SCORE Office (Maryville)
201 S. Washington St.
Maryville, TN 37804-5728
(423)983-2241
800-525-6834
Fax: (423)984-1386

SCORE Office (Memphis)
Federal Bldg., Ste. 390
167 N. Main St.
Memphis, TN 38103
(901)544-3588

SCORE Office (Nashville)
50 Vantage Way, Ste. 201
Nashville, TN 37228-1500
(615)736-7621

Texas

SCORE Office (Abilene)
2106 Federal Post Office and Court Bldg.
Abilene, TX 79601
(915)677-1857

SCORE Office (Austin)
2501 S. Congress
Austin, TX 78701
(512)442-7235
Fax: (512)442-7528

SCORE Office (Golden Triangle)
450 Boyd St.
Beaumont, TX 77704
(409)838-6581
Fax: (409)833-6718

SCORE Office (Brownsville)
3505 Boca Chica Blvd., Ste. 305
Brownsville, TX 78521
(210)541-4508

SCORE Office (Brazos Valley)
3000 Briarcrest, Ste. 302
Bryan, TX 77802
(409)776-8876
E-mail: 102633.2612@compuserve.com

SCORE Office (Cleburne)
Watergarden Pl., 9th Fl., Ste. 400
Cleburne, TX 76031
(817)871-6002

SCORE Office (Corpus Christi)
651 Upper North Broadway, Ste. 654
Corpus Christi, TX 78477
(512)888-4322
Fax: (512)888-3418

SCORE Office (Dallas)
6260 E. Mockingbird
Dallas, TX 75214-2619

(214)828-2471
Fax: (214)821-8033

SCORE Office (El Paso)
10 Civic Center Plaza
El Paso, TX 79901
(915)534-0541
Fax: (915)534-0513

SCORE Office (Bedford)
100 E. 15th St., Ste. 400
Ft. Worth, TX 76102
(817)871-6002

SCORE Office (Ft. Worth)
100 E. 15th St., No. 24
Ft. Worth, TX 76102
(817)871-6002
Fax: (817)871-6031
E-mail: fwbac@onramp.net

SCORE Office (Garland)
2734 W. Kingsley Rd.
Garland, TX 75041
(214)271-9224

SCORE Office (Granbury Chamber of Commerce)
416 S. Morgan
Granbury, TX 76048
(817)573-1622
Fax: (817)573-0805

SCORE Office (Lower Rio Grande Valley)
222 E. Van Buren, Ste. 500
Harlingen, TX 78550
(956)427-8533
Fax: (956)427-8537

SCORE Office (Houston)
9301 Southwest Fwy., Ste. 550
Houston, TX 77074
(713)773-6565
Fax: (713)773-6550

SCORE Office (Irving)
3333 N. MacArthur Blvd., Ste. 100
Irving, TX 75062
(214)252-8484
Fax: (214)252-6710

SCORE Office (Lubbock)
1205 Texas Ave., Rm. 411D
Lubbock, TX 79401
(806)472-7462
Fax: (806)472-7487

SCORE Office (Midland)
Post Office Annex
200 E. Wall St., Rm. P121
Midland, TX 79701
(915)687-2649

SCORE Office (Orange)
1012 Green Ave.
Orange, TX 77630-5620
(409)883-3536
800-528-4906
Fax: (409)886-3247

SCORE Office (Plano)
1200 E. 15th St.
PO Drawer 940287
Plano, TX 75094-0287
(214)424-7547
Fax: (214)422-5182

SCORE Office (Port Arthur)
4749 Twin City Hwy., Ste. 300
Port Arthur, TX 77642
(409)963-1107
Fax: (409)963-3322

SCORE Office (Richardson)
411 Belle Grove
Richardson, TX 75080
(214)234-4141
800-777-8001
Fax: (214)680-9103

SCORE Office (San Antonio)
Federal Bldg., Rm. A527
727 E. Durango
San Antonio, TX 78206
(210)472-5931
Fax: (210)472-5935

SCORE Office (Texarkana State College)
819 State Line Ave.
Texarkana, TX 75501
(903)792-7191
Fax: (903)793-4304

SCORE Office (East Texas)
RTDC
1530 SSW Loop 323, Ste. 100
Tyler, TX 75701
(903)510-2975
Fax: (903)510-2978

SCORE Office (Waco)
401 Franklin Ave.
Waco, TX 76701
(817)754-8898
Fax: (817)756-0776
Website: http://www.brc-waco.com/

SCORE Office (Wichita Falls)
Hamilton Bldg.
900 8th St.
Wichita Falls, TX 76307
(940)723-2741
Fax: (940)723-8773

Utah

SCORE Office (Northern Utah)
160 N. Main
Logan, UT 84321
(435)746-2269

SCORE Office (Ogden)
1701 E. Windsor Dr.
Ogden, UT 84604
(801)629-8613
E-mail: score158@netscape.net

SCORE Office (Central Utah)
1071 E. Windsor Dr.
Provo, UT 84604
(801)373-8660

SCORE Office (Southern Utah)
225 South 700 East
St. George, UT 84770
(435)652-7751

SCORE Office (Salt Lake)
310 S Main St.
Salt Lake City, UT 84101
(801)746-2269
Fax: (801)746-2273

Vermont

SCORE Office (Champlain Valley)
Winston Prouty Federal Bldg.
11 Lincoln St., Rm. 106
Essex Junction, VT 05452
(802)951-6762

SCORE Office (Montpelier)
87 State St., Rm. 205
PO Box 605
Montpelier, VT 05601
(802)828-4422
Fax: (802)828-4485

SCORE Office (Marble Valley)
256 N. Main St.
Rutland, VT 05701-2413
(802)773-9147

SCORE Office (Northeast Kingdom)
20 Main St.
PO Box 904
St. Johnsbury, VT 05819
(802)748-5101

Virgin Islands

SCORE Office (St. Croix)
United Plaza Shopping Center
PO Box 4010, Christiansted
St. Croix, VI 00822
(809)778-5380

SCORE Office (St. Thomas-St. John)
Federal Bldg., Rm. 21
Veterans Dr.
St. Thomas, VI 00801
(809)774-8530

Virginia

SCORE Office (Arlington)
2009 N. 14th St., Ste. 111
Arlington, VA 22201
(703)525-2400

SCORE Office (Blacksburg)
141 Jackson St.
Blacksburg, VA 24060
(540)552-4061

SCORE Office (Bristol)
20 Volunteer Pkwy.
Bristol, VA 24203
(540)989-4850

SCORE Office (Central Virginia)
1001 E. Market St., Ste. 101
Charlottesville, VA 22902
(804)295-6712
Fax: (804)295-7066

SCORE Office (Alleghany Satellite)
241 W. Main St.
Covington, VA 24426
(540)962-2178
Fax: (540)962-2179

SCORE Office (Central Fairfax)
3975 University Dr., Ste. 350
Fairfax, VA 22030
(703)591-2450

SCORE Office (Falls Church)
PO Box 491
Falls Church, VA 22040
(703)532-1050
Fax: (703)237-7904

SCORE Office (Glenns)
Glenns Campus
Box 287
Glenns, VA 23149
(804)693-9650

SCORE Office (Peninsula)
6 Manhattan Sq.
PO Box 7269
Hampton, VA 23666
(757)766-2000
Fax: (757)865-0339
E-mail: score100@seva.net

SCORE Office (Tri-Cities)
108 N. Main St.

Hopewell, VA 23860
(804)458-5536

SCORE Office (Lynchburg)
Federal Bldg.
1100 Main St.
Lynchburg, VA 24504-1714
(804)846-3235

SCORE Office (Greater Prince William)
8963 Center St
Manassas, VA 20110
(703)368-4813
Fax: (703)368-4733

SCORE Office (Martinsvile)
115 Broad St.
Martinsville, VA 24112-0709
(540)632-6401
Fax: (540)632-5059

SCORE Office (Hampton Roads)
Federal Bldg., Rm. 737
200 Grandby St.
Norfolk, VA 23510
(757)441-3733
Fax: (757)441-3733
E-mail: scorehr60@juno.com

SCORE Office (Norfolk)
Federal Bldg., Rm. 737
200 Granby St.
Norfolk, VA 23510
(757)441-3733
Fax: (757)441-3733

SCORE Office (Virginia Beach)
Chamber of Commerce
200 Grandby St., Rm 737
Norfolk, VA 23510
(804)441-3733

SCORE Office (Radford)
1126 Norwood St.
Radford, VA 24141
(540)639-2202

SCORE Office (Richmond)
Federal Bldg.
400 N. 8th St., Ste. 1150
PO Box 10126
Richmond, VA 23240-0126
(804)771-2400
Fax: (804)771-8018
E-mail: scorechapter12@yahoo.com
Website: http://www.cvco.org/score/

SCORE Office (Roanoke)
Federal Bldg., Rm. 716
250 Franklin Rd.
Roanoke, VA 24011

(540)857-2834
Fax: (540)857-2043
E-mail: scorerva@juno.com
Website: http://hometown.aol.com/
scorerv/Index.html

SCORE Office (Fairfax)
8391 Old Courthouse Rd., Ste. 300
Vienna, VA 22182
(703)749-0400

SCORE Office (Greater Vienna)
513 Maple Ave. West
Vienna, VA 22180
(703)281-1333
Fax: (703)242-1482

SCORE Office (Shenandoah Valley)
301 W. Main St.
Waynesboro, VA 22980
(540)949-8203
Fax: (540)949-7740
E-mail: score427@intelos.net

SCORE Office (Williamsburg)
201 Penniman Rd.
Williamsburg, VA 23185
(757)229-6511
E-mail: wacc@williamsburgcc.com

SCORE Office (Northern Virginia)
1360 S. Pleasant Valley Rd.
Winchester, VA 22601
(540)662-4118

Washington

SCORE Office (Gray's Harbor)
506 Duffy St.
Aberdeen, WA 98520
(360)532-1924
Fax: (360)533-7945

SCORE Office (Bellingham)
101 E. Holly St.
Bellingham, WA 98225
(360)676-3307

SCORE Office (Everett)
2702 Hoyt Ave.
Everett, WA 98201-3556
(206)259-8000

SCORE Office (Gig Harbor)
3125 Judson St.
Gig Harbor, WA 98335
(206)851-6865

SCORE Office (Kennewick)
PO Box 6986
Kennewick, WA 99336
(509)736-0510

SCORE Office (Puyallup)
322 2nd St. SW
PO Box 1298
Puyallup, WA 98371
(206)845-6755
Fax: (206)848-6164

SCORE Office (Seattle)
1200 6th Ave., Ste. 1700
Seattle, WA 98101
(206)553-7320
Fax: (206)553-7044
E-mail: score55@aol.com
Website: http://www.scn.org/civic/score-
online/index55.html

SCORE Office (Spokane)
801 W. Riverside Ave., No. 240
Spokane, WA 99201
(509)353-2820
Fax: (509)353-2600
E-mail: score@dmi.net
Website: http://www.dmi.net/score/

SCORE Office (Clover Park)
PO Box 1933
Tacoma, WA 98401-1933
(206)627-2175

SCORE Office (Tacoma)
1101 Pacific Ave.
Tacoma, WA 98402
(253)274-1288
Fax: (253)274-1289

SCORE Office (Fort Vancouver)
1701 Broadway, S-1
Vancouver, WA 98663
(360)699-1079

SCORE Office (Walla Walla)
500 Tausick Way
Walla Walla, WA 99362
(509)527-4681

SCORE Office (Mid-Columbia)
1113 S. 14th Ave.
Yakima, WA 98907
(509)574-4944
Fax: (509)574-2943
Website: http://www.ellensburg.com/~
score/

West Virginia

SCORE Office (Charleston)
1116 Smith St.
Charleston, WV 25301
(304)347-5463
E-mail: score256@juno.com

Organizations, Agencies, & Consultants

SCORE Office (Virginia Street)
1116 Smith St., Ste. 302
Charleston, WV 25301
(304)347-5463

SCORE Office (Marion County)
PO Box 208
Fairmont, WV 26555-0208
(304)363-0486

SCORE Office (Upper Monongahela Valley)
1000 Technology Dr., Ste. 1111
Fairmont, WV 26555
(304)363-0486
E-mail: score537@hotmail.com

SCORE Office (Huntington)
1101 6th Ave., Ste. 220
Huntington, WV 25701-2309
(304)523-4092

SCORE Office (Wheeling)
1310 Market St.
Wheeling, WV 26003
(304)233-2575
Fax: (304)233-1320

Wisconsin

SCORE Office (Fox Cities)
227 S. Walnut St.
Appleton, WI 54913
(920)734-7101
Fax: (920)734-7161

SCORE Office (Beloit)
136 W. Grand Ave., Ste. 100
PO Box 717
Beloit, WI 53511
(608)365-8835
Fax: (608)365-9170

SCORE Office (Eau Claire)
Federal Bldg., Rm. B11
510 S. Barstow St.
Eau Claire, WI 54701
(715)834-1573
E-mail: score@ecol.net
Website: http://www.ecol.net/~score/

SCORE Office (Fond du Lac)
207 N. Main St.
Fond du Lac, WI 54935
(414)921-9500
Fax: (414)921-9559

SCORE Office (Green Bay)
835 Potts Ave.
Green Bay, WI 54304
(414)496-8930
Fax: (414)496-6009

SCORE Office (Janesville)
20 S. Main St., Ste. 11
PO Box 8008
Janesville, WI 53547
(608)757-3160
Fax: (608)757-3170

SCORE Office (La Crosse)
712 Main St.
La Crosse, WI 54602-0219
(608)784-4880

SCORE Office (Madison)
505 S. Rosa Rd.
Madison, WI 53719
(608)441-2820

SCORE Office (Manitowoc)
1515 Memorial Dr.
PO Box 903
Manitowoc, WI 54221-0903
(414)684-5575
Fax: (414)684-1915

SCORE Office (Milwaukee)
310 W. Wisconsin Ave., Ste. 425
Milwaukee, WI 53203
(414)297-3942
Fax: (414)297-1377

SCORE Office (Central Wisconsin)
1224 Lindbergh Ave.
Stevens Point, WI 54481
(715)344-7729

SCORE Office (Superior)
Superior Business Center Inc.
1423 N. 8th St.
Superior, WI 54880
(715)394-7388
Fax: (715)393-7414

SCORE Office (Waukesha)
223 Wisconsin Ave.
Waukesha, WI 53186-4926
(414)542-4249

SCORE Office (Wausau)
300 3rd St., Ste. 200
Wausau, WI 54402-6190
(715)845-6231

SCORE Office (Wisconsin Rapids)
2240 Kingston Rd.
Wisconsin Rapids, WI 54494
(715)423-1830

Wyoming

SCORE Office (Casper)
Federal Bldg., No. 2215
100 East B St.

Casper, WY 82602
(307)261-6529
Fax: (307)261-6530

Venture capital & financing companies

This section contains a listing of financing and loan companies in the United States and Canada. These listing are arranged alphabetically by country, then by state or province, then by city, then by organization name.

Canada

Alberta

Launchworks Inc.
1902J 11th St., S.E.
Calgary, AB, Canada T2G 3G2
(403)269-1119
Fax: (403)269-1141
Website: http://www.launchworks.com

Native Venture Capital Company, Inc.
21 Artist View Point, Box 7
Site 25, RR 12
Calgary, AB, Canada T3E 6W3
(903)208-5380

Miralta Capital Inc.
4445 Calgary Trail South
888 Terrace Plaza Alberta
Edmonton, AB, Canada T6H 5R7
(780)438-3535
Fax: (780)438-3129

Vencap Equities Alberta Ltd.
10180-101st St., Ste. 1980
Edmonton, AB, Canada T5J 3S4
(403)420-1171
Fax: (403)429-2541

British Columbia

Discovery Capital
5th Fl., 1199 West Hastings
Vancouver, BC, Canada V6E 3T5
(604)683-3000
Fax: (604)662-3457
E-mail: info@discoverycapital.com
Website: http://www.discoverycapital.com

Greenstone Venture Partners
1177 West Hastings St.
Ste. 400
Vancouver, BC, Canada V6E 2K3
(604)717-1977
Fax: (604)717-1976
Website: http://www.greenstonevc.com

Growthworks Capital
2600-1055 West Georgia St.
Box 11170 Royal Centre
Vancouver, BC, Canada V6E 3R5
(604)895-7259
Fax: (604)669-7605
Website: http://www.wofund.com

MDS Discovery Venture Management, Inc.
555 W. Eighth Ave., Ste. 305
Vancouver, BC, Canada V5Z 1C6
(604)872-8464
Fax: (604)872-2977
E-mail: info@mds-ventures.com

Ventures West Management Inc.
1285 W. Pender St., Ste. 280
Vancouver, BC, Canada V6E 4B1
(604)688-9495
Fax: (604)687-2145
Website: http://www.ventureswest.com

Nova Scotia

ACF Equity Atlantic Inc.
Purdy's Wharf Tower II
Ste. 2106
Halifax, NS, Canada B3J 3R7
(902)421-1965
Fax: (902)421-1808

Montgomerie, Huck & Co.
146 Bluenose Dr.
PO Box 538
Lunenburg, NS, Canada B0J 2C0
(902)634-7125
Fax: (902)634-7130

Ontario

IPS Industrial Promotion Services Ltd.
60 Columbia Way, Ste. 720
Markham, ON, Canada L3R 0C9
(905)475-9400
Fax: (905)475-5003

Betwin Investments Inc.
Box 23110
Sault Ste. Marie, ON, Canada P6A 6W6
(705)253-0744
Fax: (705)253-0744

Bailey & Company, Inc.
594 Spadina Ave.
Toronto, ON, Canada M5S 2H4
(416)921-6930
Fax: (416)925-4670

BCE Capital
200 Bay St.

South Tower, Ste. 3120
Toronto, ON, Canada M5J 2J2
(416)815-0078
Fax: (416)941-1073
Website: http://www.bcecapital.com

Castlehill Ventures
55 University Ave., Ste. 500
Toronto, ON, Canada M5J 2H7
(416)862-8574
Fax: (416)862-8875

CCFL Mezzanine Partners of Canada
70 University Ave.
Ste. 1450
Toronto, ON, Canada M5J 2M4
(416)977-1450
Fax: (416)977-6764
E-mail: info@ccfl.com
Website: http://www.ccfl.com

Celtic House International
100 Simcoe St., Ste. 100
Toronto, ON, Canada M5H 3G2
(416)542-2436
Fax: (416)542-2435
Website: http://www.celtic-house.com

Clairvest Group Inc.
22 St. Clair Ave. East
Ste. 1700
Toronto, ON, Canada M4T 2S3
(416)925-9270
Fax: (416)925-5753

Crosbie & Co., Inc.
One First Canadian Place
9th Fl.
PO Box 116
Toronto, ON, Canada M5X 1A4
(416)362-7726
Fax: (416)362-3447
E-mail: info@crosbieco.com
Website: http://www.crosbieco.com

Drug Royalty Corp.
Eight King St. East
Ste. 202
Toronto, ON, Canada M5C 1B5
(416)863-1865
Fax: (416)863-5161

Grieve, Horner, Brown & Asculai
8 King St. E, Ste. 1704
Toronto, ON, Canada M5C 1B5
(416)362-7668
Fax: (416)362-7660

Jefferson Partners
77 King St. West
Ste. 4010

PO Box 136
Toronto, ON, Canada M5K 1H1
(416)367-1533
Fax: (416)367-5827
Website: http://www.jefferson.com

J.L. Albright Venture Partners
Canada Trust Tower, 161 Bay St.
Ste. 4440
PO Box 215
Toronto, ON, Canada M5J 2S1
(416)367-2440
Fax: (416)367-4604
Website: http://www.jlventures.com

McLean Watson Capital Inc.
One First Canadian Place
Ste. 1410
PO Box 129
Toronto, ON, Canada M5X 1A4
(416)363-2000
Fax: (416)363-2010
Website: http://www.mcleanwatson.com

Middlefield Capital Fund
One First Canadian Place
85th Fl.
PO Box 192
Toronto, ON, Canada M5X 1A6
(416)362-0714
Fax: (416)362-7925
Website: http://www.middlefield.com

Mosaic Venture Partners
24 Duncan St.
Ste. 300
Toronto, ON, Canada M5V 3M6
(416)597-8889
Fax: (416)597-2345

Onex Corp.
161 Bay St.
PO Box 700
Toronto, ON, Canada M5J 2S1
(416)362-7711
Fax: (416)362-5765

Penfund Partners Inc.
145 King St. West
Ste. 1920
Toronto, ON, Canada M5H 1J8
(416)865-0300
Fax: (416)364-6912
Website: http://www.penfund.com

Primaxis Technology Ventures Inc.
1 Richmond St. West, 8th Fl.
Toronto, ON, Canada M5H 3W4
(416)313-5210
Fax: (416)313-5218
Website: http://www.primaxis.com

Priveq Capital Funds
240 Duncan Mill Rd., Ste. 602
Toronto, ON, Canada M3B 3P1
(416)447-3330
Fax: (416)447-3331
E-mail: priveq@sympatico.ca

Roynat Ventures
40 King St. West, 26th Fl.
Toronto, ON, Canada M5H 1H1
(416)933-2667
Fax: (416)933-2783
Website: http://www.roynatcapital.com

Tera Capital Corp.
366 Adelaide St. East, Ste. 337
Toronto, ON, Canada M5A 3X9
(416)368-1024
Fax: (416)368-1427

Working Ventures Canadian Fund Inc.
250 Bloor St. East, Ste. 1600
Toronto, ON, Canada M4W 1E6
(416)934-7718
Fax: (416)929-0901
Website: http://www.workingventures.ca

Quebec

Altamira Capital Corp.
202 University
Niveau de Maisoneuve, Bur. 201
Montreal, QC, Canada H3A 2A5
(514)499-1656
Fax: (514)499-9570

Federal Business Development Bank
Venture Capital Division
Five Place Ville Marie, Ste. 600
Montreal, QC, Canada H3B 5E7
(514)283-1896
Fax: (514)283-5455

Hydro-Quebec Capitech Inc.
75 Boul, Rene Levesque Quest
Montreal, QC, Canada H2Z 1A4
(514)289-4783
Fax: (514)289-5420
Website: http://www.hqcapitech.com

Investissement Desjardins
2 complexe Desjardins
C.P. 760
Montreal, QC, Canada H5B 1B8
(514)281-7131
Fax: (514)281-7808
Website: http://www.desjardins.com/id

Marleau Lemire Inc.
One Place Ville-Marie, Ste. 3601
Montreal, QC, Canada H3B 3P2

(514)877-3800
Fax: (514)875-6415

Speirs Consultants Inc.
365 Stanstead
Montreal, QC, Canada H3R 1X5
(514)342-3858
Fax: (514)342-1977

Tecnocap Inc.
4028 Marlowe
Montreal, QC, Canada H4A 3M2
(514)483-6009
Fax: (514)483-6045
Website: http://www.technocap.com

Telsoft Ventures
1000, Rue de la Gauchetiere
Quest, 25eme Etage
Montreal, QC, Canada H3B 4W5
(514)397-8450
Fax: (514)397-8451

Saskatchewan

Saskatchewan Government Growth Fund
1801 Hamilton St., Ste. 1210
Canada Trust Tower
Regina, SK, Canada S4P 4B4
(306)787-2994
Fax: (306)787-2086

United states

Alabama

FHL Capital Corp.
600 20th Street North
Suite 350
Birmingham, AL 35203
(205)328-3098
Fax: (205)323-0001

Harbert Management Corp.
One Riverchase Pkwy. South
Birmingham, AL 35244
(205)987-5500
Fax: (205)987-5707
Website: http://www.harbert.net

Jefferson Capital Fund
PO Box 13129
Birmingham, AL 35213
(205)324-7709

Private Capital Corp.
100 Brookwood Pl., 4th Fl.
Birmingham, AL 35209
(205)879-2722
Fax: (205)879-5121

21st Century Health Ventures
One Health South Pkwy.
Birmingham, AL 35243
(256)268-6250
Fax: (256)970-8928

FJC Growth Capital Corp.
200 W. Side Sq., Ste. 340
Huntsville, AL 35801
(256)922-2918
Fax: (256)922-2909

Hickory Venture Capital Corp.
301 Washington St. NW
Suite 301
Huntsville, AL 35801
(256)539-1931
Fax: (256)539-5130
E-mail: hvcc@hvcc.com
Website: http://www.hvcc.com

Southeastern Technology Fund
7910 South Memorial Pkwy., Ste. F
Huntsville, AL 35802
(256)883-8711
Fax: (256)883-8558

Cordova Ventures
4121 Carmichael Rd., Ste. 301
Montgomery, AL 36106
(334)271-6011
Fax: (334)260-0120
Website: http://www.cordova
ventures.com

**Small Business Clinic of Alabama/AG
Bartholomew & Associates**
PO Box 231074
Montgomery, AL 36123-1074
(334)284-3640

Arizona

Miller Capital Corp.
4909 E. McDowell Rd.
Phoenix, AZ 85008
(602)225-0504
Fax: (602)225-9024
Website: http://www.themiller
group.com

The Columbine Venture Funds
9449 North 90th St., Ste. 200
Scottsdale, AZ 85258
(602)661-9222
Fax: (602)661-6262

Koch Ventures
17767 N. Perimeter Dr., Ste. 101
Scottsdale, AZ 85255
(480)419-3600

Fax: (480)419-3606
Website: http://www.kochventures.com

McKee & Co.
7702 E. Doubletree Ranch Rd.
Suite 230
Scottsdale, AZ 85258
(480)368-0333
Fax: (480)607-7446

Merita Capital Ltd.
7350 E. Stetson Dr., Ste. 108-A
Scottsdale, AZ 85251
(480)947-8700
Fax: (480)947-8766

Valley Ventures / Arizona Growth Partners L.P.
6720 N. Scottsdale Rd., Ste. 208
Scottsdale, AZ 85253
(480)661-6600
Fax: (480)661-6262

Estreetcapital.com
660 South Mill Ave., Ste. 315
Tempe, AZ 85281
(480)968-8400
Fax: (480)968-8480
Website: http://www.estreetcapital.com

Coronado Venture Fund
PO Box 65420
Tucson, AZ 85728-5420
(520)577-3764
Fax: (520)299-8491

Arkansas

Arkansas Capital Corp.
225 South Pulaski St.
Little Rock, AR 72201
(501)374-9247
Fax: (501)374-9425
Website: http://www.arcapital.com

California

Sundance Venture Partners, L.P.
100 Clocktower Place, Ste. 130
Carmel, CA 93923
(831)625-6500
Fax: (831)625-6590

Westar Capital (Costa Mesa)
949 South Coast Dr., Ste. 650
Costa Mesa, CA 92626
(714)481-5160
Fax: (714)481-5166
E-mail: mailbox@westarcapital.com
Website: http://www.westarcapital.com

Alpine Technology Ventures
20300 Stevens Creek Boulevard, Ste. 495
Cupertino, CA 95014
(408)725-1810
Fax: (408)725-1207
Website: http://www.alpineventures.com

Bay Partners
10600 N. De Anza Blvd.
Cupertino, CA 95014-2031
(408)725-2444
Fax: (408)446-4502
Website: http://www.baypartners.com

Novus Ventures
20111 Stevens Creek Blvd., Ste. 130
Cupertino, CA 95014
(408)252-3900
Fax: (408)252-1713
Website: http://www.novusventures.com

Triune Capital
19925 Stevens Creek Blvd., Ste. 200
Cupertino, CA 95014
(310)284-6800
Fax: (310)284-3290

Acorn Ventures
268 Bush St., Ste. 2829
Daly City, CA 94014
(650)994-7801
Fax: (650)994-3305
Website: http://www.acornventures.com

Digital Media Campus
2221 Park Place
El Segundo, CA 90245
(310)426-8000
Fax: (310)426-8010
E-mail: info@thecampus.com
Website: http://www.digital
mediacampus.com

BankAmerica Ventures / BA Venture Partners
950 Tower Ln., Ste. 700
Foster City, CA 94404
(650)378-6000
Fax: (650)378-6040
Website: http://
www.baventurepartners.com

Starting Point Partners
666 Portofino Lane
Foster City, CA 94404
(650)722-1035
Website: http://www.startingpoint
partners.com

Opportunity Capital Partners
2201 Walnut Ave., Ste. 210

Fremont, CA 94538
(510)795-7000
Fax: (510)494-5439
Website: http://www.ocpcapital.com

Imperial Ventures Inc.
9920 S. La Cienega Boulevar, 14th Fl.
Inglewood, CA 90301
(310)417-5409
Fax: (310)338-6115

Ventana Global (Irvine)
18881 Von Karman Ave., Ste. 1150
Irvine, CA 92612
(949)476-2204
Fax: (949)752-0223
Website: http://www.ventanaglobal.com

Integrated Consortium Inc.
50 Ridgecrest Rd.
Kentfield, CA 94904
(415)925-0386
Fax: (415)461-2726

Enterprise Partners
979 Ivanhoe Ave., Ste. 550
La Jolla, CA 92037
(858)454-8833
Fax: (858)454-2489
Website: http://www.epvc.com

Domain Associates
28202 Cabot Rd., Ste. 200
Laguna Niguel, CA 92677
(949)347-2446
Fax: (949)347-9720
Website: http://www.domainvc.com

Cascade Communications Ventures
60 E. Sir Francis Drake Blvd., Ste. 300
Larkspur, CA 94939
(415)925-6500
Fax: (415)925-6501

Allegis Capital
One First St., Ste. Two
Los Altos, CA 94022
(650)917-5900
Fax: (650)917-5901
Website: http://www.allegiscapital.com

Aspen Ventures
1000 Fremont Ave., Ste. 200
Los Altos, CA 94024
(650)917-5670
Fax: (650)917-5677
Website: http://www.aspenventures.com

AVI Capital L.P.
1 First St., Ste. 2
Los Altos, CA 94022

(650)949-9862
Fax: (650)949-8510
Website: http://www.avicapital.com

Bastion Capital Corp.
1999 Avenue of the Stars, Ste. 2960
Los Angeles, CA 90067
(310)788-5700
Fax: (310)277-7582
E-mail: ga@bastioncapital.com
Website: http://www.bastioncapital.com

Davis Group
PO Box 69953
Los Angeles, CA 90069-0953
(310)659-6327
Fax: (310)659-6337

Developers Equity Corp.
1880 Century Park East, Ste. 211
Los Angeles, CA 90067
(213)277-0300

Far East Capital Corp.
350 S. Grand Ave., Ste. 4100
Los Angeles, CA 90071
(213)687-1361
Fax: (213)617-7939
E-mail: free@fareastnationalbank.com

Kline Hawkes & Co.
11726 San Vicente Blvd., Ste. 300
Los Angeles, CA 90049
(310)442-4700
Fax: (310)442-4707
Website: http://www.klinehawkes.com

Lawrence Financial Group
701 Teakwood
PO Box 491773
Los Angeles, CA 90049
(310)471-4060
Fax: (310)472-3155

Riordan Lewis & Haden
300 S. Grand Ave., 29th Fl.
Los Angeles, CA 90071
(213)229-8500
Fax: (213)229-8597

Union Venture Corp.
445 S. Figueroa St., 9th Fl.
Los Angeles, CA 90071
(213)236-4092
Fax: (213)236-6329

Wedbush Capital Partners
1000 Wilshire Blvd.
Los Angeles, CA 90017
(213)688-4545
Fax: (213)688-6642
Website: http://www.wedbush.com

Advent International Corp.
2180 Sand Hill Rd., Ste. 420
Menlo Park, CA 94025
(650)233-7500
Fax: (650)233-7515
Website: http://www.adventinter
national.com

Altos Ventures
2882 Sand Hill Rd., Ste. 100
Menlo Park, CA 94025
(650)234-9771
Fax: (650)233-9821
Website: http://www.altosvc.com

Applied Technology
1010 El Camino Real, Ste. 300
Menlo Park, CA 94025
(415)326-8622
Fax: (415)326-8163

APV Technology Partners
535 Middlefield, Ste. 150
Menlo Park, CA 94025
(650)327-7871
Fax: (650)327-7631
Website: http://www.apvtp.com

August Capital Management
2480 Sand Hill Rd., Ste. 101
Menlo Park, CA 94025
(650)234-9900
Fax: (650)234-9910
Website: http://www.augustcap.com

Baccharis Capital Inc.
2420 Sand Hill Rd., Ste. 100
Menlo Park, CA 94025
(650)324-6844
Fax: (650)854-3025

Benchmark Capital
2480 Sand Hill Rd., Ste. 200
Menlo Park, CA 94025
(650)854-8180
Fax: (650)854-8183
E-mail: info@benchmark.com
Website: http://www.benchmark.com

Bessemer Venture Partners (Menlo Park)
535 Middlefield Rd., Ste. 245
Menlo Park, CA 94025
(650)853-7000
Fax: (650)853-7001
Website: http://www.bvp.com

The Cambria Group
1600 El Camino Real Rd., Ste. 155
Menlo Park, CA 94025
(650)329-8600

Fax: (650)329-8601
Website: http://www.cambriagroup.com

Canaan Partners
2884 Sand Hill Rd., Ste. 115
Menlo Park, CA 94025
(650)854-8092
Fax: (650)854-8127
Website: http://www.canaan.com

Capstone Ventures
3000 Sand Hill Rd., Bldg. One, Ste. 290
Menlo Park, CA 94025
(650)854-2523
Fax: (650)854-9010
Website: http://www.capstonevc.com

Comdisco Venture Group (Silicon Valley)
3000 Sand Hill Rd., Bldg. 1, Ste. 155
Menlo Park, CA 94025
(650)854-9484
Fax: (650)854-4026

Commtech International
535 Middlefield Rd., Ste. 200
Menlo Park, CA 94025
(650)328-0190
Fax: (650)328-6442

Compass Technology Partners
1550 El Camino Real, Ste. 275
Menlo Park, CA 94025-4111
(650)322-7595
Fax: (650)322-0588
Website: http://www.compass
techpartners.com

Convergence Partners
3000 Sand Hill Rd., Ste. 235
Menlo Park, CA 94025
(650)854-3010
Fax: (650)854-3015
Website: http://www.conver
gencepartners.com

The Dakota Group
PO Box 1025
Menlo Park, CA 94025
(650)853-0600
Fax: (650)851-4899
E-mail: info@dakota.com

Delphi Ventures
3000 Sand Hill Rd.
Bldg. One, Ste. 135
Menlo Park, CA 94025
(650)854-9650
Fax: (650)854-2961
Website: http://www.delphiventures.com

El Dorado Ventures
2884 Sand Hill Rd., Ste. 121
Menlo Park, CA 94025
(650)854-1200
Fax: (650)854-1202
Website: http://www.eldorado
ventures.com

Glynn Ventures
3000 Sand Hill Rd., Bldg. 4, Ste. 235
Menlo Park, CA 94025
(650)854-2215

Indosuez Ventures
2180 Sand Hill Rd., Ste. 450
Menlo Park, CA 94025
(650)854-0587
Fax: (650)323-5561
Website: http://www.indosuez
ventures.com

Institutional Venture Partners
3000 Sand Hill Rd., Bldg. 2, Ste. 290
Menlo Park, CA 94025
(650)854-0132
Fax: (650)854-5762
Website: http://www.ivp.com

Interwest Partners (Menlo Park)
3000 Sand Hill Rd., Bldg. 3, Ste. 255
Menlo Park, CA 94025-7112
(650)854-8585
Fax: (650)854-4706
Website: http://www.interwest.com

**Kleiner Perkins Caufield & Byers
(Menlo Park)**
2750 Sand Hill Rd.
Menlo Park, CA 94025
(650)233-2750
Fax: (650)233-0300
Website: http://www.kpcb.com

Magic Venture Capital LLC
1010 El Camino Real, Ste. 300
Menlo Park, CA 94025
(650)325-4149

Matrix Partners
2500 Sand Hill Rd., Ste. 113
Menlo Park, CA 94025
(650)854-3131
Fax: (650)854-3296
Website: http://www.matrixpartners.com

Mayfield Fund
2800 Sand Hill Rd.
Menlo Park, CA 94025
(650)854-5560
Fax: (650)854-5712
Website: http://www.mayfield.com

**McCown De Leeuw and Co. (Menlo
Park)**
3000 Sand Hill Rd., Bldg. 3, Ste. 290
Menlo Park, CA 94025-7111
(650)854-6000
Fax: (650)854-0853
Website: http://www.mdcpartners.com

Menlo Ventures
3000 Sand Hill Rd., Bldg. 4, Ste. 100
Menlo Park, CA 94025
(650)854-8540
Fax: (650)854-7059
Website: http://www.menloventures.com

Merrill Pickard Anderson & Eyre
2480 Sand Hill Rd., Ste. 200
Menlo Park, CA 94025
(650)854-8600
Fax: (650)854-0345

**New Enterprise Associates (Menlo
Park)**
2490 Sand Hill Rd.
Menlo Park, CA 94025
(650)854-9499
Fax: (650)854-9397
Website: http://www.nea.com

Onset Ventures
2400 Sand Hill Rd., Ste. 150
Menlo Park, CA 94025
(650)529-0700
Fax: (650)529-0777
Website: http://www.onset.com

Paragon Venture Partners
3000 Sand Hill Rd., Bldg. 1, Ste. 275
Menlo Park, CA 94025
(650)854-8000
Fax: (650)854-7260

**Pathfinder Venture Capital Funds
(Menlo Park)**
3000 Sand Hill Rd., Bldg. 3, Ste. 255
Menlo Park, CA 94025
(650)854-0650
Fax: (650)854-4706

Rocket Ventures
3000 Sandhill Rd., Bldg. 1, Ste. 170
Menlo Park, CA 94025
(650)561-9100
Fax: (650)561-9183
Website: http://www.rocketventures.com

Sequoia Capital
3000 Sand Hill Rd., Bldg. 4, Ste. 280
Menlo Park, CA 94025
(650)854-3927
Fax: (650)854-2977

E-mail: sequoia@sequioacap.com
Website: http://www.sequoiacap.com

Sierra Ventures
3000 Sand Hill Rd., Bldg. 4, Ste. 210
Menlo Park, CA 94025
(650)854-1000
Fax: (650)854-5593
Website: http://www.sierraventures.com

Sigma Partners
2884 Sand Hill Rd., Ste. 121
Menlo Park, CA 94025-7022
(650)853-1700
Fax: (650)853-1717
E-mail: info@sigmapartners.com
Website: http://www.sigmapartners.com

Sprout Group (Menlo Park)
3000 Sand Hill Rd.
Bldg. 3, Ste. 170
Menlo Park, CA 94025
(650)234-2700
Fax: (650)234-2779
Website: http://www.sproutgroup.com

TA Associates (Menlo Park)
70 Willow Rd., Ste. 100
Menlo Park, CA 94025
(650)328-1210
Fax: (650)326-4933
Website: http://www.ta.com

Thompson Clive & Partners Ltd.
3000 Sand Hill Rd., Bldg. 1, Ste. 185
Menlo Park, CA 94025-7102
(650)854-0314
Fax: (650)854-0670
E-mail: mail@tcvc.com
Website: http://www.tcvc.com

Trinity Ventures Ltd.
3000 Sand Hill Rd., Bldg. 1, Ste. 240
Menlo Park, CA 94025
(650)854-9500
Fax: (650)854-9501
Website: http://www.trinityventures.com

U.S. Venture Partners
2180 Sand Hill Rd., Ste. 300
Menlo Park, CA 94025
(650)854-9080
Fax: (650)854-3018
Website: http://www.usvp.com

USVP-Schlein Marketing Fund
2180 Sand Hill Rd., Ste. 300
Menlo Park, CA 94025
(415)854-9080
Fax: (415)854-3018
Website: http://www.usvp.com

Venrock Associates
2494 Sand Hill Rd., Ste. 200
Menlo Park, CA 94025
(650)561-9580
Fax: (650)561-9180
Website: http://www.venrock.com

Brad Peery Capital Inc.
145 Chapel Pkwy.
Mill Valley, CA 94941
(415)389-0625
Fax: (415)389-1336

Dot Edu Ventures
650 Castro St., Ste. 270
Mountain View, CA 94041
(650)575-5638
Fax: (650)325-5247
Website: http://www.dotedu
ventures.com

Forrest, Binkley & Brown
840 Newport Ctr. Dr., Ste. 480
Newport Beach, CA 92660
(949)729-3222
Fax: (949)729-3226
Website: http://www.fbbvc.com

Marwit Capital LLC
180 Newport Center Dr., Ste. 200
Newport Beach, CA 92660
(949)640-6234
Fax: (949)720-8077
Website: http://www.marwit.com

**Kaiser Permanente / National Venture
Development**
1800 Harrison St., 22nd Fl.
Oakland, CA 94612
(510)267-4010
Fax: (510)267-4036
Website: http://www.kpventures.com

Nu Capital Access Group, Ltd.
7677 Oakport St., Ste. 105
Oakland, CA 94621
(510)635-7345
Fax: (510)635-7068

Inman and Bowman
4 Orinda Way, Bldg. D, Ste. 150
Orinda, CA 94563
(510)253-1611
Fax: (510)253-9037

Accel Partners (San Francisco)
428 University Ave.
Palo Alto, CA 94301
(650)614-4800
Fax: (650)614-4880
Website: http://www.accel.com

Advanced Technology Ventures
485 Ramona St., Ste. 200
Palo Alto, CA 94301
(650)321-8601
Fax: (650)321-0934
Website: http://www.atvcapital.com

Anila Fund
400 Channing Ave.
Palo Alto, CA 94301
(650)833-5790
Fax: (650)833-0590
Website: http://www.anila.com

**Asset Management Company Venture
Capital**
2275 E. Bayshore, Ste. 150
Palo Alto, CA 94303
(650)494-7400
Fax: (650)856-1826
E-mail: postmaster@assetman.com
Website: http://www.assetman.com

**BancBoston Capital / BancBoston
Ventures**
435 Tasso St., Ste. 250
Palo Alto, CA 94305
(650)470-4100
Fax: (650)853-1425
Website: http://www.bancboston
capital.com

Charter Ventures
525 University Ave., Ste. 1400
Palo Alto, CA 94301
(650)325-6953
Fax: (650)325-4762
Website: http://www.charterventures.com

Communications Ventures
505 Hamilton Avenue, Ste. 305
Palo Alto, CA 94301
(650)325-9600
Fax: (650)325-9608
Website: http://www.comven.com

HMS Group
2468 Embarcadero Way
Palo Alto, CA 94303-3313
(650)856-9862
Fax: (650)856-9864

Jafco America Ventures, Inc.
505 Hamilton Ste. 310
Palto Alto, CA 94301
(650)463-8800
Fax: (650)463-8801
Website: http://www.jafco.com

New Vista Capital
540 Cowper St., Ste. 200

Palo Alto, CA 94301
(650)329-9333
Fax: (650)328-9434
E-mail: fgreene@nvcap.com
Website: http://www.nvcap.com

Norwest Equity Partners (Palo Alto)
245 Lytton Ave., Ste. 250
Palo Alto, CA 94301-1426
(650)321-8000
Fax: (650)321-8010
Website: http://www.norwestvp.com

Oak Investment Partners
525 University Ave., Ste. 1300
Palo Alto, CA 94301
(650)614-3700
Fax: (650)328-6345
Website: http://www.oakinv.com

**Patricof & Co. Ventures, Inc. (Palo
Alto)**
2100 Geng Rd., Ste. 150
Palo Alto, CA 94303
(650)494-9944
Fax: (650)494-6751
Website: http://www.patricof.com

RWI Group
835 Page Mill Rd.
Palo Alto, CA 94304
(650)251-1800
Fax: (650)213-8660
Website: http://www.rwigroup.com

Summit Partners (Palo Alto)
499 Hamilton Ave., Ste. 200
Palo Alto, CA 94301
(650)321-1166
Fax: (650)321-1188
Website: http://www.summit
partners.com

Sutter Hill Ventures
755 Page Mill Rd., Ste. A-200
Palo Alto, CA 94304
(650)493-5600
Fax: (650)858-1854
E-mail: shv@shv.com

Vanguard Venture Partners
525 University Ave., Ste. 600
Palo Alto, CA 94301
(650)321-2900
Fax: (650)321-2902
Website: http://www.vanguard
ventures.com

Venture Growth Associates
2479 East Bayshore St., Ste. 710
Palo Alto, CA 94303

(650)855-9100
Fax: (650)855-9104

Worldview Technology Partners
435 Tasso St., Ste. 120
Palo Alto, CA 94301
(650)322-3800
Fax: (650)322-3880
Website: http://www.worldview.com

Draper, Fisher, Jurvetson / Draper Associates
400 Seaport Ct., Ste.250
Redwood City, CA 94063
(415)599-9000
Fax: (415)599-9726
Website: http://www.dfj.com

Gabriel Venture Partners
350 Marine Pkwy., Ste. 200
Redwood Shores, CA 94065
(650)551-5000
Fax: (650)551-5001
Website: http://www.gabrielvp.com

Hallador Venture Partners, L.L.C.
740 University Ave., Ste. 110
Sacramento, CA 95825-6710
(916)920-0191
Fax: (916)920-5188
E-mail: chris@hallador.com

Emerald Venture Group
12396 World Trade Dr., Ste. 116
San Diego, CA 92128
(858)451-1001
Fax: (858)451-1003
Website: http://www.emerald
venture.com

Forward Ventures
9255 Towne Centre Dr.
San Diego, CA 92121
(858)677-6077
Fax: (858)452-8799
E-mail: info@forwardventure.com
Website: http://www.forward
venture.com

Idanta Partners Ltd.
4660 La Jolla Village Dr., Ste. 850
San Diego, CA 92122
(619)452-9690
Fax: (619)452-2013
Website: http://www.idanta.com

Kingsbury Associates
3655 Nobel Dr., Ste. 490
San Diego, CA 92122
(858)677-0600
Fax: (858)677-0800

Kyocera International Inc.
Corporate Development
8611 Balboa Ave.
San Diego, CA 92123
(858)576-2600
Fax: (858)492-1456

Sorrento Associates, Inc.
4370 LaJolla Village Dr., Ste. 1040
San Diego, CA 92122
(619)452-3100
Fax: (619)452-7607
Website: http://www.sorrento
ventures.com

Western States Investment Group
9191 Towne Ctr. Dr., Ste. 310
San Diego, CA 92122
(619)678-0800
Fax: (619)678-0900

Aberdare Ventures
One Embarcadero Center, Ste. 4000
San Francisco, CA 94111
(415)392-7442
Fax: (415)392-4264
Website: http://www.aberdare.com

Acacia Venture Partners
101 California St., Ste. 3160
San Francisco, CA 94111
(415)433-4200
Fax: (415)433-4250
Website: http://www.acaciavp.com

Access Venture Partners
319 Laidley St.
San Francisco, CA 94131
(415)586-0132
Fax: (415)392-6310
Website: http://www.access
venturepartners.com

Alta Partners
One Embarcadero Center, Ste. 4050
San Francisco, CA 94111
(415)362-4022
Fax: (415)362-6178
E-mail: alta@altapartners.com
Website: http://www.altapartners.com

Bangert Dawes Reade Davis & Thom
220 Montgomery St., Ste. 424
San Francisco, CA 94104
(415)954-9900
Fax: (415)954-9901
E-mail: bdrdt@pacbell.net

Berkeley International Capital Corp.
650 California St., Ste. 2800
San Francisco, CA 94108-2609

(415)249-0450
Fax: (415)392-3929
Website: http://www.berkeleyvc.com

Blueprint Ventures LLC
456 Montgomery St., 22nd Fl.
San Francisco, CA 94104
(415)901-4000
Fax: (415)901-4035
Website: http://www.blue
printventures.com

Blumberg Capital Ventures
580 Howard St., Ste. 401
San Francisco, CA 94105
(415)905-5007
Fax: (415)357-5027
Website: http://www.blumberg-
capital.com

Burr, Egan, Deleage, and Co. (San Francisco)
1 Embarcadero Center, Ste. 4050
San Francisco, CA 94111
(415)362-4022
Fax: (415)362-6178

Burrill & Company
120 Montgomery St., Ste. 1370
San Francisco, CA 94104
(415)743-3160
Fax: (415)743-3161
Website: http://www.burrillandco.com

CMEA Ventures
235 Montgomery St., Ste. 920
San Francisco, CA 94401
(415)352-1520
Fax: (415)352-1524
Website: http://www.cmeaventures.com

Crocker Capital
1 Post St., Ste. 2500
San Francisco, CA 94101
(415)956-5250
Fax: (415)959-5710

Dominion Ventures, Inc.
44 Montgomery St., Ste. 4200
San Francisco, CA 94104
(415)362-4890
Fax: (415)394-9245

Dorset Capital
Pier 1
Bay 2
San Francisco, CA 94111
(415)398-7101
Fax: (415)398-7141
Website: http://www.dorsetcapital.com

Gatx Capital
Four Embarcadero Center, Ste. 2200
San Francisco, CA 94904
(415)955-3200
Fax: (415)955-3449

IMinds
135 Main St., Ste. 1350
San Francisco, CA 94105
(415)547-0000
Fax: (415)227-0300
Website: http://www.iminds.com

LF International Inc.
360 Post St., Ste. 705
San Francisco, CA 94108
(415)399-0110
Fax: (415)399-9222
Website: http://www.lfvc.com

Newbury Ventures
535 Pacific Ave., 2nd Fl.
San Francisco, CA 94133
(415)296-7408
Fax: (415)296-7416
Website: http://www.newburyven.com

Quest Ventures (San Francisco)
333 Bush St., Ste. 1750
San Francisco, CA 94104
(415)782-1414
Fax: (415)782-1415

Robertson-Stephens Co.
555 California St., Ste. 2600
San Francisco, CA 94104
(415)781-9700
Fax: (415)781-2556
Website: http://www.omegaad
ventures.com

Rosewood Capital, L.P.
One Maritime Plaza, Ste. 1330
San Francisco, CA 94111-3503
(415)362-5526
Fax: (415)362-1192
Website: http://www.rosewoodvc.com

Ticonderoga Capital Inc.
555 California St., No. 4950
San Francisco, CA 94104
(415)296-7900
Fax: (415)296-8956

21st Century Internet Venture Partners
Two South Park
2nd Floor
San Francisco, CA 94107
(415)512-1221
Fax: (415)512-2650
Website: http://www.21vc.com

VK Ventures
600 California St., Ste.1700
San Francisco, CA 94111
(415)391-5600
Fax: (415)397-2744

Walden Group of Venture Capital Funds
750 Battery St., Seventh Floor
San Francisco, CA 94111
(415)391-7225
Fax: (415)391-7262

Acer Technology Ventures
2641 Orchard Pkwy.
San Jose, CA 95134
(408)433-4945
Fax: (408)433-5230

Authosis
226 Airport Pkwy., Ste. 405
San Jose, CA 95110
(650)814-3603
Website: http://www.authosis.com

Western Technology Investment
2010 N. First St., Ste. 310
San Jose, CA 95131
(408)436-8577
Fax: (408)436-8625
E-mail: mktg@westerntech.com

Drysdale Enterprises
177 Bovet Rd., Ste. 600
San Mateo, CA 94402
(650)341-6336
Fax: (650)341-1329
E-mail: drysdale@aol.com

Greylock
2929 Campus Dr., Ste. 400
San Mateo, CA 94401
(650)493-5525
Fax: (650)493-5575
Website: http://www.greylock.com

Technology Funding
2000 Alameda de las Pulgas, Ste. 250
San Mateo, CA 94403
(415)345-2200
Fax: (415)345-1797

2M Invest Inc.
1875 S. Grant St.
Suite 750
San Mateo, CA 94402
(650)655-3765
Fax: (650)372-9107
E-mail: 2minfo@2minvest.com
Website: http://www.2minvest.com

Phoenix Growth Capital Corp.
2401 Kerner Blvd.
San Rafael, CA 94901
(415)485-4569
Fax: (415)485-4663

NextGen Partners LLC
1705 East Valley Rd.
Santa Barbara, CA 93108
(805)969-8540
Fax: (805)969-8542
Website: http://www.nextgen
partners.com

Denali Venture Capital
1925 Woodland Ave.
Santa Clara, CA 95050
(408)690-4838
Fax: (408)247-6979
E-mail: wael@denaliventurecapital.com
Website: http://www.denali
venturecapital.com

Dotcom Ventures LP
3945 Freedom Circle, Ste. 740
Santa Clara, CA 95045
(408)919-9855
Fax: (408)919-9857
Website: http://www.dotcom
venturesatl.com

Silicon Valley Bank
3003 Tasman
Santa Clara, CA 95054
(408)654-7400
Fax: (408)727-8728

Al Shugart International
920 41st Ave.
Santa Cruz, CA 95062
(831)479-7852
Fax: (831)479-7852
Website: http://www.alshugart.com

Leonard Mautner Associates
1434 Sixth St.
Santa Monica, CA 90401
(213)393-9788
Fax: (310)459-9918

Palomar Ventures
100 Wilshire Blvd., Ste. 450
Santa Monica, CA 90401
(310)260-6050
Fax: (310)656-4150
Website: http://www.palomar
ventures.com

Medicus Venture Partners
12930 Saratoga Ave., Ste. D8
Saratoga, CA 95070

(408)447-8600
Fax: (408)447-8599
Website: http://www.medicusvc.com

Redleaf Venture Management
14395 Saratoga Ave., Ste. 130
Saratoga, CA 95070
(408)868-0800
Fax: (408)868-0810
E-mail: nancy@redleaf.com
Website: http://www.redleaf.com

Artemis Ventures
207 Second St., Ste. E
3rd Fl.
Sausalito, CA 94965
(415)289-2500
Fax: (415)289-1789
Website: http://www.artemisventures.com

Deucalion Venture Partners
19501 Brooklime
Sonoma, CA 95476
(707)938-4974
Fax: (707)938-8921

Windward Ventures
PO Box 7688
Thousand Oaks, CA 91359-7688
(805)497-3332
Fax: (805)497-9331

National Investment Management, Inc.
2601 Airport Dr., Ste.210
Torrance, CA 90505
(310)784-7600
Fax: (310)784-7605

Southern California Ventures
406 Amapola Ave. Ste. 125
Torrance, CA 90501
(310)787-4381
Fax: (310)787-4382

Sandton Financial Group
21550 Oxnard St., Ste. 300
Woodland Hills, CA 91367
(818)702-9283

Woodside Fund
850 Woodside Dr.
Woodside, CA 94062
(650)368-5545
Fax: (650)368-2416
Website: http://www.woodsidefund.com

Colorado

Colorado Venture Management
Ste. 300
Boulder, CO 80301

(303)440-4055
Fax: (303)440-4636

Dean & Associates
4362 Apple Way
Boulder, CO 80301
Fax: (303)473-9900

Roser Ventures LLC
1105 Spruce St.
Boulder, CO 80302
(303)443-6436
Fax: (303)443-1885
Website: http://www.roserventures.com

Sequel Venture Partners
4430 Arapahoe Ave., Ste. 220
Boulder, CO 80303
(303)546-0400
Fax: (303)546-9728
E-mail: tom@sequelvc.com
Website: http://www.sequelvc.com

New Venture Resources
445C E. Cheyenne Mtn. Blvd.
Colorado Springs, CO 80906-4570
(719)598-9272
Fax: (719)598-9272

The Centennial Funds
1428 15th St.
Denver, CO 80202-1318
(303)405-7500
Fax: (303)405-7575
Website: http://www.centennial.com

Rocky Mountain Capital Partners
1125 17th St., Ste. 2260
Denver, CO 80202
(303)291-5200
Fax: (303)291-5327

Sandlot Capital LLC
600 South Cherry St., Ste. 525
Denver, CO 80246
(303)893-3400
Fax: (303)893-3403
Website: http://www.sandlotcapital.com

Wolf Ventures
50 South Steele St., Ste. 777
Denver, CO 80209
(303)321-4800
Fax: (303)321-4848
E-mail: businessplan@wolf
ventures.com
Website: http://www.wolfventures.com

The Columbine Venture Funds
5460 S. Quebec St., Ste. 270
Englewood, CO 80111

(303)694-3222
Fax: (303)694-9007

Investment Securities of Colorado, Inc.
4605 Denice Dr.
Englewood, CO 80111
(303)796-9192

Kinship Partners
6300 S. Syracuse Way, Ste. 484
Englewood, CO 80111
(303)694-0268
Fax: (303)694-1707
E-mail: block@vailsys.com

Boranco Management, L.L.C.
1528 Hillside Dr.
Fort Collins, CO 80524-1969
(970)221-2297
Fax: (970)221-4787

Aweida Ventures
890 West Cherry St., Ste. 220
Louisville, CO 80027
(303)664-9520
Fax: (303)664-9530
Website: http://www.aweida.com

Access Venture Partners
8787 Turnpike Dr., Ste. 260
Westminster, CO 80030
(303)426-8899
Fax: (303)426-8828

Medmax Ventures LP
1 Northwestern Dr., Ste. 203
Bloomfield, CT 06002
(860)286-2960
Fax: (860)286-9960

James B. Kobak & Co.
Four Mansfield Place
Darien, CT 06820
(203)656-3471
Fax: (203)655-2905

Orien Ventures
1 Post Rd.
Fairfield, CT 06430
(203)259-9933
Fax: (203)259-5288

ABP Acquisition Corporation
115 Maple Ave.
Greenwich, CT 06830
(203)625-8287
Fax: (203)447-6187

Catterton Partners
9 Greenwich Office Park
Greenwich, CT 06830
(203)629-4901

Fax: (203)629-4903
Website: http://www.cpequity.com

Consumer Venture Partners
3 Pickwick Plz.
Greenwich, CT 06830
(203)629-8800
Fax: (203)629-2019

Insurance Venture Partners
31 Brookside Dr., Ste. 211
Greenwich, CT 06830
(203)861-0030
Fax: (203)861-2745

The NTC Group
Three Pickwick Plaza
Ste. 200
Greenwich, CT 06830
(203)862-2800
Fax: (203)622-6538

Regulus International Capital Co., Inc.
140 Greenwich Ave.
Greenwich, CT 06830
(203)625-9700
Fax: (203)625-9706

Axiom Venture Partners
City Place II
185 Asylum St., 17th Fl.
Hartford, CT 06103
(860)548-7799
Fax: (860)548-7797
Website: http://www.axiomventures.com

Conning Capital Partners
City Place II
185 Asylum St.
Hartford, CT 06103-4105
(860)520-1289
Fax: (860)520-1299
E-mail: pe@conning.com
Website: http://www.conning.com

First New England Capital L.P.
100 Pearl St.
Hartford, CT 06103
(860)293-3333
Fax: (860)293-3338
E-mail: info@firstnewenglandcapital.com
Website: http://www.firstnewengland capital.com

Northeast Ventures
One State St., Ste. 1720
Hartford, CT 06103
(860)547-1414
Fax: (860)246-8755

Windward Holdings
38 Sylvan Rd.
Madison, CT 06443
(203)245-6870
Fax: (203)245-6865

Advanced Materials Partners, Inc.
45 Pine St.
PO Box 1022
New Canaan, CT 06840
(203)966-6415
Fax: (203)966-8448
E-mail: wkb@amplink.com

RFE Investment Partners
36 Grove St.
New Canaan, CT 06840
(203)966-2800
Fax: (203)966-3109
Website: http://www.rfeip.com

Connecticut Innovations, Inc.
999 West St.
Rocky Hill, CT 06067
(860)563-5851
Fax: (860)563-4877
E-mail: pamela.hartley@ctin novations.com
Website: http://www.ctinnovations.com

Canaan Partners
105 Rowayton Ave.
Rowayton, CT 06853
(203)855-0400
Fax: (203)854-9117
Website: http://www.canaan.com

Landmark Partners, Inc.
10 Mill Pond Ln.
Simsbury, CT 06070
(860)651-9760
Fax: (860)651-8890
Website: http://www.landmarkpartners.com

Sweeney & Company
PO Box 567
Southport, CT 06490
(203)255-0220
Fax: (203)255-0220
E-mail: sweeney@connix.com

Baxter Associates, Inc.
PO Box 1333
Stamford, CT 06904
(203)323-3143
Fax: (203)348-0622

Beacon Partners Inc.
6 Landmark Sq., 4th Fl.
Stamford, CT 06901-2792

(203)359-5776
Fax: (203)359-5876

Collinson, Howe, and Lennox, LLC
1055 Washington Blvd., 5th Fl.
Stamford, CT 06901
(203)324-7700
Fax: (203)324-3636
E-mail: info@chlmedical.com
Website: http://www.chlmedical.com

Prime Capital Management Co.
550 West Ave.
Stamford, CT 06902
(203)964-0642
Fax: (203)964-0862

Saugatuck Capital Co.
1 Canterbury Green
Stamford, CT 06901
(203)348-6669
Fax: (203)324-6995
Website: http://www.sauga tuckcapital.com

Soundview Financial Group Inc.
22 Gatehouse Rd.
Stamford, CT 06902
(203)462-7200
Fax: (203)462-7350
Website: http://www.sndv.com

TSG Ventures, L.L.C.
177 Broad St., 12th Fl.
Stamford, CT 06901
(203)406-1500
Fax: (203)406-1590

Whitney & Company
177 Broad St.
Stamford, CT 06901
(203)973-1400
Fax: (203)973-1422
Website: http://www.jhwhitney.com

Cullinane & Donnelly Venture Partners L.P.
970 Farmington Ave.
West Hartford, CT 06107
(860)521-7811

The Crestview Investment and Financial Group
431 Post Rd. E, Ste. 1
Westport, CT 06880-4403
(203)222-0333
Fax: (203)222-0000

Marketcorp Venture Associates, L.P. (MCV)
274 Riverside Ave.
Westport, CT 06880

(203)222-3030
Fax: (203)222-3033

Oak Investment Partners (Westport)
1 Gorham Island
Westport, CT 06880
(203)226-8346
Fax: (203)227-0372
Website: http://www.oakinv.com

Oxford Bioscience Partners
315 Post Rd. W
Westport, CT 06880-5200
(203)341-3300
Fax: (203)341-3309
Website: http://www.oxbio.com

Prince Ventures (Westport)
25 Ford Rd.
Westport, CT 06880
(203)227-8332
Fax: (203)226-5302

LTI Venture Leasing Corp.
221 Danbury Rd.
Wilton, CT 06897
(203)563-1100
Fax: (203)563-1111
Website: http://www.ltileasing.com

Delaware

Blue Rock Capital
5803 Kennett Pike, Ste. A
Wilmington, DE 19807
(302)426-0981
Fax: (302)426-0982
Website: http://www.bluerockcapital.com

District of Columbia

Allied Capital Corp.
1919 Pennsylvania Ave. NW
Washington, DC 20006-3434
(202)331-2444
Fax: (202)659-2053
Website: http://www.alliedcapital.com

Atlantic Coastal Ventures, L.P.
3101 South St. NW
Washington, DC 20007
(202)293-1166
Fax: (202)293-1181
Website: http://www.atlanticcv.com

Columbia Capital Group, Inc.
1660 L St. NW, Ste. 308
Washington, DC 20036
(202)775-8815
Fax: (202)223-0544

Core Capital Partners
901 15th St., NW
9th Fl.
Washington, DC 20005
(202)589-0090
Fax: (202)589-0091
Website: http://www.core-capital.com

Next Point Partners
701 Pennsylvania Ave. NW, Ste. 900
Washington, DC 20004
(202)661-8703
Fax: (202)434-7400
E-mail: mf@nextpoint.vc
Website: http://www.nextpointvc.com

Telecommunications Development Fund
2020 K. St. NW
Ste. 375
Washington, DC 20006
(202)293-8840
Fax: (202)293-8850
Website: http://www.tdfund.com

Wachtel & Co., Inc.
1101 4th St. NW
Washington, DC 20005-5680
(202)898-1144

Winslow Partners LLC
1300 Connecticut Ave. NW
Washington, DC 20036-1703
(202)530-5000
Fax: (202)530-5010
E-mail: winslow@winslowpartners.com

Women's Growth Capital Fund
1054 31st St., NW
Ste. 110
Washington, DC 20007
(202)342-1431
Fax: (202)341-1203
Website: http://www.wgcf.com

Sigma Capital Corp.
22668 Caravelle Circle
Boca Raton, FL 33433
(561)368-9783

North American Business Development Co., L.L.C.
111 East Las Olas Blvd.
Ft. Lauderdale, FL 33301
(305)463-0681
Fax: (305)527-0904
Website: http://
www.northamericanfund.com

Chartwell Capital Management Co. Inc.
1 Independent Dr., Ste. 3120

Jacksonville, FL 32202
(904)355-3519
Fax: (904)353-5833
E-mail: info@chartwellcap.com

CEO Advisors
1061 Maitland Center Commons
Ste. 209
Maitland, FL 32751
(407)660-9327
Fax: (407)660-2109

Henry & Co.
8201 Peters Rd., Ste. 1000
Plantation, FL 33324
(954)797-7400

Avery Business Development Services
2506 St. Michel Ct.
Ponte Vedra, FL 32082
(904)285-6033

New South Ventures
5053 Ocean Blvd.
Sarasota, FL 34242
(941)358-6000
Fax: (941)358-6078
Website: http://www.newsouth
ventures.com

Venture Capital Management Corp.
PO Box 2626
Satellite Beach, FL 32937
(407)777-1969

Florida Capital Venture Ltd.
325 Florida Bank Plaza
100 W. Kennedy Blvd.
Tampa, FL 33602
(813)229-2294
Fax: (813)229-2028

Quantum Capital Partners
339 South Plant Ave.
Tampa, FL 33606
(813)250-1999
Fax: (813)250-1998
Website: http://www.quantum
capitalpartners.com

South Atlantic Venture Fund
614 W. Bay St.
Tampa, FL 33606-2704
(813)253-2500
Fax: (813)253-2360
E-mail: venture@southatlantic.com
Website: http://www.southatlantic.com

LM Capital Corp.
120 S. Olive, Ste. 400
West Palm Beach, FL 33401

(561)833-9700
Fax: (561)655-6587
Website: http://www.lmcapital
securities.com

Georgia

Venture First Associates
4811 Thornwood Dr.
Acworth, GA 30102
(770)928-3733
Fax: (770)928-6455

Alliance Technology Ventures
8995 Westside Pkwy., Ste. 200
Alpharetta, GA 30004
(678)336-2000
Fax: (678)336-2001
E-mail: info@atv.com
Website: http://www.atv.com

Cordova Ventures
2500 North Winds Pkwy., Ste. 475
Alpharetta, GA 30004
(678)942-0300
Fax: (678)942-0301
Website: http://www.cordovaventures.
com

Advanced Technology Development Fund
1000 Abernathy, Ste. 1420
Atlanta, GA 30328-5614
(404)668-2333
Fax: (404)668-2333

CGW Southeast Partners
12 Piedmont Center, Ste. 210
Atlanta, GA 30305
(404)816-3255
Fax: (404)816-3258
Website: http://www.cgwlp.com

Cyberstarts
1900 Emery St., NW
3rd Fl.
Atlanta, GA 30318
(404)267-5000
Fax: (404)267-5200
Website: http://www.cyberstarts.com

EGL Holdings, Inc.
10 Piedmont Center, Ste. 412
Atlanta, GA 30305
(404)949-8300
Fax: (404)949-8311

Equity South
1790 The Lenox Bldg.
3399 Peachtree Rd. NE
Atlanta, GA 30326

(404)237-6222
Fax: (404)261-1578

Five Paces
3400 Peachtree Rd., Ste. 200
Atlanta, GA 30326
(404)439-8300
Fax: (404)439-8301
Website: http://www.fivepaces.com

Frontline Capital, Inc.
3475 Lenox Rd., Ste. 400
Atlanta, GA 30326
(404)240-7280
Fax: (404)240-7281

Fuqua Ventures LLC
1201 W. Peachtree St. NW, Ste. 5000
Atlanta, GA 30309
(404)815-4500
Fax: (404)815-4528
Website: http://www.fuquaventures.com

Noro-Moseley Partners
4200 Northside Pkwy., Bldg. 9
Atlanta, GA 30327
(404)233-1966
Fax: (404)239-9280
Website: http://www.noro-moseley.com

Renaissance Capital Corp.
34 Peachtree St. NW, Ste. 2230
Atlanta, GA 30303
(404)658-9061
Fax: (404)658-9064

River Capital, Inc.
Two Midtown Plaza
1360 Peachtree St. NE, Ste. 1430
Atlanta, GA 30309
(404)873-2166
Fax: (404)873-2158

State Street Bank & Trust Co.
3414 Peachtree Rd. NE, Ste. 1010
Atlanta, GA 30326
(404)364-9500
Fax: (404)261-4469

UPS Strategic Enterprise Fund
55 Glenlake Pkwy. NE
Atlanta, GA 30328
(404)828-8814
Fax: (404)828-8088
E-mail: jcacyce@ups.com
Website: http://www.ups.com/sef/
sef_home

Wachovia
191 Peachtree St. NE, 26th Fl.
Atlanta, GA 30303

(404)332-1000
Fax: (404)332-1392
Website: http://www.wachovia.com/wca

Brainworks Ventures
4243 Dunwoody Club Dr.
Chamblee, GA 30341
(770)239-7447

First Growth Capital Inc.
Best Western Plaza, Ste. 105
PO Box 815
Forsyth, GA 31029
(912)781-7131

Financial Capital Resources, Inc.
21 Eastbrook Bend, Ste. 116
Peachtree City, GA 30269
(404)487-6650

Hawaii

HMS Hawaii Management Partners
Davies Pacific Center
841 Bishop St., Ste. 860
Honolulu, HI 96813
(808)545-3755
Fax: (808)531-2611

Idaho

Sun Valley Ventures
160 Second St.
Ketchum, ID 83340
(208)726-5005
Fax: (208)726-5094

Illinois

Open Prairie Ventures
115 N. Neil St., Ste. 209
Champaign, IL 61820
(217)351-7000
Fax: (217)351-7051
E-mail: inquire@openprairie.com
Website: http://www.openprairie.com

ABN AMRO Private Equity
208 S. La Salle St., 10th Fl.
Chicago, IL 60604
(312)855-7079
Fax: (312)553-6648
Website: http://www.abnequity.com

Alpha Capital Partners, Ltd.
122 S. Michigan Ave., Ste. 1700
Chicago, IL 60603
(312)322-9800
Fax: (312)322-9808
E-mail: acp@alphacapital.com

Ameritech Development Corp.
30 S. Wacker Dr., 37th Fl.
Chicago, IL 60606
(312)750-5083
Fax: (312)609-0244

Apex Investment Partners
225 W. Washington, Ste. 1450
Chicago, IL 60606
(312)857-2800
Fax: (312)857-1800
E-mail: apex@apexvc.com
Website: http://www.apexvc.com

Arch Venture Partners
8725 W. Higgins Rd., Ste. 290
Chicago, IL 60631
(773)380-6600
Fax: (773)380-6606
Website: http://www.archventure.com

The Bank Funds
208 South LaSalle St., Ste. 1680
Chicago, IL 60604
(312)855-6020
Fax: (312)855-8910

Batterson Venture Partners
303 W. Madison St., Ste. 1110
Chicago, IL 60606-3309
(312)269-0300
Fax: (312)269-0021
Website: http://www.battersonvp.com

William Blair Capital Partners, L.L.C.
222 W. Adams St., Ste. 1300
Chicago, IL 60606
(312)364-8250
Fax: (312)236-1042
E-mail: privateequity@wmblair.com
Website: http://www.wmblair.com

Bluestar Ventures
208 South LaSalle St., Ste. 1020
Chicago, IL 60604
(312)384-5000
Fax: (312)384-5005
Website: http://www.bluestarventures.com

The Capital Strategy Management Co.
233 S. Wacker Dr.
Box 06334
Chicago, IL 60606
(312)444-1170

DN Partners
77 West Wacker Dr., Ste. 4550
Chicago, IL 60601
(312)332-7960
Fax: (312)332-7979

Dresner Capital Inc.
29 South LaSalle St., Ste. 310
Chicago, IL 60603
(312)726-3600
Fax: (312)726-7448

Eblast Ventures LLC
11 South LaSalle St., 5th Fl.
Chicago, IL 60603
(312)372-2600
Fax: (312)372-5621
Website: http://www.eblastventures.com

Essex Woodlands Health Ventures, L.P.
190 S. LaSalle St., Ste. 2800
Chicago, IL 60603
(312)444-6040
Fax: (312)444-6034
Website: http://www.essexwood
lands.com

First Analysis Venture Capital
233 S. Wacker Dr., Ste. 9500
Chicago, IL 60606
(312)258-1400
Fax: (312)258-0334
Website: http://www.firstanalysis.com

Frontenac Co.
135 S. LaSalle St., Ste.3800
Chicago, IL 60603
(312)368-0044
Fax: (312)368-9520
Website: http://www.frontenac.com

GTCR Golder Rauner, LLC
6100 Sears Tower
Chicago, IL 60606
(312)382-2200
Fax: (312)382-2201
Website: http://www.gtcr.com

High Street Capital LLC
311 South Wacker Dr., Ste. 4550
Chicago, IL 60606
(312)697-4990
Fax: (312)697-4994
Website: http://www.highstr.com

IEG Venture Management, Inc.
70 West Madison
Chicago, IL 60602
(312)644-0890
Fax: (312)454-0369
Website: http://www.iegventure.com

JK&B Capital
180 North Stetson, Ste. 4500
Chicago, IL 60601
(312)946-1200
Fax: (312)946-1103

E-mail: gspencer@jkbcapital.com
Website: http://www.jkbcapital.com

Kettle Partners L.P.
350 W. Hubbard, Ste. 350
Chicago, IL 60610
(312)329-9300
Fax: (312)527-4519
Website: http://www.kettlevc.com

Lake Shore Capital Partners
20 N. Wacker Dr., Ste. 2807
Chicago, IL 60606
(312)803-3536
Fax: (312)803-3534

LaSalle Capital Group Inc.
70 W. Madison St., Ste. 5710
Chicago, IL 60602
(312)236-7041
Fax: (312)236-0720

Linc Capital, Inc.
303 E. Wacker Pkwy., Ste. 1000
Chicago, IL 60601
(312)946-2670
Fax: (312)938-4290
E-mail: bdemars@linccap.com

Madison Dearborn Partners, Inc.
3 First National Plz., Ste. 3800
Chicago, IL 60602
(312)895-1000
Fax: (312)895-1001
E-mail: invest@mdcp.com
Website: http://www.mdcp.com

Mesirow Private Equity Investments Inc.
350 N. Clark St.
Chicago, IL 60610
(312)595-6950
Fax: (312)595-6211
Website: http://www.meisrow
financial.com

Mosaix Ventures LLC
1822 North Mohawk
Chicago, IL 60614
(312)274-0988
Fax: (312)274-0989
Website: http://www.mosaix
ventures.com

Nesbitt Burns
111 West Monroe St.
Chicago, IL 60603
(312)416-3855
Fax: (312)765-8000
Website: http://www.harrisbank.com

Polestar Capital, Inc.
180 N. Michigan Ave., Ste. 1905
Chicago, IL 60601
(312)984-9090
Fax: (312)984-9877
E-mail: wl@polestarvc.com
Website: http://www.polestarvc.com

Prince Ventures (Chicago)
10 S. Wacker Dr., Ste. 2575
Chicago, IL 60606-7407
(312)454-1408
Fax: (312)454-9125

Prism Capital
444 N. Michigan Ave.
Chicago, IL 60611
(312)464-7900
Fax: (312)464-7915
Website: http://www.prismfund.com

Third Coast Capital
900 N. Franklin St., Ste. 700
Chicago, IL 60610
(312)337-3303
Fax: (312)337-2567
E-mail: manic@earthlink.com
Website: http://www.third
coastcapital.com

Thoma Cressey Equity Partners
4460 Sears Tower, 92nd Fl.
233 S. Wacker Dr.
Chicago, IL 60606
(312)777-4444
Fax: (312)777-4445
Website: http://www.thomacressey.com

Tribune Ventures
435 N. Michigan Ave., Ste. 600
Chicago, IL 60611
(312)527-8797
Fax: (312)222-5993
Website: http://www.tribuneventures.com

Wind Point Partners (Chicago)
676 N. Michigan Ave., Ste. 330
Chicago, IL 60611
(312)649-4000
Website: http://www.wppartners.com

Marquette Venture Partners
520 Lake Cook Rd., Ste. 450
Deerfield, IL 60015
(847)940-1700
Fax: (847)940-1724
Website: http://www.marquette
ventures.com

Duchossois Investments Limited, LLC
845 Larch Ave.
Elmhurst, IL 60126

(630)530-6105
Fax: (630)993-8644
Website: http://www.duchtec.com

Evanston Business Investment Corp.
1840 Oak Ave.
Evanston, IL 60201
(847)866-1840
Fax: (847)866-1808
E-mail: t-parkinson@nwu.com
Website: http://www.ebic.com

Inroads Capital Partners L.P.
1603 Orrington Ave., Ste. 2050
Evanston, IL 60201-3841
(847)864-2000
Fax: (847)864-9692

The Cerulean Fund/WGC Enterprises
1701 E. Lake Ave., Ste. 170
Glenview, IL 60025
(847)657-8002
Fax: (847)657-8168

Ventana Financial Resources, Inc.
249 Market Sq.
Lake Forest, IL 60045
(847)234-3434

Beecken, Petty & Co.
901 Warrenville Rd., Ste. 205
Lisle, IL 60532
(630)435-0300
Fax: (630)435-0370
E-mail: hep@bpcompany.com
Website: http://www.bpcompany.com

Allstate Private Equity
3075 Sanders Rd., Ste. G5D
Northbrook, IL 60062-7127
(847)402-8247
Fax: (847)402-0880

KB Partners
1101 Skokie Blvd., Ste. 260
Northbrook, IL 60062-2856
(847)714-0444
Fax: (847)714-0445
E-mail: keith@kbpartners.com
Website: http://www.kbpartners.com

Transcap Associates Inc.
900 Skokie Blvd., Ste. 210
Northbrook, IL 60062
(847)753-9600
Fax: (847)753-9090

**Graystone Venture Partners, L.L.C. /
Portage Venture Partners**
One Northfield Plaza, Ste. 530
Northfield, IL 60093

(847)446-9460
Fax: (847)446-9470
Website: http://www.portage
ventures.com

Motorola Inc.
1303 E. Algonquin Rd.
Schaumburg, IL 60196-1065
(847)576-4929
Fax: (847)538-2250
Website: http://www.mot.com/mne

Indiana

Irwin Ventures LLC
500 Washington St.
Columbus, IN 47202
(812)373-1434
Fax: (812)376-1709
Website: http://www.irwinventures.com

Cambridge Venture Partners
4181 East 96th St., Ste. 200
Indianapolis, IN 46240
(317)814-6192
Fax: (317)944-9815

CID Equity Partners
One American Square, Ste. 2850
Box 82074
Indianapolis, IN 46282
(317)269-2350
Fax: (317)269-2355
Website: http://www.cidequity.com

Gazelle Techventures
6325 Digital Way, Ste. 460
Indianapolis, IN 46278
(317)275-6800
Fax: (317)275-1101
Website: http://www.gazellevc.com

Monument Advisors Inc.
Bank One Center/Circle
111 Monument Circle, Ste. 600
Indianapolis, IN 46204-5172
(317)656-5065
Fax: (317)656-5060
Website: http://www.monumentadv.com

MWV Capital Partners
201 N. Illinois St., Ste. 300
Indianapolis, IN 46204
(317)237-2323
Fax: (317)237-2325
Website: http://www.mwvcapital.com

First Source Capital Corp.
100 North Michigan St.
PO Box 1602
South Bend, IN 46601

(219)235-2180
Fax: (219)235-2227

Iowa

Allsop Venture Partners
118 Third Ave. SE, Ste. 837
Cedar Rapids, IA 52401
(319)368-6675
Fax: (319)363-9515

InvestAmerica Investment Advisors, Inc.
101 2nd St. SE, Ste. 800
Cedar Rapids, IA 52401
(319)363-8249
Fax: (319)363-9683

Pappajohn Capital Resources
2116 Financial Center
Des Moines, IA 50309
(515)244-5746
Fax: (515)244-2346
Website: http://www.pappajohn.com

Berthel Fisher & Company Planning Inc.
701 Tama St.
PO Box 609
Marion, IA 52302
(319)497-5700
Fax: (319)497-4244

Kansas

Enterprise Merchant Bank
7400 West 110th St., Ste. 560
Overland Park, KS 66210
(913)327-8500
Fax: (913)327-8505

Kansas Venture Capital, Inc. (Overland Park)
6700 Antioch Plz., Ste. 460
Overland Park, KS 66204
(913)262-7117
Fax: (913)262-3509
E-mail: jdalton@kvci.com

Child Health Investment Corp.
6803 W. 64th St., Ste. 208
Shawnee Mission, KS 66202
(913)262-1436
Fax: (913)262-1575
Website: http://www.chca.com

Kansas Technology Enterprise Corp.
214 SW 6th, 1st Fl.
Topeka, KS 66603-3719
(785)296-5272
Fax: (785)296-1160

E-mail: ktec@ktec.com
Website: http://www.ktec.com

Kentucky

Kentucky Highlands Investment Corp.
362 Old Whitley Rd.
London, KY 40741
(606)864-5175
Fax: (606)864-5194
Website: http://www.khic.org

Chrysalis Ventures, L.L.C.
1850 National City Tower
Louisville, KY 40202
(502)583-7644
Fax: (502)583-7648
E-mail: bobsany@chrysalisventures.com
Website: http://www.chrysalis ventures.com

Humana Venture Capital
500 West Main St.
Louisville, KY 40202
(502)580-3922
Fax: (502)580-2051
E-mail: gemont@humana.com
George Emont, Director

Summit Capital Group, Inc.
6510 Glenridge Park Pl., Ste. 8
Louisville, KY 40222
(502)332-2700

Louisiana

Bank One Equity Investors, Inc.
451 Florida St.
Baton Rouge, LA 70801
(504)332-4421
Fax: (504)332-7377

Advantage Capital Partners
LLE Tower
909 Poydras St., Ste. 2230
New Orleans, LA 70112
(504)522-4850
Fax: (504)522-4950
Website: http://www.advantagecap.com

Maine

CEI Ventures / Coastal Ventures LP
2 Portland Fish Pier, Ste. 201
Portland, ME 04101
(207)772-5356
Fax: (207)772-5503
Website: http://www.ceiventures.com

Commwealth Bioventures, Inc.
4 Milk St.
Portland, ME 04101

(207)780-0904
Fax: (207)780-0913

Maryland

Annapolis Ventures LLC
151 West St., Ste. 302
Annapolis, MD 21401
(443)482-9555
Fax: (443)482-9565
Website: http://www.annapolis ventures.com

Delmag Ventures
220 Wardour Dr.
Annapolis, MD 21401
(410)267-8196
Fax: (410)267-8017
Website: http://www.delmag ventures.com

Abell Venture Fund
111 S. Calvert St., Ste. 2300
Baltimore, MD 21202
(410)547-1300
Fax: (410)539-6579
Website: http://www.abell.org

ABS Ventures (Baltimore)
1 South St., Ste. 2150
Baltimore, MD 21202
(410)895-3895
Fax: (410)895-3899
Website: http://www.absventures.com

Anthem Capital, L.P.
16 S. Calvert St., Ste. 800
Baltimore, MD 21202-1305
(410)625-1510
Fax: (410)625-1735
Website: http://www.anthemcapital.com

Catalyst Ventures
1119 St. Paul St.
Baltimore, MD 21202
(410)244-0123
Fax: (410)752-7721

Maryland Venture Capital Trust
217 E. Redwood St., Ste. 2200
Baltimore, MD 21202
(410)767-6361
Fax: (410)333-6931

New Enterprise Associates (Baltimore)
1119 St. Paul St.
Baltimore, MD 21202
(410)244-0115
Fax: (410)752-7721
Website: http://www.nea.com

T. Rowe Price Threshold Partnerships
100 E. Pratt St., 8th Fl.
Baltimore, MD 21202
(410)345-2000
Fax: (410)345-2800

Spring Capital Partners
16 W. Madison St.
Baltimore, MD 21201
(410)685-8000
Fax: (410)727-1436
E-mail: mailbox@springcap.com

Arete Corporation
3 Bethesda Metro Ctr., Ste. 770
Bethesda, MD 20814
(301)657-6268
Fax: (301)657-6254
Website: http://www.arete-
microgen.com

Embryon Capital
7903 Sleaford Place
Bethesda, MD 20814
(301)656-6837
Fax: (301)656-8056

Potomac Ventures
7920 Norfolk Ave., Ste. 1100
Bethesda, MD 20814
(301)215-9240
Website: http://www.potomac
ventures.com

Toucan Capital Corp.
3 Bethesda Metro Center, Ste. 700
Bethesda, MD 20814
(301)961-1970
Fax: (301)961-1969
Website: http://www.toucancapital.com

Kinetic Ventures LLC
2 Wisconsin Cir., Ste. 620
Chevy Chase, MD 20815
(301)652-8066
Fax: (301)652-8310
Website: http://www.kineticventures.com

Boulder Ventures Ltd.
4750 Owings Mills Blvd.
Owings Mills, MD 21117
(410)998-3114
Fax: (410)356-5492
Website: http://www.boulderventures.com

Grotech Capital Group
9690 Deereco Rd., Ste. 800
Timonium, MD 21093
(410)560-2000
Fax: (410)560-1910
Website: http://www.grotech.com

Massachusetts

Adams, Harkness & Hill, Inc.
60 State St.
Boston, MA 02109
(617)371-3900

Advent International
75 State St., 29th Fl.
Boston, MA 02109
(617)951-9400
Fax: (617)951-0566
Website: http://www.adventiner
national.com

American Research and Development
30 Federal St.
Boston, MA 02110-2508
(617)423-7500
Fax: (617)423-9655

Ascent Venture Partners
255 State St., 5th Fl.
Boston, MA 02109
(617)270-9400
Fax: (617)270-9401
E-mail: info@ascentvp.com
Website: http://www.ascentvp.com

Atlas Venture
222 Berkeley St.
Boston, MA 02116
(617)488-2200
Fax: (617)859-9292
Website: http://www.atlasventure.com

Axxon Capital
28 State St., 37th Fl.
Boston, MA 02109
(617)722-0980
Fax: (617)557-6014
Website: http://www.axxoncapital.com

BancBoston Capital/BancBoston Ventures
175 Federal St., 10th Fl.
Boston, MA 02110
(617)434-2509
Fax: (617)434-6175
Website: http://
www.bancbostoncapital.com

Boston Capital Ventures
Old City Hall
45 School St.
Boston, MA 02108
(617)227-6550
Fax: (617)227-3847
E-mail: info@bcv.com
Website: http://www.bcv.com

Boston Financial & Equity Corp.
20 Overland St.
PO Box 15071
Boston, MA 02215
(617)267-2900
Fax: (617)437-7601
E-mail: debbie@bfec.com

Boston Millennia Partners
30 Rowes Wharf
Boston, MA 02110
(617)428-5150
Fax: (617)428-5160
Website: http://www.millennia
partners.com

Bristol Investment Trust
842A Beacon St.
Boston, MA 02215-3199
(617)566-5212
Fax: (617)267-0932

Brook Venture Management LLC
50 Federal St., 5th Fl.
Boston, MA 02110
(617)451-8989
Fax: (617)451-2369
Website: http://www.brookventure.com

Burr, Egan, Deleage, and Co. (Boston)
200 Clarendon St., Ste. 3800
Boston, MA 02116
(617)262-7770
Fax: (617)262-9779

Cambridge/Samsung Partners
One Exeter Plaza
Ninth Fl.
Boston, MA 02116
(617)262-4440
Fax: (617)262-5562

Chestnut Street Partners, Inc.
75 State St., Ste. 2500
Boston, MA 02109
(617)345-7220
Fax: (617)345-7201
E-mail: chestnut@chestnutp.com

Claflin Capital Management, Inc.
10 Liberty Sq., Ste. 300
Boston, MA 02109
(617)426-6505
Fax: (617)482-0016
Website: http://www.claflincapital.com

Copley Venture Partners
99 Summer St., Ste. 1720
Boston, MA 02110
(617)737-1253
Fax: (617)439-0699

Corning Capital / Corning Technology Ventures
121 High Street, Ste. 400
Boston, MA 02110
(617)338-2656
Fax: (617)261-3864
Website: http://www.corningventures.com

Downer & Co.
211 Congress St.
Boston, MA 02110
(617)482-6200
Fax: (617)482-6201
E-mail: cdowner@downer.com
Website: http://www.downer.com

Fidelity Ventures
82 Devonshire St.
Boston, MA 02109
(617)563-6370
Fax: (617)476-9023
Website: http://www.fidelityventures.com

Greylock Management Corp. (Boston)
1 Federal St.
Boston, MA 02110-2065
(617)423-5525
Fax: (617)482-0059

Gryphon Ventures
222 Berkeley St., Ste.1600
Boston, MA 02116
(617)267-9191
Fax: (617)267-4293
E-mail: all@gryphoninc.com

Halpern, Denny & Co.
500 Boylston St.
Boston, MA 02116
(617)536-6602
Fax: (617)536-8535

Harbourvest Partners, LLC
1 Financial Center, 44th Fl.
Boston, MA 02111
(617)348-3707
Fax: (617)350-0305
Website: http://www.hvpllc.com

Highland Capital Partners
2 International Pl.
Boston, MA 02110
(617)981-1500
Fax: (617)531-1550
E-mail: info@hcp.com
Website: http://www.hcp.com

Lee Munder Venture Partners
John Hancock Tower T-53
200 Clarendon St.
Boston, MA 02103

(617)380-5600
Fax: (617)380-5601
Website: http://www.leemunder.com

M/C Venture Partners
75 State St., Ste. 2500
Boston, MA 02109
(617)345-7200
Fax: (617)345-7201
Website: http://www.mcventure partners.com

Massachusetts Capital Resources Co.
420 Boylston St.
Boston, MA 02116
(617)536-3900
Fax: (617)536-7930

Massachusetts Technology Development Corp. (MTDC)
148 State St.
Boston, MA 02109
(617)723-4920
Fax: (617)723-5983
E-mail: jhodgman@mtdc.com
Website: http://www.mtdc.com

New England Partners
One Boston Place, Ste. 2100
Boston, MA 02108
(617)624-8400
Fax: (617)624-8999
Website: http://www.nepartners.com

North Hill Ventures
Ten Post Office Square
11th Fl.
Boston, MA 02109
(617)788-2112
Fax: (617)788-2152
Website: http://www.northhill ventures.com

OneLiberty Ventures
150 Cambridge Park Dr.
Boston, MA 02140
(617)492-7280
Fax: (617)492-7290
Website: http://www.oneliberty.com

Schroder Ventures
Life Sciences
60 State St., Ste. 3650
Boston, MA 02109
(617)367-8100
Fax: (617)367-1590
Website: http://www.shroderventures.com

Shawmut Capital Partners
75 Federal St., 18th Fl.
Boston, MA 02110

(617)368-4900
Fax: (617)368-4910
Website: http://www.shawmutcapital.com

Solstice Capital LLC
15 Broad St., 3rd Fl.
Boston, MA 02109
(617)523-7733
Fax: (617)523-5827
E-mail: solticecapital@solcap.com

Spectrum Equity Investors
One International Pl., 29th Fl.
Boston, MA 02110
(617)464-4600
Fax: (617)464-4601
Website: http://www.spectrumequity.com

Spray Venture Partners
One Walnut St.
Boston, MA 02108
(617)305-4140
Fax: (617)305-4144
Website: http://www.sprayventure.com

The Still River Fund
100 Federal St., 29th Fl.
Boston, MA 02110
(617)348-2327
Fax: (617)348-2371
Website: http://www.stillriverfund.com

Summit Partners
600 Atlantic Ave., Ste. 2800
Boston, MA 02210-2227
(617)824-1000
Fax: (617)824-1159
Website: http://www.summitpartners.com

TA Associates, Inc. (Boston)
High Street Tower
125 High St., Ste. 2500
Boston, MA 02110
(617)574-6700
Fax: (617)574-6728
Website: http://www.ta.com

TVM Techno Venture Management
101 Arch St., Ste. 1950
Boston, MA 02110
(617)345-9320
Fax: (617)345-9377
E-mail: info@tvmvc.com
Website: http://www.tvmvc.com

UNC Ventures
64 Burough St.
Boston, MA 02130-4017
(617)482-7070
Fax: (617)522-2176

Venture Investment Management Company (VIMAC)
177 Milk St.
Boston, MA 02190-3410
(617)292-3300
Fax: (617)292-7979
E-mail: bzeisig@vimac.com
Website: http://www.vimac.com

MDT Advisers, Inc.
125 Cambridge Park Dr.
Cambridge, MA 02140-2314
(617)234-2200
Fax: (617)234-2210
Website: http://www.mdtai.com

TTC Ventures
One Main St., 6th Fl.
Cambridge, MA 02142
(617)528-3137
Fax: (617)577-1715
E-mail: info@ttcventures.com

Zero Stage Capital Co. Inc.
101 Main St., 17th Fl.
Cambridge, MA 02142
(617)876-5355
Fax: (617)876-1248
Website: http://www.zerostage.com

Atlantic Capital
164 Cushing Hwy.
Cohasset, MA 02025
(617)383-9449
Fax: (617)383-6040
E-mail: info@atlanticcap.com
Website: http://www.atlanticcap.com

Seacoast Capital Partners
55 Ferncroft Rd.
Danvers, MA 01923
(978)750-1300
Fax: (978)750-1301
E-mail: gdeli@seacoastcapital.com
Website: http://www.seacoast
capital.com

Sage Management Group
44 South Street
PO Box 2026
East Dennis, MA 02641
(508)385-7172
Fax: (508)385-7272
E-mail: sagemgt@capecod.net

Applied Technology
1 Cranberry Hill
Lexington, MA 02421-7397
(617)862-8622
Fax: (617)862-8367

Royalty Capital Management
5 Downing Rd.
Lexington, MA 02421-6918
(781)861-8490

Argo Global Capital
210 Broadway, Ste. 101
Lynnfield, MA 01940
(781)592-5250
Fax: (781)592-5230
Website: http://www.gsmcapital.com

Industry Ventures
6 Bayne Lane
Newburyport, MA 01950
(978)499-7606
Fax: (978)499-0686
Website: http://
www.industryventures.com

Softbank Capital Partners
10 Langley Rd., Ste. 202
Newton Center, MA 02459
(617)928-9300
Fax: (617)928-9305
E-mail: clax@bvc.com

Advanced Technology Ventures (Boston)
281 Winter St., Ste. 350
Waltham, MA 02451
(781)290-0707
Fax: (781)684-0045
E-mail: info@atvcapital.com
Website: http://www.atvcapital.com

Castile Ventures
890 Winter St., Ste. 140
Waltham, MA 02451
(781)890-0060
Fax: (781)890-0065
Website: http://www.castileventures.com

Charles River Ventures
1000 Winter St., Ste. 3300
Waltham, MA 02451
(781)487-7060
Fax: (781)487-7065
Website: http://www.crv.com

Comdisco Venture Group (Waltham)
Totton Pond Office Center
400-1 Totten Pond Rd.
Waltham, MA 02451
(617)672-0250
Fax: (617)398-8099

Marconi Ventures
890 Winter St., Ste. 310
Waltham, MA 02451
(781)839-7177

Fax: (781)522-7477
Website: http://www.marconi.com

Matrix Partners
Bay Colony Corporate Center
1000 Winter St., Ste.4500
Waltham, MA 02451
(781)890-2244
Fax: (781)890-2288
Website: http://www.matrix
partners.com

North Bridge Venture Partners
950 Winter St. Ste. 4600
Waltham, MA 02451
(781)290-0004
Fax: (781)290-0999
E-mail: eta@nbvp.com

Polaris Venture Partners
Bay Colony Corporate Ctr.
1000 Winter St., Ste. 3500
Waltham, MA 02451
(781)290-0770
Fax: (781)290-0880
E-mail: partners@polarisventures.com
Website: http://www.polar
isventures.com

Seaflower Ventures
Bay Colony Corporate Ctr.
1000 Winter St. Ste. 1000
Waltham, MA 02451
(781)466-9552
Fax: (781)466-9553
E-mail: moot@seaflower.com
Website: http://www.seaflower.com

Ampersand Ventures
55 William St., Ste. 240
Wellesley, MA 02481
(617)239-0700
Fax: (617)239-0824
E-mail: info@ampersandventures.com
Website: http://www.ampersand
ventures.com

Battery Ventures (Boston)
20 William St., Ste. 200
Wellesley, MA 02481
(781)577-1000
Fax: (781)577-1001
Website: http://www.battery.com

Commonwealth Capital Ventures, L.P.
20 William St., Ste.225
Wellesley, MA 02481
(781)237-7373
Fax: (781)235-8627
Website: http://www.ccvlp.com

Fowler, Anthony & Company
20 Walnut St.
Wellesley, MA 02481
(781)237-4201
Fax: (781)237-7718

Gemini Investors
20 William St.
Wellesley, MA 02481
(781)237-7001
Fax: (781)237-7233

Grove Street Advisors Inc.
20 William St., Ste. 230
Wellesley, MA 02481
(781)263-6100
Fax: (781)263-6101
Website: http://www.groves
treetadvisors.com

Mees Pierson Investeringsmaat B.V.
20 William St., Ste. 210
Wellesley, MA 02482
(781)239-7600
Fax: (781)239-0377

Norwest Equity Partners
40 William St., Ste. 305
Wellesley, MA 02481-3902
(781)237-5870
Fax: (781)237-6270
Website: http://www.norwestvp.com

Bessemer Venture Partners (Wellesley Hills)
83 Walnut St.
Wellesley Hills, MA 02481
(781)237-6050
Fax: (781)235-7576
E-mail: travis@bvpny.com
Website: http://www.bvp.com

Venture Capital Fund of New England
20 Walnut St., Ste. 120
Wellesley Hills, MA 02481-2175
(781)239-8262
Fax: (781)239-8263

Prism Venture Partners
100 Lowder Brook Dr., Ste. 2500
Westwood, MA 02090
(781)302-4000
Fax: (781)302-4040
E-mail: dwbaum@prismventure.com

Palmer Partners LP
200 Unicorn Park Dr.
Woburn, MA 01801
(781)933-5445
Fax: (781)933-0698

Michigan

Arbor Partners, L.L.C.
130 South First St.
Ann Arbor, MI 48104
(734)668-9000
Fax: (734)669-4195
Website: http://www.arborpartners.com

EDF Ventures
425 N. Main St.
Ann Arbor, MI 48104
(734)663-3213
Fax: (734)663-7358
E-mail: edf@edfvc.com
Website: http://www.edfvc.com

White Pines Management, L.L.C.
2401 Plymouth Rd., Ste. B
Ann Arbor, MI 48105
(734)747-9401
Fax: (734)747-9704
E-mail: ibund@whitepines.com
Website: http://www.whitepines.com

Wellmax, Inc.
3541 Bendway Blvd., Ste. 100
Bloomfield Hills, MI 48301
(248)646-3554
Fax: (248)646-6220

Venture Funding, Ltd.
Fisher Bldg.
3011 West Grand Blvd., Ste. 321
Detroit, MI 48202
(313)871-3606
Fax: (313)873-4935

Investcare Partners L.P. / GMA Capital LLC
32330 W. Twelve Mile Rd.
Farmington Hills, MI 48334
(248)489-9000
Fax: (248)489-8819
E-mail: gma@gmacapital.com
Website: http://www.gmacapital.com

Liberty Bidco Investment Corp.
30833 Northwestern Highway, Ste. 211
Farmington Hills, MI 48334
(248)626-6070
Fax: (248)626-6072

Seaflower Ventures
5170 Nicholson Rd.
PO Box 474
Fowlerville, MI 48836
(517)223-3335
Fax: (517)223-3337
E-mail: gibbons@seaflower.com
Website: http://www.seaflower.com

Ralph Wilson Equity Fund LLC
15400 E. Jefferson Ave.
Gross Pointe Park, MI 48230
(313)821-9122
Fax: (313)821-9101
Website: http://www.Ralph
WilsonEquityFund.com
J. Skip Simms, President

Minnesota

Development Corp. of Austin
1900 Eighth Ave., NW
Austin, MN 55912
(507)433-0346
Fax: (507)433-0361
E-mail: dca@smig.net
Website: http://www.spamtownusa.com

Northeast Ventures Corp.
802 Alworth Bldg.
Duluth, MN 55802
(218)722-9915
Fax: (218)722-9871

Medical Innovation Partners, Inc.
6450 City West Pkwy.
Eden Prairie, MN 55344-3245
(612)828-9616
Fax: (612)828-9596

St. Paul Venture Capital, Inc.
10400 Vicking Dr., Ste. 550
Eden Prairie, MN 55344
(612)995-7474
Fax: (612)995-7475
Website: http://www.stpaulvc.com

Cherry Tree Investments, Inc.
7601 France Ave. S, Ste. 150
Edina, MN 55435
(612)893-9012
Fax: (612)893-9036
Website: http://www.cherrytree.com

Shared Ventures, Inc.
6550 York Ave. S
Edina, MN 55435
(612)925-3411

Sherpa Partners LLC
5050 Lincoln Dr., Ste. 490
Edina, MN 55436
(952)942-1070
Fax: (952)942-1071
Website: http://www.sherpapartners.com

Affinity Capital Management
901 Marquette Ave., Ste. 1810
Minneapolis, MN 55402
(612)252-9900

Fax: (612)252-9911
Website: http://www.affinitycapital.com

Artesian Capital
1700 Foshay Tower
821 Marquette Ave.
Minneapolis, MN 55402
(612)334-5600
Fax: (612)334-5601
E-mail: artesian@artesian.com

Coral Ventures
60 S. 6th St., Ste. 3510
Minneapolis, MN 55402
(612)335-8666
Fax: (612)335-8668
Website: http://www.coralventures.com

Crescendo Venture Management, L.L.C.
800 LaSalle Ave., Ste. 2250
Minneapolis, MN 55402
(612)607-2800
Fax: (612)607-2801
Website: http://www.crescendo
ventures.com

Gideon Hixon Venture
1900 Foshay Tower
821 Marquette Ave.
Minneapolis, MN 55402
(612)904-2314
Fax: (612)204-0913

Norwest Equity Partners
3600 IDS Center
80 S. 8th St.
Minneapolis, MN 55402
(612)215-1600
Fax: (612)215-1601
Website: http://www.norwestvp.com

Oak Investment Partners (Minneapolis)
4550 Norwest Center
90 S. 7th St.
Minneapolis, MN 55402
(612)339-9322
Fax: (612)337-8017
Website: http://www.oakinv.com

**Pathfinder Venture Capital Funds
(Minneapolis)**
7300 Metro Blvd., Ste. 585
Minneapolis, MN 55439
(612)835-1121
Fax: (612)835-8389
E-mail: jahrens620@aol.com

**U.S. Bancorp Piper Jaffray Ventures,
Inc.**
800 Nicollet Mall, Ste. 800
Minneapolis, MN 55402

(612)303-5686
Fax: (612)303-1350
Website: http://www.paperjaffrey
ventures.com

The Food Fund, Ltd. Partnership
5720 Smatana Dr., Ste. 300
Minnetonka, MN 55343
(612)939-3950
Fax: (612)939-8106

Mayo Medical Ventures
200 First St. SW
Rochester, MN 55905
(507)266-4586
Fax: (507)284-5410
Website: http://www.mayo.edu

Missouri

Bankers Capital Corp.
3100 Gillham Rd.
Kansas City, MO 64109
(816)531-1600
Fax: (816)531-1334

Capital for Business, Inc. (Kansas City)
1000 Walnut St., 18th Fl.
Kansas City, MO 64106
(816)234-2357
Fax: (816)234-2952
Website: http://
www.capitalforbusiness.com

De Vries & Co. Inc.
800 West 47th St.
Kansas City, MO 64112
(816)756-0055
Fax: (816)756-0061

**InvestAmerica Venture Group Inc.
(Kansas City)**
Commerce Tower
911 Main St., Ste. 2424
Kansas City, MO 64105
(816)842-0114
Fax: (816)471-7339

Kansas City Equity Partners
233 W. 47th St.
Kansas City, MO 64112
(816)960-1771
Fax: (816)960-1777
Website: http://www.kcep.com

Bome Investors, Inc.
8000 Maryland Ave., Ste. 1190
St. Louis, MO 63105
(314)721-5707
Fax: (314)721-5135

Website: http://www.gateway
ventures.com

Capital for Business, Inc. (St. Louis)
11 S. Meramac St., Ste. 1430
St. Louis, MO 63105
(314)746-7427
Fax: (314)746-8739
Website: http://www.capitalfor
business.com

Crown Capital Corp.
540 Maryville Centre Dr., Ste. 120
Saint Louis, MO 63141
(314)576-1201
Fax: (314)576-1525
Website: http://www.crown-
cap.com

Gateway Associates L.P.
8000 Maryland Ave., Ste. 1190
St. Louis, MO 63105
(314)721-5707
Fax: (314)721-5135

Harbison Corp.
8112 Maryland Ave., Ste. 250
Saint Louis, MO 63105
(314)727-8200
Fax: (314)727-0249

Heartland Capital Fund, Ltd.
PO Box 642117
Omaha, NE 68154
(402)778-5124
Fax: (402)445-2370
Website: http://www.heartland
capitalfund.com

Odin Capital Group
1625 Farnam St., Ste. 700
Omaha, NE 68102
(402)346-6200
Fax: (402)342-9311
Website: http://www.odincapital.com

Nevada

Edge Capital Investment Co. LLC
1350 E. Flamingo Rd., Ste. 3000
Las Vegas, NV 89119
(702)438-3343
E-mail: info@edgecapital.net
Website: http://www.edgecapital.net

The Benefit Capital Companies Inc.
PO Box 542
Logandale, NV 89021
(702)398-3222
Fax: (702)398-3700

Millennium Three Venture Group LLC
6880 South McCarran Blvd., Ste. A-11
Reno, NV 89509
(775)954-2020
Fax: (775)954-2023
Website: http://www.m3vg.com

New Jersey

Alan I. Goldman & Associates
497 Ridgewood Ave.
Glen Ridge, NJ 07028
(973)857-5680
Fax: (973)509-8856

CS Capital Partners LLC
328 Second St., Ste. 200
Lakewood, NJ 08701
(732)901-1111
Fax: (212)202-5071
Website: http://www.cs-capital.com

Edison Venture Fund
1009 Lenox Dr., Ste. 4
Lawrenceville, NJ 08648
(609)896-1900
Fax: (609)896-0066
E-mail: info@edisonventure.com
Website: http://www.edisonventure.com

Tappan Zee Capital Corp. (New Jersey)
201 Lower Notch Rd.
PO Box 416
Little Falls, NJ 07424
(973)256-8280
Fax: (973)256-2841

The CIT Group/Venture Capital, Inc.
650 CIT Dr.
Livingston, NJ 07039
(973)740-5429
Fax: (973)740-5555
Website: http://www.cit.com

Capital Express, L.L.C.
1100 Valleybrook Ave.
Lyndhurst, NJ 07071
(201)438-8228
Fax: (201)438-5131
E-mail: niles@capitalexpress.com
Website: http://www.capitalexpress.com

Westford Technology Ventures, L.P.
17 Academy St.
Newark, NJ 07102
(973)624-2131
Fax: (973)624-2008

Accel Partners
1 Palmer Sq.
Princeton, NJ 08542

(609)683-4500
Fax: (609)683-4880
Website: http://www.accel.com

Cardinal Partners
221 Nassau St.
Princeton, NJ 08542
(609)924-6452
Fax: (609)683-0174
Website: http://www.cardinal
healthpartners.com

Domain Associates L.L.C.
One Palmer Sq., Ste. 515
Princeton, NJ 08542
(609)683-5656
Fax: (609)683-9789
Website: http://www.domainvc.com

Johnston Associates, Inc.
181 Cherry Valley Rd.
Princeton, NJ 08540
(609)924-3131
Fax: (609)683-7524
E-mail: jaincorp@aol.com

Kemper Ventures
Princeton Forrestal Village
155 Village Blvd.
Princeton, NJ 08540
(609)936-3035
Fax: (609)936-3051

Penny Lane Parnters
One Palmer Sq., Ste. 309
Princeton, NJ 08542
(609)497-4646
Fax: (609)497-0611

Early Stage Enterprises L.P.
995 Route 518
Skillman, NJ 08558
(609)921-8896
Fax: (609)921-8703
Website: http://www.esevc.com

MBW Management Inc.
1 Springfield Ave.
Summit, NJ 07901
(908)273-4060
Fax: (908)273-4430

BCI Advisors, Inc.
Glenpointe Center W.
Teaneck, NJ 07666
(201)836-3900
Fax: (201)836-6368
E-mail: info@bciadvisors.com
Website: http://www.bci
partners.com

Demuth, Folger & Wetherill / DFW Capital Partners
Glenpointe Center E., 5th Fl.
300 Frank W. Burr Blvd.
Teaneck, NJ 07666
(201)836-2233
Fax: (201)836-5666
Website: http://www.dfwcapital.com

First Princeton Capital Corp.
189 Berdan Ave., No. 131
Wayne, NJ 07470-3233
(973)278-3233
Fax: (973)278-4290
Website: http://www.lytellcatt.net

Edelson Technology Partners
300 Tice Blvd.
Woodcliff Lake, NJ 07675
(201)930-9898
Fax: (201)930-8899
Website: http://www.edelsontech.com

New Mexico

Bruce F. Glaspell & Associates
10400 Academy Rd. NE, Ste. 313
Albuquerque, NM 87111
(505)292-4505
Fax: (505)292-4258

High Desert Ventures, Inc.
6101 Imparata St. NE, Ste. 1721
Albuquerque, NM 87111
(505)797-3330
Fax: (505)338-5147

New Business Capital Fund, Ltd.
5805 Torreon NE
Albuquerque, NM 87109
(505)822-8445

SBC Ventures
10400 Academy Rd. NE, Ste. 313
Albuquerque, NM 87111
(505)292-4505
Fax: (505)292-4528

Technology Ventures Corp.
1155 University Blvd. SE
Albuquerque, NM 87106
(505)246-2882
Fax: (505)246-2891

New York

New York State Science & Technology Foundation
Small Business Technology Investment Fund
99 Washington Ave., Ste. 1731
Albany, NY 12210

(518)473-9741
Fax: (518)473-6876

Rand Capital Corp.
2200 Rand Bldg.
Buffalo, NY 14203
(716)853-0802
Fax: (716)854-8480
Website: http://www.randcapital.com

Seed Capital Partners
620 Main St.
Buffalo, NY 14202
(716)845-7520
Fax: (716)845-7539
Website: http://www.seedcp.com

Coleman Venture Group
5909 Northern Blvd.
PO Box 224
East Norwich, NY 11732
(516)626-3642
Fax: (516)626-9722

Vega Capital Corp.
45 Knollwood Rd.
Elmsford, NY 10523
(914)345-9500
Fax: (914)345-9505

Herbert Young Securities, Inc.
98 Cuttermill Rd.
Great Neck, NY 11021
(516)487-8300
Fax: (516)487-8319

Sterling/Carl Marks Capital, Inc.
175 Great Neck Rd., Ste. 408
Great Neck, NY 11021
(516)482-7374
Fax: (516)487-0781
E-mail: stercrlmar@aol.com
Website: http://www.serling
carlmarks.com

Impex Venture Management Co.
PO Box 1570
Green Island, NY 12183
(518)271-8008
Fax: (518)271-9101

Corporate Venture Partners L.P.
200 Sunset Park
Ithaca, NY 14850
(607)257-6323
Fax: (607)257-6128

Arthur P. Gould & Co.
One Wilshire Dr.
Lake Success, NY 11020
(516)773-3000
Fax: (516)773-3289

Dauphin Capital Partners
108 Forest Ave.
Locust Valley, NY 11560
(516)759-3339
Fax: (516)759-3322
Website: http://www.dauphincapital.com

550 Digital Media Ventures
555 Madison Ave., 10th Fl.
New York, NY 10022
Website: http://www.550dmv.com

Aberlyn Capital Management Co., Inc.
500 Fifth Ave.
New York, NY 10110
(212)391-7750
Fax: (212)391-7762

Adler & Company
342 Madison Ave., Ste. 807
New York, NY 10173
(212)599-2535
Fax: (212)599-2526

Alimansky Capital Group, Inc.
605 Madison Ave., Ste. 300
New York, NY 10022-1901
(212)832-7300
Fax: (212)832-7338

Allegra Partners
515 Madison Ave., 29th Fl.
New York, NY 10022
(212)826-9080
Fax: (212)759-2561

The Argentum Group
The Chyrsler Bldg.
405 Lexington Ave.
New York, NY 10174
(212)949-6262
Fax: (212)949-8294
Website: http://www.argentum
group.com

Axavision Inc.
14 Wall St., 26th Fl.
New York, NY 10005
(212)619-4000
Fax: (212)619-7202

Bedford Capital Corp.
18 East 48th St., Ste. 1800
New York, NY 10017
(212)688-5700
Fax: (212)754-4699
E-mail: info@bedfordnyc.com
Website: http://www.bedfordnyc.com

Bloom & Co.
950 Third Ave.

New York, NY 10022
(212)838-1858
Fax: (212)838-1843

Bristol Capital Management
300 Park Ave., 17th Fl.
New York, NY 10022
(212)572-6306
Fax: (212)705-4292

**Citicorp Venture Capital Ltd.
(New York City)**
399 Park Ave., 14th Fl.
Zone 4
New York, NY 10043
(212)559-1127
Fax: (212)888-2940

CM Equity Partners
135 E. 57th St.
New York, NY 10022
(212)909-8428
Fax: (212)980-2630

Cohen & Co., L.L.C.
800 Third Ave.
New York, NY 10022
(212)317-2250
Fax: (212)317-2255
E-mail: nlcohen@aol.com

Cornerstone Equity Investors, L.L.C.
717 5th Ave., Ste. 1100
New York, NY 10022
(212)753-0901
Fax: (212)826-6798
Website: http://www.cornerstone-
equity.com

CW Group, Inc.
1041 3rd Ave., 2nd fl.
New York, NY 10021
(212)308-5266
Fax: (212)644-0354
Website: http://www.cwventures.com

DH Blair Investment Banking Corp.
44 Wall St., 2nd Fl.
New York, NY 10005
(212)495-5000
Fax: (212)269-1438

Dresdner Kleinwort Capital
75 Wall St.
New York, NY 10005
(212)429-3131
Fax: (212)429-3139
Website: http://www.dresdnerkb.com

East River Ventures, L.P.
645 Madison Ave., 22nd Fl.

New York, NY 10022
(212)644-2322
Fax: (212)644-5498

Easton Hunt Capital Partners
641 Lexington Ave., 21st Fl.
New York, NY 10017
(212)702-0950
Fax: (212)702-0952
Website: http://www.eastoncapital.com

Elk Associates Funding Corp.
747 3rd Ave., Ste. 4C
New York, NY 10017
(212)355-2449
Fax: (212)759-3338

EOS Partners, L.P.
320 Park Ave., 22nd Fl.
New York, NY 10022
(212)832-5800
Fax: (212)832-5815
E-mail: mfirst@eospartners.com
Website: http://www.eospartners.com

Euclid Partners
45 Rockefeller Plaza, Ste. 3240
New York, NY 10111
(212)218-6880
Fax: (212)218-6877
E-mail: graham@euclidpartners.com
Website: http://www.euclidpartners.com

Evergreen Capital Partners, Inc.
150 East 58th St.
New York, NY 10155
(212)813-0758
Fax: (212)813-0754

Exeter Capital L.P.
10 E. 53rd St.
New York, NY 10022
(212)872-1172
Fax: (212)872-1198
E-mail: exeter@usa.net

Financial Technology Research Corp.
518 Broadway
Penthouse
New York, NY 10012
(212)625-9100
Fax: (212)431-0300
E-mail: fintek@financier.com

4C Ventures
237 Park Ave., Ste. 801
New York, NY 10017
(212)692-3680
Fax: (212)692-3685
Website: http://www.4cventures.com

Fusient Ventures
99 Park Ave., 20th Fl.
New York, NY 10016
(212)972-8999
Fax: (212)972-9876
E-mail: info@fusient.com
Website: http://www.fusient.com

Generation Capital Partners
551 Fifth Ave., Ste. 3100
New York, NY 10176
(212)450-8507
Fax: (212)450-8550
Website: http://www.genpartners.com

Golub Associates, Inc.
555 Madison Ave.
New York, NY 10022
(212)750-6060
Fax: (212)750-5505

Hambro America Biosciences Inc.
650 Madison Ave., 21st Floor
New York, NY 10022
(212)223-7400
Fax: (212)223-0305

Hanover Capital Corp.
505 Park Ave., 15th Fl.
New York, NY 10022
(212)755-1222
Fax: (212)935-1787

Harvest Partners, Inc.
280 Park Ave, 33rd Fl.
New York, NY 10017
(212)559-6300
Fax: (212)812-0100
Website: http://www.harvpart.com

Holding Capital Group, Inc.
10 E. 53rd St., 30th Fl.
New York, NY 10022
(212)486-6670
Fax: (212)486-0843

Hudson Venture Partners
660 Madison Ave., 14th Fl.
New York, NY 10021-8405
(212)644-9797
Fax: (212)644-7430
Website: http://www.hudsonptr.com

IBJS Capital Corp.
1 State St., 9th Fl.
New York, NY 10004
(212)858-2018
Fax: (212)858-2768

InterEquity Capital Partners, L.P.
220 5th Ave.
New York, NY 10001

(212)779-2022
Fax: (212)779-2103
Website: http://www.interequity-capital.com

The Jordan Edmiston Group Inc.
150 East 52nd St., 18th Fl.
New York, NY 10022
(212)754-0710
Fax: (212)754-0337

Josephberg, Grosz and Co., Inc.
633 3rd Ave., 13th Fl.
New York, NY 10017
(212)974-9926
Fax: (212)397-5832

J.P. Morgan Capital Corp.
60 Wall St.
New York, NY 10260-0060
(212)648-9000
Fax: (212)648-5002
Website: http://www.jpmorgan.com

The Lambda Funds
380 Lexington Ave., 54th Fl.
New York, NY 10168
(212)682-3454
Fax: (212)682-9231

Lepercq Capital Management Inc.
1675 Broadway
New York, NY 10019
(212)698-0795
Fax: (212)262-0155

Loeb Partners Corp.
61 Broadway, Ste. 2400
New York, NY 10006
(212)483-7000
Fax: (212)574-2001

Madison Investment Partners
660 Madison Ave.
New York, NY 10021
(212)223-2600
Fax: (212)223-8208

MC Capital Inc.
520 Madison Ave., 16th Fl.
New York, NY 10022
(212)644-0841
Fax: (212)644-2926

McCown, De Leeuw and Co. (New York)
65 E. 55th St., 36th Fl.
New York, NY 10022
(212)355-5500
Fax: (212)355-6283
Website: http://www.mdcpartners.com

Morgan Stanley Venture Partners
1221 Avenue of the Americas, 33rd Fl.
New York, NY 10020
(212)762-7900
Fax: (212)762-8424
E-mail: msventures@ms.com
Website: http://www.msvp.com

Nazem and Co.
645 Madison Ave., 12th Fl.
New York, NY 10022
(212)371-7900
Fax: (212)371-2150

Needham Capital Management, L.L.C.
445 Park Ave.
New York, NY 10022
(212)371-8300
Fax: (212)705-0299
Website: http://www.needhamco.com

Norwood Venture Corp.
1430 Broadway, Ste. 1607
New York, NY 10018
(212)869-5075
Fax: (212)869-5331
E-mail: nvc@mail.idt.net
Website: http://www.norven.com

Noveltek Venture Corp.
521 Fifth Ave., Ste. 1700
New York, NY 10175
(212)286-1963

Paribas Principal, Inc.
787 7th Ave.
New York, NY 10019
(212)841-2005
Fax: (212)841-3558

Patricof & Co. Ventures, Inc.
(New York)
445 Park Ave.
New York, NY 10022
(212)753-6300
Fax: (212)319-6155
Website: http://www.patricof.com

The Platinum Group, Inc.
350 Fifth Ave, Ste. 7113
New York, NY 10118
(212)736-4300
Fax: (212)736-6086
Website: http://www.platinumgroup.com

Pomona Capital
780 Third Ave., 28th Fl.
New York, NY 10017
(212)593-3639
Fax: (212)593-3987
Website: http://www.pomonacapital.com

Prospect Street Ventures
10 East 40th St., 44th Fl.
New York, NY 10016
(212)448-0702
Fax: (212)448-9652
E-mail: wkohler@prospectstreet.com
Website: http://www.prospectstreet.com

Regent Capital Management
505 Park Ave., Ste. 1700
New York, NY 10022
(212)735-9900
Fax: (212)735-9908

Rothschild Ventures, Inc.
1251 Avenue of the Americas, 51st Fl.
New York, NY 10020
(212)403-3500
Fax: (212)403-3652
Website: http://www.nmrothschild.com

Sandler Capital Management
767 Fifth Ave., 45th Fl.
New York, NY 10153
(212)754-8100
Fax: (212)826-0280

Siguler Guff & Company
630 Fifth Ave., 16th Fl.
New York, NY 10111
(212)332-5100
Fax: (212)332-5120

Spencer Trask Ventures Inc.
535 Madison Ave.
New York, NY 10022
(212)355-5565
Fax: (212)751-3362
Website: http://www.spencertrask.com

Sprout Group (New York City)
277 Park Ave.
New York, NY 10172
(212)892-3600
Fax: (212)892-3444
E-mail: info@sproutgroup.com
Website: http://www.sproutgroup.com

US Trust Private Equity
114 W.47th St.
New York, NY 10036
(212)852-3949
Fax: (212)852-3759
Website: http://www.ustrust.com/
privateequity

Vencon Management Inc.
301 West 53rd St., Ste. 10F
New York, NY 10019
(212)581-8787
Fax: (212)397-4126
Website: http://www.venconinc.com

Venrock Associates
30 Rockefeller Plaza, Ste. 5508
New York, NY 10112
(212)649-5600
Fax: (212)649-5788
Website: http://www.venrock.com

Venture Capital Fund of America, Inc.
509 Madison Ave., Ste. 812
New York, NY 10022
(212)838-5577
Fax: (212)838-7614
E-mail: mail@vcfa.com
Website: http://www.vcfa.com

Venture Opportunities Corp.
150 E. 58th St.
New York, NY 10155
(212)832-3737
Fax: (212)980-6603

Warburg Pincus Ventures, Inc.
466 Lexington Ave., 11th Fl.
New York, NY 10017
(212)878-9309
Fax: (212)878-9200
Website: http://www.warburgpincus.com

Wasserstein, Perella & Co. Inc.
31 W. 52nd St., 27th Fl.
New York, NY 10019
(212)702-5691
Fax: (212)969-7879

Welsh, Carson, Anderson, & Stowe
320 Park Ave., Ste. 2500
New York, NY 10022-6815
(212)893-9500
Fax: (212)893-9575

Whitney and Co. (New York)
630 Fifth Ave. Ste. 3225
New York, NY 10111
(212)332-2400
Fax: (212)332-2422
Website: http://www.jhwitney.com

Winthrop Ventures
74 Trinity Place, Ste. 600
New York, NY 10006
(212)422-0100

The Pittsford Group
8 Lodge Pole Rd.
Pittsford, NY 14534
(716)223-3523

Genesee Funding
70 Linden Oaks, 3rd Fl.
Rochester, NY 14625
(716)383-5550
Fax: (716)383-5305

Gabelli Multimedia Partners
One Corporate Center
Rye, NY 10580
(914)921-5395
Fax: (914)921-5031

Stamford Financial
108 Main St.
Stamford, NY 12167
(607)652-3311
Fax: (607)652-6301
Website: http://www.stamford
financial.com

Northwood Ventures LLC
485 Underhill Blvd., Ste. 205
Syosset, NY 11791
(516)364-5544
Fax: (516)364-0879
E-mail: northwood@northwood.com
Website: http://www.north
woodventures.com

Exponential Business Development Co.
216 Walton St.
Syracuse, NY 13202-1227
(315)474-4500
Fax: (315)474-4682
E-mail: dirksonn@aol.com
Website: http://www.exponential-ny.com

Onondaga Venture Capital Fund Inc.
714 State Tower Bldg.
Syracuse, NY 13202
(315)478-0157
Fax: (315)478-0158

Bessemer Venture Partners (Westbury)
1400 Old Country Rd., Ste. 109
Westbury, NY 11590
(516)997-2300
Fax: (516)997-2371
E-mail: bob@bvpny.com
Website: http://www.bvp.com

Ovation Capital Partners
120 Bloomingdale Rd., 4th Fl.
White Plains, NY 10605
(914)258-0011
Fax: (914)684-0848
Website: http://www.ovation
capital.com

North Carolina

Carolinas Capital Investment Corp.
1408 Biltmore Dr.
Charlotte, NC 28207
(704)375-3888
Fax: (704)375-6226

First Union Capital Partners
1st Union Center, 12th Fl.
301 S. College St.
Charlotte, NC 28288-0732
(704)383-0000
Fax: (704)374-6711
Website: http://www.fucp.com

Frontier Capital LLC
525 North Tryon St., Ste. 1700
Charlotte, NC 28202
(704)414-2880
Fax: (704)414-2881
Website: http://www.frontierfunds.com

Kitty Hawk Capital
2700 Coltsgate Rd., Ste. 202
Charlotte, NC 28211
(704)362-3909
Fax: (704)362-2774
Website: http://www.kittyhawk
capital.com

Piedmont Venture Partners
One Morrocroft Centre
6805 Morisson Blvd., Ste. 380
Charlotte, NC 28211
(704)731-5200
Fax: (704)365-9733
Website: http://www.piedmontvp.com

Ruddick Investment Co.
1800 Two First Union Center
Charlotte, NC 28282
(704)372-5404
Fax: (704)372-6409

The Shelton Companies Inc.
3600 One First Union Center
301 S. College St.
Charlotte, NC 28202
(704)348-2200
Fax: (704)348-2260

Wakefield Group
1110 E. Morehead St.
PO Box 36329
Charlotte, NC 28236
(704)372-0355
Fax: (704)372-8216
Website: http://www.wakefiel
dgroup.com

Aurora Funds, Inc.
2525 Meridian Pkwy., Ste. 220
Durham, NC 27713
(919)484-0400
Fax: (919)484-0444
Website: http://www.aurora
funds.com

Intersouth Partners
3211 Shannon Rd., Ste. 610
Durham, NC 27707
(919)493-6640
Fax: (919)493-6649
E-mail: info@intersouth.com
Website: http://www.intersouth.com

Geneva Merchant Banking Partners
PO Box 21962
Greensboro, NC 27420
(336)275-7002
Fax: (336)275-9155
Website: http://www.geneva
merchantbank.com

The North Carolina Enterprise Fund, L.P.
3600 Glenwood Ave., Ste. 107
Raleigh, NC 27612
(919)781-2691
Fax: (919)783-9195
Website: http://www.ncef.com

Ohio

Senmend Medical Ventures
4445 Lake Forest Dr., Ste. 600
Cincinnati, OH 45242
(513)563-3264
Fax: (513)563-3261

The Walnut Group
312 Walnut St., Ste. 1151
Cincinnati, OH 45202
(513)651-3300
Fax: (513)929-4441
Website: http://www.thewal
nutgroup.com

Brantley Venture Partners
20600 Chagrin Blvd., Ste. 1150
Cleveland, OH 44122
(216)283-4800
Fax: (216)283-5324

Clarion Capital Corp.
1801 E. 9th St., Ste. 1120
Cleveland, OH 44114
(216)687-1096
Fax: (216)694-3545

Crystal Internet Venture Fund, L.P.
1120 Chester Ave., Ste. 418
Cleveland, OH 44114
(216)263-5515
Fax: (216)263-5518
E-mail: jf@crystalventure.com
Website: http://www.crystal
venture.com

Key Equity Capital Corp.
127 Public Sq., 28th Fl.
Cleveland, OH 44114
(216)689-3000
Fax: (216)689-3204
Website: http://www.keybank.com

Morgenthaler Ventures
Terminal Tower
50 Public Square, Ste. 2700
Cleveland, OH 44113
(216)416-7500
Fax: (216)416-7501
Website: http://www.morgenthaler.com

National City Equity Partners Inc.
1965 E. 6th St.
Cleveland, OH 44114
(216)575-2491
Fax: (216)575-9965
E-mail: nccap@aol.com
Website: http://www.nccapital.com

Primus Venture Partners, Inc.
5900 LanderBrook Dr., Ste. 2000
Cleveland, OH 44124-4020
(440)684-7300
Fax: (440)684-7342
E-mail: info@primusventure.com
Website: http://www.primusventure.com

Banc One Capital Partners (Columbus)
150 East Gay St., 24th Fl.
Columbus, OH 43215
(614)217-1100
Fax: (614)217-1217

Battelle Venture Partners
505 King Ave.
Columbus, OH 43201
(614)424-7005
Fax: (614)424-4874

Ohio Partners
62 E. Board St., 3rd Fl.
Columbus, OH 43215
(614)621-1210
Fax: (614)621-1240

Capital Technology Group, L.L.C.
400 Metro Place North, Ste. 300
Dublin, OH 43017
(614)792-6066
Fax: (614)792-6036
E-mail: info@capitaltech.com
Website: http://www.capitaltech.com

Northwest Ohio Venture Fund
4159 Holland-Sylvania R., Ste. 202
Toledo, OH 43623
(419)824-8144

Fax: (419)882-2035
E-mail: bwalsh@novf.com

Oklahoma

Moore & Associates
1000 W. Wilshire Blvd., Ste. 370
Oklahoma City, OK 73116
(405)842-3660
Fax: (405)842-3763

Chisholm Private Capital Partners
100 West 5th St., Ste. 805
Tulsa, OK 74103
(918)584-0440
Fax: (918)584-0441
Website: http://www.chisholmvc.com

Davis, Tuttle Venture Partners (Tulsa)
320 S. Boston, Ste. 1000
Tulsa, OK 74103-3703
(918)584-7272
Fax: (918)582-3404
Website: http://www.davistuttle.com

RBC Ventures
2627 E. 21st St.
Tulsa, OK 74114
(918)744-5607
Fax: (918)743-8630

Oregon

Utah Ventures II LP
10700 SW Beaverton-Hillsdale Hwy.,
Ste. 548
Beaverton, OR 97005
(503)574-4125
E-mail: adishlip@uven.com
Website: http://www.uven.com

Orien Ventures
14523 SW Westlake Dr.
Lake Oswego, OR 97035
(503)699-1680
Fax: (503)699-1681

OVP Venture Partners (Lake Oswego)
340 Oswego Pointe Dr., Ste. 200
Lake Oswego, OR 97034
(503)697-8766
Fax: (503)697-8863
E-mail: info@ovp.com
Website: http://www.ovp.com

Oregon Resource and Technology Development Fund
4370 NE Halsey St., Ste. 233
Portland, OR 97213-1566
(503)282-4462
Fax: (503)282-2976

Shaw Venture Partners
400 SW 6th Ave., Ste. 1100
Portland, OR 97204-1636
(503)228-4884
Fax: (503)227-2471
Website: http://www.shawventures.com

Pennsylvania

Mid-Atlantic Venture Funds
125 Goodman Dr.
Bethlehem, PA 18015
(610)865-6550
Fax: (610)865-6427
Website: http://www.mavf.com

Newspring Ventures
100 W. Elm St., Ste. 101
Conshohocken, PA 19428
(610)567-2380
Fax: (610)567-2388
Website: http://www.news
printventures.com

Patricof & Co. Ventures, Inc.
455 S. Gulph Rd., Ste. 410
King of Prussia, PA 19406
(610)265-0286
Fax: (610)265-4959
Website: http://www.patricof.com

Loyalhanna Venture Fund
527 Cedar Way, Ste. 104
Oakmont, PA 15139
(412)820-7035
Fax: (412)820-7036

Innovest Group Inc.
2000 Market St., Ste. 1400
Philadelphia, PA 19103
(215)564-3960
Fax: (215)569-3272

Keystone Venture Capital Management Co.
1601 Market St., Ste. 2500
Philadelphia, PA 19103
(215)241-1200
Fax: (215)241-1211
Website: http://www.keystonevc.com

Liberty Venture Partners
2005 Market St., Ste. 200
Philadelphia, PA 19103
(215)282-4484
Fax: (215)282-4485
E-mail: info@libertyvp.com
Website: http://www.libertyvp.com

Penn Janney Fund, Inc.
1801 Market St., 11th Fl.
Philadelphia, PA 19103

(215)665-4447
Fax: (215)557-0820

Philadelphia Ventures, Inc.
The Bellevue
200 S. Broad St.
Philadelphia, PA 19102
(215)732-4445
Fax: (215)732-4644

Birchmere Ventures Inc.
2000 Technology Dr.
Pittsburgh, PA 15219-3109
(412)803-8000
Fax: (412)687-8139
Website: http://www.birchmerevc.com

CEO Venture Fund
2000 Technology Dr., Ste. 160
Pittsburgh, PA 15219-3109
(412)687-3451
Fax: (412)687-8139
E-mail: ceofund@aol.com
Website: http://www.ceoventure
fund.com

Innovation Works Inc.
2000 Technology Dr., Ste. 250
Pittsburgh, PA 15219
(412)681-1520
Fax: (412)681-2625
Website: http://www.innovation
works.org

Keystone Minority Capital Fund L.P.
1801 Centre Ave., Ste. 201
Williams Sq.
Pittsburgh, PA 15219
(412)338-2230
Fax: (412)338-2224

Mellon Ventures, Inc.
One Mellon Bank Ctr., Rm. 3500
Pittsburgh, PA 15258
(412)236-3594
Fax: (412)236-3593
Website: http://www.mellon
ventures.com

Pennsylvania Growth Fund
5850 Ellsworth Ave., Ste. 303
Pittsburgh, PA 15232
(412)661-1000
Fax: (412)361-0676

Point Venture Partners
The Century Bldg.
130 Seventh St., 7th Fl.
Pittsburgh, PA 15222
(412)261-1966
Fax: (412)261-1718

Cross Atlantic Capital Partners
5 Radnor Corporate Center, Ste. 555
Radnor, PA 19087
(610)995-2650
Fax: (610)971-2062
Website: http://www.xacp.com

Meridian Venture Partners (Radnor)
The Radnor Court Bldg., Ste. 140
259 Radnor-Chester Rd.
Radnor, PA 19087
(610)254-2999
Fax: (610)254-2996
E-mail: mvpart@ix.netcom.com

TDH
919 Conestoga Rd., Bldg. 1, Ste. 301
Rosemont, PA 19010
(610)526-9970
Fax: (610)526-9971

Adams Capital Management
500 Blackburn Ave.
Sewickley, PA 15143
(412)749-9454
Fax: (412)749-9459
Website: http://www.acm.com

S.R. One, Ltd.
Four Tower Bridge
200 Barr Harbor Dr., Ste. 250
W. Conshohocken, PA 19428
(610)567-1000
Fax: (610)567-1039

Greater Philadelphia Venture Capital Corp.
351 East Conestoga Rd.
Wayne, PA 19087
(610)688-6829
Fax: (610)254-8958

PA Early Stage
435 Devon Park Dr., Bldg. 500, Ste. 510
Wayne, PA 19087
(610)293-4075
Fax: (610)254-4240
Website: http://www.paearlystage.com

The Sandhurst Venture Fund, L.P.
351 E. Constoga Rd.
Wayne, PA 19087
(610)254-8900
Fax: (610)254-8958

TL Ventures
700 Bldg.
435 Devon Park Dr.
Wayne, PA 19087-1990
(610)975-3765
Fax: (610)254-4210
Website: http://www.tlventures.com

Rockhill Ventures, Inc.
100 Front St., Ste. 1350
West Conshohocken, PA 19428
(610)940-0300
Fax: (610)940-0301

Puerto Rico

Advent-Morro Equity Partners
Banco Popular Bldg.
206 Tetuan St., Ste. 903
San Juan, PR 00902
(787)725-5285
Fax: (787)721-1735

North America Investment Corp.
Mercantil Plaza, Ste. 813
PO Box 191831
San Juan, PR 00919
(787)754-6178
Fax: (787)754-6181

Rhode Island

Manchester Humphreys, Inc.
40 Westminster St., Ste. 900
Providence, RI 02903
(401)454-0400
Fax: (401)454-0403

Navis Partners
50 Kennedy Plaza, 12th Fl.
Providence, RI 02903
(401)278-6770
Fax: (401)278-6387
Website: http://www.navis
partners.com

South Carolina

Capital Insights, L.L.C.
PO Box 27162
Greenville, SC 29616-2162
(864)242-6832
Fax: (864)242-6755
E-mail: jwarner@capitalinsights.com
Website: http://www.capitalin
sights.com

Transamerica Mezzanine Financing
7 N. Laurens St., Ste. 603
Greenville, SC 29601
(864)232-6198
Fax: (864)241-4444

Tennessee

Valley Capital Corp.
Krystal Bldg.
100 W. Martin Luther King Blvd.,
Ste. 212

Chattanooga, TN 37402
(423)265-1557
Fax: (423)265-1588

Coleman Swenson Booth Inc.
237 2nd Ave. S
Franklin, TN 37064-2649
(615)791-9462
Fax: (615)791-9636
Website: http://
www.colemanswenson.com

Capital Services & Resources, Inc.
5159 Wheelis Dr., Ste. 106
Memphis, TN 38117
(901)761-2156
Fax: (907)767-0060

Paradigm Capital Partners LLC
6410 Poplar Ave., Ste. 395
Memphis, TN 38119
(901)682-6060
Fax: (901)328-3061

SSM Ventures
845 Crossover Ln., Ste. 140
Memphis, TN 38117
(901)767-1131
Fax: (901)767-1135
Website: http://www.ssm
ventures.com

Capital Across America L.P.
501 Union St., Ste. 201
Nashville, TN 37219
(615)254-1414
Fax: (615)254-1856
Website: http://
www.capitalacrossamerica.com

Equitas L.P.
2000 Glen Echo Rd., Ste. 101
PO Box 158838
Nashville, TN 37215-8838
(615)383-8673
Fax: (615)383-8693

Massey Burch Capital Corp.
One Burton Hills Blvd., Ste. 350
Nashville, TN 37215
(615)665-3221
Fax: (615)665-3240
E-mail: tcalton@masseyburch.com
Website: http://www.masseyburch.com

Nelson Capital Corp.
3401 West End Ave., Ste. 300
Nashville, TN 37203
(615)292-8787
Fax: (615)385-3150

Texas

Phillips-Smith Specialty Retail Group
5080 Spectrum Dr., Ste. 805 W
Addison, TX 75001
(972)387-0725
Fax: (972)458-2560
E-mail: pssrg@aol.com
Website: http://www.phillips-smith.com

Austin Ventures, L.P.
701 Brazos St., Ste. 1400
Austin, TX 78701
(512)485-1900
Fax: (512)476-3952
E-mail: info@ausven.com
Website: http://www.austinventures.com

The Capital Network
3925 West Braker Lane, Ste. 406
Austin, TX 78759-5321
(512)305-0826
Fax: (512)305-0836

Techxas Ventures LLC
5000 Plaza on the Lake
Austin, TX 78746
(512)343-0118
Fax: (512)343-1879
E-mail: bruce@techxas.com
Website: http://www.techxas.com

Alliance Financial of Houston
218 Heather Ln.
Conroe, TX 77385-9013
(936)447-3300
Fax: (936)447-4222

Amerimark Capital Corp.
1111 W. Mockingbird, Ste. 1111
Dallas, TX 75247
(214)638-7878
Fax: (214)638-7612
E-mail: amerimark@amcapital.com
Website: http://www.amcapital.com

AMT Venture Partners / AMT Capital Ltd.
5220 Spring Valley Rd., Ste. 600
Dallas, TX 75240
(214)905-9757
Fax: (214)905-9761
Website: http://www.amtcapital.com

Arkoma Venture Partners
5950 Berkshire Lane, Ste. 1400
Dallas, TX 75225
(214)739-3515
Fax: (214)739-3572
E-mail: joelf@arkomavp.com

Capital Southwest Corp.
12900 Preston Rd., Ste. 700
Dallas, TX 75230
(972)233-8242
Fax: (972)233-7362
Website: http://
www.capitalsouthwest.com

Dali, Hook Partners
One Lincoln Center, Ste. 1550
5400 LBJ Freeway
Dallas, TX 75240
(972)991-5457
Fax: (972)991-5458
E-mail: dhook@hookpartners.com
Website: http://www.hookpartners.com

HO2 Partners
Two Galleria Tower
13455 Noel Rd., Ste. 1670
Dallas, TX 75240
(972)702-1144
Fax: (972)702-8234
Website: http://www.ho2.com

Interwest Partners (Dallas)
2 Galleria Tower
13455 Noel Rd., Ste. 1670
Dallas, TX 75240
(972)392-7279
Fax: (972)490-6348
Website: http://www.interwest.com

Kahala Investments, Inc.
8214 Westchester Dr., Ste. 715
Dallas, TX 75225
(214)987-0077
Fax: (214)987-2332

MESBIC Ventures Holding Co.
2435 North Central Expressway, Ste. 200
Dallas, TX 75080
(972)991-1597
Fax: (972)991-4770
Website: http://www.mvhc.com

North Texas MESBIC, Inc.
9500 Forest Lane, Ste. 430
Dallas, TX 75243
(214)221-3565
Fax: (214)221-3566

Richard Jaffe & Company, Inc,
7318 Royal Cir.
Dallas, TX 75230
(214)265-9397
Fax: (214)739-1845

Sevin Rosen Management Co.
13455 Noel Rd., Ste. 1670
Dallas, TX 75240

(972)702-1100
Fax: (972)702-1103
E-mail: info@srfunds.com
Website: http://www.srfunds.com

Stratford Capital Partners, L.P.
300 Crescent Ct., Ste. 500
Dallas, TX 75201
(214)740-7377
Fax: (214)720-7393
E-mail: stratcap@hmtf.com

Sunwestern Investment Group
12221 Merit Dr., Ste. 935
Dallas, TX 75251
(972)239-5650
Fax: (972)701-0024

Wingate Partners
750 N. St. Paul St., Ste. 1200
Dallas, TX 75201
(214)720-1313
Fax: (214)871-8799

Buena Venture Associates
201 Main St., 32nd Fl.
Fort Worth, TX 76102
(817)339-7400
Fax: (817)390-8408
Website: http://www.buenaventure.com

The Catalyst Group
3 Riverway, Ste. 770
Houston, TX 77056
(713)623-8133
Fax: (713)623-0473
E-mail: herman@thecatalystgroup.net
Website: http://www.thecatalyst
group.net

Cureton & Co., Inc.
1100 Louisiana, Ste. 3250
Houston, TX 77002
(713)658-9806
Fax: (713)658-0476

Davis, Tuttle Venture Partners (Dallas)
8 Greenway Plaza, Ste. 1020
Houston, TX 77046
(713)993-0440
Fax: (713)621-2297
Website: http://www.davistuttle.com

Houston Partners
401 Louisiana, 8th Fl.
Houston, TX 77002
(713)222-8600
Fax: (713)222-8932

Southwest Venture Group
10878 Westheimer, Ste. 178

Houston, TX 77042
(713)827-8947
(713)461-1470

AM Fund
4600 Post Oak Place, Ste. 100
Houston, TX 77027
(713)627-9111
Fax: (713)627-9119

Ventex Management, Inc.
3417 Milam St.
Houston, TX 77002-9531
(713)659-7870
Fax: (713)659-7855

MBA Venture Group
1004 Olde Town Rd., Ste. 102
Irving, TX 75061
(972)986-6703

First Capital Group Management Co.
750 East Mulberry St., Ste. 305
PO Box 15616
San Antonio, TX 78212
(210)736-4233
Fax: (210)736-5449

The Southwest Venture Partnerships
16414 San Pedro, Ste. 345
San Antonio, TX 78232
(210)402-1200
Fax: (210)402-1221
E-mail: swvp@aol.com

Medtech International Inc.
1742 Carriageway
Sugarland, TX 77478
(713)980-8474
Fax: (713)980-6343

Utah

First Security Business Investment Corp.
15 East 100 South, Ste. 100
Salt Lake City, UT 84111
(801)246-5737
Fax: (801)246-5740

Utah Ventures II, L.P.
423 Wakara Way, Ste. 206
Salt Lake City, UT 84108
(801)583-5922
Fax: (801)583-4105
Website: http://www.uven.com

Wasatch Venture Corp.
1 S. Main St., Ste. 1400
Salt Lake City, UT 84133
(801)524-8939

Fax: (801)524-8941
E-mail: mail@wasatchvc.com

Vermont

North Atlantic Capital Corp.
76 Saint Paul St., Ste. 600
Burlington, VT 05401
(802)658-7820
Fax: (802)658-5757
Website: http://www.north
atlanticcapital.com

Green Mountain Advisors Inc.
PO Box 1230
Quechee, VT 05059
(802)296-7800
Fax: (802)296-6012
Website: http://www.gmtcap.com

Virginia

Oxford Financial Services Corp.
Alexandria, VA 22314
(703)519-4900
Fax: (703)519-4910
E-mail: oxford133@aol.com

Continental SBIC
4141 N. Henderson Rd.
Arlington, VA 22203
(703)527-5200
Fax: (703)527-3700

Novak Biddle Venture Partners
1750 Tysons Blvd., Ste. 1190
McLean, VA 22102
(703)847-3770
Fax: (703)847-3771
E-mail: roger@novakbiddle.com
Website: http://www.novakbiddle.com

Spacevest
11911 Freedom Dr., Ste. 500
Reston, VA 20190
(703)904-9800
Fax: (703)904-0571
E-mail: spacevest@spacevest.com
Website: http://www.spacevest.com

Virginia Capital
1801 Libbie Ave., Ste. 201
Richmond, VA 23226
(804)648-4802
Fax: (804)648-4809
E-mail: webmaster@vacapital.com
Website: http://www.vacapital.com

Calvert Social Venture Partners
402 Maple Ave. W
Vienna, VA 22180

(703)255-4930
Fax: (703)255-4931
E-mail: calven2000@aol.com

Fairfax Partners
8000 Towers Crescent Dr., Ste. 940
Vienna, VA 22182
(703)847-9486
Fax: (703)847-0911

Global Internet Ventures
8150 Leesburg Pike, Ste. 1210
Vienna, VA 22182
(703)442-3300
Fax: (703)442-3388
Website: http://www.givinc.com

Walnut Capital Corp. (Vienna)
8000 Towers Crescent Dr., Ste. 1070
Vienna, VA 22182
(703)448-3771
Fax: (703)448-7751

Washington

Encompass Ventures
777 108th Ave. NE, Ste. 2300
Bellevue, WA 98004
(425)486-3900
Fax: (425)486-3901
E-mail: info@evpartners.com
Website: http://www.encom
passventures.com

Fluke Venture Partners
11400 SE Sixth St., Ste. 230
Bellevue, WA 98004
(425)453-4590
Fax: (425)453-4675
E-mail: gabelein@flukeventures.com
Website: http://www.flukeventures.com

Pacific Northwest Partners SBIC, L.P.
15352 SE 53rd St.
Bellevue, WA 98006
(425)455-9967
Fax: (425)455-9404

Materia Venture Associates, L.P.
3435 Carillon Pointe
Kirkland, WA 98033-7354
(425)822-4100
Fax: (425)827-4086

OVP Venture Partners (Kirkland)
2420 Carillon Pt.
Kirkland, WA 98033
(425)889-9192
Fax: (425)889-0152
E-mail: info@ovp.com
Website: http://www.ovp.com

Digital Partners
999 3rd Ave., Ste. 1610
Seattle, WA 98104
(206)405-3607
Fax: (206)405-3617
Website: http://www.digitalpartners.com

Frazier & Company
601 Union St., Ste. 3300
Seattle, WA 98101
(206)621-7200
Fax: (206)621-1848
E-mail: jon@frazierco.com

Kirlan Venture Capital, Inc.
221 First Ave. W, Ste. 108
Seattle, WA 98119-4223
(206)281-8610
Fax: (206)285-3451
Website: http://www.kirlanventure.com

Phoenix Partners
1000 2nd Ave., Ste. 3600
Seattle, WA 98104
(206)624-8968
Fax: (206)624-1907

Voyager Capital
800 5th St., Ste. 4100
Seattle, WA 98103
(206)470-1180
Fax: (206)470-1185
E-mail: info@voyagercap.com
Website: http://www.voyagercap.com

Northwest Venture Associates
221 N. Wall St., Ste. 628
Spokane, WA 99201
(509)747-0728
Fax: (509)747-0758
Website: http://www.nwva.com

Wisconsin

Venture Investors Management, L.L.C.
University Research Park
505 S. Rosa Rd.
Madison, WI 53719
(608)441-2700
Fax: (608)441-2727
E-mail: roger@ventureinvestors.com
Website: http://www.venture
investers.com

Capital Investments, Inc.
1009 West Glen Oaks Lane, Ste. 103
Mequon, WI 53092
(414)241-0303
Fax: (414)241-8451
Website: http://
www.capitalinvestmentsinc.com

Future Value Venture, Inc.
2745 N. Martin Luther King
Dr., Ste. 204
Milwaukee, WI 53212-2300
(414)264-2252
Fax: (414)264-2253
E-mail: fvvventures@aol.com
William Beckett, President

Lubar and Co., Inc.
700 N. Water St., Ste. 1200
Milwaukee, WI 53202
(414)291-9000
Fax: (414)291-9061

GCI
20875 Crossroads Cir., Ste. 100
Waukesha, WI 53186
(262)798-5080
Fax: (262)798-5087

Glossary of Small Business Terms

Absolute liability
Liability that is incurred due to product defects or negligent actions. Manufacturers or retail establishments are held responsible, even though the defect or action may not have been intentional or negligent.

ACE
See Active Corps of Executives

Accident and health benefits
Benefits offered to employees and their families in order to offset the costs associated with accidental death, accidental injury, or sickness.

Account statement
A record of transactions, including payments, new debt, and deposits, incurred during a defined period of time.

Accounting system
System capturing the costs of all employees and/or machinery included in business expenses.

Accounts payable
See Trade credit

Accounts receivable
Unpaid accounts which arise from unsettled claims and transactions from the sale of a company's products or services to its customers.

Active Corps of Executives (ACE)
A group of volunteers for a management assistance program of the U.S. Small Business Administration; volunteers provide one-on-one counseling and teach workshops and seminars for small firms.

ADA
See Americans with Disabilities Act

Adaptation
The process whereby an invention is modified to meet the needs of users.

Adaptive engineering
The process whereby an invention is modified to meet the manufacturing and commercial requirements of a targeted market.

Adverse selection
The tendency for higher-risk individuals to purchase health care and more comprehensive plans, resulting in increased costs.

Advertising
A marketing tool used to capture public attention and influence purchasing decisions for a product or service. Utilizes various forms of media to generate consumer response, such as flyers, magazines, newspapers, radio, and television.

Age discrimination
The denial of the rights and privileges of employment based solely on the age of an individual.

Agency costs
Costs incurred to insure that the lender or investor maintains control over assets while allowing the borrower or entrepreneur to use them. Monitoring and information costs are the two major types of agency costs.

Agribusiness
The production and sale of commodities and products from the commercial farming industry.

America Online
An online service which is accessible by computer modem. The service features Internet access, bulletin boards, online periodicals, electronic mail, and other services for subscribers.

Americans with Disabilities Act (ADA)
Law designed to ensure equal access and opportunity to handicapped persons.

Annual report
Yearly financial report prepared by a business that adheres to the requirements set forth by the Securities and Exchange Commission (SEC).

Antitrust immunity
Exemption from prosecution under antitrust laws. In the transportation industry, firms with antitrust immunity are permitted under certain conditions to set schedules and sometimes prices for the public benefit.

Applied research
Scientific study targeted for use in a product or process.

Asians
A minority category used by the U.S. Bureau of the Census to represent a diverse group that includes Aleuts, Eskimos, American Indians, Asian Indians, Chinese, Japanese, Koreans, Vietnamese, Filipinos, Hawaiians, and other Pacific Islanders.

Assets
Anything of value owned by a company.

Audit
The verification of accounting records and business procedures conducted by an outside accounting service.

Average cost
Total production costs divided by the quantity produced.

Balance Sheet
A financial statement listing the total assets and liabilities of a company at a given time.

Bankruptcy
The condition in which a business cannot meet its debt obligations and petitions a federal district court either for reorganization of its debts (Chapter 11) or for liquidation of its assets (Chapter 7).

Basic research
Theoretical scientific exploration not targeted to application.

Basket clause
A provision specifying the amount of public pension funds that may be placed in investments not included on a state's legal list (see separate citation).

BBS
See Bulletin Board Service

BDC
See Business development corporation

Benefit
Various services, such as health care, flextime, day care, insurance, and vacation, offered to employees as part of a hiring package. Typically subsidized in whole or in part by the business.

BIDCO
See Business and industrial development company

Billing cycle
A system designed to evenly distribute customer billing throughout the month, preventing clerical backlogs.

Birth
See Business birth

Blue chip security
A low-risk, low-yield security representing an interest in a very stable company.

Blue sky laws
A general term that denotes various states' laws regulating securities.

Bond
A written instrument executed by a bidder or contractor (the principal) and a second party (the surety or sureties) to assure fulfillment of the principal's obligations to a third party (the obligee or government) identified in the bond. If the principal's obligations are not met, the bond assures payment to the extent stipulated of any loss sustained by the obligee.

Bonding requirements
Terms contained in a bond (see separate citation).

Bonus
An amount of money paid to an employee as a reward for achieving certain business goals or objectives.

Brainstorming
A group session where employees contribute their ideas for solving a problem or meeting a company objective without fear of retribution or ridicule.

Brand name
The part of a brand, trademark, or service mark that can be spoken. It can be a word, letter, or group of words or letters.

Bridge financing
A short-term loan made in expectation of intermediateterm or long-term financing. Can be used when a company plans to go public in the near future.

Broker
One who matches resources available for innovation with those who need them.

Budget
An estimate of the spending necessary to complete a project or offer a service in comparison to cash-on-hand and expected earnings for the coming year, with an emphasis on cost control.

Bulletin Board Service (BBS)
An online service enabling users to communicate with each other about specific topics.

Business and industrial development company (BIDCO)
A private, for-profit financing corporation chartered by the state to provide both equity and long-term debt capital to small business owners (see separate citations for equity and debt capital).

Business birth
The formation of a new establishment or enterprise. The appearance of a new establishment or enterprise in the Small Business Data Base (see separate citation).

Business conditions
Outside factors that can affect the financial performance of a business.

Business contractions
The number of establishments that have decreased in employment during a specified time.

Business cycle
A period of economic recession and recovery. These cycles vary in duration.

Business death
The voluntary or involuntary closure of a firm or establishment. The disappearance of an establishment or enterprise from the Small Business Data Base (see separate citation).

Business development corporation (BDC)
A business financing agency, usually composed of the financial institutions in an area or state, organized to assist in financing businesses unable to obtain assistance through normal channels; the risk is spread among various members of the business development corporation, and interest rates may vary somewhat from those charged by member institutions. A venture capital firm in which shares of ownership are publicly held and to which the Investment Act of 1940 applies.

Business dissolution
For enumeration purposes, the absence of a business that was present in the prior time period from any current record.

Business entry
See Business birth

Business ethics
Moral values and principles espoused by members of the business community as a guide to fair and honest business practices.

Business exit
See Business death

Business expansions
The number of establishments that added employees during a specified time.

Business failure
Closure of a business causing a loss to at least one creditor.

Business format franchising
The purchase of the name, trademark, and an ongoing business plan of the parent corporation or franchisor by the franchisee.

Business license
A legal authorization issued by municipal and state governments and required for business operations.

Business name
Enterprises must register their business names with local governments usually on a "doing business as" (DBA) form. (This name is sometimes referred to as a "fictional name.") The procedure is part of the business licensing process and prevents any other business from using that same name for a similar business in the same locality.

Business norms
See Financial ratios

Business permit
See Business license

Business plan
A document that spells out a company's expected course of action for a specified period, usually including a detailed listing and analysis of risks and uncertainties. For the small business, it should examine the proposed products, the market, the industry, the management policies, the marketing policies, production needs, and financial needs. Frequently, it is used as a prospectus for potential investors and lenders.

Business proposal
See Business plan

Business service firm
An establishment primarily engaged in rendering services to other business organizations on a fee or contract basis.

Business start
For enumeration purposes, a business with a name or similar designation that did not exist in a prior time period.

Cafeteria plan
See Flexible benefit plan

Capacity
Level of a firm's, industry's, or nation's output corresponding to full practical utilization of available resources.

Capital
Assets less liabilities, representing the ownership interest in a business. A stock of accumulated goods, especially at a specified time and in contrast to income received during a specified time period. Accumulated goods devoted to production. Accumulated possessions calculated to bring income.

Capital expenditure
Expenses incurred by a business for improvements that will depreciate over time.

Capital gain
The monetary difference between the purchase price and the selling price of capital. Capital gains are taxed at a rate of 28% by the federal government.

Capital intensity
The relative importance of capital in the production process, usually expressed as the ratio of capital to labor but also sometimes as the ratio of capital to output.

Capital resource
The equipment, facilities and labor used to create products and services.

Caribbean Basin Initiative
An interdisciplinary program to support commerce among the businesses in the nations of the Caribbean Basin and the United States. Agencies involved include: the Agency for International Development, the U.S. Small Business Administration, the International Trade Administration of the U.S. Department of Commerce, and various private sector groups.

Catastrophic care
Medical and other services for acute and long-term illnesses that cost more than insurance coverage limits or that cost the amount most families may be expected to pay with their own resources.

CDC
See Certified development corporation

CD-ROM
Compact disc with read-only memory used to store large amounts of digitized data.

Certified development corporation (CDC)
A local area or statewide corporation or authority (for profit or nonprofit) that packages U.S. Small Business Administration (SBA), bank, state, and/or private money into financial assistance for existing business capital improvements. The SBA holds the second lien on its maximum share of 40 percent involvement. Each state has at least one certified development corporation. This program is called the SBA 504 Program.

Certified lenders
Banks that participate in the SBA guaranteed loan program (see separate citation). Such banks must have a good track record with the U.S. Small Business Administration (SBA) and must agree to certain conditions set forth by the agency. In return, the SBA agrees to process any guaranteed loan application within three business days.

Champion
An advocate for the development of an innovation.

Channel of distribution
The means used to transport merchandise from the manufacturer to the consumer.

Chapter 7 of the 1978 Bankruptcy Act
Provides for a court-appointed trustee who is responsible for liquidating a company's assets in order to settle outstanding debts.

Chapter 11 of the 1978 Bankruptcy Act
Allows the business owners to retain control of the company while working with their creditors to reorganize their finances and establish better business practices to prevent liquidation of assets.

Closely held corporation
A corporation in which the shares are held by a few persons, usually officers, employees, or others close to the management; these shares are rarely offered to the public.

Code of Federal Regulations
Codification of general and permanent rules of the federal government published in the Federal Register.

Code sharing
See Computer code sharing

Coinsurance
Upon meeting the deductible payment, health insurance participants may be required to make additional health care cost-sharing payments. Coinsurance is a payment of a fixed percentage of the cost of each service; copayment is usually a fixed amount to be paid with each service.

Collateral
Securities, evidence of deposit, or other property pledged by a borrower to secure repayment of a loan.

Collective ratemaking
The establishment of uniform charges for services by a group of businesses in the same industry.

Commercial insurance plan
See Underwriting

Commercial loans
Short-term renewable loans used to finance specific capital needs of a business.

Commercialization
The final stage of the innovation process, including production and distribution.

Common stock
The most frequently used instrument for purchasing ownership in private or public companies. Common stock generally carries the right to vote on certain corporate actions and may pay dividends, although it rarely does in venture investments. In liquidation, common stockholders are the last to share in the proceeds from the sale of a corporation's assets; bondholders and preferred shareholders have priority. Common stock is often used in firstround start-up financing.

Community development corporation
A corporation established to develop economic programs for a community and, in most cases, to provide financial support for such development.

Competitor
A business whose product or service is marketed for the same purpose/use and to the same consumer group as the product or service of another.

Computer code sharing
An arrangement whereby flights of a regional airline are identified by the two-letter code of a major carrier in the computer reservation system to help direct passengers to new regional carriers.

Consignment
A merchandising agreement, usually referring to secondhand shops, where the dealer pays the owner of an item a percentage of the profit when the item is sold.

Consortium
A coalition of organizations such as banks and corporations for ventures requiring large capital resources.

Consultant
An individual that is paid by a business to provide advice and expertise in a particular area.

Consumer price index
A measure of the fluctuation in prices between two points in time.

Consumer research
Research conducted by a business to obtain information about existing or potential consumer markets.

Continuation coverage
Health coverage offered for a specified period of time to employees who leave their jobs and to their widows, divorced spouses, or dependents.

Contractions
See Business contractions

Convertible preferred stock
A class of stock that pays a reasonable dividend and is convertible into common stock (see separate citation). Generally the convertible feature may only be exercised after being held for a stated period of time. This arrangement is usually considered second-round financing when a company needs equity to maintain its cash flow.

Convertible securities
A feature of certain bonds, debentures, or preferred stocks that allows them to be exchanged by the owner for another class of securities at a future date and in accordance with any other terms of the issue.

Copayment
See Coinsurance

Copyright
A legal form of protection available to creators and authors to safeguard their works from unlawful use or claim of ownership by others. Copyrights may be acquired for works of art, sculpture, music, and published or unpublished manuscripts. All copyrights should be registered at the Copyright Office of the Library of Congress.

Corporate financial ratios
The relationship between key figures found in a company's financial statement expressed as a numeric value. Used to evaluate risk and company performance. Also known as Financial averages, Operating ratios, and Business ratios.

Corporation
A legal entity, chartered by a state or the federal government, recognized as a separate entity having its own rights, privileges, and liabilities distinct from those of its members.

Cost containment
Actions taken by employers and insurers to curtail rising health care costs; for example, increasing employee cost sharing (see separate citation), requiring second opinions, or preadmission screening.

Cost sharing
The requirement that health care consumers contribute to their own medical care costs through deductibles and coinsurance (see separate citations). Cost sharing does not include the amounts paid in premiums. It is used to control utilization of services; for example, requiring a fixed amount to be paid with each health care service.

Cottage industry
Businesses based in the home in which the family members are the labor force and family-owned equipment is used to process the goods.

Credit Rating
A letter or number calculated by an organization (such as Dun & Bradstreet) to represent the ability and disposition of a business to meet its financial obligations.

Customer service
Various techniques used to ensure the satisfaction of a customer.

Cyclical peak
The upper turning point in a business cycle.

Cyclical trough
The lower turning point in a business cycle.

DBA
See Business name

Death
See Business death

Debenture
A certificate given as acknowledgment of a debt (see separate citation) secured by the general credit of the issuing corporation. A bond, usually without security, issued by a corporation and sometimes convertible to common stock.

Debt
Something owed by one person to another. Financing in which a company receives capital that must be repaid; no ownership is transferred.

Debt capital
Business financing that normally requires periodic interest payments and repayment of the principal within a specified time.

Debt financing
See Debt capital

Debt securities
Loans such as bonds and notes that provide a specified rate of return for a specified period of time.

Deductible
A set amount that an individual must pay before any benefits are received.

Demand shock absorbers
A term used to describe the role that some small firms play by expanding their output levels to accommodate a transient surge in demand.

Demographics
Statistics on various markets, including age, income, and education, used to target specific products or services to appropriate consumer groups.

Demonstration
Showing that a product or process has been modified sufficiently to meet the needs of users.

Deregulation
The lifting of government restrictions; for example, the lifting of government restrictions on the entry of new businesses, the expansion of services, and the setting of prices in particular industries.

Desktop Publishing
Using personal computers and specialized software to produce camera-ready copy for publications.

Disaster loans
Various types of physical and economic assistance available to individuals and businesses through the U.S. Small Business Administration (SBA). This is the only SBA loan program available for residential purposes.

Discrimination
The denial of the rights and privileges of employment based on factors such as age, race, religion, or gender.

Diseconomies of scale
The condition in which the costs of production increase faster than the volume of production.

Dissolution
See Business dissolution

Distribution
Delivering a product or process to the user.

Distributor
One who delivers merchandise to the user.

Diversified company
A company whose products and services are used by several different markets.

Doing business as (DBA)
See Business name

Dow Jones
An information services company that publishes the Wall Street Journal and other sources of financial information.

Dow Jones Industrial Average
An indicator of stock market performance.

Earned income
A tax term that refers to wages and salaries earned by the recipient, as opposed to monies earned through interest and dividends.

Economic efficiency
The use of productive resources to the fullest practical extent in the provision of the set of goods and services that is most preferred by purchasers in the economy.

Economic indicators
Statistics used to express the state of the economy. These include the length of the average work week, the rate of unemployment, and stock prices.

Economically disadvantaged
See Socially and economically disadvantaged

Economies of scale
See Scale economies

EEOC
See Equal Employment Opportunity Commission

8(a) Program
A program authorized by the Small Business Act that directs federal contracts to small businesses owned and

operated by socially and economically disadvantaged individuals.

Electronic mail (e-mail)
The electronic transmission of mail via phone lines.

E-mail
See Electronic mail

Employee leasing
A contract by which employers arrange to have their workers hired by a leasing company and then leased back to them for a management fee. The leasing company typically assumes the administrative burden of payroll and provides a benefit package to the workers.

Employee tenure
The length of time an employee works for a particular employer.

Employer identification number
The business equivalent of a social security number. Assigned by the U.S. Internal Revenue Service.

Enterprise
An aggregation of all establishments owned by a parent company. An enterprise may consist of a single, independent establishment or include subsidiaries and other branches under the same ownership and control.

Enterprise zone
A designated area, usually found in inner cities and other areas with significant unemployment, where businesses receive tax credits and other incentives to entice them to establish operations there.

Entrepreneur
A person who takes the risk of organizing and operating a new business venture.

Entry
See Business entry

Equal Employment Opportunity Commission (EEOC)
A federal agency that ensures nondiscrimination in the hiring and firing practices of a business.

Equal opportunity employer
An employer who adheres to the standards set by the Equal Employment Opportunity Commission (see separate citation).

Equity
The ownership interest. Financing in which partial or total ownership of a company is surrendered in exchange for capital. An investor's financial return comes from dividend payments and from growth in the net worth of the business.

Equity capital
See Equity; Equity midrisk venture capital

Equity financing
See Equity; Equity midrisk venture capital

Equity midrisk venture capital
An unsecured investment in a company. Usually a purchase of ownership interest in a company that occurs in the later stages of a company's development.

Equity partnership
A limited partnership arrangement for providing start-up and seed capital to businesses.

Equity securities
See Equity

Equity-type
Debt financing subordinated to conventional debt.

Establishment
A single-location business unit that may be independent (a single-establishment enterprise) or owned by a parent enterprise.

Establishment and Enterprise Microdata File
See U.S. Establishment and Enterprise Microdata File

Establishment birth
See Business birth

Establishment Longitudinal Microdata File
See U.S. Establishment Longitudinal Microdata File

Ethics
See Business ethics

Evaluation
Determining the potential success of translating an invention into a product or process.

Exit
See Business exit

Experience rating
See Underwriting

Export
A product sold outside of the country.

Export license
A general or specific license granted by the U.S. Department of Commerce required of anyone wishing to export goods. Some restricted articles need approval from the U.S. Departments of State, Defense, or Energy.

Failure
See Business failure

Fair share agreement
An agreement reached between a franchisor and a minority business organization to extend business ownership to minorities by either reducing the amount of capital required or by setting aside certain marketing areas for minority business owners.

Feasibility study
A study to determine the likelihood that a proposed product or development will fulfill the objectives of a particular investor.

Federal Trade Commission (FTC)
Federal agency that promotes free enterprise and competition within the U.S.

Federal Trade Mark Act of 1946
See Lanham Act

Fictional name
See Business name

Fiduciary
An individual or group that hold assets in trust for a beneficiary.

Financial analysis
The techniques used to determine money needs in a business. Techniques include ratio analysis, calculation of return on investment, guides for measuring profitability, and break-even analysis to determine ultimate success.

Financial intermediary
A financial institution that acts as the intermediary between borrowers and lenders. Banks, savings and loan associations, finance companies, and venture capital companies are major financial intermediaries in the United States.

Financial ratios
See Corporate financial ratios; Industry financial ratios

Financial statement
A written record of business finances, including balance sheets and profit and loss statements.

Financing
See First-stage financing; Second-stage financing; Thirdstage financing

First-stage financing
Financing provided to companies that have expended their initial capital, and require funds to start full-scale manufacturing and sales. Also known as First-round financing.

Fiscal year
Any twelve-month period used by businesses for accounting purposes.

504 Program
See Certified development corporation

Flexible benefit plan
A plan that offers a choice among cash and/or qualified benefits such as group term life insurance, accident and health insurance, group legal services, dependent care assistance, and vacations.

FOB
See Free on board

Format franchising
See Business format franchising; Franchising

401(k) plan
A financial plan where employees contribute a percentage of their earnings to a fund that is invested in stocks, bonds, or money markets for the purpose of saving money for retirement.

Four Ps
Marketing terms referring to Product, Price, Place, and Promotion.

Franchising
A form of licensing by which the owner-the franchisor- distributes or markets a product, method, or service through affiliated dealers called franchisees. The product, method, or service being marketed is identified by a brand name, and the franchisor

maintains control over the marketing methods employed. The franchisee is often given exclusive access to a defined geographic area.

Free on board (FOB)
A pricing term indicating that the quoted price includes the cost of loading goods into transport vessels at a specified place.

Frictional unemployment
See Unemployment

FTC
See Federal Trade Commission

Fulfillment
The systems necessary for accurate delivery of an ordered item, including subscriptions and direct marketing.

Full-time workers
Generally, those who work a regular schedule of more than 35 hours per week.

Garment registration number
A number that must appear on every garment sold in the U.S. to indicate the manufacturer of the garment, which may or may not be the same as the label under which the garment is sold. The U.S. Federal Trade Commission assigns and regulates garment registration numbers.

Gatekeeper
A key contact point for entry into a network.

GDP
See Gross domestic product

General obligation bond
A municipal bond secured by the taxing power of the municipality. The Tax Reform Act of 1986 limits the purposes for which such bonds may be issued and establishes volume limits on the extent of their issuance.

GNP
See Gross national product

Good Housekeeping Seal
Seal appearing on products that signifies the fulfillment of the standards set by the Good Housekeeping Institute to protect consumer interests.

Goods sector
All businesses producing tangible goods, including agriculture, mining, construction, and manufacturing businesses.

GPO
See Gross product originating

Gross domestic product (GDP)
The part of the nation's gross national product (see separate citation) generated by private business using resources from within the country.

Gross national product (GNP)
The most comprehensive single measure of aggregate economic output. Represents the market value of the total output of goods and services produced by a nation's economy.

Gross product originating (GPO)
A measure of business output estimated from the income or production side using employee compensation, profit income, net interest, capital consumption, and indirect business taxes.

HAL
See Handicapped assistance loan program

Handicapped assistance loan program (HAL)
Low-interest direct loan program through the U.S. Small Business Administration (SBA) for handicapped persons. The SBA requires that these persons demonstrate that their disability is such that it is impossible for them to secure employment, thus making it necessary to go into their own business to make a living.

Health maintenance organization (HMO)
Organization of physicians and other health care professionals that provides health services to subscribers and their dependents on a prepaid basis.

Health provider
An individual or institution that gives medical care. Under Medicare, an institutional provider is a hospital, skilled nursing facility, home health agency, or provider of certain physical therapy services.

Hispanic
A person of Cuban, Mexican, Puerto Rican, Latin American (Central or South American), European Spanish, or other Spanish-speaking origin or ancestry.

HMO
See Health maintenance organization

Home-based business
A business with an operating address that is also a residential address (usually the residential address of the proprietor).

Hub-and-spoke system
A system in which flights of an airline from many different cities (the spokes) converge at a single airport (the hub). After allowing passengers sufficient time to make connections, planes then depart for different cities.

Human Resources Management
A business program designed to oversee recruiting, pay, benefits, and other issues related to the company's work force, including planning to determine the optimal use of labor to increase production, thereby increasing profit.

Idea
An original concept for a new product or process.

Import
Products produced outside the country in which they are consumed.

Income
Money or its equivalent, earned or accrued, resulting from the sale of goods and services.

Income statement
A financial statement that lists the profits and losses of a company at a given time.

Incorporation
The filing of a certificate of incorporation with a state's secretary of state, thereby limiting the business owner's liability.

Incubator
A facility designed to encourage entrepreneurship and minimize obstacles to new business formation and growth, particularly for high-technology firms, by housing a number of fledgling enterprises that share an array of services, such as meeting areas, secretarial services, accounting, research library, on-site financial and management counseling, and word processing facilities.

Independent contractor
An individual considered self-employed (see separate citation) and responsible for paying Social Security taxes and income taxes on earnings.

Indirect health coverage
Health insurance obtained through another individual's health care plan; for example, a spouse's employersponsored plan.

Industrial development authority
The financial arm of a state or other political subdivision established for the purpose of financing economic development in an area, usually through loans to nonprofit organizations, which in turn provide facilities for manufacturing and other industrial operations.

Industry financial ratios
Corporate financial ratios averaged for a specified industry. These are used for comparison purposes and reveal industry trends and identify differences between the performance of a specific company and the performance of its industry. Also known as Industrial averages, Industry ratios, Financial averages, and Business or Industrial norms.

Inflation
Increases in volume of currency and credit, generally resulting in a sharp and continuing rise in price levels.

Informal capital
Financing from informal, unorganized sources; includes informal debt capital such as trade credit or loans from friends and relatives and equity capital from informal investors.

Initial public offering (IPO)
A corporation's first offering of stock to the public.

Innovation
The introduction of a new idea into the marketplace in the form of a new product or service or an improvement in organization or process.

Intellectual property
Any idea or work that can be considered proprietary in nature and is thus protected from infringement by others.

Internal capital
Debt or equity financing obtained from the owner or through retained business earnings.

Internet
A government-designed computer network that contains large amounts of information and is accessible through various vendors for a fee.

Intrapreneurship
The state of employing entrepreneurial principles to nonentrepreneurial situations.

Invention
The tangible form of a technological idea, which could include a laboratory prototype, drawings, formulas, etc.

IPO
See Initial public offering

Job description
The duties and responsibilities required in a particular position.

Job tenure
A period of time during which an individual is continuously employed in the same job.

Joint marketing agreements
Agreements between regional and major airlines, often involving the coordination of flight schedules, fares, and baggage transfer. These agreements help regional carriers operate at lower cost.

Joint venture
Venture in which two or more people combine efforts in a particular business enterprise, usually a single transaction or a limited activity, and agree to share the profits and losses jointly or in proportion to their contributions.

Keogh plan
Designed for self-employed persons and unincorporated businesses as a tax-deferred pension account.

Labor force
Civilians considered eligible for employment who are also willing and able to work.

Labor force participation rate
The civilian labor force as a percentage of the civilian population.

Labor intensity
The relative importance of labor in the production process, usually measured as the capital-labor ratio; i.e., the ratio of units of capital (typically, dollars of tangible assets) to the number of employees. The higher the capital-labor ratio exhibited by a firm or industry, the lower the capital intensity of that firm or industry is said to be.

Labor surplus area
An area in which there exists a high unemployment rate. In procurement (see separate citation), extra points are given to firms in counties that are designated a labor surplus area; this information is requested on procurement bid sheets.

Labor union
An organization of similarly-skilled workers who collectively bargain with management over the conditions of employment.

Laboratory prototype
See Prototype

LAN
See Local Area Network

Lanham Act
Refers to the Federal Trade Mark Act of 1946. Protects registered trademarks, trade names, and other service marks used in commerce.

Large business-dominated industry
Industry in which a minimum of 60 percent of employment or sales is in firms with more than 500 workers.

LBO
See Leveraged buy-out

Leader pricing
A reduction in the price of a good or service in order to generate more sales of that good or service.

Legal list
A list of securities selected by a state in which certain institutions and fiduciaries (such as pension funds, insurance companies, and banks) may invest. Securities not on the list are not eligible for investment. Legal lists typically restrict investments to high quality securities meeting certain specifications. Generally, investment is

limited to U.S. securities and investment-grade blue chip securities (see separate citation).

Leveraged buy-out (LBO)
The purchase of a business or a division of a corporation through a highly leveraged financing package.

Liability
An obligation or duty to perform a service or an act. Also defined as money owed.

License
A legal agreement granting to another the right to use a technological innovation.

Limited partnerships
See Venture capital limited partnerships

Liquidity
The ability to convert a security into cash promptly.

Loans
See Commercial loans; Disaster loans; SBA direct loans; SBA guaranteed loans; SBA special lending institution categories Local Area Network (LAN) Computer networks contained within a single building or small area; used to facilitate the sharing of information.

Local development corporation
An organization, usually made up of local citizens of a community, designed to improve the economy of the area by inducing business and industry to locate and expand there. A local development corporation establishes a capability to finance local growth.

Long-haul rates
Rates charged by a transporter in which the distance traveled is more than 800 miles.

Long-term debt
An obligation that matures in a period that exceeds five years.

Low-grade bond
A corporate bond that is rated below investment grade by the major rating agencies (Standard and Poor's, Moody's).

Macro-efficiency
Efficiency as it pertains to the operation of markets and market systems.

Managed care
A cost-effective health care program initiated by employers whereby low-cost health care is made available to the employees in return for exclusive patronage to program doctors.

Management Assistance Programs
See SBA Management Assistance Programs

Management and technical assistance
A term used by many programs to mean business (as opposed to technological) assistance.

Mandated benefits
Specific treatments, providers, or individuals required by law to be included in commercial health plans.

Market evaluation
The use of market information to determine the sales potential of a specific product or process.

Market failure
The situation in which the workings of a competitive market do not produce the best results from the point of view of the entire society.

Market information
Data of any type that can be used for market evaluation, which could include demographic data, technology forecasting, regulatory changes, etc.

Market research
A systematic collection, analysis, and reporting of data about the market and its preferences, opinions, trends, and plans; used for corporate decision-making.

Market share
In a particular market, the percentage of sales of a specific product.

Marketing
Promotion of goods or services through various media.

Master Establishment List (MEL)
A list of firms in the United States developed by the U.S. Small Business Administration; firms can be selected by industry, region, state, standard metropolitan statistical area (see separate citation), county, and zip code.

Maturity
The date upon which the principal or stated value of a bond or other indebtedness becomes due and payable.

Medicaid (Title XIX)
A federally aided, state-operated and administered program that provides medical benefits for certain low income persons in need of health and medical care who are eligible for one of the government's welfare cash payment programs, including the aged, the blind, the disabled, and members of families with dependent children where one parent is absent, incapacitated, or unemployed.

Medicare (Title XVIII)
A nationwide health insurance program for disabled and aged persons. Health insurance is available to insured persons without regard to income. Monies from payroll taxes cover hospital insurance and monies from general revenues and beneficiary premiums pay for supplementary medical insurance.

MEL
See Master Establishment List

MESBIC
See Minority enterprise small business investment corporation

MET
See Multiple employer trust

Metropolitan statistical area (MSA)
A means used by the government to define large population centers that may transverse different governmental jurisdictions. For example, the Washington, D.C. MSA includes the District of Columbia and contiguous parts of Maryland and Virginia because all of these geopolitical areas comprise one population and economic operating unit.

Mezzanine financing
See Third-stage financing

Micro-efficiency
Efficiency as it pertains to the operation of individual firms.

Microdata
Information on the characteristics of an individual business firm.

Mid-term debt
An obligation that matures within one to five years.

Midrisk venture capital
See Equity midrisk venture capital

Minimum premium plan
A combination approach to funding an insurance plan aimed primarily at premium tax savings. The employer self-funds a fixed percentage of estimated monthly claims and the insurance company insures the excess.

Minimum wage
The lowest hourly wage allowed by the federal government.

Minority Business Development Agency
Contracts with private firms throughout the nation to sponsor Minority Business Development Centers which provide minority firms with advice and technical assistance on a fee basis.

Minority Enterprise Small Business Investment Corporation (MESBIC)
A federally funded private venture capital firm licensed by the U.S. Small Business Administration to provide capital to minority-owned businesses (see separate citation).

Minority-owned business
Businesses owned by those who are socially or economically disadvantaged (see separate citation).

Mom and Pop business
A small store or enterprise having limited capital, principally employing family members.

Moonlighter
A wage-and-salary worker with a side business.

MSA
See Metropolitan statistical area

Multi-employer plan
A health plan to which more than one employer is required to contribute and that may be maintained through a collective bargaining agreement and required to meet standards prescribed by the U.S. Department of Labor.

Multi-level marketing
A system of selling in which you sign up other people to assist you and they, in turn, recruit others to help them. Some entrepreneurs have built successful

companies on this concept because the main focus of their activities is their product and product sales.

Multimedia
The use of several types of media to promote a product or service. Also, refers to the use of several different types of media (sight, sound, pictures, text) in a CD-ROM (see separate citation) product.

Multiple employer trust (MET)
A self-funded benefit plan generally geared toward small employers sharing a common interest.

NAFTA
See North American Free Trade Agreement

NASDAQ
See National Association of Securities Dealers Automated Quotations

National Association of Securities Dealers Automated Quotations
Provides price quotes on over-the-counter securities as well as securities listed on the New York Stock Exchange.

National income
Aggregate earnings of labor and property arising from the production of goods and services in a nation's economy.

Net assets
See Net worth

Net income
The amount remaining from earnings and profits after all expenses and costs have been met or deducted. Also known as Net earnings.

Net profit
Money earned after production and overhead expenses (see separate citations) have been deducted.

Net worth
The difference between a company's total assets and its total liabilities.

Network
A chain of interconnected individuals or organizations sharing information and/or services.

New York Stock Exchange (NYSE)
The oldest stock exchange in the U.S. Allows for trading in stocks, bonds, warrants, options, and rights that meet listing requirements.

Niche
A career or business for which a person is well-suited. Also, a product which fulfills one need of a particular market segment, often with little or no competition.

Nodes
One workstation in a network, either local area or wide area (see separate citations).

Nonbank bank
A bank that either accepts deposits or makes loans, but not both. Used to create many new branch banks.

Noncompetitive awards
A method of contracting whereby the federal government negotiates with only one contractor to supply a product or service.

Nonmember bank
A state-regulated bank that does not belong to the federal bank system.

Nonprofit
An organization that has no shareholders, does not distribute profits, and is without federal and state tax liabilities.

Norms
See Financial ratios

North American Free Trade Agreement (NAFTA)
Passed in 1993, NAFTA eliminates trade barriers among businesses in the U.S., Canada, and Mexico.

NYSE
See New York Stock Exchange

Occupational Safety & Health Administration (OSHA)
Federal agency that regulates health and safety standards within the workplace.

Optimal firm size
The business size at which the production cost per unit of output (average cost) is, in the long run, at its minimum.

Glossary

Organizational chart
A hierarchical chart tracking the chain of command within an organization.

OSHA
See Occupational Safety & Health Administration

Overhead
Expenses, such as employee benefits and building utilities, incurred by a business that are unrelated to the actual product or service sold.

Owner's capital
Debt or equity funds provided by the owner(s) of a business; sources of owner's capital are personal savings, sales of assets, or loans from financial institutions.

P & L
See Profit and loss statement

Part-time workers
Normally, those who work less than 35 hours per week. The Tax Reform Act indicated that part-time workers who work less than 17.5 hours per week may be excluded from health plans for purposes of complying with federal nondiscrimination rules.

Part-year workers
Those who work less than 50 weeks per year.

Partnership
Two or more parties who enter into a legal relationship to conduct business for profit. Defined by the U.S. Internal Revenue Code as joint ventures, syndicates, groups, pools, and other associations of two or more persons organized for profit that are not specifically classified in the IRS code as corporations or proprietorships.

Patent
A grant made by the government assuring an inventor the sole right to make, use, and sell an invention for a period of 17 years.

PC
See Professional corporation

Peak
See Cyclical peak

Pension
A series of payments made monthly, semiannually, annually, or at other specified intervals during the lifetime of the pensioner for distribution upon retirement. The term is sometimes used to denote the portion of the retirement allowance financed by the employer's contributions.

Pension fund
A fund established to provide for the payment of pension benefits; the collective contributions made by all of the parties to the pension plan.

Performance appraisal
An established set of objective criteria, based on job description and requirements, that is used to evaluate the performance of an employee in a specific job.

Permit
See Business license

Plan
See Business plan

Pooling
An arrangement for employers to achieve efficiencies and lower health costs by joining together to purchase group health insurance or self-insurance.

PPO
See Preferred provider organization

Preferred lenders program
See SBA special lending institution categories

Preferred provider organization (PPO)
A contractual arrangement with a health care services organization that agrees to discount its health care rates in return for faster payment and/or a patient base.

Premiums
The amount of money paid to an insurer for health insurance under a policy. The premium is generally paid periodically (e.g., monthly), and often is split between the employer and the employee. Unlike deductibles and coinsurance or copayments, premiums are paid for coverage whether or not benefits are actually used.

Prime-age workers
Employees 25 to 54 years of age.

Prime contract
A contract awarded directly by the U.S. Federal Government.

Private company
See Closely held corporation

Private placement
A method of raising capital by offering for sale an investment or business to a small group of investors (generally avoiding registration with the Securities and Exchange Commission or state securities registration agencies). Also known as Private financing or Private offering.

Pro forma
The use of hypothetical figures in financial statements to represent future expenditures, debts, and other potential financial expenses.

Proactive
Taking the initiative to solve problems and anticipate future events before they happen, instead of reacting to an already existing problem or waiting for a difficult situation to occur.

Procurement
A contract from an agency of the federal government for goods or services from a small business.

Prodigy
An online service which is accessible by computer modem. The service features Internet access, bulletin boards, online periodicals, electronic mail, and other services for subscribers.

Product development
The stage of the innovation process where research is translated into a product or process through evaluation, adaptation, and demonstration.

Product franchising
An arrangement for a franchisee to use the name and to produce the product line of the franchisor or parent corporation.

Production
The manufacture of a product.

Production prototype
See Prototype

Productivity
A measurement of the number of goods produced during a specific amount of time.

Professional corporation (PC)
Organized by members of a profession such as medicine, dentistry, or law for the purpose of conducting their professional activities as a corporation. Liability of a member or shareholder is limited in the same manner as in a business corporation.

Profit and loss statement (P & L)
The summary of the incomes (total revenues) and costs of a company's operation during a specific period of time. Also known as Income and expense statement.

Proposal
See Business plan

Proprietorship
The most common legal form of business ownership; about 85 percent of all small businesses are proprietorships. The liability of the owner is unlimited in this form of ownership.

Prospective payment system
A cost-containment measure included in the Social Security Amendments of 1983 whereby Medicare payments to hospitals are based on established prices, rather than on cost reimbursement.

Prototype
A model that demonstrates the validity of the concept of an invention (laboratory prototype); a model that meets the needs of the manufacturing process and the user (production prototype).

Prudent investor rule or standard
A legal doctrine that requires fiduciaries to make investments using the prudence, diligence, and intelligence that would be used by a prudent person in making similar investments. Because fiduciaries make investments on behalf of third-party beneficiaries, the standard results in very conservative investments. Until recently, most state regulations required the fiduciary to apply this standard to each investment. Newer, more progressive regulations permit fiduciaries to apply this standard to the portfolio taken as a whole, thereby allowing a fiduciary to balance a portfolio with higher-yield, higher-risk investments. In states with more progressive regulations, practically every type of security is eligible for inclusion in the portfolio of investments made by a fiduciary, provided

that the portfolio investments, in their totality, are those of a prudent person.

Public equity markets
Organized markets for trading in equity shares such as common stocks, preferred stocks, and warrants. Includes markets for both regularly traded and nonregularly traded securities.

Public offering
General solicitation for participation in an investment opportunity. Interstate public offerings are supervised by the U.S. Securities and Exchange Commission (see separate citation).

Quality control
The process by which a product is checked and tested to ensure consistent standards of high quality.

Rate of return
The yield obtained on a security or other investment based on its purchase price or its current market price. The total rate of return is current income plus or minus capital appreciation or depreciation.

Real property
Includes the land and all that is contained on it.

Realignment
See Resource realignment

Recession
Contraction of economic activity occurring between the peak and trough (see separate citations) of a business cycle.

Regulated market
A market in which the government controls the forces of supply and demand, such as who may enter and what price may be charged.

Regulation D
A vehicle by which small businesses make small offerings and private placements of securities with limited disclosure requirements. It was designed to ease the burdens imposed on small businesses utilizing this method of capital formation.

Regulatory Flexibility Act
An act requiring federal agencies to evaluate the impact of their regulations on small businesses before the regulations are issued and to consider less burdensome alternatives.

Research
The initial stage of the innovation process, which includes idea generation and invention.

Research and development financing
A tax-advantaged partnership set up to finance product development for start-ups as well as more mature companies.

Resource mobility
The ease with which labor and capital move from firm to firm or from industry to industry.

Resource realignment
The adjustment of productive resources to interindustry changes in demand.

Resources
The sources of support or help in the innovation process, including sources of financing, technical evaluation, market evaluation, management and business assistance, etc.

Retained business earnings
Business profits that are retained by the business rather than being distributed to the shareholders as dividends.

Revolving credit
An agreement with a lending institution for an amount of money, which cannot exceed a set maximum, over a specified period of time. Each time the borrower repays a portion of the loan, the amount of the repayment may be borrowed yet again.

Risk capital
See Venture capital

Risk management
The act of identifying potential sources of financial loss and taking action to minimize their negative impact.

Routing
The sequence of steps necessary to complete a product during production.

S corporations
See Sub chapter S corporations

SBA
See Small Business Administration

SBA direct loans
Loans made directly by the U.S. Small Business Administration (SBA); monies come from funds appropriated specifically for this purpose. In general, SBA direct loans carry interest rates slightly lower than those in the private financial markets and are available only to applicants unable to secure private financing or an SBA guaranteed loan.

SBA 504 Program
See Certified development corporation

SBA guaranteed loans
Loans made by lending institutions in which the U.S. Small Business Administration (SBA) will pay a prior agreed-upon percentage of the outstanding principal in the event the borrower of the loan defaults. The terms of the loan and the interest rate are negotiated between theborrower and the lending institution, within set parameters.

SBA loans
See Disaster loans; SBA direct loans; SBA guaranteed loans; SBA special lending institution categories

SBA Management Assistance Programs
Classes, workshops, counseling, and publications offered by the U.S. Small Business Administration.

SBA special lending institution categories
U.S. Small Business Administration (SBA) loan program in which the SBA promises certified banks a 72-hour turnaround period in giving its approval for a loan, and in which preferred lenders in a pilot program are allowed to write SBA loans without seeking prior SBA approval.

SBDB
See Small Business Data Base

SBDC
See Small business development centers

SBI
See Small business institutes program

SBIC
See Small business investment corporation

SBIR Program
See Small Business Innovation Development Act of 1982

Scale economies
The decline of the production cost per unit of output (average cost) as the volume of output increases.

Scale efficiency
The reduction in unit cost available to a firm when producing at a higher output volume.

SCORE
See Service Corps of Retired Executives

SEC
See Securities and Exchange Commission

SECA
See Self-Employment Contributions Act

Second-stage financing
Working capital for the initial expansion of a company that is producing, shipping, and has growing accounts receivable and inventories. Also known as Second-round financing.

Secondary market
A market established for the purchase and sale of outstanding securities following their initial distribution.

Secondary worker
Any worker in a family other than the person who is the primary source of income for the family.

Secondhand capital
Previously used and subsequently resold capital equipment (e.g., buildings and machinery).

Securities and Exchange Commission (SEC)
Federal agency charged with regulating the trade of securities to prevent unethical practices in the investor market.

Securitized debt
A marketing technique that converts long-term loans to marketable securities.

Seed capital
Venture financing provided in the early stages of the innovation process, usually during product development.

Glossary

Self-employed person
One who works for a profit or fees in his or her own business, profession, or trade, or who operates a farm.

Self-Employment Contributions Act (SECA)
Federal law that governs the self-employment tax (see separate citation).

Self-employment income
Income covered by Social Security if a business earns a net income of at least $400.00 during the year. Taxes are paid on earnings that exceed $400.00.

Self-employment retirement plan
See Keogh plan

Self-employment tax
Required tax imposed on self-employed individuals for the provision of Social Security and Medicare. The tax must be paid quarterly with estimated income tax statements.

Self-funding
A health benefit plan in which a firm uses its own funds to pay claims, rather than transferring the financial risks of paying claims to an outside insurer in exchange for premium payments.

Service Corps of Retired Executives (SCORE)
Volunteers for the SBA Management Assistance Program who provide one-on-one counseling and teach workshops and seminars for small firms.

Service firm
See Business service firm

Service sector
Broadly defined, all U.S. industries that produce intangibles, including the five major industry divisions of transportation, communications, and utilities; wholesale trade; retail trade; finance, insurance, and real estate; and services.

Set asides
See Small business set asides

Short-haul service
A type of transportation service in which the transporter supplies service between cities where the maximum distance is no more than 200 miles.

Short-term debt
An obligation that matures in one year.

SIC codes
See Standard Industrial Classification codes

Single-establishment enterprise
See Establishment

Small business
An enterprise that is independently owned and operated, is not dominant in its field, and employs fewer than 500 people. For SBA purposes, the U.S. Small Business Administration (SBA) considers various other factors (such as gross annual sales) in determining size of a business.

Small Business Administration (SBA)
An independent federal agency that provides assistance with loans, management, and advocating interests before other federal agencies.

Small Business Data Base
A collection of microdata (see separate citation) files on individual firms developed and maintained by the U.S. Small Business Administration.

Small business development centers (SBDC)
Centers that provide support services to small businesses, such as individual counseling, SBA advice, seminars and conferences, and other learning center activities. Most services are free of charge, or available at minimal cost.

Small business development corporation
See Certified development corporation

Small business-dominated industry
Industry in which a minimum of 60 percent of employment or sales is in firms with fewer than 500 employees.

Small Business Innovation Development Act of 1982
Federal statute requiring federal agencies with large extramural research and development budgets to allocate a certain percentage of these funds to small research and development firms. The program, called the Small Business Innovation Research (SBIR) Program, is designed to stimulate technological innovation and make greater use of small businesses in meeting national innovation needs.

Small business institutes (SBI) program
Cooperative arrangements made by U.S. Small Business Administration district offices and local colleges and

universities to provide small business firms with graduate students to counsel them without charge.

Small business investment corporation (SBIC)
A privately owned company licensed and funded through the U.S. Small Business Administration and private sector sources to provide equity or debt capital to small businesses.

Small business set asides
Procurement (see separate citation) opportunities required by law to be on all contracts under $10,000 or a certain percentage of an agency's total procurement expenditure.

Smaller firms
For U.S. Department of Commerce purposes, those firms not included in the Fortune 1000.

SMSA
See Metropolitan statistical area

Socially and economically disadvantaged
Individuals who have been subjected to racial or ethnic prejudice or cultural bias without regard to their qualities as individuals, and whose abilities to compete are impaired because of diminished opportunities to obtain capital and credit.

Sole proprietorship
An unincorporated, one-owner business, farm, or professional practice.

Special lending institution categories
See SBA special lending institution categories

Standard Industrial Classification (SIC) codes
Four-digit codes established by the U.S. Federal Government to categorize businesses by type of economic activity; the first two digits correspond to major groups such as construction and manufacturing, while the last two digits correspond to subgroups such as home construction or highway construction.

Standard metropolitan statistical area (SMSA)
See Metropolitan statistical area

Start-up
A new business, at the earliest stages of development and financing.

Start-up costs
Costs incurred before a business can commence operations.

Start-up financing
Financing provided to companies that have either completed product development and initial marketing or have been in business for less than one year but have not yet sold their product commercially.

Stock
A certificate of equity ownership in a business.

Stop-loss coverage
Insurance for a self-insured plan that reimburses the company for any losses it might incur in its health claims beyond a specified amount.

Strategic planning
Projected growth and development of a business to establish a guiding direction for the future. Also used to determine which market segments to explore for optimal sales of products or services.

Structural unemployment
See Unemployment

Sub chapter S corporations
Corporations that are considered noncorporate for tax purposes but legally remain corporations.

Subcontract
A contract between a prime contractor and a subcontractor, or between subcontractors, to furnish supplies or services for performance of a prime contract (see separate citation) or a subcontract.

Surety bonds
Bonds providing reimbursement to an individual, company, or the government if a firm fails to complete a contract. The U.S. Small Business Administration guarantees surety bonds in a program much like the SBA guaranteed loan program (see separate citation).

Swing loan
See Bridge financing

Target market
The clients or customers sought for a business' product or service.

Targeted Jobs Tax Credit
Federal legislation enacted in 1978 that provides a tax credit to an employer who hires structurally unemployed individuals.

Tax number
A number assigned to a business by a state revenue department that enables the business to buy goods without paying sales tax.

Taxable bonds
An interest-bearing certificate of public or private indebtedness. Bonds are issued by public agencies to finance economic development.

Technical assistance
See Management and technical assistance

Technical evaluation
Assessment of technological feasibility.

Technology
The method in which a firm combines and utilizes labor and capital resources to produce goods or services; the application of science for commercial or industrial purposes.

Technology transfer
The movement of information about a technology or intellectual property from one party to another for use.

Tenure
See Employee tenure

Term
The length of time for which a loan is made.

Terms of a note
The conditions or limits of a note; includes the interest rate per annum, the due date, and transferability and convertibility features, if any.

Third-party administrator
An outside company responsible for handling claims and performing administrative tasks associated with health insurance plan maintenance.

Third-stage financing
Financing provided for the major expansion of a company whose sales volume is increasing and that is breaking even or profitable. These funds are used for further plant expansion, marketing, working capital,

or development of an improved product. Also known as Third-round or Mezzanine financing.

Time deposit
A bank deposit that cannot be withdrawn before a specified future time.

Time management
Skills and scheduling techniques used to maximize productivity.

Trade credit
Credit extended by suppliers of raw materials or finished products. In an accounting statement, trade credit is referred to as "accounts payable."

Trade name
The name under which a company conducts business, or by which its business, goods, or services are identified. It may or may not be registered as a trademark.

Trade periodical
A publication with a specific focus on one or more aspects of business and industry.

Trade secret
Competitive advantage gained by a business through the use of a unique manufacturing process or formula.

Trade show
An exhibition of goods or services used in a particular industry. Typically held in exhibition centers where exhibitors rent space to display their merchandise.

Trademark
A graphic symbol, device, or slogan that identifies a business. A business has property rights to its trademark from the inception of its use, but it is still prudent to register all trademarks with the Trademark Office of the U.S. Department of Commerce.

Translation
See Product development

Treasury bills
Investment tender issued by the Federal Reserve Bank in amounts of $10,000 that mature in 91 to 182 days.

Treasury bonds
Long-term notes with maturity dates of not less than seven and not more than twenty-five years.

Glossary

Treasury notes
Short-term notes maturing in less than seven years.

Trend
A statistical measurement used to track changes that occur over time.

Trough
See Cyclical trough

UCC
See Uniform Commercial Code

UL
See Underwriters Laboratories

Underwriters Laboratories (UL)
One of several private firms that tests products and processes to determine their safety. Although various firms can provide this kind of testing service, many local and insurance codes specify UL certification.

Underwriting
A process by which an insurer determines whether or not and on what basis it will accept an application for insurance. In an experience-rated plan, premiums are based on a firm's or group's past claims; factors other than prior claims are used for community-rated or manually rated plans.

Unfair competition
Refers to business practices, usually unethical, such as using unlicensed products, pirating merchandise, or misleading the public through false advertising, which give the offending business an unequitable advantage over others.

Unfunded accrued liability
The excess of total liabilities, both present and prospective, over present and prospective assets.

Unemployment
The joblessness of individuals who are willing to work, who are legally and physically able to work, and who are seeking work. Unemployment may represent the temporary joblessness of a worker between jobs (frictional unemployment) or the joblessness of a worker whose skills are not suitable for jobs available in the labor market (structural unemployment).

Uniform Commercial Code (UCC)
A code of laws governing commercial transactions across the U.S., except Louisiana. Their purpose is to bring uniformity to financial transactions.

Uniform product code (UPC symbol)
A computer-readable label comprised of ten digits and stripes that encodes what a product is and how much it costs. The first five digits are assigned by the Uniform Product Code Council, and the last five digits by the individual manufacturer.

Unit cost
See Average cost

UPC symbol
See Uniform product code

U.S. Establishment and Enterprise Microdata (USEEM) File
A cross-sectional database containing information on employment, sales, and location for individual enterprises and establishments with employees that have a Dun & Bradstreet credit rating.

U.S. Establishment Longitudinal Microdata (USELM) File
A database containing longitudinally linked sample microdata on establishments drawn from the U.S. Establishment and Enterprise Microdata file (see separate citation).

U.S. Small Business Administration 504 Program
See Certified development corporation

USEEM
See U.S. Establishment and Enterprise Microdata File

USELM
See U.S. Establishment Longitudinal Microdata File

VCN
See Venture capital network

Venture capital
Money used to support new or unusual business ventures that exhibit above-average growth rates, significant potential for market expansion, and are in need of additional financing to sustain growth or further research and development; equity or equity-type financing traditionally provided at the

commercialization stage, increasingly available prior to commercialization.

Venture capital company

A company organized to provide seed capital to a business in its formation stage, or in its first or second stage of expansion. Funding is obtained through public or private pension funds, commercial banks and bank holding companies, small business investment corporations licensed by the U.S. Small Business Administration, private venture capital firms, insurance companies, investment management companies, bank trust departments, industrial companies seeking to diversify their investment, and investment bankers acting as intermediaries for other investors or directly investing on their own behalf.

Venture capital limited partnerships

Designed for business development, these partnerships are an institutional mechanism for providing capital for young, technology-oriented businesses. The investors' money is pooled and invested in money market assets until venture investments have been selected. The general partners are experienced investment managers who select and invest the equity and debt securities of firms with high growth potential and the ability to go public in the near future.

Venture capital network (VCN)

A computer database that matches investors with entrepreneurs.

WAN

See Wide Area Network

Wide Area Network (WAN)

Computer networks linking systems throughout a state or around the world in order to facilitate the sharing of information.

Withholding

Federal, state, social security, and unemployment taxes withheld by the employer from employees' wages; employers are liable for these taxes and the corporate umbrella and bankruptcy will not exonerate an employer from paying back payroll withholding. Employers should escrow these funds in a separate account and disperse them quarterly to withholding authorities.

Workers' compensation

A state-mandated form of insurance covering workers injured in job-related accidents. In some states, the state is the insurer; in other states, insurance must be acquired from commercial insurance firms. Insurance rates are based on a number of factors, including salaries, firm history, and risk of occupation.

Working capital

Refers to a firm's short-term investment of current assets, including cash, short-term securities, accounts receivable, and inventories.

Yield

The rate of income returned on an investment, expressed as a percentage. Income yield is obtained by dividing the current dollar income by the current market price of the security. Net yield or yield to maturity is the current income yield minus any premium above par or plus any discount from par in purchase price, with the adjustment spread over the period from the date of purchase to the date of maturity.

Index

Listings in this index are arranged alphabetically by business plan type, then alphabetically by business plan name. Users are provided with the volume number in which the plan appears.

Index